Small United States and United Nations
Warships in the Korean War

ALSO BY PAUL M. EDWARDS
AND FROM MCFARLAND

*The Hill Wars of the Korean Conflict: A Dictionary of Hills,
Outposts and Other Sites of Military Action* (2006)

Small United States and United Nations Warships in the Korean War

Paul M. Edwards

McFarland & Company, Inc., Publishers
Jefferson, North Carolina, and London

LIBRARY OF CONGRESS CATALOGUING-IN-PUBLICATION DATA

Edwards, Paul M.
Small United States and United Nations warships in the Korean war/ Paul M. Edwards.
p.   cm.
Includes bibliographical references and index.

ISBN 978-0-7864-2930-1
softcover : 50# alkaline paper ∞

1. Korean War, 1950–1953 — Naval operations.   2. Korean War, 1950–1953 — Naval operations, American.   3. United States. Navy — History — Korean War, 1950–1953.   I. Title.
DS920.A2E48   2008   951.904'245 — dc22   2007049746

British Library cataloguing data are available

©2008 Paul M. Edwards. All rights reserved

No part of this book may be reproduced or transmitted in any form or by any means, electronic or mechanical, including photocopying or recording, or by any information storage and retrieval system, without permission in writing from the publisher.

On the cover: Map of Korea; *General William Weigel* at Pusan, 1953

Manufactured in the United States of America

*McFarland & Company, Inc., Publishers
Box 611, Jefferson, North Carolina 28640
www.mcfarlandpub.com*

To Carolynn Jean,
Paula Jean, Alison Jean and Cora Jean,
four generations of fabulous women

ACKNOWLEDGMENTS

It is important that I acknowledge the many sources I have used and the help I have received. Among primary sources, the following have been most helpful: the Ships History Branch, Department of the Navy, Naval Historical Center, which maintains individual ship histories as published in the invaluable *Dictionary of American Naval Fighting Ships* (DANFS, 8 volumes, 1958–81); Operational Archives Branch, Naval Historical Center, which has custody of the post–1945 action reports; Deck Logs (1941–69) located in the Modern History Branch, National Archives, at College Park; the New York Public Library, which houses a significant collection of U.S. Navy cruise books; The Naval Historical Collection in the Naval War College's archives; "United States Naval Vessels: the Official United States Navy," a reference manual prepared by the Division of Naval Intelligence (a reprint of ONI222,54,226); Korean War diaries, action reports and submarine war patrol reports located at the Operational Archives Branch at the Naval Historical Center; and Sources of Information on Ships Sources, Navy Department Library.

This work has also relied on a wide variety of secondary sources that have been painstakingly researched by their authors. First and foremost, anyone working on naval history during the Korean War must acknowledge James Field's *History of United States Naval Operations: Korea* (Washington: GPO, 1962) and Malcolm W. Cagle and Frank A. Manson, *The Sea War in Korea* (Annapolis, Maryland: United States Naval Institute, 1957). Other significant works include *U.S. Navy Ships: Sunk or Damaged in Action During the Korean Conflict*, Naval Historical Center, Washington, D.C. (now available on the Web); J. L. Christley, *United States Naval Submarine Force Information Book* and *Jane's Fighting Ships of World War II*.

The author also wishes to express his gratitude for considerable institutional help. Among those who need to be acknowledged are the staff and volunteers at the Center for the Study of the Korean War, located at the Independence, Missouri, campus of Graceland University, as well as the university librarians. Also of importance: Dr. Mike Devine and the professional staff at the Harry S. Truman Presidential Museum & Library in Independence, Missouri; the staff at the Naval Historical Center; the highly competent and friendly researchers at the Imperial War Museum in London, for information dealing with British ships, especially Royal Fleet Auxiliary (RFA) ships; the librarians at the Naval War College at Newport, Rhode Island; Duke University research librarians; the bibliographical librarian at the Nimitz Library, United States Naval Academy; and the staff at the New York Public Library. Other individuals it is important to acknowledge are Gregg Edwards, Executive Director of the Center for the Study of the Korean War, and Joni Wilson, an institution herself, whose magic purple pencil made a world of difference.

Other individuals have lent their support and expertise to the completion of this collection. High among these are my long-suffering wife Carolynn, my always attentive companion Bailey, and longtime dear friend Gregg Smith, as well as Center volunteers and associates Lisa Hecht, Lewis Oglethorpe, Cindy Roberts, Nancy Eilser, and Jack Eller.

Table of Contents

Acknowledgments — vii
Preface — 1
Introduction — 5

1. A Brief History of the Naval War — 15
2. Ship Identity and Designation — 30
3. Little Brothers — 41
4. Command and Convalescence — 57
5. Submarines — 62
6. The Landing Ships: Men and Equipment — 70
7. Feeding the Fleet — 94
8. Tenders and Tugs, Rescue, Repair, and Salvage — 127
9. Attack Transports — 139
10. Minesweepers — 151
11. Merchant Marines — 166
12. Other Ships in Action — 199
13. Allied Nations — 208
14. Analysis of the Other Ships — 222

Bibliography — 227
Index — 233

Preface

> *The Navy is on its way out. There is no reason for having a Navy and Marine Corps. General Bradley tells me that amphibious operations are a thing of the past. We'll never have any more amphibious operations. That does away with the Marine Corps. And the Air Force can do anything the Navy can do nowadays, so that does away with the Navy.*
> — Secretary of Defense Louis Johnson, 1949

Following the assault on Inchon, Korea, on 15 September 1950, General Douglas MacArthur lavished heavy praise on the naval and Marine officers who planned and executed the operation. He declared it a performance which "not only sustained our country's great naval tradition, but which in ultimate effect is probably unexcelled in the history of warfare."* While directed toward this single engagement, the praise reflects the role played by the United States Navy during the Korean War, for it was a highly significant role and one without which the outcome of the war might have been vastly different. Yet, in the decades since the war, the role of the Navy has been greatly ignored and it might easily be defined as the forgotten service of the forgotten war.

It has become popular to refer to the Korean War as the "forgotten war," and there are certainly justifications for this. While this is not the place to argue the relative merits as to how the Korean War should be addressed, it is nevertheless true that the term "forgotten" may be misleading, for "forgotten" implies the loss of memory about something that was once known. Perhaps it would be better to suggest that the war in Korea (1950–53) has been ignored. That is, it has never been properly acknowledged nor understood by the American people.

From what appeared to be a civil war between the Republic of Korea and the Democratic People's Republic of Korea, a powerful multinational war emerged. It was a war that would eventually involve more than twenty-five nations, and draw nearly five million men and women from around the world into the devastating effects of combat. It quickly became an event through which conflicting ideologies were to be tested, where the Soviet Union and international communism would be met head-on by Western nations represented by the

---

*Malcolm W. Cagle and Frank A. Manson, *The Sea War in Korea* (Annapolis, MD: United States Naval Institute Press, 1957), 105.

United Nations. It was, as Vice Admiral A. D. Struble was to comment, "a major war confined to a small area." To ignore the impact of the Korean War is to put us deeply in danger of repeating the same mistakes of history.

It is true, as well, that even among those who are familiar with the war, there are many who are vastly ignorant of many aspects of it. One such case has been the failure to comprehend the role played by naval forces in this unique conflict. Granted, in any war it is the GIs fighting on the ground who play the fundamental role. And the newly constituted United States Air Force made a significant contribution as it fought its first war, while involved in developing whole new concepts based on the emergence of jet aircraft. The role of the air force in Korea has been more easily dramatized. The marines, though officially part of the navy, nevertheless had an independent and courageous role. This role has perhaps been as well told as any. However, the story of the war will remain sketchy until significant attention is given to the important role played by the United States Navy and the naval forces of the United Nations.

The nation of Korea occupies a peninsula, which means that simple geography dictates the presence and necessary participation of a naval force if control is to be maintained. Because neither the Democratic People's Republic of Korea (North Korea) nor the Republic of China (ROC) had much of a navy with which to challenge the United Nations forces, and since the Soviet Union decided not to allow its own naval forces to become involved, it is sometimes suggested that the U.S. Navy had no one to fight.

Those who do remember the Korean War, even the naval involvement, are more inclined to consider the massive carriers with their fleets of planes, and battleships, cruisers and even some destroyers. It is human nature for us to be drawn to those whose role appears to be the most significant in the winning of these wars. But to do so is both inaccurate and unfair.

Few recall the minesweeper, the picket boat, the ammunition carrier, the rescue ship, the tugs, and the tankers. How many Americans are aware that submarines played an important role in the Korean War? Nevertheless, far more who participated in this great endeavor were involved on support ships, supplies, or maintenance, sometimes called "the train." These ships have been referred to in this work as "the little ships." But the job they did, and the performance of the men and women who made it happen, was magnificent.

The reference to these vessels as "little ships" should not be taken to mean insignificant, for these ships and their crews were an essential part of the war effort. What is little about them is generally their size and the amount of armament that they carried, or even the amount of attention they drew. They are seen as support and service vessels, and tend to occupy the periphery. In fact, some of these ships are as large or larger than the combat ships about which we hear so much more. A ship like a destroyer minesweeper supported considerable tonnage. Some, like the attack transports and cargo vessels, carried hundreds of troops or massive amounts of ammunition or equipment. Others, like tugs and minesweepers, were very small, operated with small complements, and performed very specific functions.

Much of the material used to write this book comes from the archives of the Center for the Study of the Korean War. On most days visitors come into the Center and talk of their time in Korea. The majority of the Navy men did not serve on large ships. A few, perhaps, have memories of a carrier or battleship, but most served on one of the numerous ships of support. They often want to know where they were ("much of the ocean looks very much alike," they say) and what was going on around them during their service. They have stories of incredible courage, interminable boredom, unending monotony and moments of desperate bewilderment and danger. Most of them are thankful that their lot fell into the U.S. Navy and all expressed great loyalty and affection for their ships and shipmates. Few have much of a picture of the larger combat situation, for their war focused on a variety of often-repeated functions and unglamorous jobs.

It is in the memory of these vessels and the men who sailed them that this volume has been constructed. The little ships, the auxiliary ships, the utility ships, the support ships — however it is best to identify them — all played integral roles, often unheralded because they did their work in the support of the capital ships rather than in the delivery of bombardments and intervention. These ships did everything from clearing the harbors of mines to delivering troops to the beaches of Inchon and Wonsan. The work of these ships was both excitingly dangerous and awesomely boring. Hour upon hour of sailing, loading and unloading, deliveries and evacuation, interspersed with intense action, backbreaking labor, and mind-numbing sameness.

This war was a confrontation between the Democratic People's Republic of Korea and the Republic of China on one side, and the United Nations and the Republic of South Korea on the other. In his *United States Naval Action in Korea* James Field describes the Korean War as a "surprising war in a surprising place at a surprising time, and one, which imperatively called for answers to neglected problems of national defense."*

This war was fought in a distant and seemingly strange country; unknown to most in the West, North and South Korea were rarely considered to be of any interest or value. Certainly the United States view, broadcast in Secretary of State Dean Acheson's January 1950 talk to the American Press Club, was that Korea was outside America's area of influence and concern.

First populated by people who spoke the Ural-Altaic language, Korea has remained a surprisingly homogeneous nation. Tradition suggests Tangun founded Korea in 2333 B.C., but it was the Choson dynasty, which had come into power in 1392 A.D. that ruled until the Japanese annexation in 1910. Japanese control of Korea was tight, ruthless, and executed in a manner meant to influence Korean language and culture. The Allies had divided Korea along the 38th parallel as a result of meetings among the "Big Three." Consequently, when Japan surrendered in 1945, Korea came under the control of the United States and the Soviet Union. As these Cold War nations exerted influence and control, the United Nations effort to unify Korea and establish a national government failed.

About 80 percent of North Korea consists of mountain ranges, forested hills separated by long deep valleys and small cultivated plains. The most rugged areas are in the north and east. Good harbors are found on the east coast. The capital city Pyongyang is located on the Taedong River near the west coast. South Korea's capital is Seoul. Most of the agricultural areas of the Korean Peninsula are found in South Korea, and rice is the primary product.

At the outbreak of the war, the United States, despite its power and determination, was not prepared. The CIA analysis of the North Korean invasion, supplied to the president less than a month before the invasion, provides this somewhat ambiguous description of the situation: "The U.S. does not have the military force-in-readiness to honor its commitments with U.S. military forces and equipment in many areas other than Korea (perhaps none) without a substantial increase in U.S. Military forces and industrial productivity in the military field, bringing about what would amount to at least a partial (as distinguished from a general) mobilization for war."†

---

*James A. Field, *History of United States Naval Operations: Korea* (Washington, D.C.: Office of Naval History, 1962), ix.
 †"CIA Analysis of the North Korean Invasion," Intelligence Memo No. 302, Documents R-114, Truman Presidential Library and Museum, Independence, Missouri. Quoted in Cagle and Manson, op. cit., 462.

And yet the job given the Navy was immense. Colonel Joseph H. Alexander, USMC (retired) insightfully wrote in the preface of his book *Fleet Operations in a Mobile War, September 1950–June 1951*, "On the strategic level, the Navy protected Japan and Taiwan by vigilantly guarding against threats to these countries from two powerful and implacable enemies who shared a common cause with North Korea — the Soviet Union and the People's Republic of China. Each mission in Korean waters had to be executed with one eye on the real danger of superpower intervention, the possible onset of a third world war. The situation abided throughout the war, but proved exceptionally stressful between September 1950 and June 1951."*

---

*Joseph H. Alexander, *Fleet Operations in a Mobile War* (Washington, DC: Naval Historical Center, 2001), vi.

INTRODUCTION

*In every field — amphibious, logical, aviation, operational and planning —
the impact was monumental. Korea was a naval proving ground.*
— Malcolm W. Cagle and Frank A. Manson, *The Sea War in Korea*

As World War II came to an end, the United States, following its usual postwar pattern, demobilized the armed forces as quickly as possible. The United States was tired of war and its expense, and moved quickly to cut expenditures required to maintain the armed forces. In the following five years the government reduced the size of the military considerably, with the U.S. Navy suffering a cut of about 90 percent. At the same time the navy was involved in a bitter debate with the air force over the relative merits and funding of naval versus land-based air power. In 1943, General George C. Marshall, Chairman of the Joint Chiefs of Staff, called for the unification of the services. A serious move in this direction was taken in 1947 when the National Security Act created a National Military Establishment, a National Security Council, and the Central Intelligence Agency, and approved the development of the U.S. Air Force as an independent command.

In this inter-war period, the Soviet Union was acknowledged as the potential enemy the United States would face in any future war. Russia was a land power with only a moderate sea-going navy and not susceptible to a naval blockade. As a result the U.S. Navy, as well as the British Navy, concluded that the focus of foreign policy should be along the line of national security and that the deployment of offensive naval forces, focused around the aircraft carriers, would serve as both a symbolic commitment to its allies, and the best defense. The use of naval power directed toward the Eurasian periphery fit in well with the expectations of the NATO doctrine.

During this time the Soviet Union, with more ambitious goals, had expanded its World War II strength. The United States, however, was not so concerned. The decision to put significant segments of its World War II naval strength in mothballs caused considerable criticism from those who thought the reserve fleet should be disposed of. The expense of maintaining reasonable combat-readiness for its navy seemed far too expensive. New construction of ships, as well as the completion of many ships not yet finished, was primarily halted. Commanders Malcolm W. Cagle and Frank A. Manson, in *The Sea War in Korea*, provide an excellent description of the situation:

"At the end of World War II, the goals which the United States set for itself, while commendable, were actually beyond realization within the self-imposed limits. The United States was trying to maintain a military posture, assimilate the lessons of World War II, accommodate the facts of the atomic age and jet propulsion, and simultaneously reduce military forces to peace-time levels despite expanding overseas commitments."*

Extrapolating from the success of naval air power in World War II and determined to get its share of support for aircraft capable of carrying the multi-ton nuclear bombs then in the arsenal, the navy was well into its plan for building a super-carrier, the USS *United States* (CVA 58). But there were anti-naval forces at work in the Truman administration.

In understanding the period it is important to remember that the war in Korea was America's first war fought under the newly unified Department of Defense. This unification had arrived at considerable cost to the trust level between senior officers of the navy, marine corps, air force and army. This uneasiness, in part, was the result of the so-called "revolt of the admirals."

The Revolt of the Admirals

The revolt of the admirals was hardly a revolt, but it was a passionate and public debate over the significance of the navy and naval air power. It had been building for nearly a decade and eventually resulted in the resignation of Louis E. Denfeld, Chief of Naval Operations, and John L. Sullivan, Secretary of the Department of the Navy. During the last years of World War II, General George C. Marshall had called for a postwar unification of the Department of War and the Department of the Navy. His efforts eventually led to the "unification debates" and finally to the passage of the National Security Act of 1947 and through it the unification of command.

The argument challenged the need to maintain naval and marine forces that it was believed were no longer necessary in the wake of America's emergence as an atomic nation. Underlying this was the assumption that a war, should one break out, could be won by the use of strategic bombers carrying atomic weapons, if necessary. In vital disagreement the Navy had called for the creation of a series of super carriers beginning with the USS *United States* (CVA 58) on the basis that wars could not be won by bombing alone and that even if such action became necessary these larger carriers could carry nuclear bombers. When the first Secretary of Defense, James V. Forrestal, resigned in March 1949, he was replaced by Louis A. Johnson, who supported the air force point of view. Within a few weeks of taking office Johnson cancelled plans for the USS *United States* and announced that Marine Corps assets would be transferred to the Air Force. In rebuttal, a research group, Op-23, headed by Captain Arleigh A. Burke, produced an "anonymous document" (later shown to have been written by Cedric R. Worth, a civilian employee of the Secretary of the Navy) that brought considerable criticism to bear on the capabilities of the B-36 and even suggested the concept of the large bomber was a blunder, partially based on fraud, because of Secretary Johnson's reputed contacts with the bomber's manufacturers, Consolidated Vultee.

The war continued on paper and in testimony until the national doctrine of strategic bombing came to a head on 25 June 1950 with the invasion of South Korea. The outbreak of war in Korea called for a conventional response and both the U.S. Navy and U.S. Marines Corps responded. While the argument continued in many circles of government as well as

---

*Cagle and Manson, *The Sea War in Korea*, 12.

the military, the decision in 1950 was that the United States would not use nuclear bombing to defeat North Korea, and thus ground forces, with the support of naval gunfire and amphibious activities, would be employed. Even after the war the Air Force continued its argument that the war was an aberration. However, it would appear that the wars in Korea, Vietnam, Operation Desert Storm, Kosovo, and now Iraq have proven the necessity of intra-service cooperation, and history has come down of the side of those who supported the maintenance of strong naval and marine forces.

The State of the Fleet

There remained some conflict between navy and marine officers who were deeply suspicious of the leadership of the army and the newly developed air force. Unification, despite its good intentions, had created a strain on the internal harmony of unified command.

When President Truman announced America's opposition to North Korean aggression and considered an adequate response, the naval component was far from ready. The U.S. Far East Command under General Douglas MacArthur consisted of the commander of Naval Forces Far East and twenty-nine officers. The fleet consisted of one cruiser, four destroyers, four amphibious ships, one submarine, ten minesweepers and a frigate that was on attached duty from the Australian Navy. Much of the Navy's amphibious force was a "rusty travesty" of the fleet available during World War II. Much of what would become available were the remnants of the fleet that had since been transferred to Japanese charters. Fortunately, Amphibious Group 1 ships had been involved in amphibious familiarization training in Japan just before the war started.

Conditions changed quickly when operational control of the Seventh Fleet, consisting of almost all of the navy's ships in the U.S. Pacific Fleet, was transferred to ComNavFE. The forces, which were soon to be an international mix, were quickly organized into four task forces — a carrier force; a blockade-and-escort force; Naval Forces, Japan; and the Far East Amphibious Force. Eventually all naval forces drawn together to address the North Koreans were placed under ComNavFE command. The immediate need for more ships brought about the decisions to begin withdrawing vessels from reserve fleets.

The National Defense Reserve Fleet (NDRF)

Following the end of World War II, the Merchant Ship Sales Act (1946) established a "fleet" of inactive but potentially useful merchant ships, under the custody of the Maritime Administration (MARAD), that were government owned and maintained. The MARAD was the governmental agency responsible for maintaining the merchant marine. These ships were inactive but potentially essential resources, held in fleets at Puget Sound Naval Shipyard near Bremerton, Washington; Philadelphia Naval Shipyard; on the James River near Newport News, Virginia; near Beaumont, Texas, on the Neches River; and on Suisun Bay, near Vallego, California. The estimated yearly cost for each mothballed ship was about $19,000. At the time an estimated 2,277 ships were laid up in what has been called the mothball fleet. Today the ships of the National Defense Reserve Fleet are located at the sites on the James River, the Neches River, and Suisun Bay.

At the outbreak of hostilities in Korea in 1950, ships began to be withdrawn and eventually 540 vessels were released to support military service. In the same period (1951–53) 600 vessels were reactivated to lift coal to Europe and grain to India, and finally as storage ships for the Department of Agriculture.

The Naval Register

The Naval Vessel Register (NVR), often called the navy list, is the official inventory of vessels either titled to, or in custody of, the United States Navy. Like most military things it has its own history, tracing as far back at the 1880s. It began in its modern form as the *Ships' Data: U.S. Naval Vessels* in 1911, then became the *Ships Data Book* (1952), published by the Bureau of Ordnance. The *Vessel Register* (1942) was combined with the *Ships Data Book* in 1959. A ship is registered when the hull and classification numbers are assigned, or when reinstallation is requested. Once registered, a ship remains as an asset throughout its life, and its final disposition is recorded. This information, updated weekly, is available, as required by U.S. Code 10, Section 7304–7308, and maintained under U.S. Navy Regulations 0406 (14 September 1990). The Naval Register is currently available electronically.

The Arrival of UN Ships

The Allied response to the UN call for action was quicker at sea than it was on the ground. Great Britain placed its ships located in the immediate area under the UN command. Other nations quickly followed. Sixteen countries eventually offered aid. The first blockade unit, Task Force 96.5, the East Korean Support Group, included the frigate HMAS *Shoalhaven*. The West Korean Support Group, Task Force 96.8, included the frigates HMS *Hart*, *Black*, *Swan*, and *Alacrity*. Their support consisted of thirty-two warships, five carriers, six cruisers, seven destroyers, and fourteen frigates as well as numerous cargo, troop, and supply vessels.

Japan: Friend or Enemy

Despite the fact that the United States was still officially at war with the Empire of Japan, and that Japan was not a participant in the United Nations, the Japanese played a significant role during the Korean War. At the time Japanese military facilities were under the control of the occupational government, but cooperation was generally very good. The Japanese not only supplied most necessary air and naval bases, they also provided aid through the Japanese National Railroads, the Japanese Coast Guard and the Red Cross. Naval involvement was maintained by the Shipping Control Administration of Japan (SCAJAP) and controlled by the U.S. Navy. Their sailors were involved in transporting marines to Inchon, and the Japanese Coast Guard was involved in the mine-clearing exercise at Wonsan.

The UN force assembled under Admiral Struble for the invasion of Inchon attests to the breadth of the UN commitment. It consisted of 71,339 officers and men on the assault or follow-up, 230 ships from seven navies, plus Military Sea Transportation Service (MSTS), and even 34 Japanese LSTs, one of which, it was often suggested, was commanded by a former battleship captain. There was no air force participation.

During the invasion at Inchon more than 120 Japanese barges were contracted and sent to Pusan but the crews had not been informed. When word reached them of the battle, 28 of the barge crews refused to proceed. The remaining 92, however, accompanied by a Korean light tug and minesweeper, continued. Thirty-eight LSTs, from the SCAJAP, were involved in the landing as well. The LSTs were invaluable as they represented nearly three-quarters of the LSTs available. The Japanese involvement was large enough, as well as being considered to be in violation of Japan's status as an occupied nation, that the North Koreans and Chinese identified the Japanese as a belligerent nation.

The Navy of the Republic of Korea

When the Korean War began, the Republic of Korea navy (ROKN) consisted of 6,956 officers and men with 71 vessels of various types. It had begun as a coast guard and was being developed under the leadership of U.S. Navy and Coast Guard personnel when the decision was made to reconstruct it into a navy. As it developed it was concentrated on the western and southern posts. Even given its limited capabilities, the first naval encounter and one of the few naval engagements of the war occurred when PC 701 sank a North Korean freighter trying to land invasion troops at Pusan. The following day YMS 513, a minesweeper, destroyed three Communist supply vessels near Chulpo. With the consent of the ROK government, American Vice Admiral C. Turner Joy assigned Commander Michael J. Luosey and a staff of six to take operational control of the ROKN. This was in keeping with the operating rules for the UN command during the war. Thereafter the ROKN, working in union with the UN command, carried out significant roles: minesweeping, amphibious assaults, the landing of demolition teams, carrying supplies, gathering intelligence, and most significantly patrolling the islands which were particularly vulnerable to North Korean attack and occupation along the west coast.

Special Operations

It will help to understand the role of the navy as it was involved in what is now termed Special Operations. Rather early, Admiral Joy acknowledged that air-sea interdiction efforts were not as successful in helping the deteriorating ground war as he wished, and he sought another means. In consultation with Admiral Doyle it was decided to establish a quick movement raider force to be delivered by high-speed transports, which the navy made available. In support of these activities the USS *Bass* was reconfigured to aid the parties, and the USS *Perch*, a specially designed transport submarine, was brought into play. As the war went on, these support activities, as well as the scope and complexity of the raider groups, expanded. The Central Intelligence Agency got involved, as did partisan and guerrilla groups, all of which counted on naval support to land and extract their parties.

National Policy

Not only was the inter-war period one of downsizing and disagreement, it was also a period of policy change. In what has been called "The Transoceanic Period," the navy took on a different look. World War II had vindicated the principles of U.S. sea power, but the focus on the Soviet Union as a potential enemy raised questions of how the navy would be used against a primarily ground and air power. What resulted was a shift to a policy of national security in which, according to Michael A. Palmer,

"diplomacy and military power were closely intertwined ... where forward-deployed, offensively capable naval forces, generally built around carrier battle groups, became symbols of the U.S. commitment to its allies, most notably those in the eastern Mediterranean and the western Pacific. The outbreak of war in the Korean peninsula in June 1950 further strengthened the hands of U.S. navalists. Most notably during the carrier-supported Inchon amphibious assault of September 1950, the United States demonstrated that naval power still had an important role to play in the atomic age."*

Ship Size and Assignment

We have acknowledged that those we think of as "going in harm's way" are most often cited in reports of combat or in narratives of naval history, thus blessed with a position in the memory of Americans. It is understandable why many find it exciting to consider fleets of planes rising off the deck of a carrier to attack the enemy or fight the enemy's planes; or to consider the massive flash of the USS *Missouri*'s 16-inch guns blasting against an enemy coastal position, or the fleeting movements of a sleek destroyer on the trail of a submarine contact. But, while these "ships of the line" played a highly significant role in the battles of the Korean War, they do not properly reflect the naval contribution.

Hundreds of other ships, carrying thousands of men, were involved. Their role, by virtue of design or assignment, was care, supply and maintenance. All of these ships are significant; their crews all served with efficiency, courage, and determination. Many have never been mentioned in dispatches, have not made their way into the histories of the war, and are sometimes listed, but rarely discussed, even in works about the naval war. But there would have been no war without them, and whatever good came out of the Korean War is dependent to a significant degree on the role played by these ships of service.

The concept of mobile support for the ships of the line goes back as far as the war with Tripoli when the frigate *John Adams* was put into service supplying the fighting ships. This was repeated and enlarged during the Spanish-American War when the distances involved made it necessary to take supplies and equipment to the navy rather than pulling ships off the line for replenishment. On 25 June 1950 the service support ships available consisted of an LST, a destroyer tender, a reefer, a tug and a fleet tanker. The only hospital ship and the single fleet stores issue ship had been decommissioned and the lone landing ship (dock) had only escaped the same fate by being loaned to Operation Greenhouse, the atomic testing program. The single ammunition ship, the *Mount Katmai,* was at Port Chicago.

Coast Guard

The United States Coast Guard was involved in a variety of tasks in Korea. There were twenty-four USCG cutters serving in the theater of operations during the Korean War. They

---

*Michael A. Palmer, "The Navy: The Transoceanic Period, 1945–1992," Department of the Navy, n.d.

established air positioning posts at Sangley Point in the Philippines, as well as in Guam, Wake, and Midway, and at Barbers Point in the Hawaiian islands, from which they conducted thousands of search and rescue missions to provide safety for those in transit across the Pacific. Twelve destroyer escorts were transformed to the Guard to aid in carrying out this duty. More than fifty members of the Guard were stationed in Korea to aid in the development of the ROK Navy. The Guard also provided communications support programs, plane guards, and meteorological services. Twenty-four cutters (previously destroyers) served on station and were eligible for the Korean Service Medal.

At home the Coast Guard was charged with the responsibility of the security of U.S. ports and harbors. The primary concern was to prevent disruption of military cargoes that were bound for Korea or Japan. Boat-patrolling stations were occupied 24 hours a day, and in the first two years of the war, the New York Ambrose lightship station inspected more than 1,500 ships. They were also responsible for the highly dangerous job of loading ammunition.

During the Korean War the Coast Guard nearly doubled in size since its 1947 low, rising to an active duty figure of 35,082 officers and enlisted men and women.

Eligibility for the Korean Service Medal

President Harry S. Truman, with Executive Order 10179, issued 8 November 1950, authorized the Korean Service Medal. The following rules of eligibility were established*:

1. The ship's service must be performed in Korean waters adjacent thereto, within the following limits: From a point at latitude 39.30" N., longitude 122.45"E. southward to latitude 33.N, longitude 122.45'E., thence eastward to latitude 33.N., longitude 127.55'E.; thence northeastward to latitude 37.05' N., longitude 133.E., thence northward to latitude 40.40' N., longitude 133 E.; thence northwestward to a point on the east coast of Korea at the juncture of Korea with the U.S.S.R, or in such areas as Commander, Naval Forces Far East, considers has having directly supported the military effort in Korea.

2. The duty must have been performed between 27 June 1950 and 27 July 1954. (Note that this late date takes into consideration the hostile conditions that followed the cease-fire for several months.)

3. Those on temporary duty must have served 30 consecutive days or 60 nonconsecutive days in the assigned area unless on board a vessel that was attacked or engaged in combat, in which case they shall become immediately eligible without reference to time.

4. Passengers are not eligible unless the vessel on which they are traveling is either attacked or engaged in combat, in which case they shall become immediately eligible.

5. Patients on hospital ships shall be considered as attached to the ship.

Using This Book

A few general comments about the organization of this book will make it more useful.

1. It is important to note that the time in Korea is fourteen hours ahead of Washington, D. C. That is, the invasion which occurred at 4:00 A.M. in Korea was reported in the United

---

Service Medals and Campaign Credits for the United States Navy (Department of the Navy, 1959).

States at 2:00 P.M. on the previous day. To help in clarity, the times used in this book reflect the time that is recorded at the point of the event under consideration.

2. The 38th parallel of north latitude runs 19,648 miles around the earth. Of this, 196 miles cross Korea, one percent of the whole, while the remainder crosses twelve countries, including China, Russia, and the United States.

3. The names, designations, and sometimes even the numbers of ships changed during their active life. Inasmuch as has been possible all names have been included with dates provided under the ship's primary identification. The numbers of many landing crafts were supplemented in July of 1955 with names and though these names were activated after the end of the Korean War, they are often used to discuss the ships' earlier action. Therefore the names as well as the numbers are used in accounting for these vessels.

4. Of major concern was the decision about which vessels to include and exclude. This decision was made on the basis of the best consensus between the leading reports of ship activities. The sources consulted were: ships' logs, *Dictionary of American Naval Fight Ships* (Department of the Navy, Naval Historical Center); Malcolm W. Cagle and Frank A. Munson, *The Sea War in Korea*; *The United States Coast Guard in the Korean War* (korea 50.army.mil/history/factsheets/coastguard.shtml); "The Korean Service Medal 1950–1954, Ships and Other Units of the U.S. Navy and Marine Corps"; *Navy and Marine Corps Awards Manual*; Bureau of Naval Personnel; and U.S. Marine Corps Headquarters. There is considerable disagreement between these sources; where sources conflict, every effort has been made to cross-reference them, but when some confusion remains, *United States Naval Vessels: The Official United States Navy Reference Manual* has been used as the accepted source. The primary difference between reports is reflected in armament provided, and is based on general sources. It is generally accepted that these reflect the differences in armament that was available at the time of commissioning.

5. The keys to identifying individual sources are: Malcolm W. Cagle, and Frank A. Mason, *The Sea War in Korea* [Cagle]; *Navy and Marine Corps Award Manual* [Awards]; M. P. Crocker, *West Coast Support Group* [Crocker]; and *Dictionary of American Naval Fighting Ships* [DANFS].

6. The time period needs to be determined when the question of eligibility is close. Since the official dates given for the Korean War are 27 June 1950 to 1 January 1954, some ships will be included that served in Korean waters after the armistice, but during a time when hostilities were still potential. Therefore any ship that was eligible for the Korean Service Medal, however interpreted, has been included.

7. Only one battle star is given for one or more engagement within the same campaign. The ten official awards campaigns for the U.S. Navy are as follows: North Korean Aggression: 27 June to 2 November 1950. Communist China Aggression: 3 November 1950 to 24 January 1951. Inchon Landing: 13–17 September 1950. First UN Counteroffensive: 25 January to 21 April 1951. Communist China Spring Offensive: 22 April to 8 July 1951. UN Summer-Fall Offensive: 9 July to 27 November 1951. Second Korean Winter: 28 November 1951 to 30 April 1952. Korean Defense Summer-Fall 1952: 1 May to 30 November 1952. Third Korean Winter: 1 December 1952 to 30 April 1953. Korea, Summer-Fall 1953: 1 May to 27 July 1953.

8. In order to meet the needs of its service, the U.S. Navy turned over a number of destroyer escorts to the Coast Guard. These are designated with the prefix "W." The Guard commissioned these ships as cutters. Most of them were very old and had aged while sailing on convoy duty during World War II. To better equip these ships they were fitted with a shel-

ter on the stern that was used for weather balloons, and armed with a variety of depth charges and anti-aircraft weapons. Twelve of these ships were transferred, the first two being the USS *Koiner* and the USS *Falgout*.

Their primary duty consisted of maintaining ocean stations, which served as weather stations, and to help guard the movement of troops and equipment to Korea. During 1950 the busiest of these, called *Station Nan*, reported giving 375 fixes per patrol. A patrol, the length of time a ship stayed on station, was about 700 hours, during which a ship steamed an approximate 4,000 miles. Coast Guard ships that served with the forces in Korea are listed along with the U.S. Navy vessels of the same type.

9. Naval vessels are built according to classes, and ships within the classification have the same general specification. Yet individual ships within a class may vary somewhat. The armament, for example, was dependent on what was available at the time. Therefore, even though the class is listed, the individual specifications are provided in some cases because of the variation. Even then, be aware that the technical statistics provided vary somewhat. In most cases they have been checked with the *Dictionary of American Naval Fighting Ships*, or individual ship plans, but even these sources vary. Some information is simply not available; there is no discernable record of what happens to a particular ship once it has been decommissioned. The displacements listed are those when the ship is unloaded unless otherwise indicated, and the speeds offered are often the speed reached on trials. The cruising speed of most ships was considerably slower.

Sources

Specific sources relating to ship information are varied and found in both official and unofficial records. Primary to this compilation is the *Dictionary of Naval Fighting Ships*, an excellent source even if not always up-to-date. Also important: the logs available through the Deck Log Section, Ships History Branch, Naval Historical Center; Operational Archives Branch, Naval Historical Center, and *U.S. Navy Korean War: Chronology of U.S. Pacific Fleet Operation, June-December 1950* (Washington D.C.: Naval Historical Center, 28 June 1950). The activities of the reserve fleets from 1947 through 1960 are available at the Ships Material Readiness Division, Reserve Fleet Ship Branch, Sub-Group Atlantic and Pacific Reserve Fleets, Records of Chief of Naval Operations (OP 432). It is located at Operational Archives Branch, Naval Historical Center, at the Washington Navy Yard, Washington D.C., 20374–5060. Also highly significant are two basic histories of naval operations, Cagle and Manson's *The Sea War in Korea* and James A. Field's *History of United States Naval Operations*. Both of these are old but still very useful. A fairly new and very important work is M. P. Cocker's *West Coast Support Group, Task Force 96.8*. Few histories provide as much detailed description as these three; but, as is normally the case, there is precious little in them about the secondary and support ships discussed in this volume.

1

A Brief History of the Naval War

The advent of the Korean War found the Navy in the midst of a shaky recovery from the tumultuous months of debates on its roles and missions, the "Revolt of the Admirals" and the extensive downsizing of naval forces after World War II.
— Richard Hallion

Looking back more than half a century it is hard to believe that the United States did not foresee the coming of the Korean War, but to a large extent that is apparently true. On the other hand, few in Korea had any doubt that war would break out sooner or later, but there were equally few who could predict just who would attack whom and when. The tensions in Korea, and around the world, which eventually erupted in an outbreak of hostilities have been carefully considered by many well qualified historians, and though their opinions vary they do not need to be recounted here. It is sufficient to say that the decision to divide Korea, and to allow the Soviet Union and the United States to occupy different sections, was not a good idea. Nevertheless it is true that these opposing nations, already involved in heating up the Cold War, used their positions and the general dissatisfaction of the Korean people on both sides of the 38th parallel to aggravate one another.

Despite the many efforts made by the United Nations to unify Korea, that goal was out of reach. The UN finally determined that all that could be done was to hold elections in the south, and support a government in South Korea. During the occupation, North Koreans, under the leadership of Kim Il Sung, continued to undermine the effort at unification, including taking actions to prevent the UN elections — which went off as scheduled in May 1948 — from including the North Korean vote.

A large percentage of the southern population voted. The reply that came from the north was to cut off power lines sending energy to the South, a move that was countered by two U.S. Navy power barges that furnished electricity until the Republic of Korea could compensate in its production. The government of the Republic of Korea, while certainly not the democracy the U.S. might have wanted, functioned under its president Syngman Rhee and, as arranged, both the United States and the Soviet Union withdrew their occupation forces.

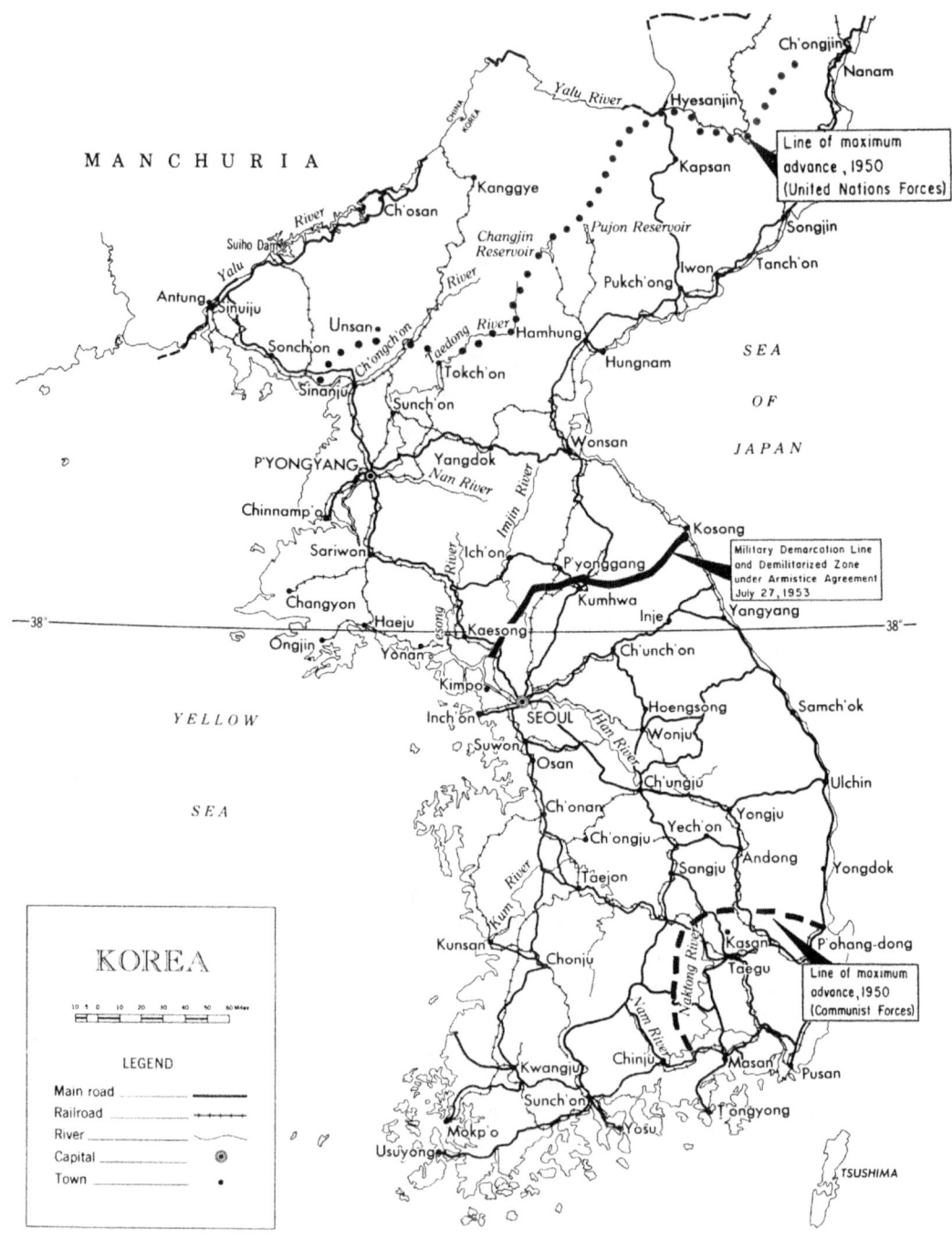

Map of Korea (courtesy Paul Wolfgeher Collection, Center for the Study of the Korean War, Graceland University).

The Democratic People's Republic of Korea, created shortly after the formation of the Republic of Korea, crossed the 38th parallel in force on the 25 June 1950, setting off hostilities between the separated states. The forces of the Republic of Korea, though beginning to gain strength, were unable to present a strong enough front to stop the communists at the parallel and were soon falling back all along the border. As North Korean troops advanced across the parallel, a border constabulary brigade of nearly 10,000 troops executed amphibious landings at Kangnung and Samchok.

In response to this crisis, President Truman, in a series of meeting in Blair House, ordered the evacuation of American dependents and authorized General MacArthur to assist in the evacuation of Americans and noncombatants. MacArthur was also authorized to use air and naval forces to prevent the Inchon-Kimpo-Seoul airfield from falling into enemy hands before the evacuation was complete. To support the ROK Army he was urged to send as much ammunition as possible. American ships, the USS *Juneau* and *De Haven*, escorted the ammunition ships *Sergeant Keathley* from Tokyo, and the USS *Collett* and *Mansfield* escorted the laden *Cardinal O'Connell* to Korea.

By 26 June the president authorized naval and air attacks against all North Korean troops south of the 38th parallel, and removed all restrictions on the use of naval forces of the Far East Command in the coastal waters of Korea. Acting alone, and then with the support of the United Nations Security Council, the United States responded to the threat. Vice Admiral Arthur D. Struble, the Seventh Fleet Commander was still in Washington, D.C., and the Commander, Carrier Division, Rear Admiral J. M. Hopkins was placed in command. Fortunately the Seventh Fleet and the forces of NavFE (Naval Forces, Far East) were within a quickly traversed distance from Korea. Also in the area was the First Amphibious Group under Rear Admiral James H. Doyle.

On 29 June 1950 Truman authorized General MacArthur to use army troops if necessary to furnish supplies and maintain control of evacuation ports. On the 31st MacArthur received instructions from the Joint Chiefs of Staff that included this statement: "The Seventh Fleet is assigned to your operational control. You are authorized to extend your military operations into North Korea against ... purely military targets if and when in your judgment this becomes essential."*

The instructions for the navy came on 26 June, Washington time:

CINCFE [commander in chief, Far East] is authorized to take such action by air and Navy to insure safe evacuation of U.S. dependents and noncombatants ... Seventh Fleet is ordered to proceed immediately to Sasebo and report to ComNavFE for operational control.... While the foregoing decisions are geared to the protection of dependents and noncombatants, further high-level decisions may be expected as military and political situation develops.†

The crossing of the 38th was accompanied by a number of small unopposed landings along the east coast as far to the south as Samchok. They were contained, as they could be, by the small but determined navy of the Republic of Korea. Located at Inchon on the day of the invasion there were four Yard Class Minesweepers (YMS), two steel-hulled ex–Japanese minecraft (JML) and the only tank landing ship (LST) in the Korean navy. At Mokpo, at the southwestern tip of Korea, some small craft and two YMS were available. At Pusan there were nine YMS and small craft. Perhaps the most significant surface battle of the war took place on the night of 25 June 1950, when PC 701 under the command of Nam Cho Yong met and sunk an armed steamer near Pusan with 680 North Korean troops on board. Since Pusan was the only port of entry available to South Korea and because it was basically defenseless at that time, a successful landing of enemy forces could have been a highly significant event.

During the nearly three months following the invasion, and prior to the landing at Inchon

---
*Walter Karig, Malcolm W. Cagle, and Frank A. Manson, *Battle Report: The War in Korea* (New York: Rinehart, 1952), 55.
†Cagle and Manson, *The Sea War in Korea*, 34.

on 15 September 1950, the war in Korea was fought as a defensive retreat, finally ending up in a perimeter around the port city of Pusan. The role of the navy during this period was composed of varied missions: the close air support missions of Task Forces 77 and 96, armed reconnaissance of enemy troops and positions, the cruiser and destroyer bombardment along the east coast, and the amphibious landing of American troops at Pohang. There 10,027 troops, 2,027 vehicles, and 2,729 tons of supplies were unloaded in less than twelve hours. The navy also conducted the evacuation of elements of the 3rd ROK division, as well as providing the vast logistical support that gradually built up the UN force in and around Pusan.

The passage of the UN resolution calling on member nations to support military action in Korea produced fairly immediate results. The first to respond was Great Britain when, on 28 June 1950, she made available the light fleet carrier HMS *Triumph*, the cruisers HMS *Belfast* and *Jamaica*, two destroyers, and the frigates, HMS *Black Swan*, *Alacrity*, and *Hart*. The Australian and New Zealand governments quickly followed suit. The UN call for support eventually resulted in the response of more than seventeen nations.

At the end of the first ten days a steam of shipping was flowing across the Korean Strait from Japan to Pusan, the one remaining open port. There, prior to the arrival of an Army Port Command, the unloading of more than fifty ships with 15,000 troops and 1,700 vehicles was accomplished by Economic Cooperation Administration (ECA) employees. The first military offensive response came with the combined efforts of Task Force 77 in the bombardment of Pyongyang. Also identified for attack were rail facilities in the areas of Kumchon, Sariwon, and Sinanju. The initial strikes, both on the enemy's capital at Pyongyang and the rail facilities, were deemed successful.

As the ROK and UN troops continued to retreat they took up defensive positions near Taejon where the 24th Division under Major General William F. Dean came under considerable fire. With the defense weakening it was necessary to bring in more troops as quickly as possible and it was determined to take them in at Pohang-dong about seventy miles north of Pusan. The scramble for landing vessels resulted in the collection of the *Oglethorpe* (AKA-100) and *Titania* (AKA-13) and six utility landing ships (LSU) reactivated from the Japanese. The assault got under way on 15 July with the fighting only seven miles to the north. A sweep of the harbor by Mine Squadron Three showed that no mines had been sown and the naval units, after avoiding a quickly forming typhoon called "Grace," arrived on 18 July and were able to land troops administratively (without opposition).

With the success of this mission it was possible to pull elements of the Seventh Fleet from their supporting role and move them north into a series of bombardment and interdiction missions at Wonsan and the Chosin oil refineries. As the fighting consolidated around Pusan, Task Force 77 sailed to the west coast and took on the major role of close air support, its planes and guns providing cover for the GIs on the ground. In support of this effort, ANGLICO (Air-Naval Gunfire Liaison Company) was assigned, and air support became the prime mission under the control of the Fifth Air Force. Second priority were targets of interdiction south of the 38th.

Then, as fighting was still going on at Pusan, the stunning landing at Inchon on 15 September 1950 altered the course of the war. This invasion, the product of the mind and perseverance of General MacArthur, called for a highly risky amphibious landing at the enemy-held port of Inchon. The goal was to cut across Korea, breaking the enemy supply lines and isolating large numbers of troops in the south. The selection of the target was highly controversial because, among other hindrances, it meant dealing with one of the highest tides in the world (as much as 33 feet) and extending mud flats that projected some 6,000 yards into the sea. As well, Flying Fish Channel, through which the landing force would need to approach the shore, was narrow and tortuous. It was so narrow that if one ship in the line grounded, the rest would be trapped. The complexity existed because as the sea approaches Inchon it is heading generally eastward since the harbor is protected by numerous islands both north and south. The Yellow Sea rushes into this pocket and piles up in the narrow channel, creating extreme conditions of high and low water.

The invasion started with bombing raids and a seventy-five minute naval bombardment against the tiny harbor island of Wolmi. Intelligence was unclear as to the extent of the mine danger in Flying Fish Channel. On 11 September 1950, ROK PC 703, commanded by Lee Sung Ho, discovered an enemy boat laying mines. But it turned out that the mines scheduled for sowing there had been delayed in arriving. The advance force, consisting of three APD and one LSD, moved up Flying Fish Channel. There were two waves of LCVP (of eight boats), and one wave of three LSU carrying tanks, and the Marines took the island against fairly light resistance. The actual invasion began on the 15th. There was no time to get in and then back out, so it was decided to leave the LSTs on the beach during the period of low tide. Eight selected from those were turned over to the Supreme Commander, Allies, Japan. The boats were old and had been heavily used. To crew these ships men were pulled in from all over the command, forming ragtag teams with limited experience.

The assault on Red and Blue Beaches were simultaneous as twenty-three waves of tracked landing vehicles (LVTs) hit the beaches. LST 973 was hit by a mortar shell as it beached, but quick work prevented further damage. LST 014, the fourth one in line, was set on fire by enemy gunfire. LSTs 857 and 859 were also hit. The landing, difficult and risky, was nevertheless a success, and within days the 7th Infantry Division, which had landed administratively, had joined the First Marine Division on the move toward Seoul. General Douglas MacArthur communicated to the Navy his appreciation: "The Navy and the Marines had never shone more brightly than this morning." The effects of the successful landing were almost immediate, not the least of which was the breakout from the Pusan Perimeter. In the long run it also had a great deal of effect on the continuing acceptance of amphibious landings, highlighted the significance of maintaining the Marine Corps, and supported the naval arguments for their role in close air support.

With the success at Inchon and Seoul, and the breakout of the Pusan Perimeter, the UN turned from defense to offense. The naval forces were focused on keeping the pressure on the enemy by blockade and bombardment. The raids were so successful that it became something of a chore to locate appropriate targets for the planes of the aircraft carriers. As UN troops approached the 38th parallel a decision had to be made about whether the fight should be taken to the enemy, pushing the retreating North Koreans across the 38th. With the Soviet Union objecting, the decision was made by President Truman and the United Nations to cross the parallel and push for the complete defeat of the North Korean army. General MacArthur was directed to feel "unhampered" from proceeding north.

MacArthur directed the Eighth Army to move north to Pyongyang as the still semi-independent Tenth Corps made the journey from the west to east coast to conduct an amphibious landing at Wonsan and Iwon. There they would proceed west and north. Wonsan had a large harbor of about 300 square miles that was naturally protected from the common typhoons and storms at sea. It was also ice-free during the winter. The bottom was mud and there was good holding ground for anchorage in six to eight fathoms. Before the war Wonsan had been a significant and popular summer resort for wealthy Asians, as well as a transportation and communication center. The planning for this landing was a near copy of the plans for Inchon.

MacArthur had briefly considered landing at the more northern point of Hungnam, but it was eventually discarded in favor of Wonsan. The navy task was large and composed of seven missions: to maintain the blockade of the east-coast ports, to provide naval gunfire in support of troops at the landing site and along the east coast, to provide bombardment on invasion day, to transport the bulk of the Tenth Corps to Wonsan, to conduct an amphibious landing at Wonsan, to defend the beachhead once achieved, and to provide initial logistical support for the Tenth Corps. To accomplish this, Admiral Struble's task force consisted of Carrier Attack Force, CTF 92, Tenth Corps, CTF 95 Advance Force, CTG 96.2 Patrol and Reconnaissance Group, CTG 96.8 Escort Carriers, CTF 77 Fast Carriers and CTF 79 Logistics Support.

But this landing did not go as well as MacArthur anticipated. Two things worked against him this time. The first was that the coast line of Korea was ideal for the use of mines. On the east coast particularly, the location of a large shelf of shallow water made mine planting very effective. The second was that his projected landing site was on the Soviet side of Korea and that the USSR had historically favored the use of defensive mines. It was soon discovered that the harbor at Wonsan was heavily mined, and authorities quickly acknowledged that the mines had to be cleared before there could be any attempt at an amphibious landing.

When the conflict began there were six AMS (wooden-hulled sweepers) and one AM (steel-hulled sweeper) in commission in the Far East. In addition there were 12 Japanese minesweepers under contract, and three AMS in caretaker status. The force available to attack the problem at Wonsan consisted of Mine Squadron Three under Lieutenant Commander D'Arcy V. Shouldice. His flagship, the *Pledge*, commanded by Lt. Richard O. Young, served also as a tender. The other ships in the command were AM-3 *Partridge*, AM-22 *Kite*, AM-28 *Osprey*, AM-32 *Redhead*, AM-40 *Chatterer* and AM-27 *Mocking Bird*. The ships were old and worn.

All in all, more than 300 mines had been spotted along the Korean coast. Some of these were drifters. On 26 September 1950 the USS *Brush* hit a mine and was rendered useless. This was followed by four or five other incidents. On 6 October 1950 Mine Squadron Three left Sasebo for Wonsan. As it turned out, the 400 square miles in the harbor area contained more than 3,000 mines, a mixture of magnetic and contact mines. Later, assault intelligence indicated that the mining of Wonsan and Chinnampo had been going on since 1 August 1950 and had been intensified after the assault at Inchon. The difficulty imposed by the mines was so discouraging that it led Rear Admiral Allan E. "Hoke" Smith to say, "The U. S. Navy has lost command of the sea in Korean waters." While the little sweepers worked, the Marines aboard the amphibious vessels were steaming around and around for fifteen days. After weeks of clearing, as well as the loss of the *Pirate* and the *Pledge*, it was determined that the amphibious landing could go forth.

As Wonsan task force was steaming about in circles, the ROK First Corps had taken Wonsan in a routine operation, so the landing at Wonsan was administrative. Once ashore, approximately 22,000 Marines started north, fanning out toward Hamhung and Hungnam. As the Marines were coming ashore at Wonsan, the 7th Infantry Division, still assigned to Tenth Corps and having been brought to the east coast, was landing at Iwon. By nightfall of 29 October, more than 27,000 army troops had dug in.

On the west coast, the 8th Army was pushing north and, as they did, lengthening their supply lines. It became necessary to open the port of Chinnampo, the primary port for the North Korean capital at Pyongyang, known to be heavily mined. Chinnampo was blocked by islands and a delta, with a muddy tide that rose a minimum of twelve feet with a five-knot current. After considerable difficulty locating sweepers, the USS *Carmick* (DMS 33) and USS *Thompson* (DMS 38) moved up the channel as volunteers. They were followed by three small AMS (Mine Division 51), the USS *Pelican* (AMS 32), USS *Swallow* (AMS 36) and USS *Guall* (AM 16). Just about every clearing technique was attempted, from dropping depth charges to set off mines, to using helicopters to help locate the mines. Finally, the small sweepers cleared the deep-water port. Ten days later, some 200 miles of channel had been cleared and more than 80 mines destroyed.

The war on the ground was sweeping north toward the Yalu River, pushing the North Korean army before it. Eighth Army was moving up on the west in a fairly even mass across the line, and the Tenth Corps progressed in four columns. The Marines went northwest, the 7th Infantry Division north, the ROK First Corps' Third and Capitol Divisions moved steadily along the east coast. By 30 October, Eighth Army was reaching Chongju. On the east coast, elements of the ROK Sixth Division began to report isolated contact with Chinese troops. The appearance of the Chinese did not seem to cause the concern that would now seem justified, and the advance continued until 15 November 1950 when the 7th Marines arrived at Hagaru-ri near the Chosin Reservoir. Soon the attacks increased and by November an all-out offensive was unleashed as Chinese forces attacked both Tenth Corps and Eighth Army.

As the Chinese poured more and more troops across the Yalu River, the fighting on both coasts intensified and eventually it led to massive withdrawals along both lines. In the east, the Tenth Corps moved back in the face of nearly impossible obstacles imposed by aggressive enemy forces and the unrelenting cold. In the west, General Walker's forces begin pulling back in the face of advancing Chinese troops; some were being evacuated by UN ships moving into the shallow inlets. The account of these two highly courageous withdrawals has been excellently narrated other places, and is beyond the scope of this account.

In support of the massive evacuation, planes of Marine Air provided the necessary air-ground protection, and military transports supplied retreating troops the necessities to survive. As the situation grew more and more desperate, plans were underway for the evacuation of Tenth Corps on the east and Eighth Army on the west. The first reaction took place in late November as Admiral Joy alerted Admiral Doyle that all ships of Task Force 90 be placed on six-hour alert. By the 30th of the month, Task Force 90 was heading back from replenishment in Japan. The situation in the west required evacuation from small harbors that would be difficult and would need to be accomplished by small craft. The larger evacuation took place at Hungnam where the port, though small, was excellent. On 9 December, General MacArthur ordered the withdrawal of all troops, and Admiral Doyle was placed in command. The plan called for the evacuation of Tenth Corps at Hungnam and Wonsan on the east coast, and for elements of Eighth Army to retreat through Chinnampo and Inchon on the west.

The withdrawal began on the 10 December 1950. During the Chosin withdrawal, *Philippine Sea*, *Valley Forge*, *Princeton*, *Leyte Gulf*, and three escort carriers provided close air support. The battleship *Missouri* and the cruisers *St. Paul* and *Rochester*, as well as rocket ships and destroyers, provided a ring of fire around the evacuating troops.

On the west coast, Rear Admiral Lyman A. Thackrey was sent to handle evacuation from Chinnampo and Inchon. Associated with him were ships of the British, Australian and Canadian navies, moving in and out of inlets. The mission was accomplished in the early days of December. The evacuation at Chinnampo was executed by the British Commonwealth, protected by Sea Furies and Fireflies flying off British carriers. By the last day of the year, 32,428 men, 1,103 vehicles, and more than 54 tons of cargo had been taken out of Inchon, after which port facilities were destroyed. The total evacuation from the west had included 68,913 troops, 1,404 vehicles and over 62 tons of cargo.

At Wonsan, UN personnel and equipment began to be out-loaded on 3 December 1950. Under covering fire from cruisers and destroyers, the operation was able to move more than 7,000 Korean civilians, 3,834 military and 1,146 vehicles. During this time, naval gunfire kept the enemy at a distance far enough away that the action was taken without loss of a single life.

At Hungnam, the withdrawal and evacuation was directed from the USS *McKinley*. Unlike Inchon, Hungnam was small but had a good harbor with a tidal range of less than a foot, and locations for berthing seven ships at the docks. During the evacuation, Navy officers double-banked ships, raising the number that could be accommodated to eleven. At the beaches, 111 LSTs could be handled. Most of the cargo was loaded along the dock where the LSTs were located. Men were loaded into the APA and AKA at close anchorage. Troops loaded in this order: the First Marine Division and the ROK regiments, the Seventh and Third infantry divisions. The last was responsible for the defense of the perimeter until the final moment. The Marines began loading on 14 December, and the ROK regiment three days later. The U.S. Seventh Division got away on 21 December and the Third took up the rear, leaving on Christmas Eve. During the evacuation, Task Force 90 embarked 105,000 troops, 17,500 tanks and vehicles, 350,000 measures of cargo, and 91,000 Korean civilians.

The evacuation was made possible not only by the excellent coordination of amphibious naval forces but by the well-planned delivery of intense bombardment around the narrowing Hungnam perimeter. During the daylight hours, close air support was provided. Battleships, cruisers, destroyers and rocket ships, beginning on 15 December, laid down a protective fire at ranges up to ten miles. As the evacuation continued, ships came closer to shore to better identify and hit targets. The gunfire continued around the clock until the last of the troops and foreign nationals were taken off. The ships loaded beyond reason — one APA had 12,000 refugees on it. On 24 December, naval gunfire maintained a strip 2,500 yards wide and 3,000 yards from the harbor. The last pilot to fly over the Hungnam area did so on Christmas Eve and reported the night clear and cold. Later analysis would prove that this amphibious effort in reverse identified as the Hungnam Redeployment was efficient and successful. In the action, six APA, six AKA, 12 TAP, 76 time-charter ships, 81 LSTs and 11 LSD were used.

Following the Chinese intervention, the UN withdrawal, and the eventual establishment of new, more permanent lines near the DMZ, the nature of the war changed once again. At this point it is easier to describe the remainder of the war by examining phases of the general campaign rather than chronologically. The remainder of the war saw the naval arm, especially the small ships, involved in battling the continuing problem of mines, sea and air interdiction, blockade, amphibious threats, as well as the massive job of supply and replenishment, and maintaining the siege of Wonsan.

Mines

As the war continued, the problem of mines came under control but maintaining this control required continuous attention. However, the inexperience of personnel available and limitations of the equipment had changed in 1950, as had the policy for mine sweeping. Where it had been necessary before to sweep where the mines were not, in order to identify the easiest channel, it now became possible to sweep where the mines were; this gave the United Nations access to any waters in which they wished to sail. The fleet available for this chore was extended to include LSTs, some carrying mine-hunting helicopters, several steel-hulled sweepers and chicks (AMS), as well as some South Korean AMS. At first, because of the danger, sweeping was only conducted by day, but it was soon acknowledged that if the blockade and bombardment ships were to do their jobs, it would be necessary to sweep both day and night. Some of the LSTs carried three or four small LCVP sweepboats. Among the major tasks was keeping the port of Wonsan clear of mines in support of the siege ordered 30 March 1951. Clearing was also conducted at Songjin's harbor entrance. Check sweeping was maintained on the west coast near Chinnampo.

Sweeping was always dangerous because of the mines themselves, but it was also a hazardous occupation due to the increasing effectiveness of North Korean shore batteries that maintained almost continuous fire against the sweepers. Communist artillery pieces, often hidden in caves along the area, would be brought out, fire a few shots, and then retreat back into their safe area. One of the more difficult spots was at Chongjin, located just 75 miles south of Vladivostok, Russia, on the east coast. Not only was the sweeping difficult but, as close as it was to the Soviet source of supply, the sweepers found that the areas once swept were quickly resown with mines.

Intelligence suggested that the Soviets were able to supply enough mines to sow the major harbors and that there were stockpiles of such mines held near Chinnampo, Chongjin, Songjin and Hungnam. Reports from defectors and spies suggested the areas were being mined at night by small sailing craft, power junks, fishing sampan, and — it was reported but not verified — by a Soviet minelayer. Some of the mines had a self-planting capability and they were being floated on the current of rivers into the harbors buoyed up by oil drums and kegs.

During the war, several warships were struck by mines. AMS *Partridge* (31) struck a mine near Sokcho and sank, the tug *Sarsi* (ATF-11) was lost to a mine near Hungnam where two destroyers, the DD *Thompson* and DD *Small*, were also hit. The USS *Barton* hit a mine 90 miles east of Wonsan and was damaged. The ROK *JMS 306* (a Japanese minesweeper) was hit and Patrol Craft 704 was destroyed off Yo-do Island. The answer was to conduct as complete a sweeping exercise as possible. Night minesweeping provided its own particular dangers. Following the sweep of Kojo, prior to the amphibious feint, fire from the increasingly accurate shore batteries forced the ships to begin night sweeps. Following that, most if not all of the major sweeps were conducted at night. Sometimes at night the sweepers would run into sampans that may well have been sowing at the same time. By June of 1952 the majority of sweeping was done under a policy of checks rather than clearance. After the armistice was signed sweeping was discontinued except for areas around major harbors like Inchon, and even that stopped in September 1953. The lesson had been learned, however, and in August 1953 the Navy ordered 125 new sweepers of a variety of descriptions and began the process of making the mine service a more attractive career choice.

Interdiction

As the war progressed, particularly after the Chinese entered, the navy was given the task of isolating the battlefield. To do this, carrier planes were to destroy the six major bridges across the Yalu River and the seventeen that joined with Manchuria. The point was to isolate the enemy forces through interdiction to cut off supplies and force Chinese into retreat. The emphasis that had been placed on interdiction of supply and transportation earlier in the war was slowly beginning to give way at the end of the war, to supporting ROK forces in the coastal areas. While the majority of the gunfire support was provided by battleships, cruisers, and destroyers, smaller vessels were involved, as well, in control of small enemy vessels, bombardment of coast lines, and the perennial needs of supply, repair, and replenishment.

The Korean coast line north of the 40th parallel is lined with mountains rising from the sea. This geographical feature had forced the North Koreans to build their railway system along the shore for more than forty miles, where it was accessible to the fire from naval guns, and raiding parties transported by naval vessels, such as the fast transport *Horace A. Bass*.

Bombardment

With the ground war very much in doubt, the bombardment during the early months of fighting was very intense. As the war continued, the bombardment never let up, but, if anything, became more selective. While this job was accomplished primarily by capital ships and thus is outside our consideration, the smaller support vessels were very much involved. Not only did some of the craft — destroyer escorts, minesweepers, frigates, etc. — add their minor weaponry to the battle, but they continued to keep the fleet at sea, and to supply whatever was needed, from ammunition to spare parts. During this time, thousands of projectiles fell on the Korean countryside, destroying military targets, bridges, troop concentrations, tunnels, marshaling yards, factories, warehouses, and oil dumps. Every pound of supplies destroyed, every soldier prevented from reaching the front, every gallon of gas that failed to arrived, eased the burden of those fighting on shore.

Blockade

The blockade, established in the opening days of the war, continued throughout the conflict. President Truman extended the blockade to include the entire Korean coast to fulfill the United Nations Security Council request that all seaborne traffic be prevented from reaching Korea. On 4 July 1950, it was announced that the United States had a naval blockade of the Korean Coast.

The decision to blockade the Korean coast was full of difficulties, not the least of them the fact that it could well have been illegal. The blockade could not, for example, prevent warships of other nations from entering, but under the decision all other ships could be. This effort was designed to prevent the enemy from the use of the sea, but also to allow UN ships to move about the coast as they wished. The blockade was a part of the control of the sea that was so important during the final two years of the war, as the communists were seeking ways to influence the negotiations at Panmunjom. It would be hard not to give considerable credit to sea power being a major factor in the final armistice agreement.

The blockade was challenged as early as 2 July 1950 when four North Korean torpedo boats in the vicinity of Chumunjin on Korea's east coast were discovered escorting ten trawlers. At first the communists made considerable effort, but they were no match for the UN ships in the area. Other than this there was little, if any, effort to challenge the blockade. There was no surface opposition, no air opposition and no submarine opposition. The opposition, when it came, was from shore batteries. It was, as Commander Cagle writes: "a crazy, mixed up, naval blockade, where trains and trucks on land were chased by ships at sea" and where communist troops as much as twenty miles from the sea were struck by naval gunfire.

Nevertheless it was a difficult blockade to maintain. Not only did UN vessels have to deal with the problem of mines, but had to deal with the distance they were from their own resources, as well as the limited number of ships available. The legal requirement meant that every portion of the coastline had to be under surveillance, by ship, once in every twenty-four hours. Nevertheless, the blockade had to be considered a success. It was maintained by frigates, minesweepers, and destroyer escorts, as well as cruisers and battleships. The blockade also made it possible for surface ships and submarines to land raiders from the U.S. Navy underwater demolitions, U.S. Marines, and British Royal Marine commandoes, as well as South Korean special forces for clandestine activity.

Amphibious Threats

The success of the landings at Inchon, Pohang, Iwon, Hungnam, and Wonsan had made the communists well aware of the threat this imposed. The United Nations took advantage of the possibility that the fear of such a landing could be a major tool. The fear of an amphibious assault would impose a heavy cost on the enemy in terms of the withdrawal of artillery and infantry units from combat in order to provide security in those areas where amphibious landings were seen as possible. To take advantage of this, the United Nations staged several amphibious feints. Among those that were considered most successful was the feint at Kojo, in northeast Korea, known as Operation Decoy. The design called for the amphibious assault, occupation and defense by the Eighth Cavalry Regimental Combat Team. The plan was to create a psychological fear, to draw enemy defense forces to the area, and to exploit the enemy's reaction. Interestingly, nowhere in the plan did it mention that it was to be only a demonstration landing. Only the top brass knew. Ships moved into the area on 1 October 1952, and, after rehearsals, the deception began on 14 October. It was never the intention to actually land troops there, but was planned in great detail and carried out until the last moment. It began with heavy naval bombardment and then the lowering of the boats. In this case the landing boats moved forward to a 5,000 yard line before returning to the ships. Unfortunately, post analysis suggested the mock exercise did not accomplish much of what was intended. Later intelligence did disclose, however, that for the next three months the communists relocated reserve divisions from inland locations to the coast.

Siege of Wonsan

On 16 February 1951 the U.S. Navy began the longest siege in American maritime history. It was part of a part of a plan devised by Admiral Smith to take and hold islands in the strategic harbor of Wonsan. From this the importance of controlling the Wonsan area became apparent. The city was the principle seaport of North Korea and was the location of the cross-peninsular railroad to the capital city of Pyongyang. It was also the center of much of the area's fishing activity. Setting up a blockade was based on the belief that the enemy would need to keep large numbers of troops in the area, and a siege would prevent the use of the vast land and sea transportation facilities. Once the area was cleared of mines, the siege began by the deployment of destroyers, but soon they were joined by heavier vessels. It became apparent that if a siege was to be conducted it would be necessary to hold the harbor islands. There were numerous small islands but the main ones occupied and used were Yo-do, Ho-do, Sin-do, Tae-do, Ung-do, Ryo-do, and Hwangto-do. Of these Hwangto was most significant, as it was used for the spotting of naval gunfire.

Once the harbor was opened, it was necessary for five or six minesweepers to remain in continual duty clearing and reclearing mines. They were accompanied by destroyers that, in case the sweepers were fired upon, would return fire in attempts to silence the shore batteries. From time to time, cruiser and destroyer gunfire would be directed into the city, and rocket attacks from the LSMR division occurred on a regular basis.

As the pressure on Wonsan continued, the communists found it necessary to give up on the movement of supplies by day and started operating at night. In response, the bombardment exercises at Wonsan moved to night missions. By the time the blockade had completed the first 100 days, the success of the effort was obvious. Significant numbers of troops had been killed, and major damage had been done to buildings, bridges, and tunnels. Trucks and railway cars had been destroyed and nearly 300 small boats either sunk or damaged.

The communists, however, did not simply accept the blockade but responded with batteries that were set up so as to fire on both anticipated landing sites and on the ships as they passed on their fire missions. In some areas tanks were placed in such a manner to fire on ships in the inland waters. Most of the enemy guns were practically invisible, often located on the reverse slopes of the hills, and could only be spotted for return fire by the flash of their guns.

The siege lasted so long that the title "Mayor of Wonsan" was bestowed on the commander of Task Unit 95.2.1, which was responsible for the siege. The siege ended as a part of the armistice agreement on 27 July 1953, with the destroyers *Wiltsie* and *Porter* and the USS *Bremerton*, a cruiser, firing until a minute before the 2200 deadline. The naval siege that had begun 16 February 1951 broke an 88-year record of continuous bombardment; 861 days. At Vicksburg, in the American Civil War, it lasted for 42 days.

Of what value was this siege other than to prove once again the courage and the tenacity of the American navy? It placed in continuous jeopardy the transportation and rail center that was critical to the North Koreans. The significance of it is perhaps best demonstrated in the effort made by the North Koreans to clear the port. But as it turned out, neither the mines nor the gunfire were successful. No matter how hard they tried, they were unable either to sink the ships or drive the navy out of the harbor.

Submarine Threats

From the beginning there was little intelligence or assurance concerning the threat of communist submarines. While neither North Korea nor China maintained large naval forces, particularly submarines, the Soviet were well equipped. By 1 July 1950 there had already been two reported contacts with submarines assumed to be Russian, one near Okinawa and one near Buckner Bay. Until the United Nations knew what was going on, the submarine situation required an investment in defensive measures. The State Department warned all involved that the events in Korea might well be but the first stage in a series of military attacks around the world. The main attack was expected in Europe, but the United States had gone on a worldwide alert and the Sixth Fleet had put to sea in the Mediterranean. During the first week of the war more than eight submarine sightings had been reported and, with more than 80 submarines based not far away in Vladivostok, Russia, VP 47 patrol planes were assigned local antisubmarine patrols. On 23 July the submarine USS *Remora,* escorted by her tender USS

Greenlet, headed out for a patrol of La Perouse Strait. On the 26 July a highly credible submarine contact occurred, and on more than one occasion exercises were abandoned because of a submarine contact on 26 August.

With the Chinese involvement and increasing evidence of Soviet support the question of submarine involvement rose again. Perhaps, it was considered, the Soviets would use the Chinese participation as an excuse for becoming involved. If the invasion was in fact accompanied by an effort to undergo undersea warfare, the United States would have faced the possibility of being cut off from its support. But as time went on the fear diminished. During the second six months of the war there had been only 16 reported submarine contacts, in contrast to more than 80 during the first six months, but on 29 April the Commander Seventh Fleet again warned his command of the danger of a surprise submarine attack from the north.

The fight in Korea was graced by the fact that it was never considered necessary to provide escorts for the trans-Pacific convoys, and this was much to the United Nations' advantage. Under the circumstances there were neither escort vessels nor tankers available for such an exercise. There had been some effort to provide escorts for the early convoys in the Tsushima Straits, but that had been stopped. Antisubmarine types were never anything more than basically adequate to provide the need for screens for the carrier force and the blockade. At this point a communist submarine offensive would have changed the nature of the war.

With the coming of autumn in 1951, the fear of submarine attack had subsided, but it did not go away and the possibility of submarine involvement continued to preoccupy naval commanders as they set about their other assigned duties.

Patrol and Reconnaissance

Throughout the war the Navy kept submarines and aircraft on patrol duty between the Soviet Union and the combat theater. While often long-term and boring, their job was not only to provide advance warning for any movement by the Soviet navy, but also in hope that their presence might discourage such an involvement. Neither detection nor communications were as good in the 1950s as we now enjoy and the possibility of a Chinese or Soviet naval force showing up unexpectedly was prevalent. Submarine patrols, long-range air flights, and naval spotters were all used to keep an eye on the Soviets.

Supply and Transportation

The ground operations in Korea were, from the beginning, totally dependent on the uninterrupted flow of troops and materials, the vast majority of which came to Korea by sea. Evidence of this can be found in the fact that six of every seven soldiers in Korea arrived by sea, bringing with them the five tons of equipment needed for operation, 64 pounds a day. During the conflict more than 54 million tons of cargo and 22 tons of petroleum went by sea.

From the 38th parallel that lay just north of the capital city of Seoul, the line dividing the Koreas, it was 225 air miles to Pusan. From Pusan, following the Great Circle route, it was 4,914 miles to the United States, and a thousand more if the ships were routed through Pearl Harbor. This was the distance that the navy had to consider, and the task of transporting troops and supplies over this distance was a chore carried out with great success by the navy and the merchant marine.

Movement of POWs

In July 1953, on the anniversary of Commodore Perry's entrance to Tokyo Bay, the navy took on a new job, this time the movement of nearly 100,000 enemy personnel. The task group consisted of two APA, six AKA, 20 LSTs, and several minor units which had been assembled. The decision meant a delay in the scheduled return of some forces of the UN Command. On 12 July, Task Force 90 was given this responsibility, and all units were placed under a 24-hour notice. The ships were ordered to Pusan where they had wood and wire cribbing installed to house the still aggressive prisoners in more manageable groups. Eleven of the LSTs, and one AKA had been fitted as they moved out.

The End Game

Perhaps the most misunderstood period of the war is what is often called "the end game," or sometimes the "Hill War" or the "Stalemate." This was a period of attrition, where both sides tried to wear each other down in hope that changing circumstances on the battlefield would change conditions at the negotiation table. Engaged in a deadly fight, the outcome of the final year and a half made it much more likely that neither side was going to exit the war victorious, or with their agenda completely met. The Chinese, apparently not able to advance in the face of American technology and dominance of the air and sea, were not willing to invest the men necessary to bring it to a successful conclusion. On the other hand, the United States and its allies, increasingly worried about the war getting out of hand, and unable or unwilling to invest the energy to bring it to a military victory, wanted to get out. But there was to be a lot of talk, face to save, and many allies to be considered, and the progress was very slow. As the talks went on, men and women were dying all over the country.

While the machinery of the truce talks remained in place, the talks themselves were off and on, as the fighting continued on a regular basis until 27 July 1953. Finally, on that date, the military commanders of the North Korean Army, the Chinese People's Army, and the United Nations Command signed a cease-fire agreement. The war had lasted for three years, one month, and two days, and had devastated Korea. Importantly, the Republic of (South) Korea was not a signatory to the cease-fire.

When the cease-fire was signed it was accomplished with little circumstance and no pomp. And, as if unwilling to believe it was really going to happen, both sides fired weapons at one another until the very minute it became effective. There are some stories of men coming out of their trenches to wave at their previous enemy, or even to converse with them, but there was not a lot of that. The war had cost the U.S. Navy. Of the more than 265,000 navy personnel who served, 475 were killed in action, another 4,043 died from injury or disease, and 1,576 were wounded in action. Once the cease-fire was signed, the hope of some long-term solution was quickly dissipated. A political conference was called to discuss a possible unification or a permanent peace treaty. It met in Geneva in April 1954 but after two months the meeting broke off. Korea remained divided.

During the war there continued to be, at some levels of naval command, a distrust of the Air Force, and the desire to maintain some distance from them. There was, at least in the planning, some degree of turf war. The complexity of providing close air-ground support causes some difficulty between the commands. But with the passage of time, and the fact that labor was divided primarily along geographical lines, the problem seemed to lessen. Unfortunately, it was not able to completely overcome the sad consequence of the long inter-service battles of the intra-war period. This is an important and not well covered aspect of the Korean War.

As well, it is important to acknowledge the difficulties of fighting a UN war. Beyond the obvious difficulties imposed by language, culture, and differences in weapons, ammunition, and even foodstuffs, there were the additional difficulties of command and national agenda. Nevertheless, during the Korean War the United Nations maintained two extremely valuable advantages. The first was an almost immediate command of the seas. The second was the ability to extend military power by attacks from the sea by means of amphibious operations. Advancing on the military precept "to take advantage of one strengths and the enemy's weaknesses," operations from the sea provided the power to unlock strategic stalemates. By controlling the sea, the Navy controlled the UN flanks.

For Task Force 77, the final days of the conflict involved strikes on northern airfields. The USS *Bremerton* and USS *St. Paul* fired their last missions at Wonsan. The Amphibious Force took on preparations for the repatriation of prisoners. When, at 2200 hours, troops came out of their bunkers all across the Korean peninsula, the ships at Wonsan turned on their running lights. On the harbor islands of Nan Do and Cho Do and Sok To, the garrisons began to demolish their facilities and begin preparations for leaving.

2

SHIP IDENTITY AND DESIGNATION

It follows that as certain as the night succeeds the day, that without decisive naval force we can do nothing definitive, and with it, everything honorable and glorious.
— George Washington

For those cognizant of the naval world, this brief chapter will be preaching to the choir, and so could well be ignored. But for the less familiar it will be helpful to acknowledge the maze of nautical terminology and references as they relate to the identification and designed responsibilities of ships. No matter how confused it looks, there is a pattern.

The Gender of Ships

The use of "she" to identify vessels is not intended to be anything but traditional, and certainly has no political or sexist implications. Perhaps the best pronoun would be "it," but for the thousands of men and women who have sailed, on everything from Egyptian skips to U.S. carriers, ships are personal and thus deserve a personal pronoun. Traditionally that identification has been "she." While there are thousands of stories about the history of this tradition, the one that seems more appropriate is simply this, those who sailed, loved their ships.

Nautical Measurements

Displacement In shipping the long ton is used rather than the more conventional American 2,000 pounds. The word comes from the English "tun" which meant a cask or barrel with a capacity of about 252 gallons. When a duty was imposed on wine coming into England, the duty led to vessels being identified by their capacity to carry such barrels. A long ton is normally referred to as 2,240 pounds. Displacement (light) is given in long tons and is figured as the weight of the ship excluding cargo, ballast, stores, etc. Displacement (full) is the empty weight of the ship, including cargo, stores, fuel, ballast, etc. The displacement of a naval vessel is most often expressed in terms of displacement while cargo ships more typically are measured in terms of deadweight. Deadweight is the difference between displacement light and displacement full.

Length Length is measured in feet and inches from the forward tip of the bow to the aft end of the stern. This is identified as the ship's Length Overall (LOA).

Width Width is usually identified as the breadth or beam width, measured in feet and inches from the outboard point on one side of the ship to the opposite point, at the widest point of the vessel.

Depth Depth is a much more involved concept when it comes to operation of a ship, but for identification purposes it is the distance from the keel upward at the lowest point of the ship. Depth is generally not given for ships in this survey.

Speed The basic measurement for speed at sea is the knot. A knot is one nautical mile per hour or in the metric 1.852 kilometers per hour. That is equal to about 1.15 survey miles, or 6,080 feet. It is, more officially, the angular distance of one minute of arc on the surface of the earth. The space of the earth at the equator is divided into 360 degrees, then broken into 60 minutes each. In this case a knot is the equivalent of one minute. When the speed is given in relation to the water in which it sailed, and not land, it is called boat speed. Traditionally this measurement dates back to the seventeenth century when speed was determined by throwing a knotted line overboard and timing the passages of the knots with an hourglass. Some sources say that the knots on the line were spaced at a distance of 47 feet 3 inches.

It is customary to state speed in knots per hour but this is not actually correct. It is redundant since the term "knot" is defined as one nautical mile per hour. To say it twice (k/h2) is to suggest acceleration.

Activation

Keel-Laying Ceremony

The keel-laying ceremony dates back several centuries to a time when a talisman was inserted into the keel of a vessel as the building began, to protect the builder and those who sailed in the ship. A ceremony of some sort still takes place, though modern shipbuilding does not take place from the keel up as it once did.

Launching and Commissioning

When a ship is ready to go into active duty it is commissioned by means of a ceremony based on decades of tradition. At this time, the ship is sponsored by a person who—since 1846, when Lavinia Fanning Watson commissioned *Germantown*—has traditionally been a woman. Wine is the usual christening fluid, but everything from water to a flock of pigeons has been used. The first specific reference to it in U.S. naval history was in 1863, but commissioning of some kind took place before then. At commissioning, the ship is formally transferred to the commanding officer and the commissioning pennant is broken out. The pennant dates back to the 17th century when—in a war between England and Holland—the Dutch admiral Tromp hoisted a broom to the masthead, suggesting he would sweep the seas, only to be countered by a British admiral raising a coach whip, suggesting he would whip the Dutch. Pennants have been the distinguishing mark of ships of war ever since.

Decommissioning

The decommissioning ceremony comes at the end of a ship's service and is designed to pay tribute to the services of the vessel and all those who sailed on her. This is not a prescribed, official ceremony, but is the product of tradition and is designed to be both formal and solemn.

Reading a Ship's Identity

The way to determine the ownership, type, and role of a ship is as follows. First begin with the prefix that identifies the nationality or services with the nationality. For the period within the scope of this book the national prefixes are as follows. The ship's identity is provided in the order in which they are read: prefix, name, classification, modifier.

Not all nations use a prefix but in most cases an unofficial designation is given in order to identify nationality and, in some cases, basic type. Today most ships have a NATO identification that follows much the same line.

ARC	Armada de la Republica de Colombia (Columbia)
JMSDF	Japanese Maritime Self-Defense Force (unofficial)
HIJMS	His Imperial Japanese Majesty's Ship (Japan)
HMS	Her/His Majesty's Ship (Great Britain)
HMT	Her/His Majesty's Troop Ship (Great Britain)
RMS	Royal Mail Ship (Great Britain)
RFA	Royal Fleet Auxiliary Ship (Great Britain)
HDMS	Her/His Danish Majesty's Ship (Denmark)
HMAS	His/Her Majesty's Australian Ship (Australia)
HMCS	His/Her Majesty's Canadian Ship (Canada)
HTMS	His/Her Thailand Majesty's Ship (Thailand)
HMT	His Majesty's Transport (Great Britain)
HNOMS	His/Her Norwegian Majesty's Ship (Norway)
HMNZS	His/Her Majesty's New Zealand Ship (New Zealand)
RNZN	Royal New Zealand Navy (New Zealand)
HNLMS	Her/His Netherlands Majesty's Ship (Netherlands)*
F	U.S. Army
FP	U.S. Army Passenger
FS	U.S. Army Supply
FS	French Ship (France/unofficial)
USS	United States Ship (United States)†
USNS	United States Naval Ship (United States)
SS	Steam Ship/Surface Ship (United States)**
USCGC	United States Coast Guard Cutter (United States)
USAT	United States Army Transport (United States)
NUSHIP	An unofficial term used to denote ships that have not been commissioned.

Naming Ships

A ship is conceived when its keel is laid, born when it is launched, and baptized when it is commissioned. After that it adopts a personality and, though it may well be but one ship from a large class of such ships, no two are alike.

---

*This is the English translation of Hr.Ms/Zr.Ms. Dutch naval vessels are usually not given prefixes.

†Only the prefixes USS, USNS, and USCGC are still use in the U.S. Navy. The nomenclature was determined by a bill signed in 1901 by President T. Roosevelt.

**This term was used primarily to define steam ships. Some sources suggest that it was used, after 1870, to define surface ships after the submarine began to be considered. Prior to the 1880 a distinction was made between propeller-driven (SS) and paddle-driven steamers (PS).

2. Ship Identity and Designation

The United States Navy was officially authorized by Congress on 13 October 1775. During its early phase ships were named primarily on whims designed to honor someone, or a place, or to suggest the power of the ships, like the USS *Wasp*. Congress, on 3 March 1819, formally placed the naming for naval vessels in the hand of the Secretary of the Navy, and established an identity system based on the size of the vessel. On 12 June 1858 the classification system for naming a ship was altered to base it on the number of guns it carried. The rapid expansion of naval vessels resulting from the Civil War led to the provision that the Secretary of Navy could change the name of vessels purchased (or captured) by the Navy Department. The source of names changed considerably when, at the beginning of the twentieth century, ships were named in accordance to their type. From 1880 on, cruisers were to be named for cities, while destroyers were named for naval leaders and heroes. In 1920, battleships were named for states, the only exception being ship #5, named in honor of the much respected Civil War sloop *Kearsarge*.

From the turn of the century until after the Korean War, ships were named, according to a fairly strict formula, by the Secretary of the Navy. Classes of ships have usually, but not always, been named for the first ship of the class built. Battleships continued to be named after states, cruisers after cities, and destroyers after American naval leaders and heroes. Patrol and escort ships have been traditionally named in honor of members of the navy killed in action. When aircraft carriers came along, it was decided to name them after famous naval ships and battles, and then after presidents. Destroyer escorts were to be named after distinguished naval or marine officers and enlisted men. The amphibious transport docks carried names in honor of pioneers, the landing ship dock after historic sites, and LST, at first only given a number, were later named primarily after American counties or parishes. Minesweepers are usually named after birds, and after they began to run out of bird names, they were given names like "Bold" and "Agile," representing abstract qualities. Ammunition ships are named after volcanoes or words that represent explosives, and combat stores ships usually after mythological figures or stars. Hospital ships are given names reflecting peace or comfort, attack cargo ships after Medal of Honor winners, and oilers named after rivers and famous battles. Transports are usually named after presidents, early colonial forefathers, distinguished leaders and famous women. Barracks ships are named after famous hotels. Tugs are usually named after Indian peoples.

Submarines have had a rather unusual history of names, beginning with the first, named after its inventor, John Holland. Originally called submarine torpedo boats, they were given fish names. In 1911 this practice was stopped and subs were given an alphanumeric designation that represented their class and sequence. They were again reclassified in 1920 when all sub hull numbers were changed from S to SS. Since 1931 submarines have again been named after fish. It was not until 1950 that training and hunter-killer submarines were given names.

A naval vessel that has been lost to enemy action is often honored by having its name reassigned to a new command, as is illustrated by the commissioning of the later generations of the *Lexington*, *Houston*, and *Shark*. New ships given a used name are, officially designated in order by Roman numeral (*Lexington II*), but this is rarely used.

In the last decade or so there have been a number of violations of tradition, especially in the naming of ships for a living person. The first was USS *Carl Vinson* (CVN 70), and others have been the USS *Arleigh Burke* (DDG 51), USS *Hyman G. Rickover* (SSN 709), USS *Ronald Reagan* (CVN 76), USNS *Bob Hope* (T-AKR 300) and USS *Jimmy Carter* (SSN 23).

Coast Guard classifications were, at the beginning, based on size; first identified as cutters, second as smaller cutters, third as smaller vessels and tugs, and fourth, primarily harbor craft, as launches. In 1942 the Coast Guard adopted the navy ship classification. In order to distinguish them from their navy counterparts they were given the prefix "W." There is no meaning to this; it was simply an open letter at the time. At this same time the Coast Guard began an exclusive hull numbering system. The Guard changed its use in 1965–66, to more closely identify the role of the ship.

Designation Designations of the various U.S. Navy vessels use an initial letter to indicate the general category, with a second letter to denote the particular species. For example, AH would be an auxiliary ship serving as a hospital ship.

Sometimes a converted or heavily modified ship may have received a new symbol and be given a new hull number. The systems have changed somewhat since they were first introduced in 1907. Some symbols have been changed or dropped. In 1920 it was determined that the ship's name would be both written and pronounced, i.e., ships should have both a name and an alphanumeric designation: for example, the USS *Missouri* is also designated as (BB-63). When this happened fleet escort destroyers (DDE) were reclassified DD. The designation PF was originally a World War II identification for frigates of the Asheville and Tacoma class. The designation DE was assigned to destroyer escorts during World War II. The *Dictionary of American Fighting Ships* and Naval Register now list DE as simply escorts. This was altered in 1975 when DEG (guided missile escorts) were redesignated as FFG (guided missile frigate) and escorts still in operation (DE) were redesignated as frigates (FF). A large number of destroyer escorts were converted, during the 1950s, to Radar Pickets (DDR). During World War II some destroyers (DD) were modified and identified as fleet escorts.

Classification Following the name of the ship — and some ships do not have names, only numbers — is the designation that begins with a general category. At the period of this inquiry, they are as follows:

A	Auxiliary
B	Battleship
C	Cruiser
CV	Aircraft Carriers (originally on a carrier base)
D	Destroyer
F	Frigate
L	Landing and Amphibious Ship
M	Minecraft
P	Patrol Craft
S	Submarine
T	Military Sealift Command (crewed primarily by civilians)
Y	Yard craft

The first letter is followed by a modifier, as follows:

AB	Crane ship (inactive)
ACM	Auxiliary minelayer (inactive)
AD	Destroyer tender
ADG	Degaussing ship
AE	Ammunition ship
AEL	Small ammunition ship
AF	Refrigerated stores ship ("Reefer")
AFS	Combat stores ship
AG	Miscellaneous
AGC	Amphibious force flagship, general communications vessel
AGF	Miscellaneous command ship
AGL	Lighthouse tender
AGP	Motor torpedo boat tender

AGR	Radar picket ship (inactive)
AGT	Target service ship
AH	Hospital
AK	Cargo ship
AKA	Attack cargo ship
AKD	Cargo ship, deep hold (dock)
AKL	Cargo ship, light
AKN	Net cargo ship
AKF	Refrigerated cargo ship
AKR	Cargo ship, vehicle
AKS	General stores issue ship
AFI	General stores ship (inactive)
AKL	Light cargo ship
AKS	General stores ship
AL	USCG lightship
AM	Fleet minesweeper (inactive)
AMC	USCG minesweeper
AMM	Motor minesweeper
AMS	Motor minesweepers, high speed; formerly YMS (inactive)
AN	Net tender
AO	Oiler
AOG	Gasoline tanker
AOE	Fast combat support ship
AOR	Replenishment oiler
AOT	Transport oiler
AP	Transport (operated by the Navy)
APA	Attack transport (also animal transport, later changed to LPA)
APD	Fast transport, destroyer escort conversion
APF	Administrative flagship
APSS	Transport submarine
AR	Repair ship
ARG	Internal combustion engine repair (inactive)
ARH	Heavy hull repair (inactive)
ARL	Landing ship repair
ARS	Salvage ship
ARVE	Aircraft repair ship, engine
AS	Submarine tender
ASR	Submarine rescue vessel
AT	Tug
ATA	Ocean auxiliary tug
ATF	Fleet tug
ATR	Ocean tug, rescue
ATS	Salvage and rescue ship
AV	Seaplane tender
AVD	Seaplane tender, destroyer
AVP	Small seaplane tender (inactive)
AW	Distilling ship
AWK	Water transport
BB	Battleship
CA	Heavy cruiser
CL	Light cruiser
CLAA	Antiaircraft light cruiser (inactive)
CV	Aircraft carrier
CVE	Escort aircraft carrier, with merchant ship hull
CVL	Light aircraft carrier, with cruiser hull
DD	Destroyer

DDC	Corvette
DDE	Escort destroyer (converted for antisubmarine warfare)
DDR	Radar picket destroyer
DE	Destroyer escort
DER	Escort vessel, radar picket
DL	Destroyer leader (dropped in 1950 in favor of "frigate")
DMS	Fast minesweeper, destroyer conversion (inactive)
DUKW	Amphibious truck
FF	Frigate
IBS	Inflatable boat, small
JMS	Japanese minesweepers (YMS type)
LCI*	Landing craft, infantry
LCP	Landing craft, personnel
LCRL	Landing craft, inflatable boat large
LCRS	Landing craft, inflatable boat small
LCS	Landing craft, support (altered in 2004 to mean littoral combat ship)
LCSR	Landing craft, swimmer reconnaissance
LCT	Landing craft, tank
LCU	Landing craft, utility
LCV	Landing craft, vehicle
LCVP	Vehicle and personnel landing craft
LHA	Amphibious assault ship, general purpose
LPH	Helicopter amphibious assault ship
LSD	Landing ship, dock
LSM	Landing ship, medium
LSMR	Landing ship, medium, rocket (a landing ship conversion)
LST	Tank landing ship
LSU	Utility landing ships
LSV	Landing ship, vehicle
LVA	Landing vehicle, assault
LVT	Tracked landing vehicle
LVTA	Armored tracked landing vehicles
MSRD	Maritime Administration
MB	Motor boat
MC	Maritime Commission
MM	Minelayer fleet
MSC	Coastal minesweepers, nonmagnetic
MSI	Inshore minesweepers, nonmagnetic
MSO	Ocean minesweepers, nonmagnetic
MSTS	Military Sea Transport Service
PB	Patrol boat
PC	Submarine chaser
PCE	Patrol escort
PCED	Amphibious control vessel, patrol escort conversion
PF	Frigate, patrol gunboat, or corvette
PG	Patrol gunboat (also used to define corvettes transferred to England in 1942)
PT	Motor torpedo boat
PTF	Fast patrol boat
RA	Seven-man rubber boat (RB-7)
RB	Ten-man rubber boat (RB-10)
SS	Submarine
SSP	Submarine transport
T-AP	Transport assigned to MSTS

*Note: Most of the ships defined as landing craft during World War II were redefined thereafter as landing ships.

2. Ship Identity and Designation

T-APC	Small coastal transport assigned to MSTS
TB	Torpedo boat
WAG	Coast Guard miscellaneous auxiliary
WAGO	Coast Guard amphibious force flag ship
WAK	Coast Guard cargo ship
WAO	Coast Guard oiler
WAS	Wartime Shipping Administration
WAT	Coast Guard oceangoing tug
WSCG	Coast Guard lighthouse ship
YAG	Degaussing vessel
XAK	MM, cargo ship
YMS	Motor minesweeper
YN	Net tender
YT	Harbor tug
YW	Water barge

Ship Numbers

The final classification is the number assigned. This is not to be confused with the hull number which is simply the manufacturing number. The classification number is traditionally, but not exclusively, assigned in the order of the ship's commissioning. The USS *Missouri* BB-63 would be the sixty-third battleship commissioned in the United States Navy. Occasionally, because of the difference in location and speed of construction, a ship will be chronologically out of order in relation to the date it is laid down.

Condition of Service

Commissioned A ship is considered on active duty when it is commissioned. The term "in service" is also used, but usually by smaller ships without permanent crews or with civilian crews.

Non-Commissioned A non-commissioned ship is usually a privately owned ship working under navy jurisdiction but with a civilian crew.

Decommissioned A decommissioned ship is one that is no longer commissioned, thus out of service.

Recommissioned Sometimes a ship is taken out of duty, put into a reserve fleet, and then recalled to active duty. This requires a recommissioning and the name returned to the Naval Register.

Reserve Fleets Reserve fleets are the so-called mothball fleets, established after World War II, in which some ships are stored for potential reuse. There are several reserve fleets and locations.

Navy Register The Navy Register, also known as the Navy List, is a listing of all ships on active duty with the United States Navy. The Congress must authorize the addition or removal of a vessel from the list. A ship that is sunk during wartime, or one sunk by accident during peacetime, is never "struck" but is no longer listed.

Stricken To be "stricken" is to be removed from the Naval Register. This retires the ship and then the name is available to be used again.

Naval Service Organization

In Korea the following naval organization was developed.

Task Group 53.7	Provisional Transport Group
Task Force 70	
70.1	Flagship Group, Wonsan
70.6	Fleet Air Wing
70.7	Service Group
70.9	Submarine Group
Task Force 77	Striking Force. Used until 25 August 1950 when the term Fast Carrier Force was introduced.
77.1	Support Force, Pohang, Inchon, Hungnam Redeployment
77.2	Screening Group, Pohang, Inchon, Hungnam Redeployment
77.3	Formosa Patrol
77.3	Carrier Group, Hungnam Redeployment
77.4	Carrier Group, Inchon, Hungnam Redeployment
Task Force 79	Logistic Support Force, Wonsan
79.1	Mobile Logistic Service Group, Inchon
79.2	Objective Area Logistic Group, Inchon
79.2	Hungnam Logistic Support Group, Hungnam Redeployment
79.3	Logistic Support Group, Inchon
79.4	Salvage and Maintenance Group, Inchon
Task Force 90	Amphibious Force Far East
90.0	Follow-up Shipping Group, Pohang
90.0	Attack Force, Wonsan
90.00	Flagship Element, Inchon, Wonsan, Hungnam Redeployment
90.01	Tactical Air Control Element, Inchon, Wonsan, Hungnam Redeployment
90.02	Naval Beach Group Element, Inchon, Wonsan
90.2	Transport Group, Hungnam Redeployment
90.21	Transport Element, Hungnam Redeployment
90.03	Control Element, Inchon, Hungnam Redeployment
90.04	Administrative Element, Inchon
90.1	Tactical Air Control Group
90.10	Flagship Element, Wonsan
90.1.1	Medical Unit, Wonsan
90.1.2	Repair and Salvage Unit, Wonsan
90.1.3	Service Unit, Wonsan
90.11	Transport Group, Inchon
90.2	Transport Group, Pohang, Inchon, Wonsan
90.20	Administrative Element
90.3	Tractor Group, Pohang, Inchon, Wonsan
90.4	Protective Group, Pohang
90.4	Transport Division, Inchon
90.4	Control Group, Wonsan
90.41	COMINRON 3
90.42	COMINDIV 31
90.43	Two ships for screen of movement only, then under 96.5, Pohang
90.5	Close Air Support Group, Pohang, Inchon
90.6	Deep Air Support Group, Pohang
90.6	Reconnaissance Group, Wonsan
90.6	Gunfire Support Group, Inchon
90.61	Cruiser Element, Inchon
90.62	Destroyer Element, Inchon
90.63	LSMR Element, Inchon
90.7	Reconnaissance Group, Pohang

2. Ship Identity and Designation

90.7	Screening and Protective Group, Inchon
90.8	Coastal Control, Pohang
90.8	Second Echelon Movement Group, Inchon
90.8	Gunfire Support Group, Hungnam Redeployment
90.9	Beach Group, Pohang
90.9	Third Echelon Movement Group, Inchon
Task Force 91	Landing Force, Pohang
Task Force 91	Blockade and Covering Fire, Inchon
Task Force 92	Logistics Support Force. Activated 3 April 1951 and included those ships operating as Task Group 701.7 and Task Force 79 under ComNavJap at 96.4.
92.1	Landing Force, Inchon, Wonsan
Task Force 95	United Nations Blockading and Escort Force. This force included ships from Australia, Canada, Colombia, France, Thailand, Great Britain, Netherlands, New Zealand, the Republic of Korea and the United States. Also called Combined Task Force (CTF) 95.
95.1	Korean Blockade Group 1, West Coast Group
95.11	Carrier Element
95.12	Surface Blockade and Patrol Element
95.2	Korean Blockade Group 2, East Coast Group
95.2	Gunfire Support Group, Wonsan
95.2	Blockade, Escort and Minesweeping Group, Hungnam Redeployment
95.21	Wonsan Element
95.22	Songjin Element
95.24	Hungnam Element
95.25	East Island Defense Element
95.28	Bombline Element
95.5	Escorts
95.6	Minesweepers Group, Pohang, Wonsan, Hungnam Redeployment
95.7	ROK Naval Forces (See also Task Group 96.7)
Task Force 96	Naval Forces Japan
96.1	Escort Group
96.2	Search and Reconnaissance, Inchon, Wonsan
96.3	Shipping Control Administration
96.4	Service Group
96.5	Gunfire Support Group, Pohang
96.5.2	Destroyer Element
96.5.3	British Commonwealth Support Element
96.5.6	Submarine Element
96.6	Task Group Minesweeping Group
96.7	ROK Naval Forces
96.8	West Coast Support Group (Commonwealth Naval Force), Wonsan, Hungnam Redeployment
96.81	Carrier Element I, Hungnam Redeployment
96.82	Carrier Element II, Hungnam Redeployment
96.83	Carrier Element III, Hungnam Redeployment
96.84	Screening Element, Hungnam Redeployment
96.9	Submarine Group
Task Force 99	Patrol and Reconnaissance Force, Pohang, Inchon

Abbreviations Used in Ship Listings

a	armament
cal	caliber
cpl.	complement

d.	displacement	
dc.	depth charges	
dcp.	depth charge projectors	
dcr.	depth charge racks	
dct.	depth charge tracks	
dep.	roll-off depth charges	
(f)	full displacement	
hh	hedgehog (type of depth charge projector)	
k.	knots	
(l)	light displacement	
mg	machine guns	
mk	Oto Melara MK 75/76mm Italian artillery piece for surface and air defense	
tt.	torpedo tubes	
l × b.	length and breadth in feet	

Armament and specific weapons are listed by number carried, followed by caliber in inches or millimeters (mm). For example, a .4-3" indicates four guns of 3 inch caliber, and 4-21" tt means four torpedo tubes, firing 21-inch caliber torpedoes.

Presentation Format

When ships have names, the ships are listed in alphabetical order. Where ships are known primarily by numbers, they are listed in numerical order. When a ship has served more than one function, both symbols and numbers (if different) are provided. When there is general agreement between sources, no source is listed. Where there is diversity, a source is given in support of the information included.

3

LITTLE BROTHERS

Uncommon valor was a common virtue.
— Admiral Chester W. Nimitz

During the Korean War, many of the duties once assumed to be within the role of the destroyer were taken over by smaller, more specifically designed ships. Among these were ships designated as destroyer escorts, frigates, cutters, patrol frigates, picket radar destroyers, and picket ships. Included, as well, are Coast Guard ships serving in one of the designated capacities.

Destroyer Escort (DE)

The destroyer escort provided a valuable service for the United States during World War II and its use was continued during the conflict in Korea. The escort is a small, comparatively slow ship, which was designed to support convoys of merchant ships. They were created in response to the threat posed by German U-boats. They were smaller and cheaper than destroyers but could accomplish most of the same missions. When World War II came to a close, most destroyer escorts were decommissioned. Many were scrapped and some were transferred to foreign navies. By 1950 the force on activity duty had been reduced to 27. During the conflict in Korea this number was increased to 52, but by 1960 the number on fleet service had dropped to just three. It is interesting to note that the primary difference between destroyer escorts in the U.S. Navy and the Royal Navy was that the British removed the ice-cream maker, water fountains, dishwashers, and laundries in order to add to the number of depth charges they could carry.

After the war, in 1954, the first of the specifically designated DE were completed. The designation was changed to distinguish between the DDE — escort destroyers that were being modified for antisubmarine duty — and the escort ships. In 1975 all destroyer escorts in commission were redesignated frigates (FF), and the DE and DDE names were discontinued. The primary armament was a battery of 3-3", 2-40mm, and 9-20mm guns, and depth charges. There were no torpedo tubes since they were primarily built as antisubmarine weapons. Generally DE carried 12–15 officers and 175–200 crew. The top speed was 20–24 knots and cruising speed was 17 knots. Six classes were built: Dealey, Buckley, Ruddrow, Cannon, Edsall and John C. Butler. Service was not easy on these small ships; the space allowed a crew member in a compartment was about a sixth of the space allowed for prisoners in U.S. federal prisons at the time. As is often the case, there is not always agreement on the service of various ships. Where there is some question, the source for inclusion in this listing is identified at the end of the entry.

Carpenter DE 825: [d. 2,425; 390'6" × 41'1"; 35 k; cpl. 367; a. 4-3", hh, 4-21" tt, 6 dcp, 2 dct; Gearing Class] The *Carpenter* was launched 28 September 1945 and after several starts was commissioned as DD 825 on 15 December 1949. The ship's designation was changed to DDE on 4 March 1950. She participated in the Korean War during the Communist China Spring Offensive, UN Summer–Fall Offensive, Second Korean Winter, Korean Defense Summer–Fall 1952, and the Korea Summer–Fall 1953 campaigns. She served during the Vietnam War. She was decommissioned 20 February 1981 and leased to the Republic of Turkey. Renamed *Anittepe*, she was purchased by Turkey on 8 June 1987.

Conway III DE 507: [d. 2,050; 376'6" × 39'7"; 36 k; cpl. 273; a. 5-5", 10-40mm, 7-20mm, 10-21" tt, 6 dcp, 2 dct; Fletcher Class] Launched 16 August 1942 and commissioned 9 October 1942 she served in the Pacific during World War II and participated at Munda, Purvis Bay, and in the "Slot." She was placed out of commission 25 June 1946 but recommissioned 8 November 1950, after which she was converted to an escort destroyer (DE 507). She served off the coast of Korea during the Communist China Spring Offensive and the UN Summer–Fall Offensive campaigns. She was awarded two battle stars. Reconverted to a destroyer (DD) on 30 June 1962, she was stricken from the navy list on 15 November 1969 and sunk as a target 26 June 1970.

Cony DDE 508: [d. 2,050; 376'6" × 39'8"; 35 k; cpl. 273; a. 5-5", 10 × 21" tt, 6 dcp, 2 dct; Class Fletcher] Launched 30 August and commissioned 30 October 1942 she was active in World War II serving in the Pacific. She was decommissioned 18 June 1946 and placed in reserves. The *Cony* was reclassified DDE 508 on 26 March 1949 and recommissioned 17 November 1949. She served in Korean waters during the Communist China Spring Offensive and the UN Summer–Fall Offensive campaign. She received two battle stars for service in Korea.

Cowell II DE 547: [d. 2,050; 376'6" × 39'8"; 35 k; cpl. 273; a. 5-5", 10-21" tt, 6 dcp, 2 dct; Class Fletcher] Launched 18 March 1943 and commissioned 23 August 1943, the *Cowell II* served in the Pacific during World War II and participated in several campaigns, including the invasion of the Gilbert Islands and Okinawa. She was taken out of commission on 22 July 1946 but recommissioned 21 September 1951 for the Korean War. In January 1953 she joined Task Group 95.2 for bombardment off the Wonsan coast. She received two battle stars for service in Korea.

Currier DE 700: [d. 1,400; 306 × 37'10"; 23 k; cpl. 186; a. 3-3", 8-20mm, 3-21" tt, 1 dpc hh, 8 dcp, 2 dct; Class Buckley] Launched 14 October 1943 and commissioned 1 February 1944, she operated with the Allies around Italy, and then in the landings in southern France. After a return to the United States she was sent to Saipan for radar picket duty, and spent the rest of the war on escort duty between Guam and Okinawa. In April 1952 she patrolled off the coast of Korea and served in Korean waters during the Korean Defense Summer–Fall 1952 campaign. She received one battle star for Korea. She was placed out of commission and into reserves 4 April 1960.

Douglas A. Munro DE 422: [d. 1,350; 306 × 36'8"; 24 k; cpl. 186; a. 2-5", 3-21" tt, 8 dcp, 1 dcp hh, 2 dct: Class John C. Butler] Launched 8 March 1944, she was commissioned 11 July 1944. During World War II she was involved in convoy and minesweeping duties. After service in World War II she was placed out of service and into reserves 15 January 1947. The ship was recommissioned on 28 February 1951 and she sailed for Korean waters where she participated in the Summer–Fall Offensive, Second Korean Winter, and the Korea Summer–Fall 1953 campaigns. She received three battle stars for Korean service. She was decommissioned and placed in reserves 24 June 1960.

Durant WDE 389/489: [d. 1,200; 306 × 36'7"; 21 k; cpl. 186; a. 3-5", 2-40mm, 8-20mm, 3-21" tt, 2 dct, 8 dcp hh; Class Edsall] Serving with the United States Coast Guard she was named for Pharmacist's Mate Durant, killed on Guadalcanal. Launched 3 August 1943 she was commissioned 16 November 1943. During her early service the Durant was a school for prospective crews. She served in Korean waters during 6–19 November 1953. She made eight voyages in convoy duty. After the war she was placed out of commission 27 February 1946. Loaned to the Coast Guard 15 May 1952, she was recommissioned as WDE 489, and served in various Pacific weather stations. Placed out of commission 10 April 1954, she was reclassified as DER 338 on 7 December 1955.

Edmonds DE 406: [1,350; 306 × 36'8"; 24 k; cpl. 186; a. 2-5", 3-21" tt, 8 dcp, 1 dcr, 2 dct; Class John C. Butler] Launched 17 December 1943 and commissioned 3 April 1944, the *Edmonds* served in the Pacific during World War II, as the flagship for Commander, Escort Division 63. She was placed out of commission and in reserves on 31 May 1946. Recommissioned for service in Korea on 28 February 1951, she served in Korean waters during the UN Summer–Fall Offensive and the Second Korean Winter campaigns. She received two battle stars for Korean service. Later she operated off the Chinese coast on patrol, screening nationalist supply convoys near Quemoy. She was decommissioned March 1965 until struck from the navy list on 15 May 1972. She was sold for scrap 28 September 1973.

Epperson DDE 719: [d. 2,425; 390'6" × 41'1"; 35 k; cpl. 336; a. 6-5", 5-21" tt, 6 dcp, 2 dct; Class Gearing] Launched 22 December 1945 and redesignated DDE 710 on 28 January 1948, she was commissioned 19 March 1949. She sailed for service in Korea on 1 June 1951, and while there participated in the Communist China Spring Offensive, UN Summer–Fall Offensive, Second Korean Winter, Third Korean Winter, and the Korea Summer–Fall 1953 campaigns. She received five battle stars for Korean service.

Falgout WDE 324: [d. 1,200; 306 × 36'7"; 21 k; cpl. 186; a. 3-3", 8 dcp, 1 dcp hh, 2 dct; Class Edsall] Launched 24 July 1943 and commissioned 15 November 1943, she performed convoy duty during World War II. In commercial reserves 9 May 1946 to 18 April 1947, she was loaned to the Coast Guard from 24 August 1951 to 21 May 1954. During this time she served in Korean waters from 10 August 1952 and 8 October 1953, at stations Victory and Sugar. Reclassified DER on 28 October 1954.

Fitch WDE 462: [d. 1,630; 347'10" × 36'1"; 38 k; cpl 208; a. 4-5", 5-21" tt, 6 dcp, 2 dct; Class Bristol] Launched 14 June 1941 and commissioned 3 February 1942, reclassified DMS-25 on 15 November 1944, she served in World War II, including the landings at French Morocco and Utah Beach. She served briefly during the Korean War, was reclassified DD 462 on 15 July 1955 and was decommissioned 24 February 1956. Identified in Cagle as a Bristol Class gunboat.

Fletcher DDE 445: [d. 2,100; 376'3" × 39'8"; 36 k; cpl. 273; a. 5-5", 10-21" tt, 6 dcp, 2 dct; Class Fletcher] Launched 3 May 1942 and commissioned 30 June 1942, the Fletcher was reclassified DDE on 26 March 1949. During World War II she saw service in the Pacific where she received fifteen battle stars. She was placed in commission in reserves 7 August

1946 and out of commission 15 January 1947. Recommissioned 3 October 1949 as an antisubmarine ship, she served in the Korean War during the North Korean Aggression, Inchon Landing, Second Korean Winter, Korean Defensive Summer–Fall 1952, and the Korea Summer–Fall 1953 campaigns. She received five battle stars for Korean service.

Forster WDE 334: [d. 1,200; 306 × 36'7"; 21 k; a. 3-3", 3-21" tt, 8 dcp, 1 dep hh, 2 dct; Class Edsall] Launched 13 November 1943 and commissioned 25 January 1944. The *Forster* served on convoy duty during World War II and was placed on loan to the Coast Guard from 20 June 1951 to 23 May 1954. She served in Korean waters from 24 July to 5 August 1952. Reclassified as DER 334 in October 1955.

Foss DE 59: [d. 1,400; 306 × 37; 24 k; cpl. 186; a. 3-3", 3-21" tt, 8 dcp, 1 dep, 2 dct; Class Buckley] Launched 10 April 1943 and commissioned 23 July 1943, she served in escort duty for convoys building up the forces in Europe for the Normandy invasion. In 1946 she was equipped with ship/shore power conversion after which she provided emergency power for a variety of places. On 17 October 1950 she sailed for the Far East where she provided power to the shore at Chinnampo, Inchon, and Hungnam. She saw service in Korean waters during the Communist China Aggression campaign, she was decommissioned and placed in reserve June 1957, stricken from the Naval Register on 1 November 1965 and sold for scrap in June 1966.

Hanna DE 449: [d. 1,350; 306 × 36'8"; 24 k; cpl. 186; a. 2-5", 4-40mm, 10-20mm, 2 dct, 8 dcp, hh; Class John G. Butler] Launched 4 July 1944 and commissioned 27 January 1945, she was assigned to the Pacific Fleet. She was decommissioned 31 May 1946 and placed in reserves. Recommissioned 27 December 1950, she sailed for the Western Pacific, and then sailed with Task Force 95 off the west coast of Korea. She served in Korean waters during the Communist China Spring Offensive, UN Summer–Fall Offensive, Korean Defense Summer–Fall 1952, Third Korean Winter, and the Korea Summer–Fall 1953 campaigns. The *Hanna* received five battle stars for Korea. She was damaged, and one man killed, when on 24 November 1952 she was hit by shore batteries at Songjin, North Korea. She was decommissioned 11 December 1959 and placed in the Pacific Reserve Fleet.

Jenkins II DDE 447: [d. 2,100; 376'4" × 39'5"; 35.5 k; cpl. 273; a. 5-5", 10-40mm, 7-20mm, 10-21" tt, 6 dcp, 2dct; Class Fletcher] Launched 21 June 1942 and commissioned 31 July 1942, she served first in the area off Casablanca and then moved to the Pacific during World War II. She was decommissioned 1 May 1946, but then recommissioned as DDE on 2 November 1951. In Korea she operated with Task Force 77. She served in Korean waters during the Korean Defense Summer–Fall 1952 campaign and received one battle star. Later she served in Vietnam. She was decommissioned 2 July 1969 and struck from the navy list the same day, then sold on 26 February 1971 for scrap.

Keppler DDE 765: [d. 2,425; 390'2" × 40'11"; 35 k; cpl. 336; a. 6-5", 12-40mm, 10-20mm; 6 dcp. 2 dct; 5-21" tt; Class Gearing] Launched 24 June 1946 and commissioned 23 May 1947, she was converted in 1949 to an antisubmarine destroyer and on 4 March reclassified as a destroyer escort. She saw service in Korean waters and participated in the Communist China Aggression and the First UN Counter Offensive campaigns. She received two battle stars. She was decommissioned 7 January 1972 and sold to Turkey where she became the *Tinaztepe*.

Koiner WDE 331/DD: [d. 1,200; 306 × 36'7"; 21 k; cpl. 186; a. 3-3", 6-40mm, 10-20mm, 9 dcp, 2 dct; Class Edsall] Launched 5 September 1943 and commissioned 27 December 1943, she served in escort duty with Britain-bound convoys during World War II. She was decommissioned 4 October 1946. From 20 June 1951 to 14 May 1954 she was on loan to the Coast Guard, commissioned WDE 431, and served as an ocean station vessel in Korean waters during periods between June 1952 to July 1953. She was struck from the navy list 23 September 1963 and sold 3 September 1969. Not listed in *DANFS* she is in the Department of Defense listing.

Lewis DE 535: [d. 1,600; 306 × 36'10"; 24 k; cpl 181; a. 2-5", 20 twin 40mm, 10-20mm, 3tt; hh, 8 K guns, 2 dcr; Class John C. Butler] Launched in 7 December 1943 and commissioned 5 September 1944, she was involved in convoy duty, including the Iwo Jima campaign. She was decommissioned May 1946. Pulled out of reserves 28 March 1952, she served in the Korean War during the Korean Defense Summer–Fall 1952 campaign. She was hit 21 October 1952 by fire from a shore battery that caused hull damage and wounded eight. She was decommissioned in May 1960 and in March of 1966 she was towed out and sunk as a target ship.

Lowe WDE 325: [d. 1,200; 306 × 36'7"; 21 k; cpl. 186; a. 3-3", 6-40mm, 10-20mm, 1 dcp, 2 dct; Class Edsall] Launched 28 July 1943 and commissioned 22 November 1943, she served on Atlantic convoy duty during World War II. Decommissioned 1 May 1946 she was recommissioned 20 July 1951 and she served in Korean waters 31 August 1952 until 31 July 1953. The *Lowe* was at weather station Victor. She was scrapped 20 September 1968.

Marsh DE 699: [d. 1,400; 306 × 36'10"; 23 k; cpl. 186; a. 3-3", 4-1.1", 6-40mm, 10-20mm, 3-21" tt, 2 dct, 8 dcp, 1 dcp hh; Class Buckley] The *Marsh* was launched 25 September 1943 and commissioned 12 January 1944. During World War II she served trans–Atlantic convoys and then was transferred to the Pacific. She supported American occupation in Korea. In June 1950 she headed for Pusan where she supplied power to the city for two weeks, then supported the Inchon defense. She served in Korean waters during the North Korean Aggression, Communist China Aggression, First UN Counter Offensive, and the Korean Defense Summer–Fall 1952 campaigns. She received four battle stars for Korea. On 16 August 1958 she was decommissioned but remained active as an antisubmarine training ship in the reserves. Placed back into service, she was recommissioned 15 December 1961 for service in South Vietnam.

McCaffery DE 860: [d. 2,425; 390'6" × 40'1"; 34.5 k; cpl. 367; a. 6-5", 4-40mm, 5-21" tt, 6 dcp, 2 dct, 1dep hh; Class Gearing] Launched on 12 April 1945 and commissioned 26 July 1945, she operated with the 7th Fleet in support of the United Nations participating in Korean waters during the Communist China Aggression and the First UN Counter Offensive campaigns. She received two battle stars for Korean service. She later served during the Cuban Missile Crisis in 1962 and the recovery missions for Gemini IX and XII, as well as fire missions during the Vietnam War. She was decommissioned and stricken from the navy list 30 September 1973 and sold for scrap in June 1974.

McCoy Reynolds DE 440: [d. 1.350; 306 × 36'8"; 24 k; cpl. 186; a. 2-5", 4-40mm, 10-20mm, 3-21" tt, 8 dcp, 1 dep; Class John C. Butler] Launched 22 February 1944 and commissioned 2 May 1944, the *McCoy Reynolds* participated in the conquest of Peleliu, Leyte, Marianas and Marshalls, and is credited with two submarine sinkings. Decommissioned 31 May 1946, she entered the Pacific Reserve Fleet. Recommissioned 29 March 1951, she deployed to the Far East, where she served in the Korean waters during the Korean Defense Summer–Fall 1952 campaign. She alternated duty off Korea with escort service from Japan and Okinawa, and with the Formosa patrol. She received one battle star for Korea. Decommissioned 7 February 1957, she was loaned to Portugal where she served as the *Corte Real*. Struck from the naval register 1 November 1968, she was sold to Portugal.

McGinty DE 365: [d. 1,350; 306 × 36'8"; 24 k; cpl. 186; a. 2-5", 4-40mm, 10-20mm

3-21" tt, 1 dpc hh, 2 dct; Class John C. Butler] Launched 5 August and commissioned 25 September 1944, she was active in the Pacific as an escort. Following World War II she was decommissioned 15 January 1947. She was recommissioned 28 March 1950 then served as the flagship of Escort Squadron 11. During three tours of duty in Korea — the UN Summer–Fall Offensive, Second Korean Winter, and Korea Summer–Fall 1953 campaigns — she served in blockade and bombardment. She received three battle stars for Korea. She was again decommissioned 23 September 1968, struck the same day, and scrapped in 1969.

Naifeh DE 352: [d. 1,350; 306 × 36'8"; 24 k; cpl. 186; a. 2-5", 4-40mm, 10-20mm, 3-21" tt, 8 dcp, 1 dcp hh, 2 dct: Class John C. Butler] Launched 29 February 1944 and commissioned 4 July 1944, she operated with the *Philippine Sea* Frontier during World War II on escort duty. She was decommissioned 27 June 1946 and put into the reserves. She was recommissioned 26 January 1951 and assigned to the United Nations Escort and Blockade Force. The *Naifeh* served in Korean waters during the Communist China Spring Offensive, UN Summer–Fall Offensive, and the Korean Defense Summer–Fall 1952 campaigns. She received three battle stars. Decommissioned 17 June 1960 and struck from the roles 1 January 1966, she was sunk as a target ship.

Newell WDE 322: Dimensions: d. 1,200; 306 × 36'7"; 21 k; cpl. 186; a. 3-3", 2-40mm, 8-20mm, 1 dcp, 2 dct; Class Edsall] Launched 29 June 1943 and commissioned 30 October 1943, she served with Atlantic convoys during World War II. Decommissioned 20 November 1945, she was recommissioned 20 July 1951 with the Coast Guard, then served in Korean waters 2 November 1952 to 18 November 1953. Decommissioned again 21 February 1954, she was brought out later for service in Vietnam, then struck from Navy list 28 September 1968. She was used in making the film *Tora! Tora! Tora!*

Nicholas II DDE 449: [d. 2,050; 376'6" × 39'8"; 37 k; cpl. 319; a. 5-5", 10-40mm, 10-21" tt, 6 dcp, 2 dct; Class Fletcher] Launched 19 February and commissioned 4 June 1942, she saw active duty in the Pacific during World War II. She was placed in inactivation 12 June 1946, reclassified as a DDE on 26 March 1949, and recalled in November 1950. Recommissioned 19 February 1951, she was active in Korean waters during the Communist China Spring Offensive, UN Summer–Fall Offensive, Korean Defense Summer–Fall 1952, Third Korean Winter, and the Korea Summer–Fall 1953 campaigns. She won five battle stars for Korea. Later she served in the Vietnam War and as support for the NASA Apollo program.

Norris DDE 859: [d. 2,425; 391 × 41; 31.5 k; cpl. 288; a. 6-5", 14-40mm, 20-20mm, 2 dct, 6 dcp, 1 dcp hh; 10-21" tt: Class Gearing] Laid 29 August 1944 and commissioned 9 June 1945, she spent several years in anti-smuggling duty along the Korean and Chinese coasts. On 4 March 1950 she was reclassified as DDE 859, and then in December 1950 joined the evacuation force at Hungnam. Later she served in Korean waters during the Communist China Aggression, First UN Counter Offensive campaigns. She received two battle stars for Korean service. She then transferred to service in the Atlantic and later saw duty in the Vietnam War.

O'Bannon II DE 450: [d. 2,700; 376'4" × 39'9"; 35 k; cpl. 273; a. 5-5", 6-20mm, 1-1.1" quad, 10-21" tt; Class Fletcher] She was launched 19 February and commissioned 26 June 1942. Based in the Pacific during World War II, she was converted to an escort destroyer and designated DDE on 26 March 1949. The *O'Bannon* was recommissioned 19 February 1951 and sailed for Korea. She served in Korean waters during the Second Korean Winters, Korean Defense Summer–Fall 1952, and Korea Summer–Fall 1953 campaigns. She received three battle stars for Korea and later served in Vietnam.

Philip II DE 498: [d. 2,050; 376'6" × 39'8"; 35 k; cpl. 273; a. 5-5", 4-40mm, 4-20mm, 10-21" tt, 6 dcp, 6 dct; Class Fletcher] Launched 13 October and commissioned 21

November 1942, she had a very active career in the Pacific during World War II. Decommissioned in January 1947 she was reclassified to a destroyer escort on 26 March 1949 and recommissioned 30 June 1950. She served as a plane guard for President Truman's visit with General MacArthur on Wake Island, and then joined Task Force 77. She participated in the Communist China Spring Offensive, UN Summer–Fall Offensive, Korean Defense Summer–Fall 1952, Third Korean Winter, and the Korea Summer–Fall 1953 campaigns. She received five battle stars for Korea. On 1 July 1962 she was redesignated DD and served briefly in Vietnam. She was decommissioned 30 September 1968 and struck from the navy list 1 October 1968.

Radford II DDE 446: [d. 2,940; 376'6" × 39'7"; 35 k; cpl. 329; a. 5-5", 10-40mm, 7-20mm, 10-21" tt, 6 dcp, 2 dct; Class Fletcher] Launched 3 May 1942 and commissioned 22 July 1942, the *Radford* participated in World War II in the Pacific Theater. She was decommissioned 17 January 1946 and converted to a destroyer escort 26 March 1949. Recommissioned 17 October 1949, she sailed for Korea. She participated in Korean waters during the North Korean Aggression, Inchon Landing, Second Korean Winter, Korean Defense Summer–Fall 1952, and the Korea Summer–Fall 1953 campaigns. She earned five battle stars for Korea. Later she served in the Vietnam War. She was decommissioned and struck from the navy list 10 November 1969 after which she was sold for scrap.

Ramsden WDE 382: [d.1,200; 306 × 36'7"; 21 k; cpl. 382; a. 3-3", 6-40mm, 8-20mm, 12-21" tt, 9 dcp, 2 dct; Class Edsall] Launched 24 May and commissioned 19 October 1943, she served Atlantic convoy duty during World War II. Decommissioned 13 June 1946, she was transferred to the Coast Guard and was recommissioned 28 March 1952. She served in Korean waters between 12 September 1951 and 16 September 1952. She was reclassified as DER in 1957 and decommissioned 23 June 1960.

Renshaw III DE 499: [d. 2,940; 376'5" × 39'8"; 35 k; cpl. 329; a. 5-5", 4-40mm, 8-20mm, 10-21" tt, 6 dcp, 2dct; Class Fletcher] Launched 13 October and commissioned 5 December 1942, she operated in the Pacific Island campaigns during World War II. She was decommissioned in February 1947 and was converted to an antisubmarine vessel and recommissioned as DDE in June 1950. She participated in the Korean War during the Communist China Spring Offensive, UN Summer–Fall Offensive, Third Korean Winter, and the Korea Summer–Fall 1953 campaigns. She was slightly damaged after being hit by shore batteries near Songjin, North Korea, on 11 October 1951. There was one casualty. She received five battle stars for Korea. She was decommissioned 13 February 1970 and struck from the navy list. She was sold for scrap in October 1970.

Richey WDE 385/485: [d. 1,490 (f); 306 × 36'7"; 21 k; cpl. 216; a. 2-5", 3-3" 10-40mm, 24-20mm, 2 dct, 8 dcp, 9-21" tt; Class Edsall] Launched 30 June and commissioned 30 October 1943, her World War II service was in Atlantic escort duty. Redesignated WDE 485, she was loaned to the Coast Guard from 1 April 1952 to June 1954. She saw limited service in Korea, but was eligible for the Korean Service Medal. She was struck 30 June 1968 and sunk as a target.

Silverstein DE 534: [d. 1,350; 306 × 36'7"; 24.3 k; cpl. 222; a. 1-5", 10-40mm: Class John C. Butler] She was launched 8 November 1943 and commissioned 14 July 1944. During the remainder of World War II she served in the Pacific. Placed out of commission 15 January 1947, she was recommissioned on 28 February 1951 to serve in Korea. She served in bombardment and patrolling duty during the UN Summer–Fall Offensive, Second Korean Winter, and Korea Summer–Fall 1953 campaigns. She earned three battle stars in Korea. She was decommissioned 1 December 1972 and struck from the navy list. On 3 December 1973 she was sold for scrap.

Sproston DDE 577: [d. 2,924; 376'3" × 39'8"; 35.2 k; cpl. 273; a. 5-5", 4-1.1", 4-20mm, 10-40mm, 10-21" tt; Class Fletcher] Launched 31 August 1942 and commissioned on 19 May 1943, she served in the Pacific during World War II. She was decommissioned 18 January 1946. Following the outbreak of war in Asia, she was recommissioned as DDE on 15 September 1950. She served in Korean waters during the Korean Defense Summer–Fall 1952 campaign. She received one battle star. She was redesignated DD in 1962 and later served in Vietnam. She was decommissioned 30 September 1968, struck from the navy lists 10 October 1960 and sold for scrap 15 September 1971.

Taylor DDE 468: [d. 2,050; 376'6" × 39'8"; 37 k; cpl. 329; a. 5-5", 10-40mm, 4-1.1", 6-20mm, 10-21" tt, 6 dcp, 2 dct; Class Fletcher] Launched 7 June 1942 and commissioned 28 August 1942, she moved to the northern Atlantic and then served as convoy escort. Transferred to the Pacific, she saw considerable service during World War II, earning 15 battle stars. She was decommissioned 31 May 1946. She was converted to an escort destroyer and designated DDE 468. She was recommissioned 3 December 1951 and joined Task Force 77 on 16 June to screen carriers. She participated in Korean waters during the Korean Defense Summer–Fall 1952 and the Korea Summer–Fall 1953 campaigns. She earned two battle stars for Korea. She later participated in the Vietnam War, having been reconverted to a destroyer on 7 June 1962. She was decommissioned and struck from the navy list in January 1971 at which time she was cannibalized to maintain a sister ship serving in the Italian navy.

Ulvert M. Moore DE 442: [d. 1,350; 306 × 36'8"; 24 k; cpl. 186; a. 2-5", 4-40mm, 3-21" tt, 8 dpc hh, 2 dct; Class John C. Butler] Launched 8 March 1944 and commissioned 11 July 1944, she served in the Pacific during World War II. Placed out of commission and in reserves 15 January 1947, she was recommissioned 28 February 1951. She served in Korea with the UN Blockading and Escort Force and, in her second tour, with Task Force 95 on escort and patrol. She served in Korean waters during the Communist China Spring Offensive and the UN Summer–Fall campaigns, and received three battle stars. She was decommissioned and placed in reserves again 24 June 1960. She was stricken 1 December 1965 and sunk as a target.

Vammen DE 664: [d. 1,400; 306 × 37; 23.5 k; cpl. 186; a. 3-3", 4-1.1", 10-20mm, 3-21" tt, 2 dct, 8 dcp hh; Class Buckley] Launched 21 May 1944 and commissioned 27 July 1944, she was inactivated on 2 April 1947. After World War II service, the USS *Vammen* was reactivated and modified as a specialized antisubmarine warfare ship. The bridge was redesigned, equipped with hedgehogs (trainable, forward-firing, ASW projectors) and improved sonar capabilities. In Korea she operated along the eastern coast of North Korea, and performed patrol and gunfire support at Wonsan from 25 August to 17 September 1952 during Korean Defense Summer–Fall 1952 campaign. She earned one engagement star for her service in Korea. She returned for a second tour of support and patrol. She saw service in Vietnam, was decommissioned on 1 August 1969, and then determined to be unfit for further service. She was utilized in a Condor missile test on 4 February 1971 and sunk on 18 February.

Walker DE 517: [d. 2,940; 376'5" × 39'4"; 35 k; cpl. 329; a. 5-5", 10-40mm, 10-21" tt; Class Fletcher] Launched 31 January and commissioned 3 April 1943, she participated first in Atlantic and then Pacific combat duty. She was decommissioned 31 May 1946 and recommissioned and converted to a destroyer escort (DE) 27 February 1951. She participated in the atomic exercise "Greenhouse" and then sailed for Korea where she took part in escort and blockade service. She participated in the Second Korean Winter and the Korean Defense Summer–Fall 1952 campaigns, earning two battle stars for Korea. She was decommissioned 2 July 1969 and taken from the navy list. Sold to the Italian Navy in 1977, she was renamed *Fante*.

Waller DE 466: [d. 2,940; 376'5" × 39'7"; 35 k; cpl. 329; a. 5-5", 10-40mm, 7-20mm, 10-21" tt; 6 dcp, 2 dct; Class Fletcher] Launched 15 August 1942 and commissioned 1 October 1942, she sailed for the Pacific war on convoy and escort duty. Placed out of commission, she was recommissioned as a destroyer escort on 5 July 1950. She set sail for Korea and participated in the Communist China Spring Offensive and the UN Summer–Fall Offensive campaigns, earning two battle stars. She was decommissioned and struck on 15 July 1969, and disposed of as a target 2 February 1970.

Walton DE 361: [d. 1,350; 306 × 36'8"; 24 k; cpl. 186; a. 1-5", 4-40mm, 10-20mm, 3-21" tt, 2 dct, 8 dcp, 1 dep hh; Class John C. Butler] Launched 20 May 1944 and commissioned 4 September 1944, the *Walton* operated in the Pacific. Converted to a DDE on 31 May 1949, she remained in reserves until the Korean War. Recommissioned 5 July 1950, she arrived and began patrol and blockade duties. She participated in the Korean Defense Summer–Fall 1952 and the Korea Summer–Fall 1953 campaigns, receiving two battle stars and the Republic of Korea Presidential Unit Citation. Decommissioned 20 September 1968, she was struck from the navy list 23 September 1968 and sunk as a target 7 August 1969.

Whitehurst DE 634: [d. 1,400; 306 × 37; 23.5 k; cpl. 186; a. 3-3", 4-1.1", 8-20mm, 3-21" tt, 2 dct, 8 dcp, 1 dep hh; Class Buckley] Launched 5 September and commissioned 19 November 1943, she participated in the campaign of the Solomon where she escorted oilers. Decommissioned 27 November 1946, she was placed in the Atlantic Reserve Fleet. Reactivated in 1950, she was recommissioned 1 September 1950 and sailed for the Far East. She served in Korean waters during the First UN Counter Offensive, Communist China Spring Offensive, and the UN Summer–Fall Offensive campaigns, remaining in the Far East until 1955, and earning three battle stars. She served as the background for the movie *The Enemy Below*. On 6 December 1958 she was decommissioned. On 12 July 1969 she was taken out of service and removed from the navy list. She was taken to sea and sunk as a target by the USS *Trigger* in April of 1971.

William Seiverling DE 441: [d. 1,350; 306 × 36'8"; 24 k; cpl. 222; a. 2-5", 4-40mm, 10-20mm, 3-21" tt, 2 dct, 8 dcp, 1 dep; Class John C. Butler] Launched 7 March and commissioned 1 June 1944, she operated in the Pacific during World War II. She was formally decommissioned 21 March 1947. She was recommissioned 27 December 1950 and joined the escort and blockade task force. She participated in Korean waters during the Communist China Spring Offensive, UN Summer–Fall Offensive, Korean Defense Summer–Fall 1952, Third Korean Winter, and the Korea Summer–Fall 1953 campaigns. On 8 September 1951 her fire room was flooded by fire from a shore battery near Wonsan, North Korea. There were no casualties. She received three battle stars. She was placed out of commission on 17 September 1957 but remained in the Pacific Reserve Fleet until she was struck from the navy list on 20 September 1973. She was sold for scrap.

Wiseman DE 667: [d. 1,400; 306 × 36'1"; 24 k; cpl. 186; a. 3-3", 4-1.1", 8-20mm; 2 dct, 8 dcp; Class Buckley] Launched 6 November 1943, she was commissioned 4 April 1944. She was converted to a floating power station, the ship-to-shore electrical facilities concept having been proven earlier in the Pacific War when she provided electric power for Manila. During this time she also provided 150,000 gallons of drinking water to the army. Decommissioned on 31 May 1944, she was deactivated 31 January 1947. Recommissioned in the autumn of 1950, she was rushed to Korea. She saw service in Korean waters during the Communist China Aggression, First UN Counter Offensive, Communist China Spring Offensive, UN Summer–Fall Offensive, Third Korean Winter, and Korea Summer–Fall 1953 campaign. During her second trip she carried out patrol assignments, blockaded, and bombarded segments of northeastern Korea. She received six battle stars for her role in Korea She was decommissioned on 16 May 1959. Later she saw service in Vietnam. She returned home and was decommissioned again on 17 July 1962, struck 15 April 1973, and later sold for scrap.

Frigate (PF)

The term "frigate" has been overused, and in the 1950s was used differently by the various navies that participated in the Korean War. The word first appeared in the fifteenth century to mean a small boat or craft. The British, in 1646, built a boat designed to counteract the growing problem with pirates. It was distinguished by the combination of her 30 guns and shallow draft. The ship was called *Constant Warwick* and she was identified as a frigate.

The term reappeared during World War II when "frigate" was used to describe ships designed for cruising and scouting. The British used the term to identify ships with a high ratio of keel to beam, then more broadly to describe medium-size warships. During World War II, some frigates, built by Canada, were transferred to the U.S. Navy. These were initially classified as corvettes and given hull numbers in the Gunboat (PG) series. On 15 April 1943, however, the navy changed the classification of the Canadian ships, as well as those proposed for construction in Great Britain and the United States, to patrol escorts or frigates, and gave them hull numbers within the newly created frigate (PF) series. These ships were not highly regarded by the navy, and, because of their "low tech" characteristics, they were sometimes called "economy destroyers" and considered to be a "duration-only" ship.

Following the war, and reflecting this idea, most ships within this classification were leased, loaned, or sold to other nations. A few were recommissioned during the Korean War but then all were eventually transferred during the war to South Korea, Japan, Thailand, and Colombia. While in service, the term "frigate" identified antisubmarine and escort vessels with little or no uniform distinction from destroyers. As the war ended, a few remained on the Naval Register, but they were on other service. The more modern navy uses the term "frigate" for destroyer leaders (DL) and guided-missile frigates.

Albuquerque PF 7: [d. 1430; 303'11" × 37'6"; 20 k; cpl. 190; a. 3-5", 4-40mm, 4-20mm, 1 hh, 8-Y guns, 2 dcr; Class Tacoma] The first ship to be named after Albuquerque, New Mexico, it was laid 20 July and commissioned 20 December 1943. She served with the Eastern Division 27 and escorted convoys around Alaska. On 16 August 1945 she was transferred to the Soviet Union where it was renamed EK 16. After four years of service with the Soviet Navy she was returned to the U.S. Navy on 15 November 1949 and recommissioned 3 October 1950. She conducted patrol and escort duty along the eastern coast of Korea, concluding on 26 October 1951. She earned three battle stars during the Korean War. She was decommissioned 28 February 1953 and loaned to Japan where she served as *Tochi* PF 16. Struck from the navy list 1 December 1961, she was transferred to Japan where she was sunk as a target in 1963.

Bayonne PF 21: [d. 1,430; 303'11" × 37'6"; 20 k; cpl. 195; a. 3-3", 2-40mm, 9-20mm, dc; Class Tacoma] Launched 11 Sept 1943 and commissioned 14 Feb 1945, hull 1487 (T-S2-SS-AO1), she served in Alaska until decommissioned and loaned 2 September 1945 to the Soviet Union where she became the EK 25. She was returned to the Navy and placed out of commission on 14 November 1949. Recommissioned 28 July 1950 at Yokosuka, Japan, in order to participate in the Inchon landing, she saw service in Korean waters during the North

Korean Aggression, Inchon Landing, UN Summer–Fall Offensive, Second Korean Winter, Korean Defense Summer–Fall 1952, Third Korean Winter, and the Korea Summer–Fall 1953 campaigns. She served in Korea until 31 January 1953 when she was decommissioned and loaned to Japan. The Bayonne received six battle stars.

Bisbee PF 46: [d. 1,430; 303'11" × 37'6"; 20.3 k; cpl. 190; a. 2-3', 4-40mm, 4-20mm, 8 dcp, 1 dcp hh, 2 dct: Class Tacoma] Launched 7 September 1943 and commissioned 14 February 1944, she was laid down as PG 146, accepted by the navy, recommissioned on the 15 February, and named *Bisbee* PF 46. During World War II she served in Pacific waters. She was decommissioned 26 August 1945 and transferred the following day to the Soviet Union. She was returned on 1 November 1949 and remained in reserve until she was recommissioned 18 October 1950. She participated with the East Coast Blockading and Escort Force. She served in Korean waters during the Communist China Aggression, First UN Counter Offensive, Communist China Spring Offensive, UN Summer–Fall Offensive, and the Korean Defense Summer–Fall 1952 campaigns. She received three battle stars for Korean service. She was decommissioned 12 February 1952 and turned over to a Colombian crew, becoming the *Capitan Tono*. She was removed from the navy list 25 February 1952.

Burlington PF 51: [d. 1430; 303'11" × 37'6"; 20 k; cpl. 190; a. 3-3"; Class Tacoma] The *Burlington* was launched 7 December 1943 and commissioned 3 April 1944. During World War II she was operated by the U.S. Coast Guard, primarily escorting convoys from New Guinea and the Philippines in support of the Leyte operation. The ship was leased to the Soviet Union on 26 August 1945, returned to the U.S. and recommissioned on 5 January 1951. While on Korean service she operated at Wonsan Harbor and Chongjin-Songjin, bombarding shore targets, performing escort and patrol, serving as a harbor entrance control vessel, and guarding minesweepers at Wonsan. From 11 May until 8 June 1951 she performed patrol and escort duty, transported casualties, and provided bombardment with Task Force 92. She was placed out of commission and in reserve 15 September 1952. The *Burlington* received five battle stars for her Korean Service.

Everett PF 8: [d. 1,264; 303'11" × 37'6"; 20 k; cpl. 190; a. 3-3"; Class Tacoma] She was launched 29 September 1943 and commissioned 22 January 1944, after which she performed patrol and escort duty in the harsh waters off the Aleutians. Decommissioned in 1945, she was transferred to the USSR under lend lease. Returned to the U.S. Navy on 15 November 1949, she was recommissioned on 26 July 1950 and then joined the UN Blockading and Escort Forces off both coasts in Korea. On 3 July 1951 she was hit by shore fire and one man was killed, and seven wounded, but the ship was not badly damaged. She received four battle stars for Korea. She was decommissioned 10 March 1953 and lent to Japan. Returned to the U.S. Navy, she was stricken from the navy list on 1 December 1961.

Glendale PF 36: [d. 1,264; 303'11" × 37'6"; 20.3 k.; cpl. 190; a. 3-3", 2 twin 40mm, 9-20mm, dc; Class Tacoma] This frigate was the only ship named for Glendale, California. She was launched on 28 May 1943 and commissioned 1 October 1943. During World War II she served escort and patrol assignments at New Guinea and the Philippines. Decommissioned 12 June 1945, she was turned over to the Soviet Navy and renamed EK 42. Returned to the United States 16 November 1949, she was recommissioned 11 October 1950. She patrolled off the coast at Hungnam, Pusan, and Inchon in support of ground troops. For her service she was awarded the Presidential Unit Citation and four battle stars. Decommissioned and transferred to Thailand to serve as the *Tachin*, she was struck from the navy list on 20 November 1951.

Gloucester II PF 22: [d. 1,430; 303'11" × 37'6"; 20 k; cpl. 190; a. 3-3", 4-40mm, 9-20mm, 8 dcp, 1 dcp hh, 2 dct: Class Tacoma] Launched 12 July 1943, she served in Alaska and then was loaned to Russia where she was renamed EK 26. Returned and recommissioned 11 October 1950, she sailed to Korea 27 November 1950. She suffered a direct hit off Kojo on 11 November 1951, and one man was killed. She was decommissioned 15 September 1952 and loaned to Japan. Returned to the United States on 1 October 1953, she was sold 1 December 1961.

Hoquiam PF 5 : [d. 1,430; 303'11" × 37'6"; 20 k; cpl. 190; a. 3-3", 4-40mm, 9-20mm, 8 dcp, 1 dcp hh; 2 dct; Class Tacoma] The *Hoquiam* was launched 31 July 1943 under MC contract and commissioned 8 May 1944. During the remainder of World War II she patrolled along the Alaskan coast. On 16 August she was transferred to Russia under lend lease. Returned 1 November 1949, she was recommissioned 27 September 1950 and sent to join forces in Korea. She served as a harbor control and screening ship, performed patrol, escort and communications duty. She participated in the evacuation of Hungnam, and operations along the east coast from Wonsan to Songjin. On 7 May 1951 she was damaged by gunfire but was quickly returned to Wonsan to resume bombardment. She received five battle stars for service in Korea. She was decommissioned 8 October 1951 and leased to the Republic of Korea where she served as *Nae Tong*.

Tacoma III PF 3: [d. 1,430; 303'11" × 37'6"; 20.3 k; cpl. 190; a. 3-3", 4-40mm, 9-20mm, 2 dct, 8dcp, 1 dcp hh; Class Tacoma] She was the third ship named for Tacoma, Washington, and the lead ship of the Tacoma-class frigate. Launched 7 July 1943, she was commissioned 6 November 1943. During World War II she conducted antisubmarine patrols and escorted convoys among the Alaskan and Aleutian islands. She was decommissioned on 16 August 1945 when she was transferred to the Soviet Union where she served as EK 12. She was recommissioned, and on 30 January 1951 joined the bombardment force at Kansong and later at Kosong, Pusan, Kangnung, Yangyang and Hawangpo. On 9 October 1951 she was transferred to the Republic of Korea Navy where she served as *Taedong*. She was struck from the navy list 2 April 1973 and donated to the ROK Navy on 1 June 1973 as a museum ship. She earned three battle stars while on service in Korea.

Patrol Gunboat, Cutter

A gunboat is defined as a small craft with one or more guns. Made famous by the movie *The Sand Pebbles*, the gunboat was the ship on the spot for America's early involvement in foreign affairs, what would become known as "gunboat diplomacy." In significance use during the American Civil War, they provided access to areas where larger boats could not go. Versions of the gunboat were used widely in Europe and the Far and Middle East during the twentieth century. While the use was limited by the United Nations in Korea, both North and South Korea used gunboats. Later, in Vietnam, the ships of the "Brown Water Navy" were, to a large degree, gunboats. Listed here, in alphabetical order, are the American gunboats in service. These are primarily Coast Guard ships.

Chautauqua WPG 41: [d. 1,342; 254 × 43'1"; 17 k; cpl. 143; a. 1-5", 1 mk] Commissioned 4 August 1945, she saw Korean service during periods from 31 May 1951 until 6 April 1954. She was decommissioned 1 August 1973.

Escanaba WPG 64: [d. 1,978; 254 × 43'1"; 17 k; cpl. 143; a. 1-5", hh, 2 mk 32 ASW tt; Class Indian] Originally *Otsego*, she was commissioned 20 March 1946. In Korean waters during periods from 2 December 1951 until 29 October 1953. She was decommissioned 28 June 1954.

Iroquois WPG 43: [d. 1,978; 254 × 43'1"; 17 k; cpl. 143; a. 1-5", hh] Commissioned 9 February 1946, she saw service in Korean waters, on ocean station duty, during periods from 21 October 1951 until 13 February 1953. She ran aground in Korea, was decommissioned, and stored through 13 January 1965, after which she was scrapped.

Klamath WPG 66: [d. 1,978; 254 × 43'1"; 17 k; cpl. 143; a. 1-5", hh; Indian Class] Commissioned 19 June 1946, she saw service in the North Korean Aggression, Communist China Aggression, Inchon Landing, First UN Counter Offensive, and the Korean Defense Summer–Fall 1952, serving from 23 August 1951 to 11 September 1953 at stations Sugar and Victor. She was decommissioned on 1 May 1978 and sold for scrap on 18 November 1974.

Minnetonka WPG 67: [d. 1,978; 254 × 43'1"; 17 k; cpl. 143; a. 1-5", hh] Originally named the *Sunapee*, she was commissioned 11 July 1946, then served in Korean waters at stations Sugar and Victor during periods from 13 January 1952 until 13 January 1954. A crew member was killed 20 June 1972 and two injured when a hot-water heater exploded. She was decommissioned 31 May 1974.

Pontchartrain WGP 70: [d. 1,978; 254 × 43'1"; 17 k; cpl. 143; a 1-5", hh, 2 mk 32 ASWT TT] Originally named *Okeechobee,* she was commissioned 28 July 1945. She was decommissioned and stored until 5 September 1948. She served during periods from 30 March 1951 to 27 March 1953 at stations Victor and Sugar. She later served in Vietnam. She was decommissioned 19 October 1973.

Taney WAG 37: [d. 2,700; 327 × 41; 21 k; cpl. 120; a. 2-5"] Originally *Roger B. Taney* when launched and commissioned 3 June 1936, her name was shortened in 1940. She served briefly in Korea. The ship was decommissioned 7 December 1986 and now serves as a museum ship in Baltimore, Maryland.

Wachusett WPG 44: [d. 1,342; 254 × 43'1"; 17 k; cpl. 143; a. 1-5", hh] Originally named *Huron,* she was commissioned 23 March 1946. She served during periods from 11 March 1951 to 8 May 1953 at stations Victor and Sugar. Decommissioned 30 August 1973, she was sold November 1974.

Winnebago WPG 40: [d. 1,342; 254 × 43'1"; 17 k; cpl. 143; a. 1-5", hh] She was commissioned 21 June 1945. The *Winnebago* served in Korean waters, on ocean station duty, during periods from 6 December 1951 until 31 August 1953. Decommissioned 27 February 1973, she was sold 17 October 1974.

Winona WPG 64: [d. 1,978; 254 × 43'1"; 17 k, cpl. 143; a. 1-5", hh, 2 mk 32] Commissioned 19 April 1946, she saw service in Korean waters during periods from 26 October 1951 until 19 November 1952. She later served in Vietnam, then was decommissioned 31 May 1974.

Radar Picket Destroyer (DDR)

Some ships were designed and used to extend the radar detection range around the larger forces in order to prevent surprise attack. These were identified as radar picket destroyers. Most were converted late in the Korean War. The ships that are designated here are those whose primarily role was as a radar picket destroyer. The armament varied considerably.

Chevalier II DDR 805: [d. 2,425; 390'6" × 41'1"; 35 k; cpl. 367; a. 6-5", 10-21" tt, 6 dcp, 2 dct; Class Gearing] Launched 29 October 1944 and commissioned 9 January 1945, she saw some service in the Pacific during World War II. She was reclassified DDR on 18 May

1949 and served in Korean waters during the North Korean Aggression, Communist China Aggression, Inchon Landing, First UN Counter Offensive, UN Summer–Fall Offensive, Second Korean Winter, Korean Defense Summer–Fall 1952, Third Korean Winter, and the Korea Summer–Fall 1953 campaigns. She received nine battle stars.

Duncan III DDR 874: [d. 2,425; 390'6" × 41'1"; 34 k; cpl. 367; a. 6-5", 5-21" tt, 6 dcp, 2 dct; Class Gearing] Launched 27 October 1944 and commissioned 25 February 1945, the Duncan III was converted and reclassified as a radar picket destroyer (DDR 874) on 18 May 1949. She served in Korean waters during the Communist China Aggression, First UN Counter Offensive, Communist China Spring Offensive, UN Summer–Fall Offensive, Korean Defense Summer–Fall 1952, and the Korea Summer–Fall 1953 campaigns. She received seven battle stars.

Ernest G. Small DDR 838: [d. 2,425; 390'6" × 41'1"; 35 k; cpl. 345; a. 6-5", 10-21" tt, 6 dcp, 2 dct; Class Gearing] Launched as DD 838 on 14 June 1945 and commissioned 21 August 1945, she was decommissioned on 15 January 1952, and the bow of the unfinished *Seymour D. Owens* (DD 767) was grafted to her hull. Converted to a radar picket ship, she was reclassified DDR on 18 July 1952. Following peacetime duties and midshipman cruises, she joined the 7th Fleet as war broke out in Korea. She participated at the Hungnam redeployment where she was struck by a mine on 7 October 1951, which caused considerable damage and broke the bow. She suffered 27 casualties. The *Ernest G. Small* served in Korean waters during the North Korean Aggression, Communist China Aggression, Inchon Landing and the UN Summer–Fall Offensive campaigns. She received four battle stars for service in Korea.

Fiske II DDR 842: [d. 2,425; 390'6" × 41'1"; 35 k; cpl. 367; a. 6-5", 10-21" tt, 6 dcp, 2 dct; Class Gearing] Launched 8 September 1945 and commissioned 28 November 1945, she served in the Atlantic and Mediterranean during and following World War II. She was decommissioned 1 April 1952 and placed in reserves. Recommissioned 25 November 1952, she was active in Korean waters during the First UN Counter Offensive and the Communist China Spring Offensive campaigns. She received two battle stars for Korean service. She was loaned to Turkey and renamed *Piyale Pasa*.

Frank Knox DDR 742/DD 742: [d. 2,425; 390'6" × 41'1"; 35 k; cpl. 367; a. 6-5", 10-21" tt, 6 dcp, 2 dct; Class Gearing] Launched 17 September 1944 and commissioned 11 December 1945, she served in the Pacific during World War II. Reclassified as a DDR on 18 May 1948, she was active in Korean waters during the North Korean Aggression, Communist China Aggression, Inchon Landing, First UN Counter Offensive, and the Korean Defense Summer–Fall 1952 campaigns. She received five battle stars. She was decommissioned in January 1971.

Hanson DDR 832: [d. 2,425; 390'6" × 41'1"; 35 k; cpl. 367; a. 6-5", 10-21" tt, 6 dcp, 2 dct; Class Gearing] Launched 11 May 1945 and commissioned the same day, she was assigned to the Pacific following World War II. She was reclassified DDR on 8 May 1949 and participated in Korean waters during North Korean Aggression, Communist China Aggression, Inchon Landing, First UN Counter Offensive, UN Summer–Fall Offensive, Second Korean Winter, Third Korean Winter and the Korea Summer–Fall 1953 campaign. She received eight battle stars for service in Korea. The *Hanson* was redesignated as a destroyer in 1964.

Hawkins DDR 873/DD 873: [d. 2,425; 390'6" × 41'1"; 35 k; cpl. 367; a. 6-5", 10-21" tt, 6 dcp, 2 dct; Class Gearing] Originally named *Beatty*, she was renamed 22 June 1944, launched 7 October 1944, and commissioned 10 February 1945. She was converted to a picket ship 23 March 1945 and saw service in Korean waters during the First UN Counter Offensive and the Communist China Spring Offensive, receiving two battle stars for Korea. She was reclassified a destroyer 1 April 1964, and served during the Cuban Missile Crisis.

Henry Tucker DDR 875: [d. 2,425; 390'6" × 41'1"; 34 k; cpl. 367; 6-5", 16-40mm, 2 dct, 6 dcp; Class Gearing] Launched 29 May 1944 and commissioned 12 May 1945, she served in Korean waters during the Communist China Aggression, Inchon Landing, First UN Counter Offensive, Communist China Spring Offensive, UN Summer–Fall Offensive, Second Korean Winter, Korean Defense Summer–Fall 1952, and the Korea Summer–Fall 1953 campaigns. She won seven battle stars. On 28 June 1951 she was hit near Wonsan by shore batteries; two men were wounded and some damage suffered. Radar was added 14 April 1953.

Herbert J. Thomas DDR 833: [d. 2,425; 390'6" × 40'10"; 35 k; cpl. 435; a. 6-5", 14-40mm, 16-20mm, 6 dcp; Class Gearing] Launched 25 March 1945 and commissioned 29 May 1945, the *Herbert J. Thomas* joined the Western Pacific Forces supporting the occupation of Japan and Korea. When war broke out in Korea she was immediately dispatched and joined Task Force 77 (Fleet Striking Force), providing gunfire support for the landing at Pohang. Listed as damaged by a hit near Wonsan on 12 May 1952, there were no casualties. She won six battle stars for service in Korea. She was decommissioned 4 December 1970 and transferred to the Republic of Taiwan on 1 June 1974 where she served as the *Han Yang*.

Higbee DDR 806: [d. 2,425; 390'6" × 41'1"; 35 k; cpl. 367; a. 6-5", 10-21" tt, 6 dcp, 2 dct; Class Gearing] Launched 13 November 1944 and commissioned 27 January 1945, she was assigned to the Pacific. Reclassified as a DDR on 18 Mar 1949, the *Higbee*, known as the "leaping Lenah," served in the Korean War during the North Korean Aggression, Communist China Aggression, Inchon Landing, UN Summer–Fall Offensive, Second Korean Winter, and the Third Korean Summer campaigns. She won seven battle stars for Korean service. She took part in the Gemini Recovery and was redesignated a destroyer on 1 June 1963.

McKean II DDR 784: [d. 2,425; 390'6" × 40'11"; 35 k; cpl. 336; a. 6-5", 16-40mm, 10-20mm, 5-21" tt, 2 dct, 6 dep: Class Gearing] She was launched 31 March 1945 and commissioned 9 June 1945. During the end of World War II she operated with occupational forces in the Pacific. When war broke out in Korea she was assigned to the 7th Fleet, and participated at Inchon, Chinnampo, the blockade at Wonsan and Songjin. She saw service in Korean waters during the Korea, Summer–Fall 1953 campaign and received one battle star for Korea. Later she served in the Vietnam War.

Perkins DDR 877: [d. 3,479; 390'6" × 40'10"; 35 k; cpl 345; a. 6-5", 12-40mm, 5-21" tt; Class Gearing] Launched 7 December 1944 and commissioned 5 April 1945, she served in Korean waters during the First UN Counter Offensive, Communist China Spring Offensive, UN Summer–Fall Offensive, and the Korean Defense Summer–Fall 1952 campaigns. Slightly damaged by shore batteries off Kojo, North Korea, on 13 October 1952, the *Perkins* crew suffered 18 casualties. She received three battle stars and later served in Vietnam.

Rogers DDR 876/DD 876: [d. 2,425; 390'6"× 40'11"; 35 k; cpl. 336; a. 6-5", 12-40mm, 8-20mm, 5-21" tt, 2 dct, 6 dep: Class Gearing] Launched 20 November 1944 and commissioned 26 March 1945, she was converted to a picket ship shortly after her shakedown cruise. During the interwar period she served in the Far East. On 18 March 1949 she was converted to a radar picket destroyer and her torpedo tubes removed. She served in Korean waters during the First UN Counter Offensive, Communist China Spring Offensive, UN Summer–Fall Offensive, and the Korean Defense Summer–Fall 1952 campaigns. The *Rogers* served as the "lifeguard" for President Truman's flight to Wake Island in 1950 and President-elect Eisenhower's return trip from Korea in 1952. She earned five battle stars for Korea and later served in Vietnam. She was struck from the navy list on 1 October 1980 and transferred to the Republic of Korean Navy on 11 August 1981 where she became the *Jeong Ju*. *DANFS* reports that it is now a museum ship at Dangjin-Gun, Chung Nam Province.

Southerland DDR 743/DD 743: [d. 2,425; 390'6" × 41'1"; 34 k; cpl. 367; 6-5", 16-40mm, 2 dct, 6 dcp; Class Gearing] Launched 5 October 1944 and commissioned 22 December 1944, she served in the Pacific during World War II. She was operating in Hawaiian waters when war broke out in Korea. The *Southerland* participated in the North Korean Aggression, Communist China Aggression, Inchon Landing, First UN Counter Offensive, Communist China Spring Offensive, Second Korean Winter, the Korean Defense Summer–Fall 1952, and the Korean Summer–Fall 1953 campaign. She was slightly damaged by shore fire 16 September 1950. After receiving eight battle stars, she was struck from the navy list 23 February 1981 and sunk as a target on 2 August 1997.

William R. Rush DDR 714: [d. 2,425; 390'6" × 41'1"; 35 k; cpl. 336; a. 6-5", 12-40mm, 20-20mm, 5-21" tt, 6 dcp, 2 dct; Class Gearing] Launched 8 July 1945 and commissioned 21 September 1944, she served in Europe during World War II. She sailed for the Far East on 3 January 1951 and participated in the First UN Counter Offensive and the Communist China Spring Offensive campaigns. In July 1952 she was reclassified DDR 714. After a full deployment she was decommissioned 1 July 1978 and removed from the navy list, transferred that day to the Republic of Korea Navy, and named *Rang Won*.

4

COMMAND AND CONVALESCENCE

From where I could see, it was hard to know if anyone was in charge.
— Bruce Oglethorpe, GI

Command Ship

The role of the amphibious command ship is to provide commanders with control facilities during an amphibious exercise. They contain very sophisticated and up-to-date facilities for the navy amphibious task force commander and the commander of the marine landing force, allowing the senior officers to direct the complexities of an amphibious landing. Command ships have a crew of 700–800 and are usually named after mountains.

The USS *McKinley,* during operations at Hungnam, maintained an illustrative staff: the flagship's operations officer, who bore responsibility for the coordination of all shipments, assigned anchorage, issued docking instructions, prepared sailing orders, and supervised all operations-control stations; the beach master, who controlled LST operations; the port director, who berthed the ships; and the embarkation-control liaison officer, who coordinated between the navy staff and marine command. The Military Sea Transportation Service officer handled all shipping by command ships.

Eldorado AGC 11: [d. 12,690; 459 × 64; 17 k; cpl. 50–54 officers and 562–632 enlisted; a. 2-5", 4-twin 40mm, 10-twin 20mm; Class McKinley] Launched 26 October 1943 as the *Monsoon*, she was converted and commissioned 25 August 1944, and served in the Pacific where she participated in Iwo Jima, Leyte, and Okinawa. With the outbreak of the Korean War she served as the command vessel in charge of beach port control at Inchon, as the flagship for Admiral Lyman Thackrey and the standby for the USS *McKinley*. In service in Korean waters during North Korean Aggression, Communist China Aggression, Inchon Landing, First UN Counter Offensive, Communist China Spring Offensive, UN Summer–Fall Offensive, Third Korean Winter, and the Korea Summer–Fall 1953 campaigns, she received eight battle stars for Korea. In January 1969 she was redesignated as LCC-11. Her fate is unclear.

Estes AGC 12: [d. 12,690; 459 × 64; 17 k; cpl. 50–54 officers and 562–632 enlisted; a. 2-5", 4-twin 40mm, 10-twin 20mm; Class McKinley] Launched 1 November 1943 as the *Morning Star* and commissioned 9 October 1944, she sailed for the Pacific where she served as the flagship for three succeeding commanders of the 7th Fleet. She was decommissioned and put in reserves 30 June 1949, then recommissioned on 31 January 1951. She served as the flagship for Rear Admiral Ingolf N. Kiland, commander Amphibious Force, Pacific. The command ship participated during the UN Summer–Fall Offensive, and the Second Korean Winter campaign. She received two battle stars for Korea. Her eventual fate is unknown.

Frybarger DE 705: [d. 1,400; 306 × 36'10"; 24 k; cpl. 186; a. 3-3", 3-21" tt, dcs; Class Buckle] Launched 25 January 1944 and commissioned 18 May 1944, she was assigned to the Pacific during World War II where she provided escort duty in and around the Philippines, Carolinas, Hollandia, and Okinawa. She was decommissioned and placed in reserves 30 June 1947. She was recommissioned 6 October 1950 as a control escort vessel. Though *DANFS* does not include the *Frybarger*, nor is she mentioned in Cagle, there is evidence in Awards that she was in Korean waters controlling landing and amphibious craft, during periods from 23 March 1952 until 17 May 1954. She was decommissioned 9 December 1954 and placed in reserves.

Mt. McKinley AGC 7: [d. 12,690; 459 by 64; 17 k; cpl. 50–54 officers and 562–632 enlisted; a. 2-5", 4-twin 40mm, 10-twin 20mm; Class McKinley] Laid as the *Cyclone* 31 July 1943, she was commissioned as the *Mt. McKinley* 1 May 1944. During World War II she participated in the assault at Peleliu and later served as the command ship for the atomic testing at Eninetok. The *Mt. McKinley* served as the command flagship for the amphibious landings at Inchon and Pohang, housing the staffs of both Lt. General Edward Mallory Almond and Major General O. P. Smith. During the Inchon invasion, General Smith and his staff had established an advance command post aboard the *Mt. McKinley*. Later she was a part of the armada that carried the marines back to Wonsan where, with General Almond aboard, Tenth Corps landed on the east coast. She would serve as Rear Admiral James Doyle's flagship during the Hungnam Redeployment. She was in Korean waters during the North Korean Aggression, Communist China Aggression, Inchon Landing, First UN Counter Offensive, Communist China Spring Offensive, Second Korean Winter, Korean Defense Summer–Fall 1952, Third Korean Winter, and Korea Summer–Fall 1953 campaigns, and received 8 battle stars for her service in Korea.

Amphibious Control Vessel (PCEC)

Asheboro PC/PCEC 882: [d. 375; 173'8" × 23; 22 k; cpl. 80; a. 1-3", 1-40mm, 2-20mm, 2 dct, 4 dcp; Class PC 592]. Launched 27 December 1943 and commissioned 2 June 1944, she served in World War II on convoy duty and saw service in Korean waters during the Communist China Aggression, First UN Counter Offensive, Korean Defense Summer–Fall 1952 and Third Korean Winter campaign. She was transferred to the South Korean navy on 1 November 1974 and struck from the Navy Register 15 November 1974. Listed in the *U.S. Navy and Marine Corps Awards Manual* (*Awards*) but not in *DANFS*.

Banning PC/PCEC 886: [d. 903; 184'6" × 31'1"; 15.7 k; cpl. 99; a. 1-3", 3-40mm, 4 dcp, 1 dcp hh; Class PCC 842] Launched 10 July 1944 and commissioned 31 May 1945 as a submarine chaser, she saw duty as a weather station ship in the Philippines during World War II. She was decommissioned 30 December 1949 and then recalled 7 September 1950 as an amphibious control vessel and served in Korean waters during the Korean Defense Summer–Fall 1952 and the Third Korean Winter campaigns. She earned two battle stars. Her name was struck on 1 May 1961 and she was turned over to the Hood River Port Commission for use as a memorial.

PCEC 896 (Unnamed): [d. 903; 184'6" × 31'1"; 15.7 k; cpl. 99; a. 1-3", 3-40mm, 4 dcp, 1dcp hh; Class PCC 842] Launched 22 May 1943 and commissioned 27 November 1944, she saw service in Korean waters during the North Korean Aggression, Communist China Aggression, Inchon Landing, Second Korean Winter, Korean Defense Summer–Fall, and the Korea Summer–Fall 1953 campaigns. She was decommissioned 28 May 1964, transferred to the Coast Guard 29 July 1964, and eventually sold to the South Korean navy 1 November 1974.

PCEC 898 (Unnamed): [d. 903; 184'6" × 31'1"; 15.7 k; cpl. 99; a. 1-3", 3-40mm, 4 dcp, 1dcp hh; Class PCC 842] Launched 3 August 1943 and commissioned 24 January 1945, she saw service in Korean waters and participated in the Second Korean Winter, Third Korean Winter, and the Korea Summer–Fall 1953 campaigns. She was transferred to the South Korean navy 1 November 1974 and struck 15 November 1974.

Hospital Ship

The essential goal of military medical service is to returned a wounded man or woman to duty as quickly as possible. Notwithstanding the humanitarian efforts, it is necessary to return them as soon as they are ready. In Korea the survival of those who were wounded in combat surpassed the records of those saved in any previous wars. This was much to the credit of the medical evacuation system, and key to this system was the presence of hospital ships. The obstacles facing the evacuation system were massive, and included the initial shortage of medical supplies and personnel, the burden of huge casualties in short periods of time, and limitations imposed by difficult ground conditions and unpredictable weather. During the length of the war —1,128 days — only a low percentage of American forces in Korea were killed or died of wounds. By the end of 1952, records suggest that a high percentage of wounded men were returned to duty.

The evacuation of the wounded has always had a high priority and in Korea there were numerous ships involved in providing this and other medical services. Among these would be the LST that went ashore at Inchon carrying a mobile surgical team. But the primary hospital ships were those designed for that purpose and put into action almost immediately after the outbreak of war.

The first hospital ship in the U.S. Navy was most likely the *Intrepid*, a ketch, which was used for that purpose during the Tripolitan War. The first commissioned hospital ship was the *Red Rover*, a side-wheeler. These ships have always served to provide seaborne ambulances and later, to take on the task of mobile hospitals. In Korea, however, they played a somewhat different role. Their primary mission remained to transport patients while giving care in route, but in Korea they became useful as floating hospitals. Patients were brought directly to the ship either by lighter or helicopters that landed on the ship, where they had available the advantages of a completely modern hospital. As it turned out, the hospital ship usually remained in Korean ports for extended periods of time, moving only when they were needed somewhere else. While in port, they could also serve as medical clinics, the same as would be available from a land-based hospital where a large number of wounded and injured were treated as outpatients. By September 1952 the number of admissions to the three hospital ships on duty numbered 40,662, or about 35 percent of those wounded in battle.

The ships worked in conjunction with other efforts. At Inchon, for example, the USS *Consolation* provided medical aid via two LST, converted to hospital ships, which were anchored in the assault area. Because of the expectations of high casualties, eight APA, as well as the command ship *Mount McKinley*, were equipped to receive major battle casualties.

Benevolence AH 13: [d. 15,000'f; 520 × 71'6"; 18 k; cpl. 564, Class Haven] The *Benevolence* could care for 800 patients. Perhaps the *Benevolence* should not be included here because she never actually made it to Korea, though she was slated for service there. Returning from a shakedown cruise on 25 August 1950, at about two miles west of Seal Rock, in a San Francisco fog, she collided with a civilian cargo ship, the *Mary Lunkenback*, and sank within half an hour. There were fourteen nurses on board. Of the 526 people on board all but 18 survived. The ship had been launched on 10 July 1944 as the *Marine Lion*, and had been converted to a hospital ship and commissioned 12 May 1945. She served in World War II and in April 1946 was assigned as the medical ship for Operation Crossroads, the first atomic bomb test at Bikini. She was placed out of commission on 13 September 1947 and recommissioned for expected use in Korea.

Consolation AH 15: [d. 11,141; 520 × 71'6"; 18 k; cpl. 564; Class Haven] This ship was originally launched August 1944 as the *Marine Walrus*. She was acquired by the navy 30 August 1944 and commissioned 22 May 1945. Departing San Francisco in July 1950, the ship had the capacity to provide medical and surgical care to 786 patients. It boasted three operating rooms with at least two tables in each. The USS *Consolation*, the first American hospital ship to arrive in Korean waters, was also the first hospital ship to include a female doctor on its

Helicopter bringing in the wounded

staff, the first to use a electroencephalograph brain-wave machine at sea, the first to install and use a blood bank as standard equipment, the first to mount a helicopter flight deck on the ship, and the first to receive casualties direct from battlefield to ship. The *Consolation* rendered key service at the invasion of Inchon, and the evacuation of Hungnam. She served 12,000 patients and treated 17,000 as outpatients. She participated in Korean waters during North Korean Aggression, Communist China Aggression, Inchon Landing, First UN Counter Offensive, Communist China Spring Offensive, UN Summer Fall Offensive, Second Korean Winter, Korean Defense Summer–Fall 1952, Third Korean Winter, and the Korea Summer–Fall 1953 campaigns and received nine battle stars for service in Korea. The hospital ship would later serve in Vietnam. She was chartered 16 March 1960 to the People to People Health Foundation, and renamed *Hope*, serving from 1960–74 for Project HOPE.

Haven AH 12: [d. 11,141; 520 × 71'6"; 18 k; cpl 564; Class Haven] This 11,141-ton hospital ship was built in 1944 as the freighter *Marine Hawk*, then converted and commissioned 5 May 1945. She served during World War II and during the atomic bomb tests. She was decommissioned in July 1947. Following the sinking of the USS *Benevolence*, the *Haven* was recommissioned and sailed to Korea where she arrived at Inchon 18 October 1950 and served as a base hospital for six weeks. There she saw an average of 530 patients a day, with each of the ship's 35 doctors scheduled to perform up to 20 surgeries per day. She saw service at Pusan and Inchon and participated in the North Korean Aggression, Communist China Aggression, first UN Counter Offensive, Communist China Spring Offensive, UN Summer Fall Offensive, Second Korean Winter, Korean Defense Summer–Fall 1952, Third Korean Winter, and the Korea Summer–Fall 1953 campaign. Her medical crew averaged six surgeons, four anesthesiologists, 23 nurses and six corpsmen. She had a helicopter port added prior to her reassignment. She was decommissioned in June 1957 and struck from the list March 1967. She was sold in 1968 and renamed *Clendenin*, later *Alaskan*, until scrapped in 1987.

Repose AH 16: [d. 11,141; 520 × 71'6"; 18.7; cpl 564; Class Haven] Formerly the *Marine Beaver*, she was laid on 22 October 1943 and commissioned 26 May 1945. The USS *Repose*, known as the "Angel of the Orient," served during World War II in the Pacific Theater and was inactivated 28 October 1949 and put in reserve 19 January 1950. She was recalled and arrived in Korea on 26 October 1950. She was a 782-bed ship, with 25 doctors, 30 nurses, and 199 enlisted corpsmen. She served in Korean waters during North Korean Aggression, Communist China Aggression, First UN Counter Offensive, Communist China Spring Offensive, UN Summer–Fall Offensive, Second Korean Winter, Korean Defense Summer–Fall 1952, Third Korean Winter, and the Korea Summer–Fall 1953 campaign. She maintained station at Yokohama, Inchon, Chinnampo and Pusan. After three tours in Korea, the *Repose* was decommissioned 21 December 1954. She was reactivated in the 1960s and served in Vietnam. She was decommissioned once again and placed in reserve May 1970, and remained in the Pacific Reserve Fleet until 1974. Since September 1950, her first year of service, the *Repose* handled 9,487 bed patients and thousands of outpatients. She spent 82 days at Pusan from 8 February to 30 April 1951 during which she saw 3,432 patients. She received nine battle stars for service in Korea.

5

SUBMARINES

Without a respectable Navy, alas America!
—John Paul Jones, October 1776

Certainly one of the least known of the services that took part in the Korean War was the undersea service, the submariners. The submarine does not even warrant an index entry in Cagle and Manson's *The Sea War in Korea*, and James Field's semi-official *History of United States Naval Operations in Korea* lists submarine threats, but little to nothing about American submarines that served.

Nevertheless, during the Korean War, fleet submarines were among the first of the United States forces to take the war to the enemy. The submarines available during the Korean War were an improved version of those that fought in World War II. Between the end of World War II and the signing of a cease-fire in 1953, the submarine underwent considerable change that took it from the role of a surface ship that could occasionally dive, to a more practical vessel that could move underwater at good speed, and do so for a considerable period of time. The difference was to be found in improvements in habitability, underwater endurance, electronics, and in the submarine's ability to fight. Perhaps the most significant improvement was the GUPPY (Greater Underwater Propulsive Power) Program. Having learned a great deal from captured German XXI submarines, the United States was able to provide an advantage of speed and endurance. The conversion started in 1947 and continued through 1952. It consisted of streamlining the hull, making an increase in the battery power available, and providing an improved version of the German snorkel air-breathing system. The ships were also equipped with high-speed-drive motors with reduction gears. A further update, called GUPPY III, consisting of longer hulls, new sonar, and electronics, was begun in 1959.

Fleet snorkel boats were often considered to be GUPPYs and they were much like converted GUPPY IIs, but they did not have the internal modifications. In the main, they were simply a fleet boat with a snorkel induction, an ESM mast, and an exhaust-piping mast. Most had some form of BQR-2 sonar. One of the drawbacks of the snorkel boat became evident during the winter. The water was often so cold in the Japanese Sea, that patrols had to be abandoned in December 1950 because the snorkels froze. It was not until April 1951 that the patrols were reestablished.

5. Submarines

The role of the submarine during the Korean War was varied. Submarines provided most of the reconnoitering of Soviet shipping and aided in the neutralization of maritime activity in both the Sea of Okhotsk and the Straits of Formosa. In addition they performed significant photo reconnaissance, and participated in the selection of landing sites for potential amphibious landings. They provided screening service for surface forces, surveyed Soviet and North Korean mine fields, and engaged in a variety of special forces raids. One of the roles primarily taken over by submarines was the emergence of the radar picket submarine. This came as a result of the increasing vulnerability of the surface ships that had been performing this service. The submarine, unlike the surface ship, could dive at the first indication of the enemy, particularly enemy planes, and avoid detection and damage. The change took place by installing the electronic equipment from the Edsall-class destroyers on the submarines. The improvement took up so much space, however, that they were known as Migraines.

The nature of the submarines was to change considerably following the end of the Korean War. The USS *Blueback* (SS 581) was the last American diesel sub created for the Navy, while the USS *Albacore,* completed in 1953, was the first boat built with underwater speeds that ranged as fast as 25 knots. On 21 August 1951, the Navy granted the first contract for a nuclear-powered submarine, the Nautilus, which was launched on 21 January 1954.

The Submarine Threat

The United States had little intelligence concerning the potential involvement of the Soviet Union. The Truman administration maintained the fear, if not the belief, that the outbreak in Korea was the beginning of World War III. The danger imposed by the Soviet submarines was taken seriously. What if the estimated 80 submarines that were based in the Vladivostok area were turned loose on American shipping? The UN shortage of antisubmarine units was acute, and the general fear was not improved as the first week of the conflict brought reports, all unconfirmed, of Soviet submarine activity. On the morning of 26 June 1950, the authorities had a convincing report of submarine presence in Korean waters. The first five months of the war brought 80 more reports of possible submarine sightings; the second five-month period, however, provided only 16 such reports. There was no doubt that if the Soviet Union had committed its submarines to the defense of North Korea or China, it would have been a much different war.

Concerned about the presence of enemy submarines, Admiral C. Turner Joy had quickly established the policy that any unidentified submarines should be attacked and driven off defensively, or, if indicated, offensive action could be taken. In most cases when a sound contact was made, an attack was launched at once. In the Korean waters, as well as in the Ryukyu-Formosa area, such attacks were fairly common during the first months of the war.

The submarines available to the Seventh Fleet on 25 June 1950 consisted of the USS *Remora* (SS 487), *Catfish* (SS 339) and *Pickerel* (SS 524), which immediately went into action, taking off on a reconnaissance patrol.

It is sometimes hard to determine what a war patrol consists of and how they are reported. Three kinds of patrols are recognized — war patrols, special operations, and surveillance patrols. The boats identified as having participated in the Korean War are listed in alphabetical order.

Bashaw SSK 241: [d. 1,526; 311'8" × 27'3"; 20 k; cpl. 60; a. 1–3", 10–21" tt; Class Gato] She was launched 25 July and commissioned 25 October 1943. In her short life during World

War II she sank three Japanese merchant vessels. She was decommissioned 1 March 1946. Between May 1951 and July 1952 she was converted to a "killer" submarine, received BQR-4 sonar, and was recommissioned as SSK 28 March 1953. She was in Korean waters from 11 April to 27 July 1954. Finally redesignated as an auxiliary submarine (AGSS 241) she was decommissioned and struck from the navy list 13 September 1969. She was sunk as a target July 1972. Not listed in *DANFS*.

Besugo SS 321: [d. 1,526; 311'9" × 27'3"; 20.3 k; cpl. 81; a. 1-5", 2-20mm, 10-21" tt; Class Balao] Launched 27 February and commissioned 19 June 1944, she was assigned to the Pacific Fleet and made five war patrols in the Java Sea and the South China Sea. She was one of the last of the World War II fleet class submarines and one of the very few who remained in service during the period between World War II and Korea. In 1950 the *Besugo* was one of the first ships to enter Korean waters in support of the United Nations. She served in Korea from 21 May 1950 until 11 April 1951, and earned one battle star.

Blackfin SS 322: [d. 1,525; 311'9" × 27'3"; 20 k; cpl. 66; a. 1-5", 10-21" tt, 2-20mm, 2-.50 cal. mg; Class Balao] Launched 12 March and commissioned 4 July 1944, she completed five war patrols during World War II. In November 1950 the *Blackfin* was converted to a GUPPY submarine and recommissioned on 15 May 1951. She participated in two tours of duty in the Far East (December 1951–June 1952 and January–June 1955). The *Blackfin* had a brief experience in the movie business. She was used in the filming of the movie *Move Over Darling* with Doris Day, and for the surface scenes in the movie *Ice Station Zebra*. The USS *Blackfin* was finally sunk 15 September 1972 as a target in the SubSinkEx Project Thurber.

Blenny SS 324: [d. 1,525; 311'9" × 27'3"; 20 k; cpl. 66; a. 1-3", 1-5", 10-21" tt; Class Balao] Commissioned 27 July 1944 she reported to the Pacific during World War II where she conducted four war patrols in the Java and China Seas. Converted to GUPPY class in 1951, she arrived at Yokosuka on 24 May 1952 and took part in routine 7th Fleet operations, and then was in Korean waters 25 May to 18 October 1952. She received five battle stars for action in Korea. She remained active for another decade and a half, and sometime in 1969 was redesignated an auxiliary submarine (AGSS 324) and placed in reserves. Dropped from the navy list 15 August 1973, in 1987 the *Blenny* was given to the state of Maryland to be used as an artificial reef. *DANFS* does not list her Korean service.

Bluegill SS 242: [d. 1,526; 311'9" × 17'3"; 20 k; cpl. 80; a. 1-5", 10-21" tt; Class Gato] Launched 8 August and commissioned 11 November 1943, she was decommissioned 1 March 1946 and returned to commission 3 May 1951. She conducted war patrols in the Pacific during World War II and on 7 July 1952 was converted to a killer submarine, received sonar, and was recommissioned as SSK. She was in commission from 2 May 1953 until 28 June 1969, serving in Korean waters from 28 November to 9 December 1953. She was struck from the navy list on 28 June 1969 and used as a salvage trainer in Hawaii. Not listed in Korea by *DANFS*.

Bugara SS 331: [d. 1,525; 311'8" × 27'3"; 20 k; cpl. 66; a. 1-5", 10-21" tt, 4 mg; Class Balao] She was launched 2 July 1944 and commissioned 15 November 1944, after which she served in the Pacific, completing three war patrols during World War II. She completed conversion to a fleet snorkel in 1951. She supported Korean operations until 7 December 1954. She was decommissioned and struck from the Naval Register 1 October 1970, then she accidentally swamped and sank shortly after.

Cabezon SS 334: [d. 1,526; 311'9" × 27'3"; 20 k; cpl. 66; a. 1-5", 10-21" tt; Class Gato] Launched 27 August 1944 and commissioned 30 December 1944, she conducted her first war patrol from May to July 1945. On 25 June 1950 was with 7th Fleet, only to be relieved by the *Pickerel* on 11 July. She was in Korean waters 28 June to 12 July 1950 and 3 May to 6 October 1952, the second in the area of La Perouse Strait, between Hokkaido, Japan, and Sakhalin, USSR. She was placed out of commission 24 October 1953, and struck 15 May 1970. In recording Korean action, the *U.S. Navy and Marine Corps Awards Manual*, 1954, lists slightly different dates. She was sold for scrap 28 December 1971.

Caiman SS 323: [d. 1,526; 311'9" × 27'3"; 18 k; cpl. 66-72; a. 1-5" gun, 10-21" tt; Class Balao] Originally named the *Blanquillo*, she was renamed the *Caiman*. Launched 30 March 1944, she was commissioned 17 July 1944 and made four war patrols during World War II. In April 1951 she began conversion to a GUPPY. She headed for Korea in February 1952 and began six months of deployment, making three war patrols in Korea, 16 February to 27 July 1952. She was decommissioned and transferred to the Turkish navy 3 June 1972, becoming the TCG *Dumlupinar* (S-325), and was decommissioned by them on 23 December 1983.

Carp SS 338: [d. 1,526; 311'8" × 27'3"; 20 k; cpl. 66; a. 10-21" tt, 1-5" deck gun and 4-mg. Class Balao] The *Carp* was launched 12 November 1944 and commissioned 28 February 1945. She conducted one war patrol during World War II. She was converted to a fleet snorkel in 1952. From 22 September 1952 to April 1953 she participated in three Korean patrols, and then remained on active duty after the war until July 1959. She was decommissioned 18 March 1968 and struck from the navy list 20 December 1971.

Catfish SS 339: [d. 1,526; 311'8" × 27'3"; 20 k.; cpl. 66; a. 10-21" tt, 1-5", 4 mg; Class Balao] She was in Subic Bay when the war broke out, and she and the *Pickerel* were the first two subs in the area. She was launched on 6 January 1944 and commissioned 19 March 1945. Her conversion to a GUPPY II was completed in 1949. The *Catfish* was on two war patrols in Korea. On 17 July 1950 she sailed on a reconnaissance mission along the China coast, joined the next day by the *Pickerel*. She was in Korean waters from 27 June to 18 July 1950. She was struck on 1 July 1971, sold to the Argentine navy, and renamed the *Santa Fe*. She was damaged by the British in May 1982 during the Falkland War. The British considered keeping her as a prize but ended up sinking her because of the extent of the damage.

Charr SS 328: [d. 1,526; 311'9" × 17'3"; 20 k; cpl. 66; a. 1-5", 10-21" tt; Class Balao] Designed originally as the *Bocaccio*, she was launched and renamed 24 September 1942. She was commissioned 23 September 1944 and conducted two war patrols during World War II. She was converted to a snorkel 19 November 1951, following which she sailed on 26 March 1952 for Korean waters. She served for a period with Task Group York and is credited with three Korean War Patrols from 20 April to 9 September 1952, and 7 to 27 July 1954. She received one battle star. She was decommissioned 1 October 1970, and was sold for scrap 17 August 1972.

Diodon SS 349: [d. 1,526; 311'8" × 27'3"; 20.2 k; cpl. 66; a. 1-5", 4 mg, 10-21" tt; Class Balao] Launched 10 September 1945 and commissioned 18 March 1946, she was too late for World War II service. She completed conversion to a GUPPY II in 1948. In September 14, 1950, she rescued three downed aviators near Guam on her route to Korea. She served two Korean War Patrols, 19 October 1950 to 12 January 1951. Decommissioned and struck from the Navy register on 15 January 1971, the *Diodon* was sold for scrap 12 May 1972.

Greenfish SS 351 [d. 1,525; 311'9" × 27'3"; 20 k; cpl. 66; a. 10-21" tt, 1-5"; Class Balao] Originally the *Doncella*, she was launched 21 December 1945 and commissioned 7 June 1946, too late for operation during World War II. The *Greenfish* completed conversion to a GUPPY II in 1948. She operated out of Pearl Harbor through 1951 when she sailed for Korean War duty. She rescued six aviators off Guam during her passage. The *Greenfish* conducted war patrols 29 August 1951 to 27 April 1952. After operations with the 7th Fleet, including participation in the Cuban Missile crisis, she was decommissioned and struck from the register on 19 December 1973. She was transferred to Brazil to be renamed the *Amazon River*, spent some time as a museum, and was scrapped in 2001.

Menhaden SS 377: [d. 1,525; 311'9" × 17'3"; 20 k; cpl. 66; a. 1-5", 1-40mm, 10-21" tt; Class Balao] Launched 20 December 1944 and commissioned 22 June 1945, she operated out of Pearl Harbor and was at one time the transition flagship for Fleet *Admiral Chester W. Nimitz*. She was decommissioned 31 May 1946. She was recommissioned at Mare Island 7 August 1951, and operated out of Yokosuka, ranging the East and South China Sea until 11 February 1953. The *Menhaden* completed GUPPY II conversion in 1953. She was in Korean waters 7 August 1951 to 13 August 1952 and from 6 March 1953 to 13 August 1953. Later she saw service with a Taiwan patrol force. There was some question about her participation in the Korean War, but evidence is that she was awarded the United National Medal and the Korean Service Medal. She appears on the list of submarines that saw service in *A Hundred Years of the U.S. Navy Submarine Force*. The *Menhaden* was decommissioned on 13 August 1971. In 1972 she underwent modifications for use by the Naval Underwater Systems Center in Newport, Rhode Island. She was sold for scrap in 1988. She was painted yellow as a test vessel for the Naval Weapons Station and finally scrapped in 1988.

Perch II SS 313/SSK 313: [d. 1,525; 311'9" × 27'3"; 20 k; cpl. 80; a. 1-5", 10-21" tt; 1-40mm; Class Balao] Launched 12 September 1943, she was commissioned on 7 January the following year. She saw service during World War II and was the submarine that dropped the raiders on Japanese-held Makin Island. Decommissioned January 1947, she was recommissioned in January 1948 and redesignated a submarine transport. Her silhouette was altered by the addition of a bulbous projection, a hanger deck capable of carrying a small motor launch. Afterwards she was often called the "Pregnant Perch." The removal of the torpedo tubes and main deck gun left the *Perch* with only two 40mm cannon. Picked for a daring raid on North Korean railway lines at the northeast corner of Korea, west of Tanchon, she carried sixty Royal Marine commandos on the strike on 30 September 1950. While the raid was going on, the *Perch* remained on the surface for two hours waiting for the commandos. There was only one casualty in the mission. The *Perch* was awarded the war patrol combat pin (Submarine Combat Insignia), and the Commanding officer, Lt. Commander R. D. Quinn, was the only submarine commander to receive a combat award, the Bronze Star. Chuck Elliott, who was on board in 1951 as auxiliary man, discovered three pennies placed around the hatch preventing the seal. A crew member was arrested; not wanting to go, he had endangered the whole ship. The *Perch* was in Korean waters from 8 August 1950 to 17 October 1950. Decommissioned, she was sold for scrap on 15 January 1973.

Pomodon SS 486: [d. 1,550 tons; 312 × 27; 20 k; cpl. 76 officers; a. 1-5", 1-40mm, 10-21" tt; Class Balao] She was launched 12 June and commissioned 11 September 1945. After alterations in 1946–47, she was converted to the first GUPPY type submarine in the Pacific fleet. The *Pomodon* departed November 1951 for six months in Korea during which she conducted two patrols, 9 December 1951 to 20 April 1952 and 27 February to 29 June 1954. She served in the Vietnam War and was stricken from the Naval Register on 1 August 1970, after which she was sold.

Pickerel II SS 524: [d. 1,525; 311'8" × 27'3"; 20 k.; cpl. 76; a. 1-5", 2-20mm, 10-21" tt; Class Trench] The second *Pickerel* was launched 15 December 1944 and commissioned 4 April 1949. She completed her conversion to GUPPY II in 1949. She was on three war patrols in four months in the Korean War Zone. She was one of the first submarines to enter the conflict area. She sailed 23 August to 27 October 1950 and 11 August 1953 to 10 January 1954.

The *Pickerel II* was awarded one of two Submarine Combat Patrol pins given for a commando raid with UN personnel. Decommissioned 5 December 1977, she was loaned to Italy and then sold to them on 18 August 1972.

Queenfish I SS 393: [d. 1,525; 311'6" × 27'3"; 20 k; cpl. 66; a. 1-5", 1-40mm, 10-21" tt; Class Balao] She was launched in 30 November 1943 and commissioned 11 March 1944. After service during World War II, during which she was for a time the force flagship at Pearl Harbor, she participated in two Korean War patrols, in 1951 and 1953. She did not receive GUPPY, snorkel, or SSG conversion. The *Queenfish* achieved questionable notoriety when she was used for distance shots in the movie *Operation Petticoat*. She was reclassified as auxiliary submarine (AGSS-393) on 1 July 1960, struck from the list 1 March 1960, and sold for scrap after being used as a target ship.

Remora SS 487: [d. 1,570; 311'8" × 27'3"; 20 k; cpl. 76 officers; a. 1-5" and 10-21" tt; Balao Class] Laid 5 March 1945 and commissioned on 3 January 1946, she completed conversion to a GUPPY II in February 1947, then operated off the eastern Pacific. In May 1950 she headed for Korea where she was conducting antisubmarine warfare (ASW) training when the war broke out. As a unit of Task Force 96, she patrolled Soya Strait. She participated in two Korean War patrols from 27 June to 28 August 1950. After the war she was updated to GUPPY III and on 29 October 1973 she was transferred to the Hellenic navy and recommissioned as *Katsonis* (S-115). The *Remora* appeared in the 1956 film *The Colonel and I*.

Ronquil SS 396: [d. 1,525; 311'8" × 27'3"; 20 k; cpl. 81; a. 1-5", 1-40mm, 1-20mm, 10-21" tt; Class Balao] Launched 27 January and commissioned 22 April 1944, she participated in five war patrols during World War II. In the summer of 1951 she was deployed to WESTPAC and conducted operations in Korea monitoring Soviet and Chinese air and seaborne activity from 12 June to October. In May 1952 was converted to a GUPPY IIA after which she was recommissioned 16 January 1953 and participated in antisubmarine and other operations in the waters near Japan. She was struck from the Naval Register on 1 July 1971 and transferred to the Spanish navy where she served as the *Isaac Peral* (S-32) until being stricken in 1982. She received the Presidential Unit Citation for developing destroyer and destroyer escorts in hunter-killer techniques. The *Ronquil* was used for deck scenes in *Ice Station Zebra*. Not in *DANFS*, she is listed in *Awards* as serving in Korea 29 from October to 11 November 1950 and 11 July to 3 October 1953.

Sabalo II SS 302: [d. 1,525; 311'8" × 27'3"; 20 k; cpl. 81; a. 1-5", 1-40mm, 10-21" tt; Class Balao] Launched on 4 June 1944 she was commissioned 19 June 1945. She was decommissioned on 7 August 1946 and placed in reserve, and then recommissioned in June 1951. In February 1952 she was converted to a "fleet snorkel" and deployed to Korea from 26 December 1962 to 26 June 1953, during which she served in two war patrols. Later deployed to service in Alaska, in 1966 she resumed a training mission. Finally decommissioned 1 July 1971, she was struck from the navy list the same day and sunk as a target in February 1973. Dates given for service differ in *Awards*.

Scabbardfish SS 397: [d. 1,525; 311'8" × 27'3"; 20 k; cpl. 80; a.1-40mm, 1-20mm, 10-21" tt; Class Balao] Launched 27 January and commissioned 24 April 1944, she participated in five war patrols during World War II. During the Korean War she made one war patrol, 31 July to 2 December 1952. Decommissioned in February 1948, she remained in the reserve fleet. She was transferred to the Royal Hellenic Navy on 26 February 1965 and served as the *Triaina*. She was sold for parts in 1976. *DANFS* identifies the *Scabbardfish* as being in mothballs during the Korean War but it is listed among those receiving the Korean Service Medal.

Sea Devil I SS 400: [d. 1526; 311'6" × 27'3"; 20 k; cpl. 66; a. 1-5", 1-40mm, 1-20mm,

10-21" tt; Class Balao] She was laid 18 November 1943 and commissioned 24 May 1944. After active service during World War II she was assigned ASW training duties. She was decommissioned 9 September 1945. Recommissioned 3 March 1951, she conducted one war patrol in Korean waters, 7 October 1952 to 3 March 1953. She also served under commission 3 March 1953 to 19 February 1954. She was decommissioned 17 February 1964 and sunk as a target ship in November of that year.

Sea Fox SS 402: [d. 1,526; 311'6" × 27'3"; 20 k; cpl. 66; a. 1-5", 1-40mm, 1-20 mm, 10-21" tt; Class Balao] She was laid 2 November 1943 and commissioned 13 June 1944. The *Sea Fox* was in Korea for six months and participated in two patrols, 15 September 1951 to 18 February 1952 and 17 November 1953 to 17 April 1954. In March 1951 she completed conversion to a GUPPY IIA. On 15 October 1951 the *Sea Fox* was decommissioned and recommissioned with her new GUPPY condition on 5 June 1953. She served briefly in Vietnam. Decommissioned and struck 14 December 1970 and sold to Turkey, she was renamed *Burak Reis* (S-335).

Segundo SS 398: [d. 1,526; 311'8" × 27'3"; 20 k; cpl. 66; a.1-5", 1-4", 1-20mm, 10-21" tt; Class Balao] Launched 5 February 1944, she was originally commissioned 9 May 1944. She provided some World War II service and was in Manila when war broke out. She was equipped with a snorkel in 1951. She joined the 7th Fleet Task Force 70.9 off Korea, from 6 July to 7 October 1950 and from 9 September 1952 to 17 January 1953. She conducted four Korean War patrols, and earned one battle star for operations in Korean waters. Determined unfit for further service, she was decommissioned and struck from the list on 8 August 1970. She was sunk by the USS *Salmon* as a target

Sterlet SS 392: [d. 1,525; 311'8" × 27'3"; 20.25 k; cpl. 81; a. 1-5", 10-21" tt; 1-40mm; Class Balao] Originally called *Pudiano,* she was launched 27 October 1943 and commissioned 4 March 1944. During World War II she served with the Pacific Fleet, and accredited herself with several successful missions. She was placed out of commission and in reserves on 18 September 1948. Recalled on 7 August 1950, she took time out to take part in the movie *Submarine Command* and then was deployed to Korea. She was in Korean waters from 25 January to 23 May 1953. She was decommissioned on 31 January 1969 and was sunk as a target ship by the nuclear submarine USS *Sargo.*

Stickleback SS 415: [d. 1,625; 311'8" × 17'3"; 20 k; cpl. 81; a. 1-40mm, 1-20mm, 1-5", 10-21" tt; Class Balao] Launched 1 January and commissioned 29 March 1945, she saw limited activity during the final days of World War II. She was decommissioned 26 June 1946 and attached to the Pacific Fleet Reserve. She was recommissioned 6 September 1946 and completed conversion to a GUPPY IIA in 1953. The *Stickleback* supported naval forces in Korea from 19 January to 4 May 1954. She was struck by the destroyer escort USS *Silverstein* (DE 534) in May of 1958, during a simulated torpedo run, and sank while being towed after the collision. She was removed from the navy list on 30 June 1958.

Tang SS 563: [d. 1,870; 311'7" × 27; 20.5; cpl. 66; a. 1-5", 6-21" tt, Class Balao] Launched 18 April 1949 and commissioned 25 October 1951, she was decommissioned 8 February 1980, loaned to Turkey 18 February 1980, and struck from the navy list 6 August 1987. According to Christley's *United States Naval Submarine Force Information Book,* the *Tang* was involved in one Korean War patrol, 1 April to 10 August 1953; however this is not confirmed by either *DANFS* or *Awards.*

Tilefish SS 307: [d. 1,526; 311'10" × 27'3"; 20.25 k; cpl. 66; a. 1-5", 10-21" tt; Class Balao] Laid on 10 March 1943, she was commissioned 28 December 1943. On 5 September 1950 she departed Pearl Harbor for Japan and from 28 September 1950 to 24 March 1951

operated out of Japanese ports, conducting two patrols in Korean waters. She made a series of reconnaissance patrols to keep Naval Forces Far East informed of Soviet naval activities. She was decommissioned 12 October 1959, and then recommissioned on 30 January 1960 and decommissioned again in May 1960. She was sold to Venezuela on 4 May 1960 after which she was known as *Arv Carite* (S-11). The *Tilefish* later appeared in the film *Murphy's War* in 1969. She received one battle star for Korean War service.

Tiru SS 416: [d. 1,525; 311'7" × 27'3"; 20 k; cpl. 81; a. 1-5", 1-40mm, 10-21" tt; Class Balao] Laid on 17 April 1944, she remained incomplete for three years until completed as a GUPPY snorkel boat and launched 16 September 1947. She was commissioned on 1 September 1948 and operated in support of UN forces from 9 June 1951 to 26 November 1951, and 1 April to 10 August 1953, conducting four patrols. Between 1951 and 1952 she conducted four more WesPac deployments. On 4 May 1959 she was converted to a GUPPY III. On 1 July 1975 she was decommissioned and struck from the navy list to be sold to Turkey; however, political considerations delayed the sale and she was sunk as a target.

Volador II SS 490: [d. 1,870; 306 × 27'3"; 20 k; cpl. 85; a. 1-5", 10-21" tt; Class Trench] She was launched 21 May 1948 and commissioned on 1 October 1948. She completed GUPPY II conversion in 1948. When the Korean War broke out, the *Volador* left on 18 August 1951 for special operations, to conduct an undetected reconnaissance patrol in the area of Hokkaido, Japan, for a 4-week period. Her job was to watch and give early warning of any airborne or seaborne Soviet activity. In November she conducted ASW operations. From 16 November to 9 December she participated in a hunter-killer operation en route to Okinawa from Japan. After later service in the Vietnam War, the *Volador* was decommissioned and loaned to the Italian navy on 18 Aug 1972. She was sold to Italy on 5 December 1977 and renamed *Primo Longobordo*. The *Volador* was used in the filming of the movie *On the Beach* in 1959.

Wahoo II SS 565: [d. 1,560; 269'2" × 27'2"; 15.5 k; cpl. 83; a. 8-21" tt; Class Tang] Launched 16 October 1951 and commissioned 30 May 1952, she was assigned to the Pacific theater. She was in Korean waters between 29 January and 29 May 1954. She later served during the Vietnam War. Stricken from the navy list 15 July 1983, she was sold for scrap.

6

THE LANDING SHIPS: MEN AND EQUIPMENT

I predict that large-scale amphibious operations will never occur again.
—General of the Army Omar Nelson Bradley, 1949

During the first six months of the war, the United Nations forces conducted four major amphibious operations: the landings at Pohang-Dong, Inchon and Wonsan-Iwon, plus the evacuations at Hungnam-Wonsan-Songjin-Inchon-Chinnampo. As military historian Donald Chisholm has pointed out, the amphibious operation against a hostile beach is the most technical and organizationally complex of all military operations. These operations began with the organization of the Fleet Marine Force in 1933 and the training manuals developed over the years, through much experience, on such landings. The process was further defined during World War II and put into practice in Korea. Key to such operations was the design and construction of boats especially created or redeveloped for this purpose. The first of the amphibious ships, built in 1942, was designed primarily to carry tanks, bulldozers, artillery and general cargo, but the variety quickly expanded to meet the needs of special efforts.

The smallest landing craft were the DUKW, basically an amphibious truck, and the Landing Vehicle Tracked, an amphibious armored personnel carrier. Each had the capacity of about three tons. These were operated by army personnel. The British produced the Landing Craft Assault (LCA) which was a small boat that was transported by a larger vessel and then lowered into the water at the target beach. These were designed to carry 36 soldiers. The Landing Craft Vehicle/Personnel (LCVP) was larger and capable of carrying 30 troops or small vehicles. The larger version — the Landing Craft, Mechanized — had a ramp, and could carry a tank or about 100 troops. More maneuverable and seaworthy the LCA did not have a ramp. These close support vessels were not designed for long voyages and were limited by fuel capacity.

Larger amphibious craft were capable of sea voyages, and often made them. Basic to these was the Landing Craft Infantry (LCI). These vessels were usually 160 feet long and about 23 feet at the beam. They could carry approximately 250 troops. Variations of this craft included the LCI (L), a larger version of the LCI; the LCI (R), designed as a rocket platform; and the

6. The Landing Ships

DUKW coming ashore

LCI (M), for mortars, as well as the LCI (G), a gun ship. These had a normal bow with stepped ramps on both sides designed for troop disembarkation. In 1949 the LCI was reclassified Landing Ship Infantry (LSI).

Still larger versions of the landing craft were the Landing Craft Tank (LCT) that were capable of carrying up to four tanks and were designed with a ramp that dropped, to allow unloading on the beach. There were several varieties of this craft. A larger version, the Landing Ship Tank (LST) had doors at the bow that opened for the lowering of the ramp. These ships, when loaded, could displace more than 3,000 tons. The Landing Ship Dock had its opening at the stern and flooding compartments through which LCI-sized vessels could enter and leave.

Numerous types of landing ships were produced by both the British and Americans during World War II: the Landing Ship Infantry, large (LSIL); Landing Ship Dock; and Landing Ship, Medium (LSM). Most were diesel-powered Newport LSTs. The majority of these vessels, because there were so many of them were given only numbers, but some were later named. The armament on these vessels was varied, with the DUKW, LCA, and LCM having no fixed weapons, but LCI and LCT often carrying Oerlikon 20mm cannon.

The Shipping Control Administration, Japan (SCAJAP), an occupational agency, was responsible for inter-island trade and the return of Japanese POWs from other parts of Asia. They operated 39 LST. When Vice Admiral C. Turner Joy, commander U.S. Naval Force, Far East Command, was put on the spot, he quickly pressed into service these SCAJAP and Army LST. Many of the ships, however, were in bad repair. The crews of the American-manned LST and the 30 Japanese-manned SCAJAPs of James Doyle's Task Force 90 performed well just to keep their ships in action.

DUKW

The DUKW was a 1942 utility, amphibious, front-wheel drive, and two-rear-driving axial truck. Built on a 353 General Motors chassis, it was a 6 × 6 light-heavy truck, with a 270 cubic-inch, 6-cylinder engine, and a maximum speed of 50 mph on the road and 6 knots in water. It had a complement of two—driver and assistant driver—and one in four was armed with a .50 caliber machine gun. They went into quantity production in 1943 and about 21,000 were built. The DUKW had a capacity of 5,000 pounds or 25 fully-equipped soldiers, and a range of 240 miles. Six Marine Corps DUKW companies were formed during World War II, and first used in Sicily and in the Pacific in 1943. The significance of the vehicle carried over to the Korean War. At Hungnam, for example, the 1st Marine Division, Company A, 1st Amphibian Truck Battalion hurried the evacuation by making hundreds of round trips from the docks to the ships in their DUKWs. Later, at Pusan, DUKWs assumed the responsibility for unloading the 1st Marine Division personnel and equipment. The army stopped using them in the 1960s.

Landing Craft Infantry/Landing Ship, Infantry (LCI)

LCI were reclassified as Landing Ship, Infantry, in 1949. There were at least two (some say three) LCI series built. Those with numbers from 1 through 350 were to be built from British plans and 305 were actually completed. The final 45 were cancelled. They are distinguished by their rather square-looking conning tower. Those from hull number 351 to 1098 had a rounded conning tower, and 607 were built. Since some were never completed, there are gaps in the allotted hull numbers. The second series had hot water, heating, and excellent berthing and messing for the crew. The third series, if it can be so identified, is called the Queen Mary Class and began with LCI 402.

Landing Craft Tank (LCT)

Used by the navy in World War II, LCT went under a different designation in the Korean and Vietnam Wars. During World War II they were commonly called LCT and were available in two versions, the Mark V and Mark VI. The Vs have only a bow ramp while the VIs had both a bow and aft ramp. They were much smaller than the LST, and were unarmored and lightly armed. They were nicknamed the "Prairie Ships" because most were built in the West Bottoms of Kansas City, Kansas, and were floated more than 1,000 miles down the Missouri and Mississippi rivers to New Orleans for shipment. After World War II, the Mark V were sold for scrap or civilian use but the Mark VIs were redesignated as Landing Craft Utility. Some were modified for specific assignments, like the six that were sent into Arctic service. The Mark VI has the following dimensions: d. 143 tons; 199 × 32; 8 k; cpl. 1 officer and 12 enlisted men; a. 2 × 20mm; capacity 4 medium or 3 50-ton tanks or 150 tons cargo, accommodations for 8 troops.

Landing Craft Utility (LCU)

The Mark V LCU had a displacement of 143 tons, 309 (landing) and were 119 feet long with a beam of 32 feet. Propelled by three Gray 225-hp diesels, they had a speed of eight knots and a complement of one officer and 12 enlisted men. They were generally armed with two 20mm guns, and could carry four medium or three 50-ton tanks, or about 150 tons of cargo, as well as accommodate eight men. The LCU quickly became the navy's all-purpose ship, primarily used for amphibious transportation to move troops and equipment from sea to shore, and to deliver and retrieve personnel and their equipment (tanks, artillery, and motor vehicles) to the beaches. Each LCU has its own galley and berthing spaces and can operate at sea for approximately seven days. The following boats, listed numerically, served in Korea.

LCU 520: Participated during the Communist China Aggression and the First UN Counter Offensive campaigns.

LCU 531: Participated in the Communist China Aggression, First UN Counter Offensive, Second Korean Winter, and Korean Defense Summer–Fall 1952 campaigns, and was awarded two battle stars.

LCU 539: Participated during the Communist China Spring Offensive, Second Korean Winter, Korean Defense Summer–Fall 1952, and Korea Summer–Fall 1953 campaigns, and was awarded four battle stars.

LCU 562: In service in Korean waters 2 July 1951 to 27 July 1954.

LCU 608: Participated in the North Korean Aggression, Communist China Aggression, Inchon Landing, First UN Counter Offensive, UN Summer–Fall Offensive, and the North Korean Defense Summer–Fall 1952 campaigns. She was awarded five battle stars.

LCU 629: Participated in the North Korean Aggression, Communist China Aggression, Inchon Landing, and the Second Korean Winter campaigns. She was awarded four battle stars.

LCU 634: Served in Korean waters from 22 September 1951 to 30 April 1952.

LCU 637: Participated in the North Korean Aggression, Communist China Aggression, Inchon Landing, First UN Counter Offensive, and Korean Defense Summer–Fall 1952 campaigns. She received four battle stars.

LCU 638: Participated in the North Korean Aggression, Communist China Aggression, Inchon Landing, First UN Counter Offensive, Second Korean Winter, and Korean Defense Summer–Fall 1952 campaigns. She received six battle stars.

LCU 674: Served in Korean waters during periods from 1 December 1951 to 3 November 1953.

LCU 675: Participated in the Communist China Aggression and the First UN Counter Offensive campaigns. She was awarded two battle stars.

LCU 677: Served in Korean waters during periods from 22 September 1951 until 27 July 1954.

LCU 684: Served in Korean waters from 22 September 1951 until 4 August 1952.

LCU 686: Served in Korean waters from 22 September 1951 until 27 July 1954.

LCU 742: Participated in the Communist China Aggression and First UN Counter Offensive campaigns. She was awarded two battle stars.

LCU 783: Participated in the North Korean Aggression, Communist China Aggression, First UN Counter Offensive, UN Summer–Fall Offensive, and Second Korean Winter campaigns. She was awarded five battle stars.

LCU 788: Participated in the North Korean Aggression, Communist China Aggression, and the First UN Counter Offensive campaigns. She was awarded three battle stars.

LCU 810: Participated in the Second Korean Winter, Korean Defense Summer–Fall 1952, and Korea Summer–Fall 1953 campaigns. She was awarded three battle stars. **LCU 840**: Participated during the UN Summer–Fall Offensive campaign. She was awarded one battle star.

LCU 859: Participated in the Second Korean Winter, Korean Defense Summer–Fall 1952, and the Korea Summer–Fall 1953 campaigns. She was awarded three battle stars.

LCU 869: Participated in the North Korean Aggression, Communist China Aggression, Inchon Landing, First UN Counter Offensive, Communist China Spring Offensive, UN Summer–Fall Offensive, Second Korean Winter, and Korean Defense Summer–Fall 1952 campaigns. She was awarded eight battle stars.

LCU 870: Participated in the North Korean Aggression and the Inchon Landing campaigns. She was awarded two battle stars.

LCU 877: Participated in the Second Korean Winter and the Korean Defense Summer–Fall 1952, campaigns. She was awarded three battle stars.

LCU 893: Participated in the Inchon Landing. She was awarded a battle star.

LCU 960: Participated in the North Korean Aggression, Communist China Aggression, Inchon Landing, Communist China Spring Offensive, UN Summer–Fall Offensive. She was awarded seven battle stars.

LCU 974: Served in Korean waters from 1 December 1951 to 27 July 1954.

LCU 979: Served in Korean waters from 22 September 1951 until 27 July 1954.

LCU 980: Participated in the UN Summer–Fall Offensive and the Second Korean Winter campaigns. She was awarded two battle stars.

LCU 1009: Participated in the North Korean Aggression, Inchon Landing, First UN Counter Offensive, UN Summer–Fall Offensive, Second Korean Winter, Korean Defense Summer–Fall 1952, and the Korea Summer–Fall 1953 campaigns. She was awarded six battle stars.

LCU 1056: Served in Korean waters between 22 September 1951 until 27 July 1954.

LCU 1080: Participated in the North Korean Aggression, Communist China Aggression, Inchon Landing, First UN Counter Offensive, UN Summer–Fall Offensive, Second Korean Winter, Third Korean Winter, and the Korea, Summer–Fall 1953 campaigns. She was awarded eight battle stars.

LCU 1082: Participated in the North Korean Aggression, Communist China Aggression, Inchon Landing, and the UN Summer–Fall Offensive campaigns. She was awarded four battle stars

LCU 1085: Participated in the North Korean Aggression, Communist China Aggression, Inchon Landing, First UN Counter Offensive, UN Summer–Fall Offensive, Second Korean Winter, Korean Defense Summer–Fall 1952, and the Korea Summer–Fall 1953 campaigns. She was awarded seven battle stars.

LCU 1086: Participated in the North Korean Aggression, Communist China Aggression, and the Inchon Landing campaigns. She was awarded three battle stars.

LCU 1103: Served in Korean waters from 22 September 1951 until 27 July 1954.

LCU 1124: Participated in the Second Korean Winter campaign. She was awarded a battle star.

LCU 1125: Participated in the North Korean Aggression, Communist China Aggression, Inchon Landing, First UN Counter Offensive, UN Summer–Fall Offensive, Second Korean Winter, Korean Defense Summer–Fall 1952, Third Korean Winter, and the Korea Summer–Fall 1953 campaigns. She was awarded nine battle stars.

LCU 1136: Served in Korean waters from 22 September 1951 to 27 July 1954.

LCU 1156: Participated in the North Korean Aggression, Communist China Aggression, Inchon Landing, and the First UN Counter Offensive campaign. She was awarded four battle stars.

LCU 1160: Participated in the North Korean Aggression, China Aggression, Inchon Landing, Communist China Spring Offensive, UN Summer–Fall Offensive, Second Korean Winter, and the Korean Defense Summer–Fall 1952 campaigns. She was awarded seven battle stars.

LCU 1162: Participated in the First UN Counter Offensive, UN Summer–Fall Offensive, and the Second Korean Winter campaigns. She was awarded three battle stars.

LCU 1195: Participated in the North Korean Aggression, Communist China Aggression, Inchon Landing, First UN Counter Offensive, and the UN Summer–Fall Offensive campaigns. She was awarded five battle stars.

LCU 1236: Participated in the Second Korean Winter, Korean Defense Summer–Fall 1952, and the Korea Summer–Fall 1953 campaigns. She was awarded three battle stars.

LCU 1255: Participated in the UN Summer–Fall Offensive, Second Korean Winter, and the Korean Defense Summer–Fall 1952 campaigns. She was awarded three battle stars.

LCU 1273: Participated during the Third Korean Winter campaign. She was awarded a battle star.

LCU 1286: Participated in the North Korean Aggression, Communist China Aggression, Inchon Landing, First UN Counter Offensive, and the UN Summer–Fall Offensive campaigns. She was awarded five battle stars.

LCU 1287: Served in Korean waters from 22 September 1951 to 27 July 1954.

LCU 1317: Served in Korean waters from 22 September 1951 to 11 May 1952. She was awarded a battle star.

LCU 1374: Participated in the Korean Defense Summer–Fall campaign. She was awarded a battle star.

LCU 1387: Participated in the Second Korean Winter and the Korean Defense Summer–Fall 1952 campaigns. She was awarded two battle stars.

LCU 1396: Participated in the Third Korean Winter and the Korea Summer–Fall 1953 campaign. She was awarded two battle stars.

LCU 1402: Participated in the North Korean Aggression and the Inchon Landing campaigns. She was awarded two battle stars.

LCU 1421: Participated in the Second Korean Winter, Korean Defense Summer–Fall 1952, and Korea Summer–Fall 1953 campaigns. She was awarded three battle stars.

LCU 1446: Participated in the

Onloading landing craft

Second Korean Winter, Korean Defense Summer–Fall 1952, and Third Korean Winter campaigns. She was awarded three battle stars.

LCU 1451: Participated in the Second Korean Winter, Korean Defense Summer–Fall 1952, and Third Korean Winter campaigns. She was awarded three battle stars.

Landing Ship Medium (LSM)

The Landing Ship Medium was designed to operate as an oceangoing tank landing ship that could operate with LCI (L) convoys. The military needed a landing ship somewhere between the size and displacement of the small Landing Craft, Infantry (LCI) and the Landing Ship, Tank (LST) and it was designed by combining some of the significant features of the two. The result was a compact and highly maneuverable amphibious landing ship. The ship was able to carry five medium or three heavy tanks, 6 LVT, or, if necessary, 9 DUKW. It had a complement of four officers and 54 enlisted men, and could accommodate two officers and 46 enlisted men. Fully loaded, the ships had a displacement of 900–1,095 tons, and was 203'6" by 34'6". It was propelled by two Fairbanks-Morse or GM Cleveland diesels and could reach a speed of 13.2 knots. The small ships were armed with one twin 40mm and four 20mm guns. Occasionally this ship is referred to as "Landing Ship, Men." During the Korean War the following LSM took part in various campaigns.

LSM 58: Recommissioned and served in the Korean War, participating in the Second Defense Summer–Fall 1952 campaign. Received two battle stars.

LSM 110: Recommissioned and served in the Korean War, participating in the UN Summer–Fall Offensive, Korean Defense Summer–Fall 1952, and Third Korean Winter campaigns. She received three battle stars.

LSM 125: Recommissioned and served in the Korean War, participating in Korean Waters during the Korean Defense Summer–Fall 1952 campaign. She received battle stars.

LSM 161: *Kodiak*. Recommissioned and served in the Korean War, participating in the Second Korean Winter and the Korean Defense Summer–Fall 1952 campaigns. She received battle stars.

LSM 175: *Oceanside*. Recommissioned and went on to serve in the Korean War. Not listed in *Awards*, but LSM newsletter *Alligator Alley* identifies its service.

LSM 226: Recommissioned and served in Korean War, participating in the Second Korean Winter and the Korean Defense Summer–Fall 1952 campaigns. She received battle stars.

LSM 236: Recommissioned and served in Korean War, participating in the Korean Defense Summer–Fall 1952 campaign. She received a battle star.

LSM 316: Recommissioned and served in Korean War, participating in the UN Summer–Fall Offensive, Second Korean Winter, Third Korean Winter, and the Korea, Summer–Fall 1953 campaigns. She received four battle stars.

LSM 335: Operated in Korea between 6 October 1951 and 27 July 1954.

LSM 355: Recommissioned and served in Korean War, participating in the UN Summer–Fall Offensive, and the Korean Defense Summer–Fall 1952 campaigns. She received two battle stars.

LSM 362: Recommissioned and served in Korean War, participating in the UN Summer–Fall Offensive, Korean Defense Summer–Fall 1952, and Third Korean Winter campaigns. She received three battle stars.

LSM 397: Was not decommissioned between the wars and went on to serve in the Korean War. Listed in *Alligator Alley* but not in *Awards*.

LSM 399: Was not decommissioned between the wars and went on to serve in the Korean War, according to *Alligator Alley*, but not listed in *Awards*.

LSM 419: Was not decommissioned between the wars and went on to serve in the Korean War, during the North Korean Aggression, Communist China Aggression, Inchon Landing, and the First UN Counter Offensive campaigns. She received four battle stars.

LSM 422: Recommissioned and served in Korean War, participating in the UN Summer–Fall Offensive, Second Korean Winter, Third Korean Winter and the Korea Summer–Fall 1953 campaigns.

LSM 429: Recommissioned and served in Korean War, participating in the First UN Counter Offensive campaign. She received a battle star.

LSM 448: Was not decommissioned between the wars and went on to serve in the Korean War. Active in Korean waters during periods from September 1951 to 8 October 1953.

LSM 463: Active in Korean waters from 17 March to 1 May 1951.

LSM 546: Recommissioned and served in Korean War, participating in Korea during the UN Summer–Fall Offensive, Second Korean Winter, Korean Defense Summer–Fall 1952, and Korea Summer–Fall 1953 campaigns. She received four battle stars.

LSM 547: Recommissioned and served in Korean War, participating in Korea during UN Summer–Fall Offensive, Second Korean Winter, Third Korean Winter, and Korea Summer–Fall 1953 campaigns. She received four battle stars.

Landing Ship Tank (LST)

Designed by the British after the evacuation at Dunkirk in 1940, and at the request of Prime Minister Winston Churchill, they were first employed by the British in Operation Torch, the invasion of North Africa in 1942. An American version was designed by John Niedermair of the Bureau of Ships, and LST 1 was first laid in June 1942. Mass-produced LSTs were in commission 14 December 1942. Eventually 1,051 were produced. They were designed for the primary purpose of deploying troops, vehicles, and supplies onto beaches in offensive military operations. They were to be the largest of the vessels designed to deliver men and equipment directly to the beach. They were used at Normandy, in the Southwest Pacific theater, in the invasion of the Philippines, in the Central Pacific at Iwo Jima and Okinawa. They served in a variety of capacities: troop ships, ammunition ships, hospital ships, repair ships and other special purposes. Some were even fit with flight decks for small reconnaissance aircraft. During World War II, 26 were lost in action and 13 more due to accidents and high seas.

It was necessary for the ship being designed to meet the need of a deep draft for ocean travel, and a shallow draft for beaching. To accomplish this it was built with a large ballast system into which water could be accumulated for deepwater operations, and pumped out for beaching. The final plan called for a ship 328 feet long with a 50' beam, with the weight distributed over a large area and enabling a shallow draft. The size of the bow doors and the ramp was increased to 14 feet. An elevator was installed to enable vehicles to be lowered to the tank deck for disembarking.

Three separate acts of Congress (6 February 1942, 26 May 1943, and 17 December 1943) provided the authority for the construction of the LSTs. Of the 1,051 LSTs built during World War II, 670 of them were constructed by five inland builders. While every effort was made to keep the construction constant, some modifications were made as they went along. Among these was to replace the elevator with a ramp, to reinforce the main deck and add a distilling plant. It turned out to be a highly adaptable ship and over time many were redesigned to fill other roles. The LST "Mother Ship" modification had two Quonset huts erected on the main deck to accommodate 40 officers. Bunks in the tank deck berthed an additional 196 men. Thirty-eight LSTs were converted to serve as small hospital ships during World War II. On D-Day, LSTs brought 4,035 wounded men back across the channel to England. A few were fitted with small flight decks that allowed small observer plans to go up during amphibious exercises.

Designed primarily for transporting tanks, bulldozers, road-building equipment, artillery and general cargo, the LST was basically a large floating box designed to ground itself on the beach and then move off it again under its own power. The LST could carry four tanks or other vehicles. Behind the ramp was an open space known as the tank deck. Able to beach itself where there were no ports, and to take on and discharge men and equipment through the bow without the use of a winch or stevedores, the LST proved extremely valuable.

The successful landing at Inchon in September 1950 emphasized the important role played by the LST. This stood in remarkable contrast to the often expressed opinion that the availability of atomic weapons made amphibious landings unnecessary. Specially designed to transport and deploy troops, vehicles, and supplies during offensive action, the ships involved in the landings both at Wonsan and Inchon were well below the approved standards. Some of the LSTs at Inchon were recommissioned less than two weeks before the invasion, some with as low as 30 percent of the complement on board. The majority of the crews, and even some of the commanding officers, had little to no experience with this type of ship. But the success of the amphibious landing at Inchon proved the value of the later American version and eventually led to the construction of 15 LSTs of the Terrebonne Parish class. They were 56 feet longer, with four diesel engines, and a speed of 15 knots. Three-inch 50-caliber twin mounts replaced the 40mm guns. In July 1955 the LSTs were assigned county and Louisiana parish names and were often called "parishes."

At the end of the war, hundreds were scrapped, sunk, or put in mothballs. In January 1950 only 135 of the 1,051 LSTs the United States produced during the war remained in commission. Those used in the Korean War were of two classes. Class 511 (1) had a displacement of 1,780 tons unloaded, were 326–328 feet by 50 feet, had a loaded draft bow of 8'2" and stern of 14'1", a speed of 12 knots, and a complement of 8 to 10 officers and 100 to 115 enlisted men. They had a troop capacity of 140 men and carried 2-6 LCVP. They were propelled by two General Motors 12-568 diesel engines, two shafts with twin rudders. They were armed with 1-3", 6-40mm, 6-20mm, 2-.50 and 4-.30 caliber machine guns. Class 542 (3) had a displacement of 1,625 tons, were 328 by 50 feet, had a speed of 12 knots, had a complement of 97–110, were armed with 8-40mm and 12 20mm guns and could transport 14 officers and 90 men. There was considerable variation on the armament since many were fitted with what was available at the time of construction.

The success of the LST during the Korean War led to the construction of 15 new ships of the Terrebonne Parish class, which were 56 feet longer and had four rather than two engines. On 1 July 1955, just after the war, parish names were assigned to them. The following craft were involved in the Korean War.

Calaveras County LST 516 (Class 511): The LST 516 served in World War II and participated in the Normandy landing. She was decommissioned 28 February 1947 and recommissioned 22 September 1950. She operated in Korean waters during the UN Summer–Fall

Offensive, Second Korean Winter, Third Korean Winter, and Korea Summer–Fall 1953 campaigns. The ship won four battle stars for Korea. It was renamed *Calaveras County* on 1 July 1955. It was struck from the navy list on 10 October 1958.

Cassia County LST 527 (Class 511): Launched on 3 January 1944, she served during World II and participated in the Normandy landing. Decommissioned 28 February 1945, she was recommissioned 21 September 1950 for service in the Korean War. She was in operation during the Second Korean Winter and the Korea Summer–Fall 1953 campaigns, and received 2 battle stars. She was renamed *Cassia County* on 1 July 1955, and eventually sunk as a target.

Cayuga County LST 529 (Class 511): She was laid down 8 November 1943 and commissioned on 29 February 1944. During World War II she was assigned to the European theater and participated in the D-Day invasion. She was decommissioned 7 June 1946 and reactivated 22 September 1950 to serve in Korea. She took part in three tours — July and August 1951, December 1951 through March 1952, and June and July 1953 — and was involved in the UN Summer–Fall Offensive and Korea Summer–Fall 1953 campaign. She earned three battle stars for service in Korea. In July 1955 renamed USS *Cayuga County*, she was decommissioned and transferred to the Republic of Vietnam on 17 December 1963 and renamed *Thi Nai*. After Saigon fell in 1975 she was transferred to the Philippine navy on 17 November 1975 and renamed *Cotabato Del Sur*. Scrapped in 2003.

Chittenden County LST 561: Laid down 24 February and commissioned 15 May 1944, she was assigned to the European theater where she took part in the invasion of southern France. Decommissioned 30 April 1946, she was recommissioned 18 September 1950 because of the Korean War. She operated in Korea during the Second Korean Winter and the Korean Defense Summer–Fall 1952 campaigns. She earned two battle stars while in Korea. Redesignated *Chittenden County* in July 1955, after a county in Vermont, she was decommissioned 2 June 1958 and struck from the navy list 27 June 1958. She was sunk as a target on 21 October 1958.

Clearwater County LST 602 (Class 542): Launched 9 March and commissioned 31 March 1944, she participated in the European theater during World War II. She was decommissioned in 1946 and recommissioned from the Pacific Reserve Fleet in 1950. She participated in operations in Korea during the Second Korean Winter and the Korea Summer–Fall 1953 campaign. She received two battle stars. In July 1955 she was renamed *Clearwater County* and decommissioned. Temporarily assigned to the air force, she was transferred to the Maritime Administration. Struck from the Naval Register 1 May 1972 and sold to Mexico on 20 May of that year, she was renamed *Manzanillo*.

Crook County LST 611 (Class 542): Launched 28 April and commissioned on 15 May 1944, she was assigned to the Asiatic-Pacific theater where she participated in several operations, including the Leyte and Mindoro landings. She was in operation during the defense of the Pusan Perimeter, took part in the Inchon Landing, and participated in the North Korean Aggression, UN Summer–Fall Offensive, and the Second Korean Winter campaigns. She was damaged by a hit from shore batteries on 22 December 1951, but there were no casualties. She earned three battle stars for service in Korea. On 1 July 1955 she was redesignated *Crook County* after counties in Oregon and Wyoming. Decommissioned 26 October 1956, she was placed in reserve 26 October 1958.

Daviess County LST 692: Launched 31 May 1944 and commissioned 10 March 1945, she was assigned to the European theater. Decommissioned 1946, she was recommissioned in 1951, and sailed 4 June 1952 with Seabees debarking at Yo-do to commence building an airstrip on 9 June 1952. Participating in Korean waters in 1952 and 1953, she was awarded two battle stars. She was renamed July 1955, struck 1 June 1964, and transferred to the Philippines on 12 September 1976.

DeKalb County LST 715 (Class 542): She was launched 20 July and commissioned 15 August 1944. During World War II she participated in the Iwo Jima and Okinawa operations. Decommissioned 17 April 1946, she was transferred to the U.S. Army on 28 June 1948. Reacquired by the navy 25 July 1950, she was recommissioned on 30 August of that year. During the Korean War she participated in the Inchon invasion, and served during the North Korean Aggression, Communist China Aggression, First UN Counter Offensive, Second Korean Winter, and Korean Defense Summer–Fall 1952 campaigns, earning six battle stars. She was renamed *De Kalb County* in July 1955. Assigned to MSTS in December 1965, she was placed out of service and struck from the navy list 1 November 1973. She was disposed by the Maritime Administration 30 April 1984.

Dukes County LST 735 (Class 511): Laid 30 January and commissioned 26 April 1944, during World War II she participated in Saipan, Lingayen Gulf, and Okinawa. She was decommissioned in March 1946. Reactivated 3 November 1950 she was in operation in Korea during the Korean Defense Summer–Fall 1952, Third Korean Winter, and the Korea Summer–Fall 1953 campaigns. She earned three battle stars for her service in Korea.

Dunn County LST 742 (Class 542): Laid 12 March and commissioned 23 May 1944, she took part in the Lingayen Gulf and Tarakan island campaigns. LST 742 was decommissioned 26 April 1946 and transferred to U.S. Army on 28 June 1946. Returned to the navy 1 September 1950, she was in operation in Korea, taking part in the Inchon Landing, and serving during the North Korean Aggression, Communist China Aggression, First UN Counter Offensive, and Korea Summer–Fall 1953 campaigns. She earned five battle stars. On 1 July 1955 she was redesignated *Dunn County* for counties in North Dakota and Wisconsin. The ship was sold on 6 Sept 1961.

Duval County LST 758 (Class 511): Laid 5 June and commissioned 19 August 1944, she participated in the assaults on Iwo Jima and Okinawa. The ship was decommissioned 13 July 1946 and recommissioned 3 November 1950. In operation in Korea during UN Summer–Fall Offensive, Korean Defense Summer–Fall 1952, Third Korean Winter, and the Korea Summer–Fall 1953 campaigns, she earned four battle stars, serving until late July 1953. Redesignated on 1 July 1955 as *Duval County*, after counties in Florida and Texas, she was decommissioned 28 October 1969 and sold for scrap in 1981.

Floyd County LST 762 (Class 511): Laid 24 June and commissioned 5 September 1944, she participated in the assault on Okinawa. Decommissioned in 1946, she was reactivated 3 November 1950. She served in Korea in operations during the Second Korean Winter campaign, earning one battle star. She was redesignated *Floyd County* on 1 July 1955, after counties in Georgia, Indiana, Iowa, Kentucky, Texas and Virginia. After service in Vietnam, the LST 762 was decommissioned 3 September 1969 and struck from the navy list.

Ford County LST 772 (Class 511): Laid 3 August and commissioned 13 November 1944, she was assigned to the Pacific where she participated at Okinawa. She was placed out of commission and in reserve on 3 July 1946. Recommissioned 3 November 1950, she saw service in Korea where she participated during the First UN Counter Offensive, UN Summer–Fall Offensive, Second Korean Winter, Korean Defense Summer–Fall 1952, Third Korean Winter and Korea Summer–Fall 1953 campaigns, earning six battle stars. On 1 July 1955 she was redesignated *Ford County*, for counties in Illinois and Kansas. She was sunk as a target on 19 March 1958.

Greer County LST 799 (Class 542): This landing ship was laid on 25 August and commissioned 28 October 1944, then saw significant service in the Asiatic-Pacific theater during World War II. A veteran of Eniwetok, Saipan, and Okinawa, she was reduced to service with the Japanese as a nameless SACJAP ship as a transport, and then was decommissioned and transferred to Army on 6 May 1946. She was returned to the U.S. Navy and recommissioned 26 August 1950. At that time she was rusty and rat infested. Her armament consisted of secondhand guns taken from lend-lease Russian corvettes. She was at Inchon at Beach Red and became the first helicopter conversion LST in the Navy. She saw extensive duty in Korea, loaded a tank unit of the 5th Marines for the landing at Inchon, later went to Wonsan, and evacuated Americans at Hungnam, taking elements of the 3rd on 24 December 1950. She remained to perform logistic support for minesweepers on the east coast, performed helicopter rescue operations, engaged in coastal blockade and participated in the Wonsan Harbor Control System. She took part in the North Korean Aggression, Communist China Aggression, Inchon Landing, First UN Counter Offensive, Communist China Spring Offensive, UN Summer–Fall Offensive, Second Korean Winter, Korean Defense Summer–Fall 1952, and the Korea Summer–Fall 1953 campaigns. She earned the Navy Unit Commendation, the Korean Presidential Unit Citation, and nine battle stars for her service in Korea. As the flagship of COMINRON 3, she may well have logged more sea miles than any other ship during the war. On 1 July 1955 she was redesignated *Greer County* for a county in Oklahoma, and was struck from navy list 1 November 1960 and sold for scrap.

Hamilton County LST 802 (Class 511): Laid 2 September, she was commissioned 13 November 1944. Decommissioned in 1946, she was recommissioned for Korean service on 30 August 1950. She was in Korean waters during the North Korean Aggression, Communist China Aggression, Inchon Landing, First UN Counter Offensive, Communist China Spring Offensive, UN Summer–Fall-Offensive, Second Korean Winter, Korean Defense Summer–Fall 1962, and the Korea Summer–Fall 1953 campaigns. During that time she took part in the invasion at Inchon and Wonsan, and the evacuation at Hungnam. She earned seven battle stars for Korean service. After the war she was redesignated as *Hamilton County*, after a county in Florida. She was struck from the navy list 1 July 1960. LST 802 does not appear on all lists of vessels in Korea.

Hampden County LST 803 (Class 542): LST 803 was laid 14 September and commissioned 17 November 1944. She was decommissioned on 26 March 1949 and then recommissioned on 15 November 1950 for service in the Korean War. During the war she operated during the Communist China Spring Offensive, UN Summer–Fall Offensive, Second Korean Winter, Third Korean Winter, and the Korea Summer–Fall 1953 campaigns, earning five battle stars. On 1 July 1955 she was redesignated *Hampden County,* and then sunk as a target ship on 26 September 1958. LST 803 does not appear on all lists of vessels in Korea.

Hampshire County LST 819 (Class 542): Laid 12 September and commissioned 14 November 1944, she was decommissioned on 15 November 1946. She was recommissioned 8 September 1950 for service in the Korean War. She was in Korean waters during the First UN Counter Offensive, Communist China Spring Offensive, Second Korean Winter, and the Korean Defense Summer–Fall 1952 campaigns. She received four battle stars for service in Korea. On 1 July 1955 she was redesignated *Hampshire County* and then decommissioned 24 June 1955. She was later called back into service during the Vietnam War. She was finally struck from the navy list in April 1975.

Harris County LST 822 (Class 511): She was laid 20 September and commissioned 23 November 1944. Following World War II, she was decommissioned in August 1946, then recommissioned 23 November 1950 to participate in the Korean War. She was in operation in Korean waters during the First UN Counter Offensive, Communist China Spring Offensive, Korean Defense Summer–Fall 1952, and Third Korean Winter, and participated in prisoner of war exchange. She earned four battle stars. On 1 July 1955 she was redesignated *Harris County* after counties in Georgia and Texas. She was transferred to the Philippine navy on 13 Sept 1976.

Hickman County LST 825 (Class 542): Laid 2 October and commissioned 8 December 1944, she was decommissioned 22 May 1946 and then recommissioned 3 November 1950 for extensive service in Korea. In operation in Korean waters during the Korean Defense Summer–Fall 1952 and the Third Korean Winter campaign, she earned two battle stars. She would later serve in the Vietnam War. On 1 July 1955 she was redesignated *Hickman County*, for counties in Kentucky and Tennessee, and then sold to the Philippine government.

Hillsborough County LST 827 (Class 511): Launched 9 October and commissioned 12 December 1944, she was decommissioned 7 June 1949. Recommissioned on 3 November 1950, she saw extensive service in the Korean War, during the First UN Counter Offensive, Communist China Spring Offensive, and the Korean Defense Summer–Fall 1952 campaigns. The LST earned three battle stars. On 1 July 1955 she was redesignated *Hillsborough County* for counties in Florida and New Hampshire. She was decommissioned and struck from the navy list 28 March 1958, then sunk as a target ship on 14 August 1958. LST 827 is not on all lists of vessels in the Korean War.

Holmes County LST 836: Laid on 1 September and commissioned 25 November 1944, the *Holmes County* saw considerable service with the Pacific Fleet during World War II. At the end of the war she was decommissioned on 25 July 1946 and assigned to the Pacific Reserve Fleet. Needed for service, she was recommissioned 3 Nov 1950 and arrived in Korea on 28 March 1951. She served two tours and was awarded three battle stars in Korea for operation during the Communist China Spring Offensive, UN Summer–Fall Offensive, and Korea Summer–Fall 1953 campaigns. Between tours in Korea she took part in Operation Ivy in August of 1952 as a part of the U.S. Atmospheric Nuclear Weapons Test of two nuclear devices called Mike and King. On 1 July 1955 LST 836 was redesignated USS *Holmes County*, after counties in Florida, Mississippi, and Ohio. She served in the Vietnam War, receiving several awards for service and gallantry. Decommissioned once again, she was given to the Singapore navy on 1 July 1971 where she was renamed RS *Endurance*. She was finally decommissioned after taking part in four wars. The LST 836 is not on all lists that report ships in Korea during the war, but there is evidence that she served two tours.

Iron County LST 840 (Class 511): Laid on 28 September 1944, she was commissioned 11 Dec 1944. During World War II she served in the Asiatic-Pacific theater. After the war she was decommissioned on 1 June 1946. Recommissioned 3 Nov 1950, she saw service in the Korean War, participating in the Communist China Spring Offensive, UN Summer–Fall Offensive, and the Korea Summer–Fall 1953 campaigns, earning four battle stars. On 1 July 1955 she was redesignated *Iron County* for counties in Michigan, Missouri, Utah, and Wisconsin. She was decommissioned 23 November 1967 and transferred to the Republic of China Navy, as *Chung Fu*. LST 840 is not on all lists of vessels in the Korean War.

Jefferson County LST 845 (Class 511): Laid on 23 October 1944, she was commissioned 9 January 1945 and was too late for combat during World War II. After the war she was assigned to the Asiatic-Pacific theater. She participated in the Inchon invasion, and was in service in Korea during the North Korean Aggression, Communist China Aggression, Inchon Landing, First UN Counter Offensive, and Korean Defense Summer–Fall 1952 campaigns, earning six battle stars. On 1 July 1955 she was redesignated *Jefferson County* for counties in twenty-five states, decommissioned in early 1961, and then struck from the navy list on 1 February 1961.

Jennings County LST 846 (Class 542): Launched 12 December 1944 and commissioned 9 January 1945, she was decommissioned 14 October 1949. Recommissioned 3 November 1950, she served in Korean waters during the UN Summer–Fall Offensive campaign, receiving one battle star. She was renamed USS *Jennings County* on 1 July 1955, and went on to serve with distinction during the Vietnam War. Decommissioned and struck from the navy list 25 September 1970, her final disposition is unknown.

Kemper County LST 854 (Class 542): Launched 20 November 1944, she was commissioned in December the same year, then assigned to the Pacific theater. She was decommissioned 21 October 1949 and recommissioned 20 November 1950. In operation in Korea during the Communist China Spring Offensive, UN Summer–Fall Offensive, Second Korean Winter, Third Korean Winter, and Korea Summer–Fall 1953 campaigns, she earned five battle stars. She was renamed 1 July 1955.

Kent County LST 855 (Class 542) Launched 27 November and commissioned 21 December 1944, she served in the Okinawa operation during World War II and was decommissioned 15 February 1950. She was recommissioned from the Pacific Reserve Fleet on 3 November 1950, then served in Korea during the Communist China Spring Offensive, UN Summer–Fall Offensive, Second Korean Winter, Korean Defense Summer–Fall 1952, Third Korean Winter, and Korea Summer–Fall 1953 campaigns, receiving five battle stars. Renamed *Kemper County* on 1 July 1955, she later served in the Vietnam War. Decommissioned 28 May 1969, she was transferred to the Government of Barbados in July 1975, renamed *Northpoint*, and then to the government of Panama, renamed *El Gato Blanco*, in the 1980s.

King County LST 857 (Class 542): Commissioned 29 December 1944, she was in the Asiatic-Pacific theater during World War II. She served in Korean waters during the North Korean Aggression, Inchon Landing, UN Summer–Fall Offensive, Second Korean Winter, Korean Defense Summer–Fall 1952, Third Korean Winter, and Korea Summer–Fall 1953 campaigns. At one point she collided with ROK PC 702 that was anchored in the fairway; there was no damage, although shore fire from the beach killed one man. She received seven battle stars. Renamed *King County* on 1 July 1955, she was converted in 1957 to an experimental guided missile test ship. Decommissioned 8 July 1960, she was sold 25 April 1961.

Lafayette County LST 859 (Class 511): She was launched 15 December 1944 and commissioned 6 January 1945. During World War II she participated in the assault and occupation of Okinawa in June 1945. During the Korean War she was the first to land on Red Beach during the Inchon invasion, and was in Korean operations during the North Korean Aggression, Inchon Landing, Communist China Spring Offensive, Second Korean Winter, Korean Defense Summer–Fall 1952, Third Korean Winter, and the Summer–Fall 1953 campaigns, receiving six battle stars. On 1 July 1955 she was renamed the USS *Lafayette County*; she was decommissioned, struck from the navy list, and transferred to the Republic of China Navy on 15 August 19.

Lamoure County LST 883 (Class 511): She was launched 30 December 1944, commissioned 23 January 1945, and decommissioned 20 April 1946. Recommissioned 1 July 1950, she was at Red Beach at Inchon in September 1950. She was in operations in Korea during the North Korean Aggression, Communist China Aggression, Inchon Landing, First UN Counter Offensive, Second Korean Winter, Korean Defense Summer–Fall 1952, and the Korea Summer–Fall 1953 campaigns, winning seven battle stars and the Navy Unit Citation.

Lawrence County LST 887 (Class 511): Launched 7 October 1944, she was commissioned the following November. During World War II she operated in the Asiatic-Pacific theater. Decommissioned 23 July 1946 and laid up with the Pacific Reserve Fleet, she was recommissioned 3 November 1950 and participated in the Korean War during the UN Summer–Fall Offensive, Second Korean Winter, Korean Defense Summer–Fall 1952, and the Third Korean Winter campaigns, receiving three battle stars. She was renamed *Lawrence County* on July 1955. Decommissioned again on 22 March 1960, she was sold to Indonesia and renamed *Tandjung Nusanive*. She was struck from the navy list 1 November 1960.

Lincoln County LST 898 (Class 542) She was launched 25 November 1944 and commissioned 9 May 1946. Decommissioned 9 May 1946, custody was transferred to the U.S. Army. Reacquired by the navy for the MSTS on 1 May 1950, she was placed in service and recommissioned 26 August 1950. LST 898 participated in the Inchon invasion, and was in operation in Korean waters during the North Korean Aggression, Communist China Aggression, First UN Counter Offensive, Second Korean Winter, and Korean Defense Summer–Fall 1952 campaigns. At Inchon, LST 898 was set up as a hospital ship and took on a mobile surgical team consisting of a medical officer, three doctors, one Medical Service Corp officer and ten corpsmen, then remained there, beached, to serve the wounded. Renamed *Lincoln County* 1 July 1955, she was decommissioned 24 March 1961, transferred to Thailand and renamed *Chang* on 3 August 1962.

Litchfield County LST 901 (Class 542): Launched 9 December 1944, she was commissioned 11 January 1945. After World War II, during which she saw no action, she was decommissioned 9 August 1946. On 30 November 1950, she was recommissioned for service in the Korean War, operating in Korean waters during the Korean Defense Summer–Fall 1952 and Third Korean Winter campaigns, earning two battle stars and one Navy Unit Commendation. Renamed *Litchfield County* 1 July 1955, she participated in the Vietnam War, was decommissioned 7 March 1969, struck from the navy list 1 April 1975, and finally scrapped in 1996. LST 901 is not included on all lists.

LST 918: Launched 7 May 1944, she is listed in *Awards* as having been in Korea 19 November 1953 to 8 March 1954 where she received one battle star. According to *DANFS*, however, she was sold in 1947.

Luzerne County LST 902: Laid on 5 November 1944 and commissioned 15 February 1945, she was decommissioned after World War II. Recommissioned on 18 January 1952 , she reached Japan on 15 September 1952 when she began transporting supplies to the peninsula. She saw service during the Korean Defense Summer–Fall 1952 and the Third Korean Winter campaigns, earning two battle stars. On 1 July 1955 she was renamed *Luzerne County* for a county in Pennsylvania. She was decommissioned 29 August 1955, later served in Vietnam, and was finally struck from the navy list on 12 August 1970.

Mahoning County LST 914 (Class 542): Laid on 16 February, she was commissioned 18 May 1944. She was in duty with the Pacific Fleet during World War II. Following the war she was decommissioned 26 June 1946 and, with a Japanese crew, transported general cargo in the Far East. She was recommissioned 26 August 1950, and by mid September she transported units of the 1st Marine Division to Inchon. She participated in the Inchon invasion, and later worked in the Wonsan operations and in the evacuation of Hungnam. After a brief overhaul she returned to Korea to serve in six campaigns. She was in operation in Korea during the North Korean Aggression, Communist China Aggression, First UN Counter Offensive, Communist China Spring Offensive, Second Korean Winter, and Korean Defense Summer–Fall 1952 campaigns. For her Korean service she was awarded four battle stars and the Navy

Unit Commendation. In July 1955 she was given the name *Mahoning County*. Decommissioned 5 September 1959, she was sold for scrap on 22 June 1960.

Marion County (542) LST 975: Laid 1 December 1944 and commissioned 3 February 1946, she arrived late for World War II, but conveyed troops and equipment. She was decommissioned 16 April 1946 and turned over to the army. She was recommissioned 28 August 1960 and saw extensive service in Korea. She participated in the Inchon invasion and was in Korean waters during the North Korean Aggression, Communist China Aggression, First UN Counter Offensive, Second Korean Winter, and the Korean Defense Summer–Fall 1952 campaigns. She earned six battle stars. On 1 July 1955 she was renamed *Marion County* after counties in seventeen states. She was transferred to Vietnam on 12 April 1962 where she served as *Cam Ranh*. She was struck from the navy list on 1 June 1963.

Morgan County LST 1048 (Class 511): Launched 17 February and commissioned 15 March 1945, she was decommissioned 14 May 1946 and struck from the navy list. She was transferred to the U.S. Army and then, reacquired by the U.S. Navy, reinstated and recommissioned 26 August 1950. During the storm Kezia on 12 September 1950, she lost her port engine. Salvage ship *Consever* (ARS 39) secured a towing table and, making only six knots, the two ships proceeded to Inchon were they were in time for the invasion. She was in Korea during the North Korean Aggression, Communist China Aggression, and the Korean Defense Summer–Fall 1952 campaigns, receiving three battle stars for Korea. Decommissioned 10 May 1956, she was placed in service with the MSTS. Placed out of service and removed from the navy list 1 August 1959, she was sold for scrap 10 June 1960. LST 1048 is not included on all lists.

Orange County LST 1068 (Class 511): Launched 3 March 1945 and commissioned on the 27 March, she was decommissioned 9 August 1946 and laid up in the Pacific Reserve Fleet. The ship was recommissioned 8 September 1950. She operated in Korean waters during the First UN Counter Offensive, Communist China Spring Offensive, Second Korean Winter, and the Korean Defense Summer–Fall 1952 campaigns. She earned four battle stars. Renamed *Orange County* 1 July 1955, she was decommissioned 27 September 1957, struck from the navy list the same day, and sunk as a target vessel 18 June 1958.

Outagamie County LST 1073 (Class 542): Launched 22 March 1945, she was commissioned 17 April of the same year. Decommissioned 5 August 1946, she was recommissioned from the Pacific Reserve Fleet 3 November 1950. During the Korean War she participated during the First UN Counter Offensive, Communist China Spring Offensive, UN Summer–Fall Offensive, Korean Defense Summer–Fall 1952, Third Korean Winter, and Korea Summer–Fall 1953 campaigns. She earned six battle stars. Refitted with wooden partitions, she participated in the massive POW exchange between North and South Korea, picking up disembarking returnees from the islands of Cheju Do, Koje Do, Pongam Do, Yongcho Do, and Chogju. Renamed *Outagamie County* on 1 July 1955, she participated in the Vietnam War and was decommissioned 21 May 1971. Transferred on loan to Brazil, then sold to them on 1 December 1973, she was struck from the navy list the same day. Rechristened the *Garcia D'Avilla*, she was sold for scrap by Brazil in 1999.

Park County LST 1077 (Class 511): Launched 18 April, she was commissioned 8 May 1945, then decommissioned 31 July 1946 and laid up in the Pacific Reserve Fleet. She was recommissioned 6 September 1950 and operated in Korea during the Communist China Aggression, First UN Counter Offensive, Communist China Spring Offensive, Second Korean Winter, and Korean Defense Summer–Fall 1952 campaigns. On 1 July 1950 she was renamed *Park County*; decommissioned and struck from the navy list, 15 April 1978, she was sold to Mexico on 1 July 1978 and renamed *Rio Panuco*.

Pender County LST 1080 (Class 542): Launched 2 May 1945 and commissioned 29 May 1945, she was too late for service during World War II. She was decommissioned 29 August 1946 and laid up in the Pacific Reserve Fleet, then recommissioned 3 October 1950. During the Korean War she participated in the First UN Counter Offensive, Communist China Spring Offensive, UN Summer–Fall Offensive, Korean Defense Summer–Fall 1952, and Third Korean Winter campaigns, earning five battle stars. On 1 July 1955 she was named the *Pender County*. Decommissioned 2 January 1958, she was transferred to the Republic of Korea Navy, then struck from Naval Register 6 February 1959.

Pitkin County LST 1082 (Class 542): Launched 26 January 1945, she was commissioned 7 February 1945. During World War II she took part in the Okinawa operation and was decommissioned 5 August 1946. Recommissioned from the Pacific Reserve Fleet 6 September 1950, she served in Korean waters during the First UN Counter Offensive, Communist China Spring, and the Korean Defense Summer–Fall 1952 campaigns. She received four battle stars. On 1 July 1950 she was renamed *Pitkin County* and she was decommissioned 1 September 1955. Recommissioned 9 July 1966, she went on to earn ten campaign stars for Vietnam War service. Struck from the navy list 1 April 1975, she was sold and later served Greece. She was demolished 16 April 1988.

Plumas County LST 1083 (Class 511): Launched 14 January and commissioned 13 February 1945, she was assigned to the Asiatic-Pacific theater and took part in the Okinawa Gunto operation. Decommissioned in 1946, she was recalled 8 September 1950 and in Korean waters during the First UN Counter Offensive, Communist China Spring Offensive, and Korean Defense Summer–Fall 1952 campaigns, receiving three battle stars. Renamed *Plumas County* on 1 July 1955, she was decommissioned 22 August 1961. Placed in service by the MSTS in December 1965, she was struck from the navy list 1 June 1972 and sold for scrap.

Polk County LST 1084 (Class 511): Launched 19 January 1945 and commissioned 19 February 1945, she was decommissioned 13 August 1946. Recommissioned from reserves 3 November 1950, she operated in Korean waters during the UN Summer–Fall Offensive, Third Korean Winter, and Korea Summer–Fall 1953 campaigns, earning three battle stars. Refitted with wooden partitions, she participated in the massive POW exchange between North and South Korea, picking up disembarking returnees from the islands of Cheju Do, Koje Do, Pongam Do, Yongcho Do, and Chogu. Renamed *Polk County* 1 July 1955, she participated in the Vietnam War. Decommissioned 30 October 1969 and struck from the navy list 15 September 1974, she was sold the following year for scrap.

Rice County LST 1089 (Class 542): Launched 17 February and commissioned 28 March 1945, she was decommissioned 16 August 1946. Recommissioned 6 September 1950, during the Korean War she served in the First UN Counter Offensive, Communist China Spring Offensive, Second Korean Winter, and Korean Defense Summer–Fall 1952 campaigns, winning four battle stars. Renamed *Rice County* on 1 July 1955 and decommissioned 9 March 1960, she was sold to West Germany and renamed *Bochum*. Struck from the navy list 1 November 1960, she was finally sold by Germany to Turkey in 1972 and renamed *Sancaktar*.

Russell County LST 1090 (Class 1081): Laid 28 Dec 1944 and commissioned 2 April 1945, she supported the occupation of Japan and Okinawa during World War II. Decommissioned 22 July 1946 and placed in the reserves, she was recommissioned 3 November 1950 for service in Korea. She embarked ROK troops at Pohang Dong, and was involved in operations Big Switch and Little Switch, carrying more than 85 percent of the prisoners during Little Switch. Refitted with wooden partitions, she participated in the massive POW exchange between North and South Korea, picking up disembarking returnees from the islands of Cheju

Do, Koje Do, Pongam Do, Yongcho Do, and Chogu. She was in Korea during the First UN Counter Offensive, Communist China Spring Offensive, UN Summer–Fall Offensive, Third Korean Winter, and Korea Summer–Fall 1953 campaigns, earning five battle stars. She was named the *Russell County* on 1 July 1955, decommissioned 5 April 1960, and struck from the navy list on 1 November 1960.

St. Clair County LST 1096 (Class 542): Launched on 10 January 1945, she was commissioned 2 February 1945. During World War II she was in the Asiatic-Pacific area and participated in the Okinawa operation. The LST was decommissioned 24 August 1946 and assigned to the Pacific Reserve Fleet until recommissioned on 3 October 1950. During the Korean War she participated in the Communist China Spring Offensive, UN Summer–Fall Offensive, Korean Defense Summer–Fall 1952, Third Korean Winter, and Korea Summer–Fall 1953 campaigns, winning five battle stars. She was renamed *St. Clair County* on 1 July 1955. After participating in four campaigns during the Vietnam War, she was decommissioned 26 September 1969, struck from the navy list 1 April 1975, and sold for scrap 20 September 1980.

Saline County LST 1101 (Class 542): Launched 3 January 1945 and commissioned on the 29th of that month, she served during World War II. She was decommissioned 6 June 1946. Recommissioned 3 November 1950, she was in Korean waters during the First UN Counter Offensive, Communist China Spring Offensive, UN Summer–Fall Offensive, Third Korean Winter, and Korea Summer–Fall 1953 campaigns, and received five battle stars. Refitted with wooden partitions, she participated in the massive POW exchange between North and South Korea, picking up disembarking returnees from the islands of Cheju Do, Koje Do, Pongam Do, Yongcho Do, and Chogu. On 1 July 1955 she was renamed *Saline County*. Decommissioned 9 March 1960, she was transferred to Germany, and named *Bottrop*, then returned to U.S. custody in September 1971. In December 1972 she was sold to Turkey and renamed *Bay Raktar*.

San Joaquin County LST 1122 (Class 542): Launched on 24 January 1945, she was commissioned 14 February 1945 and assigned to the Asiatic-Pacific during World War II. She was decommissioned 15 June 1949 and then recommissioned 8 November 1950. During the conflict in Korea she participated in the First UN Counter Offensive, Communist China Spring Offensive, UN Summer–Fall Offensive, Third Korean Winter, and Korea Summer–Fall 1953 campaigns, receiving five battle stars. In July 1955 she was renamed *San Joaquin County*. Later she served in Vietnam. Decommissioned 26 September 1969, she was struck from the navy list 1 May 1972 and sold for scrap 1 September 1974.

Sedgwick County LST 1123 (Class 542): Launched 29 January 1945, she was commissioned 19 February 1945. She was in Korea during the North Korean Aggression, Communist China Aggression, Inchon Landing, First UN Counter Offensive, Korean Defense Summer–Fall 1952, and Third Korean Winter campaigns, receiving six campaign stars. Her name was changed to *Sedgwick County* 1 July 1955 and she was decommissioned 9 September 1955. Recommissioned 4 June 1966 for service in Vietnam, she was decommissioned 6 December 1969 and struck on 15 May 1975. Sold to Malaysia on 1 August 1976, she was renamed *Rajah Jaro*.

Stark County LST 1134 (Class 542): Launched 16 March 1945 and commissioned 7 April 1945, she served in Korean waters during the North Korean Aggression, Communist China Aggression, and the Inchon Landing, earning three battle stars. Renamed *Stark County* on 1 July 1955, she was decommissioned on 16 May 1966 and transferred to Thailand where she was renamed *Pangan*.

Steuben County LST 1138 (Class 511): She was launched 5 April 1945 and commissioned 24 April 1945. Following World War II she served in the Far East. She saw extensive service in the Korean War, participating during the North Korean Aggression, Communist China Aggression, Inchon Landing, Second Korean Winter, and Korea Summer–Fall 1953 campaigns. She earned five battle stars for service in Korea. Renamed *Steuben County* 1 July 1955, she was decommissioned and struck from the navy list 1 February 1961, then sold for scrap 11 August 1961.

Stone County LST 1141 (Class 542): Launched 18 April and commissioned 9 May 1945, the 1141 was decommissioned 24 August 1949 and then recommissioned 3 November 1950 for the Korean War. In Korea she participated in the UN Summer–Fall Offensive, Second Korean Winter, Third Korean Winter, and Korea Summer–Fall 1953 campaigns. She received four battle stars. In 1955 she was renamed *Stone County*. She transferred to Thailand 12 March 1970 and was renamed *Lanta*, then struck from the navy list 15 August 1973.

Summit County LST 1146 (Class 542): Launched 11 May and commissioned 30 May 1945, she saw service in Korean waters during the Second Korean Winter campaign, winning one battle star. Renamed *Summit County* 1 July 1951, she was decommissioned in late 1969, struck from the navy list 1 November 1976, and sold to Ecuador 13 February 1977, renamed *Hualcopo*.

Sumner County LST 1148 (Class 542): Launched 22 May and commissioned 9 June 1945, she was decommissioned 11 May 1946 and berthed in the Columbia River. Recommissioned 3 October 1950, she operated in Korean waters during the UN Summer–Fall Offensive and Third Korean Winter campaigns. She received four battle stars for Korean service. On 1 July 1955 she was renamed *Sumner County*, after counties in Kansas and Tennessee. In 1959 she participated in Operation Totem Pole in Kodiak. After serving in Vietnam, she was decommissioned 9 October 1969, struck from the navy list 15 September 1974 and sold for non–commercial use 1 August 1975.

Trapp LST 973 (Class 542): Laid on 25 November 1944 and commissioned 27 January 1945, she was decommissioned on 24 May 1946 and transferred to the army. She was struck from the navy list on 29 September 1947. Reinstated on 6 September 1950, she participated in the Inchon Landing, and later served during the North Korean Aggression, Communist China Aggression, First UN Counter Offensive, Communist China Spring Offensive, Second Korean Winter, and Korean Defense Summer–Fall 1952 campaigns. LST 973 earned four battle stars and one award of the Navy Unit Commendation. She was the worst hit of all the LSTs that went in to Red Beach at Inchon when a mortar shell hit right after they beached. They were carrying gas drums, but fortunately there was no fire. Damage control cut off electric motors throughout the ship and she was saved.

Landing Ship Dock (LSD)

The LSD supported amphibious operations by transporting and launching amphibious craft and vehicles. They also provided docking and repair services. The LSD saw considerable service during the Korean deployment. Capable of carrying loaded LSU, LVT or LCM this ship had the distinct advantage of being able to discharge pre-loaded, smaller craft quickly. The keel of the first LSD was laid 22 June 1942 and she was commissioned as the USS *Ashland*. The LSD were to be named after the homes of famous people. The ship had a large docking well, a vast 44' × 396' opening from stern to bridge. The ship was 457 feet long. In it would fit 27 LCVP and 18 LCM with one LCVP in each, three LCU, and one LSM. On one occasion during the Korean War an LSD took a destroyer escort aboard for repairs.

In general 330 crew and 18 officers staffed the LSD and it took most of them to keep it in operation during embarkation and debarkation. It was necessary for the LSD to take on ballast water in order to dock the small craft, an exercise that took about an hour and a half. The 45 foot steel gate at the stern settled the ship as the sea water began to roll in. The gates folded nearly in half and then doubled back under the stern. The boats were able to emerge three at a time. The LSD's ability to take aboard small boats and ships made her perfect for a dry dock, but in Korea she performed a variety of duties; not the least important was that of being the mother of minesweepers.

The LSD had a docking well just 60 feet short of the length of the vessel, and it could accommodate anything narrow enough to get through the stern gate. It had a super deck of steel grating that covered her garage area, and she could carry 350 tons of cargo there, including tanks and jeeps. Her 7000-horsepower reciprocating engines allowed her to gain 16 knots on a regular basis.

The LSD was built in several classes. Beginning with LSD 13, the ships were a part of the Casa Grande Class. These included the *Rushmore, Shadwell, Cabildo, Catamount, Colonial* and *Comstock*. The Thomaston class, beginning with LSD 28, included the *Plymouth Rock, Snelling, Point Defiance, Spiegel Grove, Alamo, Hermitage,* and *Monticello*.

Cabildo LSD 16: [d. 4,032; 457'9" × 72; 17 k; cpl 254; a. 1-5", 2-40mm quad, 2-40mm twin, 16-20mm single; Class Cabildo] Launched 28 February 1945 and commissioned 15 May 1945, she was decommissioned 15 January 1947. Recommissioned 5 October 1950 for Korean service, in Korea she landed men and tanks at Inchon, Wonsan and Iwon. She was the mother ship for sweepers on the Korean east coast. During her second tour she supported minesweeping and took part in amphibious landings. She received seven battle stars for service in Korea. She was struck from the register on 15 October 1976.

Catamount LSD 17: [d. 4,490; 457'9" × 72'2"; 15 k; cpl 326; a. 1-5"; Class Casa Grande]. Launched 27 January 1945, she was commissioned 9 April 1945, and during the remainder of World War II served in the Pacific. When the war broke out in Korea, she participated in the landing at Wonsan. At the port of Chinnampo, the *Catamount* became the first LSD to be involved in minesweeping operations, serving as a tanker and mother ship. She also served at Hungnam. She had two additional tours in Korea, from 3 November 1951 to 24 July 1952, and from 29 October 1952 to 8 April 1953. She was in Korean waters during the North Korean Aggression, Communist China Aggression, First UN Counter Offensive, Communist China Spring Offensive, Second Korean Winter, Korean Defense Summer–Fall 1952, and Third Korean Winter campaigns. She received seven battle stars for Korean War service.

Colonial LSD 18: [d. 4,032; 457'9" × 72; 17 k; cpl 254; a. 1-5", 2-40mm quad, 2-40mm twin, 16-20mm single; Class Ashland] Laid down on 1 August 1944, commissioned 15 May 1945, she served in Korean waters during the North Korean Aggression, Communist China Aggression, First UN Counter Offensive, Communist China Spring Offensive, UN Summer–Fall Offensive, Second Korean Winter, and Korean Defense Summer–Fall 1952 campaigns, earning seven battle stars. She was decommissioned and disposed of in 1970.

Comstock LSD 19: [d. 4,032; 457'9" × 72; 17 k; cpl 254; a. 1-5", 2-40mm quad, 2-40mm twin, 6-20mm; Class Casa Grande] The *Comstock* was launched 28 April and commissioned 2 July 1945. In Korea, she participated in the Inchon and Wonsan invasions, supporting British commando raids along the coast. She served in Korean water during the

North Korean Aggression, Communist China Aggression, First UN Counter Offensive, Communist China Spring Offensive, UN Summer–Fall Offensive, Second Korean Winter, Korean Defense Summer–Fall 1952, Third Korean Winter, and Korea Summer–Fall 1953 campaigns, earning ten battle stars. She was decommissioned in 1970 and struck from the Naval Register 30 June 1976. Transferred to the Republic of China, she was renamed *Chung Cheng* as a replacement for the former *White Marsh*, LSD 8.

Epping Forest LSD 4: [d. 4,490; 457 × 72'2"; 15 k; cpl 326; a. 1-5"; Class Ashland] She was launched 2 April and commissioned 11 October 1943. She served in the Pacific theater during World War II and was decommissioned 25 March 1947. Recommissioned 1 December 1960, she saw service in Korean waters during the UN Summer–Fall Offensive, Second Korean Winter, Korean Defense Summer–Fall 1952, and Korea Summer–Fall 1953 campaigns.

Fort Marion LSD 22: [d. 4,490; 467'9" × 72'2"; 15 k; cpl. 326; a. 1-5"; Class Ashland] Commissioned 29 January 1946, she spent three years repairing landing craft. When war broke out in Korea, she sailed for Pusan with marines and their equipment, arriving on 2 August 1950. She delivered men to the assault on Wolmi Do and remained to receive casualties and to care for small craft. She was at Wonsan, both for the landing and the evacuations. She deployed on a second tour during which she operated with a mine squadron at Wonsan Harbor. During her third tour she resumed her responsibilities tending minesweepers. She saw service in Korean waters during the North Korean Aggression, Communist China Aggression, Inchon Landing, First UN Counter Offensive, Korean Defensive Summer–Fall 1952 campaigns, receiving five battle stars for Korea.

Gunston Hall LSD 5: [d. 4,032; 457'9" × 72; 17 k; cpl. 254; a. 1-5", 2-40mm quad, 2-40mm twin, 16-20mm single; Class Whidby Island] Originally authorized as APM-5, Mechanized Artillery Transport, she was reclassified LSD on 1 July 1941 and commissioned as *Gunston Hall* on 10 Nov 1943. Decommissioned 7 July 1947, she was sent to the Pacific Reserve Fleet, and then converted for Arctic service 5 March 1949. In Korea she was involved in four campaigns, including the Inchon Landing, and earned nine battle stars. She was again decommissioned and struck from the navy list on 1 May 1970, then transferred to Argentina and renamed *Candido de Lasala*.

Tortuga LSD 26: [d. 4,490; 457'9" × 72; 17 k; cpl. 254; a. 1-5", 2-40mm quad, 2-40mm twin, 16-20mm single; Class Casa Grande] She was laid down 16 October 1944 and commissioned 8 June 1945, too late for World War II. She operated in Korean and Chinese waters, serving in the mobile support unit of Amphibious Forces, Pacific Fleet. Recommissioned 15 September 1950, she had three deployments to Korea during which she supported mine craft at Wonsan, engaged in POW exchange, took part in the amphibious feint at Kojo, and operated off Wonsan. She received five engagement stars for Korean service. Decommissioned and then struck from the navy list on 26 January 1970, her name was struck in 1977 and she was scuttled 21 August 1988.

Whetstone LSD 27: [d. 9,375; 457'9" × 72'2"; 15 k; cpl. 326; a. 1-5", 12-40mm quad, 24-20mm; Class Casa Grande] Launched 18 July 1945, she was commissioned 12 February 1946, too late for participation in World War II. She was decommissioned 20 October 1948 and then, with the outbreak of war, recommissioned 25 June 1950. The *Whetstone* took part in the recovery of a downed MiG 15 fighter from 19 to 22 July 1951 and she served two deployments in Korean waters. She served in Korean waters during the Communist China Spring Offensive, UN Summer–Fall Offensive, Third Korean Winter, and Korea Summer–Fall 1953 campaigns. She earned four battle stars while in Korea. Decommissioned on 2 April 1970, she was removed from the navy list 1 September 1971.

Landing Ship, Medium, Rocket (LSMR)

The specifications for LSMR varied during construction. This was particularly true when it came to armament, for they were often armed with what was most readily available. In general, however, they were built as follows: displacement 758 tons, length 203'6", beam 34', powered by GM diesel, non-reversing with airflex clutch, direct drive, that delivered 720 rpm to each of the two screws. They had an endurance of 3,000 miles at 12 knots, and could reach 13 knots. They were armed with 20 continuous loading 5" ship-to-shore (SS) rocket launchers, 2-40mm twins, 4-20mm twins and 4-4.2" mortars. During World War II and much of Korea they held a complement of six officers and 137 enlisted men. They could carry a full load of 1175 tons that required a draft of 7'9". The classes were Class 401: d. 1,175; 203.6" × 35; 13 k; cpl. 143; a. 1-5", 2-40mm, 4-20mm, 4-4.2 mortar, 20 continuous loading 5" SS rocket launchers; Class 501: d. 994; 206 × 35.6"; 12.k; cpl. 141; a. 1-5", 4-20mm, 2-40mm 4-4.2.

***Big Black River*/LSM 401** LSMR/LSM 401: Launched 22 January and commissioned 7 April 1945, she was too late for service against Japan. She was, however, not decommissioned, and when the Korean War broke out she joined Task Force 90, the attack force for the Inchon invasion. She provided rocket support for the attack on Wolmi Do and then on the mainland. Later she was involved in the landing at Wonsan, and provided rocket fire during the evacuation at Hungnam. During a second tour she supported UN troops on the isolated islands along the North Korean shore, and on Songjin, Chinnampo, Inchon and Taeju. She and her sister ship LSMR 403 fired a total of 4,903 rockets at Wonsan in a 35 minute period. She operated in Korean waters during the North Korean Aggression, Communist China Aggression, Inchon Landing, First UN Counter-Offensive, UN Summer–Fall Offensive, Second Korean Winter, and Korean Defense Summer–Fall 1952 campaigns. Placed out of commission in 1954, she remained in reserve, was named *Big Black River* on 1 October 1969, and struck from the navy list on 1 May 1973. She earned seven battle stars in Korea.

Black Warrior River LSMR404: Class 401. Launched 20 January and commissioned 25 April 1945, she was not decommissioned after World War II, and was in operation in Korean waters during the North Korean Aggression, Communist China Aggression, Inchon Landing, First UN Counter offensive, UN Summer–Fall Offensive, Second Korean Winter and Korean Defense Summer–Fall 1952 campaigns. She fired during the Inchon invasion and participated with the Hungnam gunfire support group, providing cover for the evacuation. She received seven battle stars. Decommissioned 1 October 1955, she was struck 1 October 1958.

Blackstone River LSMR/LAM 403: LSM 401 Class, she was launched 26 January 1945 and commissioned 25 April 1945, too late for duty in World War II. However she was not decommissioned, and she was assigned to the Korean War zone where she served with elements of Task Force 90, the attack force for Operation Chromite. She and sister ship LSMR 401 fired 4,903 rockets against Wonsan on the night of 20–21 May 1951. Later she was at Wonsan, provided rocket fire to cover the evacuation at Hungnam, and then went back to Wonsan in support of the siege. She operated in Korean waters during the North Korean Aggression, Communist Chinese Aggression, Inchon Landing, First UN Counter Offensive, UN Summer–Fall Offensive, Second Korean Winter, and Korean Defense Summer–Fall 1952 campaigns. Decommissioned 13 May 1955 and on 1 October 1955 named *Blackstone River*, she was struck from the navy list three years later. She earned seven battle stars for service in Korea.

Broadkill River LSMR 405: Class LSM 401. She was launched 6 January and commissioned 2 May 1945. She was decommissioned 10 February 1947 and recommissioned 28 March 1951. According to *Alligator Alley*, she served in Korea. Not listed in *Awards*, however.

Clarion River LSMR 409: Class LST 401. Commissioned on 16 May 1945, she did not see action in World War II. She was recommissioned 5 Oct 1950 and reported to Wonsan Task Force 95. In operation in Korea during the Communist China Spring Offensive, UN Summer–Fall Offensive, Third Korean Winter, and Korea Summer–Fall 1953 campaigns, she fired rockets in support of Blue Beach 15 September 1950. She acted as radar picket ship, fired star shells to illuminate targets for planes from carriers, and guarded the inner harbor from Communist junks. She received minor damage after two hits from a shore battery at Walsa-ri, North Korea, from 30 rounds of 76mm, suffering five casualties, 4 June 1953. She received four battle stars. Redesignated *Clarion River* on 1 October 1955, she was decommissioned 26 October 1955.

Des Plaines River LSMR 412/LSM: Class LSM 401. She was commissioned 23 May 1945, decommissioned after the war, and then recommissioned to serve in Korea. She was in operation in Korean waters during the Communist China Spring Offensive, UN Summer–Fall Offensive, Korean Defense Summer–Fall 1962 and Third Korean Winter campaigns. She received four battle stars. She was hit by gunfire in July of 1951 but the damage was limited. She was struck 9 January 1972.

St. Francis River LSMR525: Class 501. Launched on 16 June and commissioned 14 August 1945, she was deactivated shortly after her shakedown cruise. Recommissioned 16 September 1950 for service in Korea, she carried out fire missions at Wonsan, the island of Sok To, and Chinnampo, and operated in Korean waters during the UN Summer–Fall offensive, Korean Defense Summer–Fall 1952 and Korea Summer–Fall 1953 campaigns. She was hit by fire from the shore at Wonsan in July 1951 but was not badly damaged. She received three battle stars for service in Korea. She was decommissioned 21 November 1955 and then recommissioned 18 September 1965 for service in Vietnam. Reclassified as an LFR on 1 January 1969 and named *St. Francis River*, she was decommissioned and removed from the navy list on 17 April 1970. She was sold for scrap.

St. Joseph River LSMR527: Class LSM 501. Launched 16 June and commissioned 21 August 1945, she was only active for three months before being decommissioned 28 March 1946. She was recommissioned 14 October 1950. On 19 June 1952 she headed for Korea. She was in operation in Korean waters during the Korean Defense Summer–Fall 1952 campaigns. She was involved in the amphibious feint at Kojo and in fire support activities at Taenchon-Do. She earned two battle stars in Korea. She was decommissioned on 5 August 1955. Named the *St. Joseph River* on 1 October, she was reactivated in the summer of 1960 and transferred to the Republic of Korea Navy as *Si Hung*.

White River LSMR536: Class LSMR 501. Launched 14 July and commissioned 28 November 1945, she was placed in reserves and out of commission 31 July 1946. Recommissioned 16 September 1950, she began a series of combat cruises in Korean waters. She participated in action near Taenchong Do, Paenguyong Do, and Kirin Do. In operation in Korean waters during the Korean Defense Summer–Fall 1952 and the Third Korean Winter campaigns, she was awarded two battle stars. She was decommissioned 7 September 1956 and was recommissioned 2 October 1965 for the Vietnam War. She was decommissioned again 22 May 1970 and her name was struck from the navy list. She was sold that year for scrap.

Landing Ship Infantry, Light (LSIL)

LSIL 1091: Commissioned 21 January 1944, this 158.5-foot-long ship took part in World War II, backed up other ships in the Bikini atomic testing, and was in Korean waters during the First UN Counter Offensive, Communist China Spring Offensive, UN Summer–Fall Offensive, and the Second Korean Winter campaigns, winning four battle stars. She was sold in 1961.

Landing Craft Vehicle, Personnel (LCVP)

More that 22,000 LCVP were built during World War II, based on the design of Higgins Industries of New Orleans. Considered expendable, many were disposed of overseas after the war, or declared surplus. The design was wood, 35.9' to 36.3' long and 10.6' to 10.10' wide. They had a draft of 3 feet 5 inches and a displacement of 15,000 to 18,000 pounds light. They had a complement of three and a capacity of 36 troops or a vehicle. They were armed with two 30 caliber machine guns. Used to transport armed troops and light vehicles during amphibious operations, these boats were called into service again in Korea.

Landing Vehicle Tracked (LVT)

The largest use of the LVT was at the Leyte landing. At Okinawa more than 1,000 vessels were involved. Usually associated with the Pacific, some LVT were used in Europe. Beginning in 1949, 1,200 LVT3 were converted to LVT3C, which involved mounting a .30 caliber machine gun in a turret on the vehicle. An aluminum cargo cover was installed and armor added to the vehicle's side. In addition to the LVT3C, some LVT (A)-5 were also used in Korea. LVT were carried to the location by LSTs. The LVT began as a civilian rescue craft called the Alligator. It was adopted by the United States Marine Corps who redesigned it for military use. The first LVT could hold 24 men or 4,500 pounds of cargo. Designed at first to carry replenishment from ships ashore, they were discovered not to be tough enough for the terrain, but were recognized as an extremely advantageous amphibious assault vessel. More than 18,600 were produced during World War II, and the modernized LVT3 and LVT (A)-5 were kept in service until late 1950.

While used at Guadalcanal, they got their first real test on Tarawa where only 35 remained operational of the 125 used. They proved their worth in taking men through the shallows and across coral reefs to the beach. Over 1,000 LVT took part in the Battle of Okinawa. Some LVT3C and modified LVT (A)-5 saw action in the Korean War. The generic LVT weighed 18.1 tons, was 26'1" in length and 10'8" in width, had a crew of six, and was armed with a 75mm M3 howitzer and three 30 caliber M1919A4 machine guns. The LVT had a road speed of 40km/h and 11 km/h in water with a range of 200 km on road and 120 km on water. The LVT3 had an armored roof fitted to the bow. The LVT3C also had an armored roof fitted and the bow extended to improve buoyancy. It was armed with a .30 caliber machine gun in a turret and a .30 at the bow in a ball mount. Twelve hundred LVT3 were converted in this fashion. The LVT (A)-5 were modified LVT (A)-4, with powered turrets and gyrostabilizers for the howitzers. Two hundred sixty-nine of this design were produced.

7

Feeding the Fleet

A military maxim has it that amateurs talk about strategy while professionals talk about logistics.
—*Time* magazine, August 20, 1990

Supply meant meeting the needs of the armed forces in Korea during the long, cold winters and hot summers, in the mountains and valleys, making available the construction materials for ports, railways, bridges, pipelines, storage, hospitals, and motor transport, as well as clothing, food and water. Of the 640,000 items that were required to keep the naval force in action, more than 83,000 of the most necessary were carried by the replenishment ships. Other items, particularly large ones, were stocked ashore.

In this battle of supplies the port of Pusan was essential. During the early fighting, the port was fifteen miles or so southeast of the critical Naktong and Masan areas. But during the period between 2 July and 31 July 1950 the naval transportation system was able to deliver 309,314 tons of supplies and equipment. This was a daily average of more than 10,000 tons. During the last fifteen days of July 1950, 230 ships arrived and were unloaded.

When war broke out, the United States had very few logistical ships to support the war effort, and, even among those available, the same jury-rigged replacement methods created during World War II were unsatisfactory. Using merchant ships rearranged as combat vessels simply did not work. Nevertheless the naval response provided support across the world's largest ocean by methods pretty well worked out during the early months of the war. From that time on, it ran with relative ease under the supervision of the U.S. Navy and MSTS.

With limited base facilities available in the Western Pacific, it was obvious that it would be necessary to provide floating support. But no matter how important such mobility was, it was at first beyond the ability of the navy to provide. Fortunately, auxiliary ships — oilers, reefers, and ammunition ships — were soon on their way and by August of 1950 replenishment at sea was becoming routine. By mid–1951 night-time resupply was established and this allowed ships to work around the clock, firing during the day and reloading after dark.

One other note about supply and shipment is needed here. Never before in the history of the United States military had it been deemed necessary to conduct mass evacuation of the remains of men killed in action, even while the fighting was still going on. The long-accepted practice was to leave men in battlefield cemeteries until the cessation of hostilities allowed for careful processing, identification and shipping. But in December 1950 it was determined that bodies should be shipped home. Most remains were delivered from the battlefield to Kokura, Japan, and then shipped to the United States. By 1 April 1952 more than 16,000 remains had been shipped and the number of transports grew to match the casualty rates. These remains returned on many of the same ships that first took them alive to Korea.

Military Sea Transportation Service

The base of logistic support came from the ships of the Merchant Marine (covered in chapter 11) and the Military Sea Transport Service (MSTS).

In what might be considered a foreshadowing of the coming of the Korean War, on 1 October 1949, the Military Sea Transport Service was started. Secretary of Defense James Forrestal had set the new program in motion on 15 December 1948 by announcing that "all military sea transports including army transports would be placed under Navy command." Because it was the army that used the largest percentage of supplies, the army had maintained its own fleet of cargo ships since 1898. They continued to do so until 1950, however, the newly created MSTS inherited the responsibility for all transportation activities that took place on the water, and some 320 vessels were transferred from various sources to form the fleet. As it turned out, the takeover date was just days after the war in Korea broke out.

MSTS became the single agency for providing ocean transport to all the services. Nine months after its organization of MSTS, and after the transfer of some 105 army ships and 12,000 marine civil service personnel had expanded the 92 existing ships of the newly defunct Naval Transportation Service, the new role was tested in Korea. The advantages of the new system seem to be self-evident: the military control of at least these small fleets guaranteed that there would always be vessels to carry vital supplies in the event that other shipping was unavailable. As well, the control of all ships meant a higher degree of operational standards and avoided the duplication of services. It also provided better relations between the military and the merchant fleets, and even allowed for the creation of vessels to meet the particular needs identified by the armed services.

As the war in Korea was moving into its third year, Rear Admiral William M. Callaghan, commander of the MSTS, took time to assess the success of the service. He acknowledged that despite the fact that the MSTS was run by the navy, and was on the same administrative level as that of a fleet operating under the chief of naval operations, there were three significant differences to be considered.*

In the first place, all the personnel, ships, and equipment belonged to the navy, and they carried the responsibility for providing ocean transportation for all the services, as well as other government agencies authorized by the secretary of defense. Thus, it had to meet vastly different needs created by the requirements of these different services.

The second distinction was that MSTS operated under both military and industrial standards and was therefore subject to the regulations of the U.S. Navy, the Civil Service Commission, and the policies of the Coast Guard, the American Bureau of Shipping and the Public Health Service. This is because MSTS employed both navy and maritime civilian personnel, and it had to meet demands placed on them by these military and civilian authorities.

The third aspect is the degree to which MSTS relied on commercial shipping, illustrated

---

*"Military Sea Transportation Service," address by Vice Admiral William M Callaghan, USN, Commander Military Sea Transportation Service, to the Naval War College, Newport, Rhode Island, 2 December 1952.

by the fact that in 1952, 74 percent of the MSTS operating budget went to private shipping interests.

Finally, Admiral Callahan acknowledged that there was always some concern among naval leaders that the MSTS did not operate as a naval unit should. The answer to this charge, of course, was that they were not like any other part of the navy. The demands of variation and cross-theater control, as well as civilian and union contracts, meant that the MSTS was a unique service. Nevertheless, during the Korean War more than 85 percent of all personnel, supplies, and equipment sent to Korea were delivered by the MSTS. During the war they transported more than 54 million measured tons of cargo, nearly five million troops and other passengers, and over 22 million long tons of petroleum. It is to the credit of Callaghan and members of his staff and services, that only eleven days after the invasion his command was able to deliver the 24th Infantry Division from occupation duty in Japan to the fighting in and around Pusan, Korea. By the middle of the month, both the 1st Cavalry and the 25th Infantry Division were also put ashore.

By 1952 there were 28,860 personnel in the MSTS, 61 percent of them in civil service. In addition there were 24,355 at sea, 14,610 of which were marine civil service personnel. As of late November 1952 MSTS operated 164 ships, 27 commissioned USS ships with navy personnel, and 137 with civil service on board, called United States Naval Ships (USNS). They also maintained 62 tankers manned by merchant marines under contract to commercial companies. As well they had control of 38 navy-owned LST (also USNS) in the Far East, with Japanese crews.

It is perhaps important to note, however, that MSTS did not seek the Korean emergency as an opportunity to expand unreasonably. The increase in MSTS-owned ships, by 1952, was just 89 and consisted mostly of tankers taken from the Reserve Fleet because of the lack of commercial tankers available. This number also includes the 38 Japanese-manned LST which came to MSTS as a result of the peace treaty signed with Japan in early 1952. The MSTS was renamed Military Sealift Command in 1970.

Combat Stores Ship: Refrigerator Stores (AF) and Combat Stores (AFS)

Alstede AF 48: [d. 15,500 (f); 459'2" × 63; 16 k; cpl. 292; Class Alstede] Laid down originally as the *Ocean Chief*, she was launched 28 November 1944. Acquired by the navy on 10 May 1945, she was renamed *Alstede,* designated a store ship, and commissioned on 17 May 1946. Following World War II she supplied the men in occupational duty in the Far East. During the Korean War she supported the UN Forces operating in Korean waters during the Second Korean Winter, Korean Defense Summer–Fall 1952, Third Korean Winter, and Korea Summer–Fall 1953 campaigns. The *Alstede* was decommissioned 31 October 1960 and scrapped 2 June 1970.

Aludra AF 55: [d. 7.050; 459'2" × 63; 16 k; cpl. 292; a. 12-3"; Class Alstede] The first *Aludra* (AK 72) was sunk during World War II. The second *Aludra* was laid as the cargo ship *Matchless* and commissioned 23 August 1944. She operated as a bar boat charter during the rest of the war and until 11 August 1949 when she was returned to the Maritime Commission and laid up in the National Defense Reserve Fleet. In November 1950 the *Matchless* was reactivated, converted to a stores ship, and assigned to underway replenishment. She was renamed *Aludra* on 16 January 1951 and commissioned by the navy on 19 June 952. She sailed in support of Task Force 77 along the east coast of Korea and with TF 72 in patrols off Formosa. The *Aludra* was in Korean waters during the Third Korean Winter campaign and received one battle star. After that she operated for the next sixteen years with tours, primarily in the Far East. Decommissioned 12 September 1969, she was returned to the reserve fleet, then withdrawn for sale in November 1977.

Arequipa AF 31: [d. 7,434(l); 338'6" × 50; 11.5 k; cpl. 98; a. 1-3"; Class Adria] Laid down 17 January 1944, she was transferred to the navy on 19 December 1944 and commissioned 14 January 1945. She shuttled provisions to a variety of Pacific stations, and by the end of 1945 had serviced more than nine hundred ships and 40 shore stations and traveled more than 35,000 miles. The *Arequipa* was in Korean waters during the North Korean Aggression, Communist China Aggression, Inchon Landing, Second Korean Winter, and Korean Defense Summer–Fall 1952 campaigns. She was active in the Pacific until November 1954. Decommissioned 25 August 1955, her name was struck from the navy register. She was sold in December 1972 to StarKist Foods, Inc.

Escanaba Victory AF 57: (VC2-S-AP3). Hull 112. Built for the Maritime Commission, she was launched 7 June 1944 as an AP freighter and delivered 29 June 1944. She was placed in reserves 18 August 1948, and recalled in 1952 as a refrigerator ship. She served in Korean waters twice from 18 May to 20 September 1951. In 1952 she was renamed *Regulus* (AF 57) for the U.S. Navy and she was scrapped in 1972.

Graffias AF 29: [d. 7,770; 468'11" × 63; 16 k; cpl. 292; a. 1-5", 12-3"; Class Hyades] Laid as the *Topa*, she was acquired by the navy in February 1944 and converted to a refrigerator-cargo ship. She sailed to the Pacific on 25 November and began runs with valuable foodstuffs. She followed a routine of pick-up and delivery until the war broke out in Korea when she began provisioning the UN ships in at-sea replenishment. She remained on duty after the end of the war, after which she provisioned American and Chinese nationalist forces and the 7th Fleet. She participated in two deployments during the Vietnam conflict, then was decommissioned in 1969.

Karin AF 33: [d. 3,139; 338'6" × 50; 11.5 k; cpl. 85; a. 6-20mm; Class Adria] Built as a refrigerator ship, she was turned over to the navy in January 1945 and commissioned the next month. During World War II she served three tours delivering supplies in the Pacific area. While in Korea she supported combat activities, and operated in Korean waters during the Communist China Aggression and the Korean Defense Summer–Fall 1952 campaigns. Later she participated in the rescue of Vietnamese refugees. Placed out of commission in December 1958, she was put in reserves, and sold in 1967, after which she was converted to a deepwater oil-drilling rig.

Merapi AF 38: [d. 3,139; 338'6" × 50; 11.5 k; cpl. 85; a. 6-20mm; Class Adria] Laid 11 August 1944, she was commissioned 21 March 1945. Specializing in refrigerated stores, she sailed to Okinawa. In postwar years she supported U.S. occupation forces. During the Korean conflict she operated with units of the 7th Fleet, and participated in action off Pusan Perimeter, Wonsan and Inchon, and aided in the evacuation of troops from Hungnam. She was involved in the Communist China Aggression, First UN Counter Offensive, Communist China Spring Offensive, UN Summer–Fall Offensive, and Korean Defense Summer–Fall 1952 campaigns. She earned five stars and was twice awarded the Korean Presidential Unit Citation. She was decommissioned 16 January 1959 and struck from the navy list 1 July 1960.

Pictor AF 54: [d. 13,876; 459'1" × 63; 14 k; cpl. 241; a. 8-40mm, 12-20mm; Class Adria] Laid down 18 March 1942, she served as the *Great Republic* for several private companies. In September 1950 the navy acquired her for conversion to a stores ship. She was commissioned

13 September 1950 and sent to the Pacific Fleet. She supplied foodstuffs to UN personnel in Korea and those on the Taiwan patrol. She was in Korean waters during the Korea Summer–Fall 1953 campaign. She served later during the Vietnam War and was decommissioned in December 1969.

Polaris AF 11: [d. 13,876; 459'1" × 63; 16 k; cpl. 253; a. 1-5", 4-3"; Class Polaris.] Originally the *Donald McKay*, she was laid by the Maritime Commission and then acquired from them on 27 January 1941. She was commissioned by the navy on 4 April 1941. During World War II she operated in the Caribbean, Mediterranean, and the Pacific islands. Struck from the Naval Register 7 February 1946, she was transferred to the Maritime Commission on 30 June 1946. Reacquired, she was recommissioned 1 July 1949 and made six cruises to Korea, operating in Korean waters during the First UN Counter Offensive, Communist China Spring Offensive, UN Summer–Fall Offensive, Second Korean Winter, Korean Defense Summer–Fall 1952, and the Korea Summer–Fall 1953 campaigns. She received six battle stars for her Korean War service. She remained in the Pacific until being decommissioned 12 January 1957. Struck from the Naval Register in October of that year, she was transferred to the Maritime Administration.

Regulus see *Escanaba*

Zelima AF 49: [d. 15,500; 459'2" × 63; 16 k; cpl. 292; Class Alstede] Laid on 5 December 1944 as the *Golden Rocket*, she was operated by the United Fruit Company under contract. She was then converted to a provisions store ship and commissioned *Zelima* on 27 July 1946. Following the end of World War II she was decommissioned and put in the reserve fleet. Recalled, she operated in Korean waters during the First UN Counter Offensive campaign. The *Zelima* was an auxiliary freight ship, a reefer for frozen foods. On one run the ship cracked across the middle from port to starboard and had to be repaired at sea. She earned one battle star for service in Korea. She was struck from the navy list on 1 June 1976.

Miscellaneous Auxiliary (AG)

John L. Sullivan YAG 37: Hull 1121. This Liberty ship launched 26 Mary 1943 saw service in Korean waters during the Second Korean Winter and Korean Defensive Summer–Fall 1952 campaigns. It was transferred to the navy as YAG 37 in 1957, and scrapped in 1958.

Whidbey AG 141: [d. 540; 176 × 33; 10 k, cpl. 24, no arms; Class Whidbey] Completed as FS-S95, an inter-island freighter for the army, she was accepted for naval service, named *Whidbey*, and classified as a miscellaneous auxiliary, AG 141. She was commissioned 8 August 1947. She saw service in the Pacific with duties with the commissioner of the UN Trust Territories. In 1948 she assumed duties as a medical survey ship. These duties came to an end in 1951 and she was reassigned as a fleet epidemiological disease control ship. This unique ship saw service in Korean waters during periods between 15 June 1951 and 18 May 1954. She was decommissioned 15 November 1954 and struck from the navy list on 1 May 1959.

Ammunition Ship (AE)

When war broke out in Korea, the authorized ammunition reserve for the Far East Command was only 45 days. This figure was based on the amount of ammunition used by ground forces in the Pacific during World War II. After the North Koreans invaded, the authorized supply went up to 75 days, which was to be held in addition to the reserves to be held in Japan. In addition to the following ships, the AKA *Diphda* 59 and the AKA *Yancy* 95, though listed among the AKA, also served to carry ammunition. They are listed in Cagle as AKA and so are considered here (see chapter 9).

Firedrake AE 14: [d. 13,910; 459'2" × 63; 16 k; cpl. 267; a. 1-5", 4-3"; Class Wrangell] Built originally as the *Winged Races*, a produce vessel, she delivered ammunition during World War II. She was decommissioned 21 February 1946, and when war broke out in Korea was recommissioned in October 1951. She served for two deployments in Korea and saw service in Korean waters during the Second Korean Winter, Korean Defensive Summer–Fall 1952, Third Korean Winter, and Korea Summer–Fall 1953 campaigns. She received four battle stars for Korea, and went on to serve in Vietnam.

Mount Baker AE 3: [d. 6,100; 459 × 62; 18 k; cpl. 265; a. 1-5", 4-3", 4-.30 cal. mg; Class Lassen] Laid as *Kilauer* (AE-4), she was acquired by the navy and converted and commissioned on 16 May 1941. During World War II she carried ammunition. She was renamed *Mount Baker* on 17 March 1943 to avoid confusion with another ship. She was decommissioned and place in reserves in January 1947. She was recommissioned 5 December 1951 and moved into the battle zone to deliver ammunition. She was in Korean waters during the Second Korean Winter, Korean Defense Summer–Fall 1952, Third Korean Winter, and the Korea Summer–Fall 1953 campaigns. She received four battle stars for service in Korea. She later served during the Vietnam War. She was stricken from the Naval Register on 2 December 1969.

Mt. Katmai AE 16: [d. 14,400; 459'1" × 63; 15.5 k; cpl. 290; a. 4-3"; Class Mount Hood] She was commissioned 21 July 1945 and served in the Leyte area. She was the only ammunition ship in the Korean area when war broke out. She saw service during the North Korean Aggression, Communist China Aggression, Inchon Landing, First UN Counter Offensive, Communist China Spring Offensive, UN Summer–Fall Offensive, Korean Defense Summer–Fall 1952, Third Korean Winter, and the Korea Summer–Fall 1953 campaigns. She received nine battle stars. She later served a period as Yankee Station for aircraft in Vietnam.

Paricutin AE 18: [d. 15,295; 459'2" × 63; 16.4 k; cpl. 267; a. 1-5", 4-3", 4-40mm; Class Mount Hood] Laid under Maritime Commission contract on 7 December 1944, she was acquired by the navy and commissioned 3 March 1945. She engaged in the transfer of extra ammunition from Pacific ports, and on 30 April was placed out of commission. She was called out in response to the Korean War and recommissioned 24 June 1950. Operating out of Sasebo, she rearmed carriers, bombardment and blockading forces, and shore-based Marine units. During the Korean War was she was in Korean waters during the Communist China Aggression, First UN Counter Offensive, Communist China Spring Offensive, UN Summer–Fall Offensive, Second Korean Winter, Korean Defense Summer–Fall 1952, and the Third Korean Winter campaigns. She was struck from the navy list on 1 June 1973 and transferred to the Maritime Administration (MARAD) for disposal.

Rainier AE 5: [d. 13,876; 459 × 63; 15.5 k; cpl. 281; a.1-5", 4-3", 4-40mm, 10-20mm; Class Lassen] The *Rainier* was laid on 14 May 1940 and commissioned 21 Dec 1941. After service in World War II she was decommissioned on 30 April 1946. Recommissioned for the Korean War on 25 May 1951, she sailed for Korea on 3 November 1951. Operating out of Sasebo, Japan, she replenished ships and shore facilities at Pohang and Pusan. She returned to Korea for a second tour in February 1953. She operated in Korean waters during the Second Korean Winter, Korean Defense Summer–Fall 1952, Third Korean Winter, and Korea Summer–Fall 1953 campaigns. She earned four battle stars in Korea. She would later serve in Vietnam.

Vesuvius IV AE 15: [d. 5,504; 459 × 63; 16 k; cpl. 256; a. 1-5", 4-3", 2-40mm; Class Wrangell] The *Vesuvius* was the fourth ship with this name, and was launched 26 May 1944. She was acquired by the navy and commissioned on 16 January 1945. During World War II she replenished ammunition to the fleet in the waters around Okinawa. She was placed out of commission and in the reserves on 20 August 1946. Recommissioned on 15 November 1951, she supplied ammunition along the Korean east coast to ships of Task Force 77 from May 1952 to 1 December 1952. She was in Korean waters during the Korean Defense Summer–Fall 1952 and the Korean Summer–Fall 1953 campaigns, receiving two battle stars. She later saw service during the Vietnam War. She was decommissioned and transferred to the Inactive Ship Maintenance Facility at Mare Island on 14 August 1973 and was struck from the navy list. Not listed in Cagle, she is in *DANFS*.

Cargo Ship (AK, AKL, AKV)

Banner II TAKL 25: [d. 550 (l); 177 × 33; 12 k; cpl. 40; Class Camano] The second *Banner* was built as a small cargo ship for the army (FS 345) in 1944. She was acquired from the army and assigned to the Military Sea Transportation Service where, in August 1952, she was designated a light cargo ship. She was in Korean waters during periods from 10 March 1953 to 29 June 1954. She was decommissioned on 14 November 1969 and struck from the navy list the same day. On 5 June 1970 she was sold for scrap.

Brute II TAKL 28: [d. 550; 177 × 33; 12 k; cpl. 42; Class Camano] Launched in 1944 as FS 370 for the army, she served as a small freighter until turned over to the MSTS as USNS AK 8 and commissioned 31 October 1952 as *Brute*. She served in Korean waters during periods between 7 February 1953 and 12 April 1954. She was decommissioned 6 December 1956.

Cardinal O'Connell TAKV: (EC2-S-C5) [d. 550; 177 × 33; 12 k; cpl. 42; Class Camano] A Liberty ship, she was launched as an aircraft cargo ship and was transferred from the Army Transportation Service to MSTS on 1 March 1950. In theater when the war broke out, she was called on, in July 1950, to deliver emergency rations of ammunition to Pusan. She then went on to serve in Korean waters during the North Korean Aggression, Second Korean Winter, and Korean Defense Summer–Fall 1952 campaigns.

Dalton Victory TAK 216/AP3/AK 256: (VC2-S-AP3) [d. 500; 177 × 33; 12.5 k; cpl. 26; a. 6-20mm; Class Camano] She served in Korean waters during the Second Korean Winter, Korean Defense Summer–Fall 1952, and Third Korean Winter campaigns.

Deal AKL 2: [d. 520; 177 × 33; 13 k; cpl. 26; Class Camano] Laid in 1944 for the army as a Freight Supply Ship (FS 263), she was acquired by the navy 2 March 1947, reclassified as AKL 2, and commissioned 31 March 1947. She carried cargo to the islands in the Marianas, Marshalls, and Carolines. At the outbreak of war she arrived in Japan 8 November 1950 and operated with the 7th Fleet in logistic support of the United Nations forces. She saw service in Korean waters during the Communist China Aggression, First UN Counter Offensive, Communist China Spring Offensive, UN Summer–Fall Offensive, Korean Defensive Summer–Fall 1952, Third Korean Winter, and Korea Summer–Fall 1953 campaigns. She was decommissioned and placed in reserves 8 September 1955 and sold 18 December 1961.

Estero AKL 5: Built in 1944, she was acquired by the navy in March 1947 and she served in the UN Trust Territories. Earlier FS 275 and the USN AG 134, on 31 March 1949 she was reclassified as AKL 5 and made an ammunition ship in the Korean War. She was converted to a refrigerator ship in 1951. She was in Korean waters during the North Korean Aggression,

Inchon Landing, UN Summer–Fall Offensive, Second Korean Winter, Korean Defense Summer–Fall 1952, Third Korean Winter, and Korean Summer–Fall 1953 campaigns, receiving seven battle stars. Decommissioned 22 January 1960, she was struck from the navy list on 1 February 1960.

Grainger AK 184: [d. 7.125; 338'6" × 50; 11.5; cpl. 85; a. 1-3"; Class Alamosa] Set as MC Hull 2115, she was commissioned 26 January 1945. After serving as a training ship she was decommissioned 25 July 1946. Taken into the navy again 9 May 1947, she was recommissioned 12 June 1947. She carried out deliveries to the Marianas and Eastern Carolines as well as Kodiak and Adak, Alaska. During the Korean War she participated in the Inchon Landing. She received two battle stars for Korean service. She was decommissioned 7 February 1956 and stricken from the navy list on 1 April 1960.

Hennepin TAK 187: (C1-M-AV1) [d. 7,435 (f); 339 × 50; 12 k; cpl. 79; a. 1-3", 6-20mm; Class Alamosa] Built in 1945, she was completed for the navy as AK 187 and served in Korean waters from 23 January to 20 April 1952, participating in the Second Korean Winter campaign.

Hewell AKL 145: [d. 515; 177 × 33; 13 k; cpl. 52; a. 2-.50 cal. mg; Class Camano] Originally launched by the United States Concrete Pipe Corporation in 1944, she was acquired by the navy 2 February 1948 and commissioned 5 June that year. She worked the Pacific around Guam, Midway and Saipan. She was reclassified AKL-14. In June 1950 she shifted her operations to Japan, supplying stores and ammunition. She was in Korean waters during the North Korean Aggression, Communist China Aggression, Inchon Landing, Second Korean Winter, Korean Defensive Summer–Fall 1952, Third Korean Winter, and Korea Summer–Fall 1953 campaigns. She received seven battle stars for Korea. After the war she continued to work in the Far East, then was decommissioned on 15 March 1955 and joined the Pacific Reserve Fleet. She was stricken 1 November 1949 and sold to Steve Pickard 1 June 1960.

Lt. George W. G. Boyce TAK 251: Launched 19 September 1945 as a Maritime Commission contract, Hull 852, she was transferred to the MSTS in 1950. She served in Korean waters during the First UN Counter Offensive, Communist China Spring Offensive, UN Summer–Fall Offensive, and Second Korean Winter campaigns. She was stricken 15 July 1973 and disposed of on 1 October the following year.

Ryer AKL 9: [d. 935; 177 × 32; 13 k; cpl. 26; a. 2-.50 cal. mg; Class Camano] A light cargo ship built for commercial use by the Sturgeons Bay Ship Building and Dry Docking Company, she was taken over by the navy on 22 February 1947, named *Ryer*, designated AG 138, then commissioned on 8 June 1947. On 31 March 1949 she was redesignated AKL 9. She saw service in the Marianas, the Bonins and the Marshall Islands. When the Korean War broke out, she carried ammunition between Sasebo and Korean ports, including Pusan and Inchon. She performed service in Korean waters during the North Korean Aggression, Communist China Aggression, Inchon Landing, First UN Counter Offensive, Communist China Spring Offensive, and UN Summer–Fall Offensive campaigns, earning six battle stars. She was put into reserves on 18 June 1955 and on 1 July 1961 returned to her original owner.

Sgt. Andrew Miller TAK 242: (VC2-S-AP2) [d. 15,199 (f); 455'3" × 62; 16 k; cpl. 52; a. 4-40mm; Class Boulder Victory] Built as the *Radcliffe Victory* (Hull 743) and launched on 4 April 1945, she was commissioned by the War Shipping Administration (WSA) on 28 April 1945. Renamed *Andrew Miller* on 31 October 1947, in 1950 she was assigned to the MSTS. She participated in the Hungnam deployment and was in Korea 18 July to 20 December 1950. She was disposed of by MARAD on 2 February 1983.

Sgt. Jack J. Pendleton TAKV 5/AK 276: (VC-2S-AP2) [d. 16,199 (f); 455'3" × 62; 16

k; cpl. 55; Class James E. Robinson] Launched as *Mandan Victory* (Maritime Commission Hull 109) on 26 May 1944, she was delivered to the Maritime Commission's WSA 19 June 1944. Transferred 23 April 1945 to the army and renamed *Sgt. Jack J. Pendleton*, then to the navy on 1 March 1950 to serve in the Military Sea Transportation Service (MSTS). She served in Korean waters during the UN Summer–Fall Offensive, operating with a civilian crew. She was disposed of 1 November 1974.

Sgt. Truman Kimbro TAK 254: (VC2-S-AP2) [d. 15,199 (f); 455'3" × 62; 17 k; cpl. 53; a. 4-40mm; Class Boulder Victory] Laid as a Maritime Commission (MC) contract (Hull 254) named *Hastings Victory*, she was launched 30 November 1944, and commissioned for the WSA on 22 December 1944. On 31 October 1947 she was transferred to U.S. Army Transport (USAT) and renamed. Laid up in reserves until 19 January 1950 when she was reactivated, on 5 August 1950 she was assigned to the MSTS with civilian crew. In Korea she participated in the Communist China Aggression and the First UN Counter Offensive campaigns. Stricken 16 January 1981, she was disposed of 1 June 1982.

Sharps AKL 139: [d. 500; 177 × 33; 12.4 k; cpl. 26; Class Camano] Built in 1944 and operated as a freight supply ship (FS 385) by the army, she was transferred to the navy in 1947. She provided logistic support for the Marshall and Caroline Islands. After an overhaul she saw service in Korean waters during the UN Summer–Fall Offensive, Second Korean Winter, and the Korean Defensive Summer–Fall 1952 campaigns. She received three battle stars. On 3 April 1956 she was leased to the South Korean Navy as the *Kun San*.

General Stores Ship (AKS)

Castor AKS 1: [d. 5,500; 435 × 63; 16 k; cpl. 315; a. 1-5"; Class Castor] Launched under an MC contract as the *Challenge* on 20 May 1939, she was acquired by the navy on 23 October 1940 and commissioned on the 29th. She survived the Japanese attack on Pearl Harbor, and conducted operations in the Pacific, calling at Guam, Saipan, and Tsingtao. She was decommissioned 30 June 1947. Taken out of reserves and recommissioned 24 November 1950, she operated in Korean waters during the Communist China Spring Offensive and the UN Summer–Fall Offensive campaigns, receiving two battle stars for Korean service.

Electron AKS 27: [d. 2,179; 328 × 50; 12 k; cpl. 119; a. 8-40mm; Class LST 1470] Laid 9 March 1945 as LST 1470, she was commissioned 5 April 1945. She carried occupation cargo until December 1945 when she was converted to an electronics parts issue ship. On 27 January 1949 she was reclassified AG 146, decommissioned, and assigned the name *Electron*. Recommissioned 6 October 1950, she sailed for the Far East in December and operated from Japan, supplying and supporting allied forces. She was reclassified AKS 27 on 18 August 1951 and operated in Korean waters during the First UN Counter Offensive campaign. She was placed out of commission 16 November 1956, struck 1 April 1960, and sold in December of that year.

League Island AKS 30: [d. 1,625; 328 × 50; 12 k; cpl. 119; a. 2-40mm, 12-20mm Class LST 511] *League Island* was to have many names and distinctions during its career. She began as LST 1097 which was commissioned 9 February 1945. On 27 January 1949 she was reclassified AG 149 and named *League Island*. Decommissioned 19 December 1946, she was recommissioned for service in the Korean War. She supplied spare parts to the fleet in the Far East and operated in Korean waters from 7 July 1951 to 27 July 1954. Following the war she was reclassified as AKS 30 and decommissioned 14 December 1956. She was scrapped on 24 April 1961.

Pollux III AKS 4: [d. 13,910 (f); 459'2" × 63; 17 k; cpl. 199; a. 1-5", 4-3"; Class Castor] The third *Pollux*, she was laid 2 October 1941 and commissioned 27 April 1942. During World War II she operated with the Atlantic Fleet and in August 1943 sailed for the Pacific. She lifted the first POWs freed from the Manila area. Between the wars she participated in the atomic tests at Bikini. She was placed in reserve 3 April 1950 but recommissioned 5 August 1950. She served in Korean waters during the North Korean Aggression, Communist China Aggression, First UN Counter Offensive, and the UN Summer–Fall Offensive campaigns, receiving four battle stars for Korea. She was decommissioned 31 December 1968 and struck from the register 1 January 1969.

Oilers (AO, AOE, TAO)

At the beginning of the war there was a shortage of oilers. Because of this it was necessary, during the first days of action, for the fighting ships to return to port for refueling. But as quickly as possible every effort was made to refuel at sea. The first fueling at sea took place on 23 July 1950 with Task Force 77. By the end of the year the COMSERVRON's three oilers had managed to refuel 100 carriers, 11 battleships, 50 cruisers, and 546 destroyers. As the war continued, one oiler was stationed at Keelung to supply the Formosa Strait Patrol, while units operating in the Yellow Sea were serviced independently. The fuel consumption of the jets strained the capacity; nevertheless, by mid–1952 the oilers were able to replenish a fast carrier force in less than nine hours. Even nighttime replenishment, considered very dangerous during World War II, became a rather routine activity. In the Sea of Japan one or two oilers were kept on station.

At the height of the war the amount of fuel necessary, and carried by the AO, AOE, and AOG (gasoline tankers), required 34 deliveries a month which meant keeping between 60 and 61 ships in the pipeline all the time. By careful allocation it was possible midway through the war to maintain a maximum of ten to fifteen days' supply of bulk products in Pusan. At that point drum-filling capacity at the Pusan POL Terminal was running about 8,000 55-gallon drums a day. Delivery of POL products (petroleum, oil, and lubricants) to Inchon was more difficult because of the tide conditions. Much of that area continued to be supplied by rolling stock delivery of 55-gallon cans.

In understanding the delivery situation during the Korean War it is important to keep in mind that the distribution of motor gasoline was made primarily in 55-gallon drums. They were readily available at the time the war broke out. In World War II it had been distributed in 5-gallon cans, but this was considered too difficult. While vast numbers of 55-gallon drums were shipped to Korea, it was hard to get the empty ones returned. It became evident that the supply would be deleted if they could not find a way, and transportation returning from forward areas were forced to return fully loaded with empty drums. During the second evacuation from Seoul empty drums were given a high priority so that needed stores could be maintained.

Because of the harsh conditions in Korea it was soon determined that consumption factors of lubricating oils were greater than for World War II and had been underestimated. The extreme heat, dust, mud and rough terrain meant that oil requirements for vehicles sometimes doubled the rates used in World War II. This was made even more difficult by the fact that the United States supplied the ROK whose vehicles tended to be worn out. To add to this demand, the lack of diesel fuel meant that large numbers of troops were using gasoline for heating purposes, and the extreme cold meant that tanks and other equipment had to be kept running all night to insure they would be ready the following morning. Consequently the requirements for oil products grew a good deal during the winter months.

Anacostia TAO 94: (T2-SE-A2) Class Escambia. Built as an MC contract, Hull 1829, she was launched 24 September 1944 and commissioned 25 February 1945. Assigned to MSTS 18 July 1950, she was redesignated TAO with a civilian crew. The oiler made five trips from 20 December 1951 to 21 March 1953. She was stricken 17 December 1957.

Ashtabula AO-51: (T3-S2-T3) [d. 25,440; 553 × 75; 18.3 k; cpl. 298; a. 1-5", 4-3", 8-40mm, 8-20mm; Class Ashtabula] Acquired by the navy from the Maritime Commission, she was commissioned on 7 August 1943. During World War II she operated in the Pacific. She suffered damage from a torpedo dropped on her port side. During the Korean War she operated between Japan and Korea in the Communist China Aggression, First UN Counter Offensive, Communist China Spring Offensive, UN Summer–Fall Offensive 1952, Second Korean Winter, Korean Defense Summer–Fall 1952, and Third Korean Winter campaigns, receiving four battle stars. Later she would serve in Vietnam. Decommissioned at Pearl Harbor 30 September 1982, she joined the Maritime Administration's National Defense Reserve Fleet.

Aucilla AO 56: (T3-S2-A3) [d. 23,235; 553 × 75; 18 k; cpl. 313; a. 1-5", 4-3"; Class Ashtabula] Laid on 25 May 1943 for the MC and commissioned 22 December 1943, she operated in the Atlantic until moving to Pacific waters where she refueled warships for the 5th Fleet. During the conflict in Korea she operated in Korean waters during 25–29 November 1950. She was placed out of commission on 18 December 1970 and her name struck from the navy list on 1 December 1976.

Cacapon AO 52: (T3-S2-A3) [d. 7,470; 553 × 75; 18 k; cpl. 302; a. 1-5", 4-3"; Class Ashtabula] Launched 12 June 1943, she was acquired by the navy and commissioned on 21 September 1943. She served as a station tanker during World War II, supporting strikes against Luzon, Formosa, and the Philippines. She was grounded during Operations Crossroads. After the Korean War broke out, she completed four lengthy tours, sailing with the 7th Fleet, operating in Korean waters during the North Korean Aggression, Communist China Aggression, Inchon Landing, Communist China Spring Offensive, UN Summer–Fall Offensive, Second Korean Winter, Korean Defense Summer–Fall 1952, Third Korean Winter, and Korea Summer–Fall 1953 campaigns. She received nine battle stars and the Navy Unit Commendation.

Cache TAO 67: (T2-SE-A1) [d. 5,730; 523'6" × 68; 15 k; cpl 275; Class Suamico] Launched 7 September 1942, the ex–*Stillwater* was acquired by the Navy on 28 September and commissioned 3 November 1942. She was decommissioned 14 January 1946, then reactivated by the navy and transferred to MSTS 1 October 1949. She made four trips into Korean waters between 27 February and 29 March 1954.

Cahaba TAO 82: (T2-SE-A2) [d. 5,782; 623'6" × 68; 15 k; cpl. 225; a. 1-6", 4-3"; Class Escambia] Launched 19 May 1943 as *Laokawapan*, she was transferred to the navy, commissioned 14 January 1944 and served in the Marianas during World War II. Decommissioned 15 May 1946, she was reacquired by the MSTS 31 July 1950 and served in a non-commissioned status with civilian crew. She made sixteen trips in the Korean theater between 2 March 1951 and 9 June 1953.

Caney TAO 95: (T2-SE-A2) [d. 22,380 (f); 523'6" × 68; 15 k; cpl. 225; a. 1-5" 4-3"; Class Escambia] Launched 8 October 1944, she was acquired by the navy 25 May 1945 and commissioned the same day. The *Caney* saw considerable service in World War II. Decommissioned 27 February 1947 and reactivated in February 1948, the ship was transferred to MSTS 18 July 1950 as a noncommissioned vessel with a civilian crew. She made six trips into Korean waters between 17 May 1953 and 3 July 1954.

Caliente AO 53: (T3-S2-A3) [d. 7,236; 553 × 75; 18 k; cpl. 304; a. 1-5", 4-3", 8-40mm, 8-1l1AA, 12-20mm; Class Ashtabula] Launched 25 August 1943 on a MC contract, she was commissioned 22 October 1943 and served in the Pacific during World War II. She was assigned to the Formosa Patrol, then 7th Fleet duties, and finally operated in Korean waters during the Communist China Spring Offensive, UN Summer–Fall Offensive, Korean Defense Summer–Fall 1952, and Korea Summer–Fall 1953 campaigns, earning four battle stars. She was decommissioned 15 December 1973, transferred to the Maritime Administration, and finally sold 5 April 1976.

Cedar Creek TAO 138: (T2-SE-A1) Built in 1943 she was leased to the USSR and then returned to the Maritime Commission in June 1948. She was assigned to the navy and classified AO 138 in July 1948 and operated in non-commissioned status with a civilian crew. Listed in *Awards* as having made two trips into Korean waters between 19 October 1950 and 22 May 1953, she was struck 14 October 1957.

Chemung II AO-30: [d. 7,295; 553 × 45; 18 k; cpl. 304; a. 1-5"; Class Cimarron] This oiler was launched 9 September 1939 as the *Esso Annapolis*, then was acquired by the navy 5 June 1941 and commissioned 3 July of 1941. During World War II she operated in the Atlantic and off North Africa. She was decommissioned and placed in reserves 3 July 1950. Recommissioned 1 December 1950, she headed for the Far East in January 1951, then operated in Korean waters during the UN Summer–Fall Offensive, Second Korean Winter, Korean Defense Summer–Fall 1952, Third Korean Winter campaigns. The *Chemung* received four battle stars.

Chepacket TAO 78: (T2-SE-A1) [d. 6,782; 620 × 68; 15 k; cpl. 232; a. 1-6", 4-3"; Class Suamico] Launched 10 March 1943 and commissioned 27 April 1943, she served in both the Atlantic and Pacific during World War II. Decommissioned 16 May 1946, she was reactivated and transferred to MSTS in July 1950. She served in Korean waters 6–9 May 1953.

Chikaskia TAO-54: (T3-S2-A3) [d. 7,470; 553 × 75; 18 k; cpl. 298; a. 1-5", 4-3"; Class Ashtabula] Launched 2 October 1942 under a Maritime Commission, she was acquired by the navy on 10 January 1943 and commissioned 10 November 1943. During World War II, she joined Task Force 58 and provided logistic support during the strikes on Turk and Kwajalein. She served in support of fast cruisers and battleships. She entered Tokyo Bay 20 August 1945. She remained in the Far East and returned to the Service Force, Pacific Fleet, operating ships in Korea. She participated in Korean operations during the Korea Summer–Fall 1953 campaign, earning one battle star. She was placed out of commission and in reserves 7 November 1955, then recommissioned 12 December 1956. She was returned to the reserves in 1957 and again recommissioned on 17 December 1960.

Chipola TAO 63: (T2-S2-A3) [d. 7,470; 553 × 45; 18 k; cpl. 304; a. 1-5", 4-3"; Class Ashtabula] Launched 21 October 1944 and commissioned 30 November 1944, during World War II she operated in the Netherlands West Indies, and in preparation for the assault on Iwo Jima. When war broke out in the Far East she operated in Korea from 20 November 1950 until 2 January 1951. She was placed in commission in reserve and decommissioned 1 August 1955. Recommissioned 29 December 1956 for service with the MSTS, she was placed back in the reserve fleet in November 1957 and then recommissioned again 17 December 1960.

Cimarron II AO-22: (T3-S2-A1) [d. 7,470; 553 × 45; 18 k; cpl. 304; a. 1-5", 4-3"; Class Cimarron] One of the first navy oilers, she was commissioned in March 1939. She was involved in the war in the Atlantic, but in 1942 was transferred to the Pacific where she took part in the Doolittle Raid on Japan. She made four deployments to Korea in 1950–53 and operated in Korean waters during the North Korean Aggression, Communist China Aggression, First UN Counter Offensive, UN Summer–Fall Offensive, Korean Defense Summer–Fall 1952, Third Korean Winter, and Korea Summer–Fall 1953 campaigns. She won four battle stars for Korea. The *Cimarron* continued to support the 7th Fleet for an additional sixteen years, including service in Vietnam. She was decommissioned in San Diego in October 1968, the oldest ship on continuous active duty in the Navy, and was sold for scrap in 1969.

Cohocton TAO 101: [d. 5,730; 523'6" × 68; 15 k; cpl. 225; a. 1-5"; Class Cohocton] Launched 28 July and commissioned 25 August 1945, she served in the Pacific during World War II. Decommissioned 14 June 1946, she was reacquired by Wartime Shipping Administration. She made twelve trips into Korean waters between 1 August 1953 and 23 January 1954.

Cossatot TAO 77: [d. 6,782; 620 × 68; 16 k; cpl 229; a. 1-6", 4-3"; Class Suamico] Launched as *Fort Necessity* 28 February 1943 for the Maritime Commission, she was assigned to the navy 17 May 1943 and commissioned 20 April 1943. On 7 March 1946 she was decommissioned, but she was reactivated in February 1948 and assigned to MSTS on 10 October 1949, serving in non-commissioned status with civilian crew. She made eight trips into Korean waters between 17 February 1953 and 22 July 1954.

Cowanesque TAO 79: (T2-SE-A1) [d. 5,782; 520 × 68; 15 k; cpl. 229; a. 1-5", 4-3"; Class Suamico] Launched by the Maritime Commission (Hull 79) as *Fort Duquesne* on 11 March 1943, she was acquired by the navy 25 March 1943 and commissioned 1 May. Decommissioned 30 January 1946, she was reacquired 18 January 1948 for the Naval Transportation Service and 18 July 1950 transferred to the MSTS where she served as a non-commissioned ship with a civilian crew. She was in Korean waters 19–21 July 1951.

Guadalupe AO-32: (T3-S2-A1) Hull 12. [d. 7,256; 552 × 75'3"; 18 k; cpl. 285; a. 1-5", 4-3"; Class Cimarron] Launched as the *Esso Raleigh* by the Maritime Commission 26 January 1940, she was acquired by the navy and commissioned 19 June 1941. She sailed for the Pacific where she was involved in most of the major campaigns of the war. She remained in the area after the war, and when the Korean conflict began she sailed along the Korean coast to support the siege of Wonsan Harbor. Later she served in Vietnam.

Kankakee TAO-39 (T2) [d. 6,013; 501'5" × 68; 17 k; cpl. 261; a. 1-5", 4-3", 8-40mm, 8-20mm; Class Kennebec] Previously the *Colina,* she was launched 29 September 1941, then acquired by the navy and commissioned 4 May 1942. During World War II she serviced ships in the Pacific, including campaigns at Saipan, Guam and Taiwan. After the war she ferried oil and gasoline from the west coast to the Far East. When the Communists invaded South Korea, the *Kankakee* headed to the Far East where she fueled ships of the blockading and bombardment command. She participated in Korean operations during the Second Korean Winter campaign and received one battle star. She was transferred to MSTS. In March 1965 she was one of the recovery ships for NASA's Gemini 4 space flight.

Kaskaskia AO-27: (T3-S2-A1) [d. 7,256; 553 × 75; 18 k; cpl. 272; a. 2-5", 2-3"; Class Cimarron] The ex–*Richmond,* she was launched 29 September 1939 and commissioned 29 October 1940, then served in the Pacific during World War II. Following that, she operated in Korean waters during the North Korean Aggression, Communist China Aggression, First UN Counter Offensive, Second Korean Winter, Korean Defense Summer–Fall 1952, Third Korean Winter, and the Korea Summer–Fall 1953 campaigns, earning seven battle stars. She was decommissioned in December 1969 and sold for scrap in 1970.

Manatee II TAO-58: (T3-S2-A1) [d. 7,470; 553 × 75; 18 k; cpl. 314; a. 1-5", 4-3", 8-40mm; Class Ashtabula] The second *Manatee* was laid 28 August 1944 and commissioned 6

April 1944. She carried fuel to the Pacific through several battles, including Peleliu and in the Philippines. After the war she continued to move oil to ships in the Far East. During the Korean War she deployed to the Far East where she functioned out of Sasebo, Japan, in support of fleet activities. She operated in Korean waters during the Communist China Spring Offensive, UN Summer–Fall Offensive, Second Korean Winter, and the Korean Defense Summer–Fall 1952 campaign. She received six battle stars for Korea and would later serve in Vietnam.

Marias TAO 57: (T3-S2-A3) [d. 7,470; 533 × 75; 18 k; cpl. 315; a. 1-5", 4-3"; Class Ashtabula] A Maritime Commission tanker launched 21 December 1943, she was commissioned 12 February 1944 and participated in the Pacific during World War II, serving as a station tanker. Listed in *Awards* as being in Korean waters between 10 and 14 August 1950.

Mascoma TAO 83: (T2-SE-A2) [d. 5,532; 523'6" × 68; 18 k; cpl. 267; a. 1-5", 4-3", 8-40mm, 12-20mm; Class Escambia] Launched 31 May 1943 and accepted by the navy, she was commissioned 3 February 1944. Decommissioned 17 December 1945 and stricken from the lists, she was reactivated and assigned to the Maritime Commission 8 January 1946. She was in Korean waters nine times between 14 February and 13 August 1953. She was scrapped in 1959.

Mattaponi AO 41: (T2A) [d. 5,809; 520 × 68; 17.5 k; cpl. 242; a. 1-5", 4-3", 8-40mm; Class Mattaponi] Built under Maritime contract as *Kalkay*, she was commissioned 11 May 1942. She spent most of World War II in the Atlantic and Mediterranean theaters. During the next five years she serviced convoys, and on 17 April 1950 she was decommissioned. Recommissioned 28 December 1950, she spent four years in the MSTS (TAO 41). She sailed in Korean waters from 13 to 16 March 1952, thus was eligible for the Korean Service medal. She was struck from the navy list October 1970 and scrapped 1972.

Millicoma TAO 73: (T2-SE-A1) [Class Suamico] Hull 573. Laid down under Maritime Commission contract 5 March 1943 as the *King's Mountain*, renamed *Conestoga*, then launched as the *Millicoma*, she was in Korean waters seven times between 2 June 1953 and 14 June 1954.

Mispillion AO 105: (T3-S2-A2) [d. 7,163; 553 × 75; 18 k; cpl. 220; a. 1-5", 4-3"; Class Ashtabula] Laid down 14 February 1945 under a Maritime Commission contract and commissioned 29 December 1945, she was too late to see action in World War II, but worked the Pacific in a variety of posts, took part in Operation Sandstone and an atomic test, and did weather work in Alaska. When war came to Korea, she joined Task Force 90 and supported the Inchon Landing and the bombardment and blockade of Wonsan. She operated in Korean waters during the North Korean Aggression, Communist China Aggression, First UN Counter Offensive, Communist China Spring Offensive, Second Korean Winter, Korean Defense Summer–Fall 1952, Third Korean Winter, and the Korea Summer–Fall 1953 campaigns, receiving eight battle stars. She later served in the Vietnam War. The *Mispillion* was stricken 15 February 1995.

Mission Buenaventura TAO 111: (T2-SE-A2) [d. 5,532; 524 × 68; 16 k; cpl. 52; no a; Class Mission] This Esso Fleet oiler built by the Marinship Corporation of California for the Maritime Commission was launched 28 May 1944 and commissioned 28 June 1944. In 1947 she went to the Naval Transportation Service. She served in Korea and was decommissioned 31 March 1972.

Mission Capistrano TAO 112: (T2-SE-A2) [d. 5,532; 524 × 68; 16 k; cpl. 52; no a; Class Mission] This Esso Fleet oiler built by Marinship for the Maritime Commission was launched 29 February 1944 and commissioned 14 June 1947. In 1947 she was transferred to the Naval Transportation Service. According to the Merchant Marine Association she was in Korea in June 1954. She was scrapped in 1980.

Mission Carmel TAO 113: (T2-SE-A2) [d. 5,532; 524 × 68; 16 k; cpl. 52; no a; Class Mission] An Esso Fleet oiler built by Marinship, she was launched 28 March 1944 and commissioned 17 May 1944. She was transferred to the Naval Transportation Service in 1947. She served in Korean waters and was eventually scrapped in 1984.

Mission De Pala TAO 114: (T2-SE-A2) [d. 5,532; 524 × 68; 16 k; cpl. 52; no a; Class Mission] Launched 25 August 1944 and commissioned November 1943, she was an Esso Fleet Mission Series built by Marinship of California. She served in Korean waters.

Mission Dolores TAO 115: (T2-SE-A2) [d. 5,532; 524 × 68; 16 k; cpl. 52; no a; Class Mission] Launched 26 April and commissioned 31 May 1944, she was acquired by the navy in 1947. She served in Korean waters and was eventually scrapped in 1984.

Mission Loreto TAO 116: (T2-SE-A2) [d. 5,532; 524 × 68; 16 k; cpl. 52; no a; Class Mission] Launched 25 June and commissioned 22 July 1944, she was built by Marinship of California. She was transferred to the navy in 1947 and served in Korean waters. She was decommissioned 12 November 1957.

Mission Los Angeles TAO 117: (T2-SE-A2) [d. 5,532; 524 × 68; 16 k; cpl. 52; no a; Class Mission] Launched 10 August 1945 and commissioned 29 October 1945, she was in Korean waters fifteen times between 15 July 1952 and 20 December 1953. She was decommissioned 12 November 1957 and finally scrapped in 1975.

Mission Purisima TAO 118: (T2-SE-A2) [d. 5,532; 524 × 68; 16 k; cpl. 52; no a; Class Mission] Launched 25 August 1943 and commissioned 24 December 1947, she was an Esso Fleet oiler. She was transferred to the navy in 1947, and served in the Korean war. She was decommissioned 4 December 1957.

Mission San Antonio TAO 119: (T2-SE-A2) [d. 5,532; 524 × 68; 16 k; cpl. 52; no a; Class Mission] Launched 8 April and commissioned 24 May 1944, she was an Esso Fleet oiler built by Marinship of California. She was transferred to the navy in 1947 and served in Korean waters.

Mission San Carlos TAO 120: (T2-SE-A2) [d. 5,532; 524 × 68; 16 k; cpl. 52; no a; Class Mission] She was launched 12 February and commissioned 15 April 1944. An Esso Fleet Mission oiler built by Marinship for the Maritime Commission, she served in Korean waters.

Mission San Diego TAO 121: (T2-SE-A2) [d. 5,532; 524 × 68; 16 k; cpl. 52; no a; Mission Series, Class Buenaventure] This Esso Fleet Mission Series oiler was built by Marinship for the Maritime Commission, and commissioned in April 1944. In 1947 she was transferred to the navy and saw service in Korea. She was scrapped in 2001.

Mission San Fernando TAO 122: (T2-SE-A2) [d. 5,532; 524 × 68; 16 k; cpl. 52; no a; Class Mission] Launched 25 November 1943 and commissioned 29 February 1944, she was an Esso Fleet oiler built by Marinship for the Maritime Commission. Transferred to the navy in 1947, she served in Korean waters.

Mission San Francisco TAO 123: (T2-SE-A2) [d. 5,532; 524 × 68; 16 k; cpl. 52; no a; Class Mission] An Esso Fleet oiler commissioned in October 1945, she was transferred to the navy in 1947, and served in Korea from 29 June to 4 July 1953. In 1957 she exploded and sank after a collision.

Mission San Gabriel TAO 124: (T2-SE-A2) [d. 5,532; 524 × 68; 16 k; cpl. 52; no a; Class Mission] Launched 17 April and commissioned 27 March 1944, she was an Esso Fleet oiler built for the Maritime Commission. Transferred to the navy in 1947, she served in Korean waters.

Mission San Jose TAO 125: (T2-SE-A2) [d. 5,532; 524 × 68; 16 k; cpl. 52; no a; Class Mission] Launched 7 October 1943 and commissioned 29 January 1944, she was an Esso Fleet oiler built for the Maritime Commission, and she served in the Korean War. She was decommissioned 15 October 1957.

Mission San Juan TAO 126: (T2-SE-A2) [d. 5,532; 524 × 68; 16 k; cpl. 52; no a; Class Mission] Launched 18 October 1943 and commissioned 31 January 1944, she was an Esso Fleet oiler built for the Maritime Commission. In 1947 she was transferred to the navy and she subsequently saw service in Korean waters during the war.

Mission San Luis Obispo TAO 127: (T2-SE-A2) [d. 5,532; 524 × 68; 16 k; cpl. 52; no a; Class Mission] An Esso Fleet oiler, she was launched 18 January and commissioned 15 July 1944 for the Maritime Commission. In 1947 she was acquired by the navy. She later served in Korean waters and was scrapped in 1986.

Mission San Miguel TAO 129: (T2-SE-A2) [d. 5,532; 524 × 68; 16 k; cpl. 52; no a; Class Mission] Launched 31 October 1943 and commissioned 19 February 1944, she was an Esso Fleet oiler built for the Maritime Commission. She served in Korean waters and was sunk in 1957.

Mission San Rafael TAO 130: (T2-SE-A2) [d. 5,532; 524 × 68; 16 k; cpl. 52; no a; Cass Mission] Launched 31 December 1943 and commissioned 22 March 1944 she was an Esso Fleet oiler built for the Maritime Commission. In 1947 she was transferred to the navy. She served in Korean waters and was eventually scrapped in 1957 after grounding.

Mission Santa Ana TAO 137: (T2-SE-A2) [d. 5,532; 524 × 68; 16 k; cpl. 52; no a; Class Mission] Launched 7 October 1943 and commissioned 29 June 1944, she was an Esso Fleet oiler built for the Maritime Commission. She was transferred to navy in 1947. She served in Korean waters and was finally scrapped in 1975.

Mission Santa Barbara TAO 131: (T2-SE-A2) [d. 5,532; 524 × 68; 16 k; cpl. 52; no a; Class Mission] Launched 8 June and commissioned 8 July 1944, she was an Esso Fleet oiler built for the Maritime Commission. She participated in Korean wasters during the UN Summer–Fall Offensive, Second Korean Winter, Korean Defense Summer–Fall 1952, Third Korean Winter, and Korean Summer–Fall 1953 campaigns. She was sold in 1985.

Mission Santa Cruz TAO 133: (T2-SE-A2) [d. 5,532; 524 × 68; 16 k; cpl. 52; no a; Class Mission] Launched 9 September and commissioned 31 December 1943, she was an Esso Fleet oiler built for the Maritime Commission. She participated in Korean waters during the UN Summer–Fall Offensive, Second Korean Winter, Korean Defense Summer–Fall 1952, Third Korean Winter, and the Korean Summer–Fall 1953 campaigns.

Mission Soledad TAO 136: (T2-SE-A2) Launched 14 January and commissioned 30 May 1944, it was operated by the MSTS. An Esso Fleet Mission tanker, she was in Korean Waters during the First UN Counter Offensive, the Chinese Communist Spring Offensive, the Second Korean Winter, and the Korean Defense Summer–Fall 1952 campaigns.

Monongahela II TAO 42: (T2-SE-A2) [d. 5,882; 520 × 68; 16.5 k; cpl. 249; a. 1-4", 4-3", 12-20mm; Class Mattaponi] The second *Monongahela* was built as the *Ellkay*, a commercial oil tanker, in 1941, acquired by the navy and commissioned 11 September 1942. Assigned to the Pacific Fleet, she serviced ships all during World War II. She was recommissioned for the Korean conflict and assigned to the MSTS supplying UN forces in the Far East. She operated in Korean waters during the First UN Counter Offensive and Communist China Spring Offensive campaigns. In March 1953 she was transferred to the Atlantic Fleet. She was decommissioned 10 June 1955, then recommissioned 28 December 1956, operating along the Atlantic Coast, only to be decommissioned 22 August 1957. She was struck from the navy list 1 February 1959.

Muir Woods TAO 139: (T2-SE-A2) Hull 139. Built for the Maritime Commission and laid down on 6 January 1945, she was launched 9 March 1945. She was delivered to the Soviet

Union 22 March 1945 and returned in February 1948. In 1948 she was acquired by the navy, as AO 139, and then transferred to the MSTS in October of that year. She was in Korean waters three times between 11 February and 18 April 1952.

Navasota AO 106: [d. 7,423; 553 × 75; 16 k; cpl. 304; a. 1-5", 4-3", 8-40mm; Class Ashtabula] She was launched 30 August 1945 and commissioned 27 February 1946. She operated in Korean waters during the North Korean Aggression, Inchon Landing, First UN Counter Offensive, Communist China Spring Offensive, UN Summer–Fall Offensive, Second Korean Winter, Korean Defense Summer–Fall 1952, Third Korean Winter, and Korea Summer–Fall 1953 campaigns, earning nine battle stars. The ship was decommissioned 13 August 1975. Placed in service with the Maritime Commission in 1975 (USNS *Navasota*), she served until 1991. She was struck from the Naval Register 2 January 1992 and sold for scrapping 25 October 1995.

Passumpsic AO 107: (T3-S2-A3) [d. 7,423; 553 × 75; 18.3 k; cpl. 304; a. 1-5", Class Ashtabula] It was laid 8 March 1945 and commissioned 1 April 1946. During World War II she serviced Pacific Fleet units in Southeast Asia, the Fiji Islands, Philippines, Midway and others. From June 1950 through February 1954 she spent 34 months outside the United States. She operated in Korean Waters during the North Korean Aggression, Communist China Aggression, Inchon Landing, First UN Combat Offensive, UN Summer–Fall Offensive, Second Korean Winter, Korean Defense Summer–Fall 1952, Third Korean Winter, and Korea Summer–Fall 1953 campaigns. She received nine battle stars for service in Korea. Later she served off the coast of Vietnam.

Pecos II TAO 65: (T2-SE-A1) [d. 5,730; 523 × 68; 15 k; cpl. 200; a. 1-5", 4-3", 12-20mm; Class Suamico] Laid as *Corsicana II*, Maritime Commission hull 325, she was launched 17 August 1942, acquired by the navy on 29 August of that year, and commissioned 5 October. Decommissioned 14 March 1946, she was struck 23 April 1947. Reacquired 20 May 1950 for the MSTS, she served as a noncommissioned ship with a civilian crew. She was in Korean waters from 16 to 19 February 1952. She disappeared 17 June 1974.

Pioneer Valley TAO 140: (T2-SE-A1) [d. 21,880 (f); 524 × 68; 16 k; cpl. 52; no a] Launched 6 April 1944, she was loaned to the Soviet Union, then returned to United States on 26 February 1948. Reactivated and assigned to the MSTS as a non-commissioned ship with a civilian crew on 1 October 1950, she was in the Korean theater 18 October 1950 to 10 June 1953. She was scrapped in 1973.

Platte AO 24: (T3-S2-A1) [d. 25,440; 553 × 75; 18 k; cpl. 276; a. 4-5"; Class Cimarron] The *Platte* was laid 8 July 1939 and commissioned 1 December 1939. She was at Pearl Harbor when the Japanese attacked. She spent World War II fueling ships in the Pacific. Following the breakout of war in Korean, she fueled 7th Fleet ships and acted as a station tanker for those on the Formosa Patrol. She was in Korean waters during the First UN Counter Offensive, Communist China Spring Offensive, UN Summer–Fall Offensive, Second Korean Winter, Korean Defense Summer–Fall 1952, and the Korean Summer–Fall 1953 campaigns. She received six battle stars for service in Korea. She later served in the Vietnam War.

Sappa Creek TAO 141 (T2-AE-A1) [d. 5,782; 523'6" × 68; 14.5 k; Class Suamico] Laid by the Maritime Commission as hull 544, launched 15 September 1943, and commissioned 28 April 1948, she was transferred to the Navy 28 the same day, 28 April. She made four trips to the Korean theater between 28 February and 28 March 1952. She was inactivated 7 December 1959.

Saugatuck TAO 75: (T2-SE-A1) [d. 5,782; 523'6" × 68; 15 k; cpl. 251; a. 1-5", 4-3", 4-40mm, 12-20mm; Class Suamico] Laid as a Maritime Commission hull 335, launched as the *Newton* 7 December 1942, she was commissioned 19 February 1943. Decommissioned 19 March 1946 and reactivated 22 January 1948, she served as a noncommissioned ship with a civilian crew. She was in theater three times between 7 December 1951 and 3 June 1953.

Schuylkill TAO 76: (T2-SE-A1) [d. 21,500 (f); 523'6" × 68; 15 k; cpl 253; a. 1-5", 4-3", 8-40mm; Class Suamico] Laid for the Maritime Commission (Hull 306), she was launched 6 February 1943 as the *Louisburg* USN AO 76, and was commissioned 9 April of that year. She was decommissioned 14 February 1946 and reactivated 30 January 1948 with assignment to MSTS. She was in Korean waters six times between 23 January 1951 and 17 February 1954.

Sebec TAO 87: (T2-SE-A2) [d. 22,380 (f); 523'6" × 68; 15 k; cpl. 267; a. 1-5", 1-4", 8-40mm; Class Escambia] Laid as Maritime Commission hull 1266, she was launched 29 July 1943 and commissioned 29 March 1944, after which she served in the Pacific during World War II. Decommissioned 7 February 1946 and struck from the navy list 26 February the same year, she was reacquired 28 April 1950 as a noncommissioned ship with a civilian crew, and she served in Korean waters between 22 and 28 January 1954. She was transferred to the army 9 June 1966.

Severn TAO 61: (T3-S2-A3) [d. 7,136; 553 × 75; 18 k; cpl. 298; a. 1-5", 4-3", 8-1.1", 12-20mm; Class Ashtabula] This oiler was the fourth *Severn* and was laid on 24 November 1943 and commissioned on 19 July 1944. During World War II she served with the 7th Fleet preparing for the Leyte invasion, delivering fresh water. Later she provided oil and water to the ships involved in the landings in Lingayen Gulf. She participated in Operation Crossroads (the atomic test series) conducted at Bikini. Decommissioned on 3 July 1950, she was reactivated on 29 December of that year and, although assigned to the Atlantic Fleet, she made deliveries in Korean waters from 20–23 February 1951. She was decommissioned on 1 July 1973 and a year later her name was struck from the navy list.

Shawnee Trail TAO 142: (T2-SE-A1) [d. 5, 730; 524 × 68; 15 k; cpl. 52; Class Suamico] Launched 31 May 1944, on 28 June 1944 she was loaned to the Soviet Union. Returned 25 May 1948, she was assigned as an AO to the MSTS on 1 October 1949 with a civilian crew. She made eleven trips to the Korean theater between 17 July 1951 and 8 April 1954. She was stricken 10 August 1973.

Soubarissen TAO 93: (T2-SE-A1) [d. 21,650 (f); 523'6" × 68; 15 k; cpl. 255; 1-5", 4-3", 8-40mm. Class Escambia] Laid as *Mission Santa Ana* on MC Hull 1818, she was launched 12 August 1944 and commissioned 5 January 1945. In May 1946 she was decommissioned and then reactivated 19 February 1948 and assigned to MSTS. She made thirteen trips to Korean waters between 8 November 1950 and 6 May 1954. She was stricken 1 July 1961.

Suamico TAO 49: (T2-SE-A1) [d. 21,650; 523'6" × 68, 12 k; cpl. 318; a. 2-5", 4-3", 8-40mm; Class Suamico] Launched as the *Harlem Heights* 30 May 1942 and commissioned 10 August 1942, she served primarily in the Pacific during World War II. Decommissioned 20 January 1946 and reacquired by the navy 24 January 1948, she was in Korean waters six times between 20 December 1952 and 28 November 1953.

Taluga TAO 62: (T3-S2-A3) [d. 23,235; 530 × 75; 18 k; cpl. 313; a. 1-5", 4-3"; Class Ashtabula] Laid under an MC contract on 23 December 1943, she was commissioned on 25 August 1944. During World War II she served out of Ulithi until the end of the war. When war broke out in Korea she headed to the Far East where she supported the blockade and siege of Wonsan and Songi and ranged up and down the west coast. She participated in Korean waters during the UN Summer–Fall Offensive, Second Korean Winter, Korean Defense Summer–Fall 1952, and Third Korean Winter campaigns. She earned four battle stars in Korea. For the next ten years she participated in deployment with the 7th Fleet, including a tour in

Vietnam. She participated in Operation Charger Log II, an experiment in which navy personnel were replaced by a civilian crew. In February 1976 she was placed in reserves, only to be reactivated in October to serve with the 3rd Fleet.

Tamalpais TAO 96: (T2-SE-A2) [Class Escambia] Built for the Maritime Commission, she was laid as *Mission San Francisco,* launched in 1944, and commissioned 20 May 1945. She was in Korean waters from 29 June to 4 July 1953.

Tolovana TAO 64: (T3-S2-A3) [d. 25,440; 553 × 75; 18.3 k; cpl. 313; a. 1-5", 4-3", 8-40mm; Class Ashtabula] Laid down under a Maritime Commission contract, she was commissioned 24 February 1945. During World War II she delivered gasoline and fuel oil. She supported Operation Crossroads, the atomic bomb test at Bikini Atoll. When the Korean War broke out she was called from MSTS for general logistic duties. She operated in Korean waters during the UN Summer–Fall Offensive and the Second Korean Winter campaigns, earning two battle stars for Korea. She was decommissioned 15 April 1975 and her name struck from the naval list.

Tomahawk TAO 88: (T2-SE-A2) [d. 21,660 (f); 523'6" × 68; 16 k; cpl. 267; a. 1-6", 4-3"; Class Escambia] Built on MC hull 1267, launched 1 October 1943, and commissioned 16 April 1944, she was decommissioned 6 January 1946 and served with the MSTS as a decommissioned ship with a civilian crew. She was in Korean waters on six occasions between 10 December 1953 and 30 April 1954, and was placed in the reserve 1961.

Gasoline Tanker (AOG)

Elkhorn AOG 7: [d. 4,130; 310'9" × 48'6"; 14 k; cpl. 131; a. 4-3"; Class Patapsco] Launched 16 May 1943 and commissioned 12 February 1944, the *Elkhorn* arrived in the Far East for duty as a station tanker. She remained in service with the Pacific Fleet, operating in Japanese waters and off the Korean coast during the Korean Summer–Fall 1953 campaign.

Kishwaukee AOG 9: [d. 4,130; 311 × 49; 15.5 k; cpl. 127; a. 12-20mm; Class Patapsco] Launched 24 July 1943, she was commissioned 27 May 1944. She joined the Service Squadron at Pearl Harbor and supported the Philippine campaign until 1945. During the Korean War she supplied fuel to Pacific staging areas and operated as a station ship. She was in Korean waters from 19 November 1950 to 16 March 1951, primarily at Wonsan. She served later in the Vietnam War.

Natchaug AOG 54: [d. 4,335; 310'9" × 48'6"; 14 k; cpl. 124; a. 14-3" Class Patapsco] Commissioned 16 July 1945, the *Natchaug* supplied lubricants to bases in Midway, Canton and the Christmas Islands during World War II. During the Korean War she operated with Task Force 95 and units of the 7th Fleet. She was in service in Korean waters during the Communist China Spring Offensive campaign and received one battle star for service in Korea. She was decommissioned 24 July 1959 and transferred to the government of Greece. She was struck from the Naval Register 1 August 1959.

Patapsco AOG 1: [d. 4,335; 310'9" × 48'6"; 14 k; cpl. 124; a. 14-3"; Class Patapsco] Laid down 25 May 1944 as the sixth *Patapsco*, she was commissioned 4 February 1943. She began the transportation of fuel to the Allies in the Solomons and New Hebrides. She was decommissioned 29 May 1946, and then called back 19 October 1950 to begin refueling ships off the coast of Korea. In service during the Second Korean Winter campaign, she received one battle star. Later she would serve in Vietnam.

Petaluma TAOG 79: (T1-M-BG2). Hull 2647. [d. 6,647; 325 × 48; 10 k; cpl. 28; Class

Ricon] Laid as *Tavispan* under a Maritime Commission contract, she was launched 9 August 1945, acquired 14 August, and commissioned 11 September 1950. She served as a noncommissioned ship with a civilian crew. She was in Korean waters during the Second Korean Winter and received a battle star. Later she served in Vietnam.

Piscataqua IV TAOG 80: [d. 6,647; 352'2" × 48'4"; 10'2 k; cpl. 38; Class Tontij] Originally *Taveta*, she was launched as *Cisne* on 10 September 1945 and commissioned 13 December 1945. Decommissioned and reactivated 19 August 1950, she served in Korean waters during the UN Summer–Fall Offensive, Second Korean Winter and Korean Defense Summer–Fall 1952 campaigns. She received three battle stars.

Rincon AOG 77: [d. 6,047; 312 × 48; 10 k; cpl. 38; Class Rincon] Laid down 24 February 1945, she was transferred to the MSTS on 1 July 1950 and assigned to the Far East. Immediately she began shuttling fuel to UN forces. In three years she interrupted her Korean duty only once. She was in Korean service during the Second Korean Winter and the Korean Defense Summer–Fall 1952 campaigns. Loaned to the Republic of Korea 21 February 1982, she was renamed *So Yang*. Returned, she was struck from the navy list 23 October 1998.

Rio Grande AOG 3: [d. 4,142; 310 × 48'6"; 14 k; cpl. 133; a. 4-3"; Class Patapsco] Laid 30 June 1942 and commissioned 10 April 1943, she was assigned to the Pacific Fleet and operated there supplying fuel in the advance across the Pacific. She was decommissioned 28 June 1950. Recommissioned 12 October 1950, she served in Korea, providing oil products to the struggling UN forces. She was in Korean waters during the Korean Defense Summer–Fall 1952 and Third Korean Winter campaigns, earning two battle stars. She was decommissioned 6 January 1956 and on 30 June 1960 entered the Maritime Administration Reserve Fleet. She later served in Vietnam.

Transferring hose during "at-sea replenishment"

Tombigbee AOG 11: [d. 4,142; 310'9" × 48'6"; 14 k; cpl. 120; a. 4-3"; Class Patapsco] Laid 23 October 1942, she was commissioned 13 July 1944. Beginning with fresh water rather than oil, she worked with ships near Guam and Ulithi. Later, carrying oil as she was designed to do, she was present in Japan as the war ended. She was placed out of commission on 12 December 1949. Then, with the outbreak of war, she was recommissioned 28 July 1950 and deployed in Korea 19 October 1951 to 23 January 1952. She received eleven engagement stars for her service in Korea. She later served in Vietnam. The ship was decommissioned in July 1972 and transferred to the Greek navy where she was renamed *Ariadni*.

Wabash III AOG 4: [d. 4,142; 310'9" × 48'6"; 14 k; cpl. 120; a. 4-3"; Class Patapsco] Laid 30 June 1942, she was commissioned 10 May 1943. During World War II she provided fuel to Alaskan ports, then to the Pacific carrying high-test gasoline to Midway, Palmyra Island, and Canton. Decommissioned on 29 July 1946, she was transferred to the Army Transportation Corps and struck from the naval list on 23 April 1947. Crewed by Japanese until 1950, she was reinstated on 1 June 1950 and enrolled in the Military Sea Transportation Service. Designated T-AOG 4, she supported UN air operations and served throughout the Korean War. She participated during the Second Korean Winter and the Korean Defense Summer–Fall 1952 campaigns, receiving two battle stars for her service. She was struck from the navy list for the second time on 8 May 1958 and remained in the reserves until the 1970s.

Transport (AP, TAP)

Aiken Victory TAP 188: (VC2-AP2) Hull 616. Launched 30 November 1944 for the MC, it was delivered 30 December 1944 as a troop transport ship. Transferred to the U.S. Navy as AP 188, then TAP 188, she participated in delivering the 7th Infantry Division during the Inchon Landing, and earned eight battle stars by participating also in the North Korean Aggression, Communist China Aggression, First UN Counter Offensive, Communist China Spring Offensive, UN Summer–Fall Offensive, Second Korean Winter, Korean Defense Summer–Fall 1952, and Third Korean Winter campaigns. She was scrapped in 1971.

Archer T. Gammon TAP 243: (VC2-S-AP2) [15,199 (f); 1,455 × 62, 16 k, cpl. 51; Class Boulder Victory] Launched 31 January 1945 and commissioned 24 February 1945, she was transferred to the army on 31 October 1947. In March 1950 she was transferred to the navy. The attack transport served in Korean waters during 19 November 1950 to April 1952.

Barrett TAP 196: (P2-S1-DN) [d. 6,720; 534 × 73; troop capacity 1900] This Maritime Administration Barrett class ship was laid down as *President Jackson II*. Taken over by the navy she was renamed *Barrett* for a Marine Corps general. She became a troop transport in Korea and served from 13 to 16 February 1953. Transferred to the Maritime Administration in 1973, she was renamed *Empire State V*.

Canton Victory TAP 765: (VC2-S-AP2) Launched 20 June 1945 and delivered 21 July 1945. Jaffee suggests she was in reserves during the Korean War but she is listed in *Navy and Marine Corps Awards Manual* as having served during the Communist Chinese Aggression and First UN Counter Offensive campaigns. She participated in the Hungnam redeployment.

Fred C. Ainsworth TAP 181: [d. 14,750 (f); 492 × 70; 15 k; cpl. 576; a. 1-5", 2-3", 2 twin 40mm, 11 twin 20mm] Built on a C-3 hull, she was a U.S. Army troop transport built in 1943 that operated in the Pacific during World War II. She continued to serve the army until she was transferred to the MSTS on 1 March 1950 after which she became USNS *Fred C. Ainsworth*, TAP 181. She participated in the landing at Pohang and the defense of Pusan

Perimeter, was in the second echelon group at the Inchon Landing, and served in Korean waters during the North Korean Aggression and Communist China Aggression campaigns. The ship was scrapped 1 July 1961.

Frederick Funston TAP 178 : [d. 7,000; 492 × 69'6"; 16 k; cpl. 596; a. 1-5", 2-3"; Class Frederick Funston] Built on a C-3 Hull and acquired from the Army on 8 April and commissioned 26 April 1943, she was transferred to the MSTS from the Naval Transportation Service on 1 October 1949 and served in a noncommissioned status with a civilian crew. She participated in shipping the 2nd Division to Korea in July 1950, and served during the North Korean Aggression campaign.

General A. E. Anderson TAP 111: [d. 11, 450; 622'7" × 75'6"; 20.6 k; cpl. 507, transport 5,289; a. 4-5", 16-1.1", 20-20mm; Class General Pope] Launched 2 May 1943 and acquired by the Navy on 25 August 1943, she was commissioned 5 October 1943. During the final days of World War II and in the following years she steamed between the United States, India, China, Japan and the Philippines. Assigned to MSTS in October 1949, she moved to supply men to Korea, delivering the troops of the Marine Air Group 33 and later the 1,800 men of the 11th Airborne Division. She saw service in Korean waters during the Communist China Aggression and the First UN Counter Offensive campaigns, receiving a battle star for Korean service. She was decommissioned 10 November 1958 and entered the reserves.

General A. W. Brewster TAP 155: (TC4-S-A) [d. 9,930; 522'10" × 71'6"; 16 k; cpl. 356; transport 3,823; a. 4-5", 4-40mm, 16-20mm; Class Squire] She was laid for the Maritime Commission on 2 January 1945 and commissioned 23 April 1945. Decommissioned 10 April 1946, she was transferred to the army. Reacquired by the navy on 1 March 1950, through MSTS, she participated in the Hungnam evacuation and served in Korean waters during the Communist China Spring Offensive, Korean Defense Summer–Fall 1952, Third Korean Winter, and Korea Summer–Fall 1953 campaigns. During the course of the war she moved more than 62,000 troops.

General A. W. Greeley TAP 141: (TC4-S-A) [d. 9,930; 522'10" × 71'6"; 16 k; cpl. 356; transport 3,823; a. 4-5", 4-40mm, 16-20mm; Class Squire] She was launched 5 November 1944 and commissioned 22 March 1945. Decommissioned 29 March 1946, she was reacquired by the MSTS to operate as a noncommissioned ship with a civilian crew, 1 October 1949. She participated in transferring the 2nd Infantry Division to Korea, and served there from 20–22 April 1951. She returned to the Maritime Commission 4 June 1958.

General D. E. Aultman TAP 156: (TC4-S-A) [d. 9,930; 522'10" × 71'6"; 16 k; cpl. 356; transport 3,823; a. 4-5", 4-

Lifeboat drill aboard troopship, 1952

40mm, 16-20mm; Class Squire] Launched 18 February 1945 and commissioned 20 March 1945, she was transferred to the MSTS from the Naval Transportation Service on 1 October 1949. Reacquired by the Navy on 1 March 1950, she served in Korean waters with a civilian crew from 1–3 June 1954. She returned to the Maritime Commission 4 June 1958.

General B. M. Blatchford TAP 153: (C4-S-A1) [d. 9,950 (l); 522'10" × 71'6"; 16.5 k; cpl. 256; troops 3823; a. 4-5", 8-1.1", 16 quad 20mm. Class Squire] Launched 27 August 1944 under MC, she was commissioned 26 January 1945. After transferring to the MSTS from the Naval Transportation Service on 1 October 1949, she served in Korean waters during Third Korean Winter and the Korea Summer–Fall 1953 campaigns, receiving two battle stars. Later she served in Vietnam.

General C. C. Ballou TAP 157. (TC4-S-A1) [d. 9,960; 522'10" × 71'6"; 16 k; cpl. 356; troops 3823; a. 4-5", 40-40mm, 16-20mm; Class General Squire] Launched 7 March 1945, she was transferred to the MSTS from the Naval Transportation Service on 1 October 1949, and served in Korean waters during the First UN Counter Offensive, UN Summer–Fall Offensive, Korean Defense Summer–Fall 1952, Third Korean Winter, and Korea Summer–Fall 1953 campaigns, earning five battle stars. Struck 1 July 1960, she remains in reserves.

General C. G. Morton TAP 138: [d. 9,960; 522'10" × 71'6"; 16 k; cpl. 356; troops 3823; a. 4-5", 40-40mm, 16-20mm; Class General Squire] Launched 18 May 1944 and commissioned 7 July 1944, she was transferred to the MSTS from the Naval Transportation Service on 1 October 1949. Moved the 9th Regimental Combat Team to Pusan in July 1950, and participated in the North Korean Aggression, Communist China Aggression, and First UN Counter Offensive campaigns, earning three battle stars. She was struck 29 May 1958.

General C. H. Muir TAP 142: [d. 9,960; 522'10" × 71'6"; 16 k; cpl. 356; troops 3823; a. 4-5", 40-40mm, 16-20mm; Class General Squire] Launched 24 November 1944 and commissioned 12 April 1945, she transferred to the MSTS from the Naval Transportation Service 1 October 1949, then served in Korean waters during the Korean Defense Summer–Fall 1952 and Korea Summer–Fall 1953 campaigns, earning two battle stars. She entered reserves 30 June 1960.

General Daniel L. Sultan TAP 120: (P2-SE-R2) [Class Admiral W. S. Benson] Launched 22 November 1942 and commissioned 23 August 1944, on 3 June 1946 she was turned over to the Maritime Commission. She was transferred to the MSTS from the Naval Transportation Service 1 October 1949. Originally named *Admiral W. S. Benson*, that changed when she was transferred. Reacquired by the navy on 1 March 1950, she aided in moving the 2nd Division to Korea in July of that year, participated in the Hungnam Evacuation, and served during the North Korean Aggression and Communist China Aggression campaigns, earning two battle stars.

General E. T. Collins TAP 147: [d. 9,960; 522'10" × 71'6"; 16 k; cpl. 356; troops 3823; a. 4-5", 40-40mm, 16-20mm; Class General Squire] Launched 22 January 1944 and commissioned 20 July 1944, she was decommissioned 17 June 1946 and transferred to the Maritime Commission from the Naval Transportation Service 1 October 1949. Reactivated 1 March 1950 by the U.S. Navy, she helped move the 2nd Infantry Division to Korea in 1950, participated in the Hungnam deployment, and served in Korean waters during the Communist China Aggression, First UN Counter Offensive, Korean Defense Summer–Fall 1952, Third Korean Winter, and Korea Summer–Fall 1953 campaigns, earning five battle stars.

General Edwin D. Patrick TAP 124: (P2-S20-R2) [d. 4,500; 608 × 75'5"; 19 k; troops 4,600–5,000] Originally *Admiral C. F. Hughes*, she was transferred to the MSTS from the Naval Transportation Service on 1 October 1949. A Maritime Administration design, her name

General E. T. Collins en route to Korea, 1952

was changed when she was transferred. She headed out 17 July 1950 with first elements of the 2nd Infantry Division to Pusan and later participated in the North Korean Aggression, Communist China Aggression, and Communist China Spring Offensive campaigns, winning three battle stars for Korean service.

General George M. Randall TAP 115: (P2-S2-R1) [d. 11,828; 622'7" × 75'6"; 20.6 k; cpl. 507, troops 5289; a. 4-5", 16-1.1", 20-20mm; Class General John Pope] She was laid as AP 115, launched 30 January 1944 and commissioned 15 April 1944. During World War II she saw service in both the European and Pacific theaters. She was transferred to the MSTS from the Naval Transportation Service 1 October 1949. During the Korean War she participated in the amphibious assault on Inchon and the evacuation at Hungnam, and made several trips to Korea between 1950 and 1954, carrying men and supplies. She was decommissioned 2 June 1961 and joined the National Defense Reserve Fleet (NDRF).

General H. B. Freeman TAP 143: [d. 9,960; 522'10" × 71'6"; 16 k; cpl. 356; troops 3823; a. 4-5", 40-40mm, 16-20mm; Class General Squire] Launched 11 December 1944 and commissioned 26 April 1945, she was transferred to the MSTS from the Naval Transportation Service 1 October 1949. She helped move the 2nd Infantry Division to Pusan in July 1950, and participated in the Hungnam deployment, and the North Korean Aggression, Communist China Aggression, and First UN Counter Offensive campaigns. She was struck 24 July 1958.

General Hugh J. Gaffey TAP 121: (P2-SE-R2) [d. 20,120; 608 × 75'5"; 19 k; troops 4,600 to 5,000] Launched 20 February 1944, a Maritime Administration design, she was originally named *Admiral W. L. Capps*, but that changed when she was transferred. She was struck June 1946 and assigned to the MSTS from the Naval Transportation Service 1 October 1949. Staffed by civilian crews, she made several deliveries to Korea during 1951–1952 and later served in Vietnam.

General H. W. Butner TAP 113: [d. 11,828 (f); 622'7" × 75'6"; 19 k; cpl. 477; troops 5,289; a. 4-5", 16-1.1"; 18-20mm; Class General John Pope] A Maritime Commission contract for the U.S. Army, she was commissioned 11 January 1944. She was renamed when she was transferred to the MSTS from the Naval Transportation Service 1 October 1949. She participated during the North Korean Aggression and Inchon Landing campaigns, receiving two battle stars, and was decommissioned 28 January 1960.

General J. C. Breckinridge TAP 176: (P2-S2-R2) [d. 11,828 (f); 622'7" × 75'6"; 19 k; cpl. 477; troops 5,289; a. 4-5", 16-1.1"; 18-20mm; Class General John Pope] Operated as a commissioned ship with navy crews, she was transferred to the MSTS from the Naval Transportation Service on 1 October 1949. She was involved in the Wonsan and Hungnam evacuations and participated in the North Korean Aggression, Communist China Aggression, Inchon Landing, and the First UN Counter Offensive campaigns, receiving four battle stars. She was placed in reserves December 1966.

General J. H. McRae TAP 149: [d. 9,960; 522'10" × 71'6"; 16 k; cpl. 356; troops 3823; a. 4-5", 40-40mm, 16-20mm; Class General Squire] Launched 26 April 1944 and commissioned 8 August 1944, she was busy during World War II and decommissioned 27 February 1946. She was transferred to the MSTS from the Naval Transportation Service on 1 October 1949. Reactivated on 1 March 1950, she participated in the Communist China Spring Offensive, UN Summer–Fall Offensive, Second Korean Winter, and Korean Defense Summer–Fall 1952 campaigns, winning four battle stars.

General John Pope TAP 110: (P2-S2-R1) [d. 11,828; 622'7" × 75'6"; 20.6 k; cpl. 507; troops 5,289; a. 4-5", 16-1.1", 20-20mm; Class General John Pope] Launched 21 March 1941, acquired by the navy 2 July 1943 and commissioned 5 August 1943, she was decommissioned

General Hugh J. Gaffey en route to Korea, 1952

12 June 1946 and reinstated 20 July 1950 when assigned to the MSTS. She participated in the Communist China Spring Offensive, UN Summer–Fall Offensive, Second Korean Winter, Korean Defense Summer–Fall 1952, Third Korean Winter, and Korea Summer–Fall 1953 campaigns. She won six battle stars.

General Leroy Elting TAP 154: [d. 9,960; 522'10" × 71'6"; 16 k; cpl. 356; troops 3823; a. 4-5", 40-40mm, 16-20mm; Class General Squire] Launched 20 September 1944, she was commissioned 21 February 1945. Decommissioned 29 May 1946, she was reactivated by the MSTS in 1950. She participated in the second echelon movement at the Inchon Landing, and served in Korean waters during the First UN Counter Offensive and the Korean Defense Summer–Fall 1952 campaigns. She transported Dutch, Ethiopian and Greek troops to Korea. She later served in Vietnam and was placed in reserves January 1967.

General M. B. Stewart TAP 140: [d. 9,960; 522'10" × 71'6"; 16 k; cpl. 356; troops 3,823; a. 4-5", 40-40mm, 16-20mm; Class General Squire] Launched 15 October 1944 and commissioned 3 March 1945, she was decommissioned 24 May 1946 and turned over to the army. Reacquired 1 March 1950 by the MSTS, she made a trip to Korean waters 2–8 October 1953, earning one battle star. She was placed in reserves 21 May 1958.

General M. C. Meigs TAP 116: (P2-S2-R1) [d. 11,828; 622'7" × 75'6"; 20.6 k; cpl. 507, troops 5,500; a. 4-5", 16-1.1", 20-20mm; Class General John Pope] Launched 13 March 1944 for the War Shipping Administration, she was acquired by the navy 2 June 1944 and commissioned on 3 June. She participated in the Communist China Spring Offensive, UN Summer–Fall Offensive, Second Korean Winter, Korean Defense Summer–Fall 1952, Third Korean Winter and Korea Summer–Fall 1953 campaigns, receiving six battle stars.

General M. L. Hersey TAP 148: [d. 9,960; 522'10" × 71'6"; 16 k; cpl. 356; troops 3823; a. 4-5", 40-40mm, 16-20mm; Class General Squire] Launched under a Maritime Commission contract 1 April 1944 and commissioned 29 July 1944, she was transferred to the MSTS from the Naval Transportation Service 1 October 1949. Required by the Navy 1 March 1950, she was placed in service with a civilian crew, and during 1952–1954 made four trips to the Far East in support of the Korean War. She received two battle stars for service in Korea. Placed out of service 11 June 1954, she entered the National Defense Reserve 3 September 1959.

General M. M. Patrick TAP 150: (TC4-S-A1) [d. 9,960; 522'10" × 7'6"; 16 k; cpl. 356; troops 3823; a. 4-5", 40-40mm, 16-20mm; Class General Squire] Launched 21 June 1944 and commissioned 4 September 1944, she was decommissioned 8 March 1946 and transferred to Army transport. Reacquired by the navy 1 May 1950 for MSTS transport use, she participated in the North Korean Aggression and the Communist China Aggression campaigns, earning two battle stars. She was placed in reserves 17 October 1958.

General Nelson M. Walker TAP 125: (P2-S2-R2) [d. 23,380 (f); 608'11" × 76; 23 k; cpl. 617; troops 4,587; a. 4-5", 8-4", 28-20mm; Class Admiral Benson] Originally named *Admiral H. T. Mayo*, this transport was transferred to the MSTS from the Naval Transportation Service on 1 October 1949. Renamed *General Nelson M. Walker*, she served in Korean waters during the Korean Defense Summer–Fall 1952, Third Korean Winter, and Korea Summer–Fall 1953 campaigns. She steamed 35,000 miles in less than three months transporting Colombian, Greek, Turkish, and Dutch troops to Korea. She made eight transpacific round trips, and brought home the first U.S. POWs from Korea in 1953.

General R. L. Howze TAP 134: [d. 9,960; 522'10" × 71'6"; 16 k; cpl. 356; troops 3,823; a. 4-5", 40-40mm, 16-20mm; Class General Squire] Launched 23 May 1943 and commissioned 7 February 1944, she was transferred to the MSTS from the Naval Transportation Service on October 1, 1949. Reactivated 1 March 1950, she participated in the First UN Counter

Offensive, Communist China Spring Offensive, Second Korean Winter, Korean Defense Summer–Fall 1952, Third Korean Winter, and Korea Summer–Fall 1953 campaigns, earning six battle stars. She was placed in reserves 17 June 1958.

General S. D. Sturgis TAP 137: [d. 9,960; 522'10" × 71'6"; 16 k; cpl. 356; troops 3,823; a. 4-5", 40-40mm, 16-20mm; Class General Squire] Launched 12 November 1943 and commissioned 10 July 1944, she was decommissioned 24 May 1946 and transferred to the WSA for army transportation. She was reacquired by the navy on 1 March 1950 and participated in the Korean Defense Summer–Fall 1952, Third Korean Winter, and Korea Summer–Fall 1953 campaigns, earning three battle stars.

General Simon B. Buckner TAP 123: (P2-SE-R1) [d. 20,110; 608 × 75'5"; 19 k; troops 4,600-5,000] Launched 14 June 1944, she was transferred to the army and then reacquired by the navy March of 1950. Originally named *Admiral E. W. Eberle*, she was renamed when she was transferred to the MSTS from the Naval Transportation Service on 1 October 1949. She participated in the Inchon Landing, and served in the Communist China Spring Offensive, Second Korean Winter, Korean Defense Summer–Fall 1952, Third Korean Winter, and Korea Summer–Fall 1953 campaigns.

General Stuart Heintzelman TAP 159: [d. 9,960; 522'10" × 71'6"; 16 k; cpl. 356; troops 3,823; a. 4-5", 40-40mm, 16-20mm; Class General Squire] Launched 21 April 1945 and commissioned 12 September 1945, she was decommissioned 12 June 1946 and transferred to the Army Transport Service. Reacquired 1 March 1950 by the MSTS from the Naval Transportation Service, she participated in the Hungnam deployment and was in Korean waters in August, November and December of 1950.

General W. A. Mann TAP 112: (P2-S2-R1) [d. 11,828; 622'7" × 75'6"; 20.6 k; cpl. 507, troops 5,289; a. 4-5", 16-1.1", 20-20mm; Class General John Pope] Commissioned 13 October 1953, she was renamed from *General William A. Mann* when she was transferred to the MSTS from the Naval Transportation Service 1 October 1949. She participated in the North Korean Aggression, Communist China Aggression, Communist China Spring Offensive, UN Summer–Fall Offensive, Korean Defense Summer–Fall 1952, Second Korean Winter, Korean Defense Summer–Fall 1952, and Third Korean Winter campaigns. She was struck 1 December 1966.

General W. C. Langfitt TAP 151: [d. 9,960; 522'10" × 71'6"; 16 k; cpl. 356; troops 3,823; a. 4-5", 8-1.1", 16-20mm; Class General Squire] Launched 17 July 1944 and commissioned 30 September 1944, she was decommissioned

A break in the routine: sailors staging a boxing match on an unidentified freighter.

6 June 1946, transferred to the MSTS from the Naval Transportation Service, 1 October 1949 and reactivated 1 March 1950. She participated in the Communist China Spring Offensive, UN Summer–Fall Offensive, Second Korean Winter, and Korean Defense Summer–Fall 1952 campaigns. She was deactivated 30 September 1957.

General W. F. Hase TAP 146: [d. 9,960; 522'10" × 71'6"; 16 k; cpl. 356; troops 3,823; a. 4-5", 8-1.1", 16-20mm; Class General Squire] Launched 15 December 1943 and commissioned 6 June 1944, she was decommissioned 11 January 1946 and then reactivated 1 May 1950. She saw service during the North Korean Aggression, Communist China Aggression, First UN Counter Offensive, Communist China Spring Offensive, Second Korean Winter, Korean Defense Summer–Fall 1952, Third Korean Winter, and Korea Summer–Fall 1953 campaigns, earning eight battle stars. She was assigned to the Maritime Administration in January 1960.

General W. H. Gordon TAP 117: [d. 11,828; 622'7" × 75'6"; 20.6 k; cpl. 507; troops 5,289; a. 4-5", 16-1.1", 20-20mm; Class General John Pope] Launched 7 May 1944 and commissioned 29 June 1944, she was decommissioned 29 January 1947 and transferred to the Maritime Commission, then reactivated 8 November 1951. She participated, with a civilian crews, in the Second Korean Winter, Korean Defense Summer–Fall 1952, Third Korean Winter and Korea Summer–Fall 1953 campaigns.

General W. M. Black TAP 135: [d. 9,960; 522'10" × 71'6"; 16 k; cpl. 356; troops 3,823; a. 4-5", 8-1.1", 16-20mm; Class General Squire] Launched 23 July 1943 and commissioned 24 February 1944, she was decommissioned 28 January 1946 and transferred to the army. She was reactivated 1 March 1950 for the Korean War, then served in Korean waters during the Communist China Spring Offensive, UN Summer–Fall Offensive, Second Korean Winter, Korean Defense Summer–Fall 1952, Third Korean Winter, and Korea Summer–Fall 1953 campaigns, earning six battle stars.

General W. O. Darby TAP 127: (P2-S2-R2) [d. 20,120; 608'11" × 75'6"; 19 k; cpl. 495; troops 4,985; Class Admiral Benson] Originally built as the *Admiral W. S. Sims*, she was commissioned 21 June 1946. She was struck from the Naval Register on 3 July 1946, transferred to the Army Transport Service and renamed *General W. O. Darby*, then assigned to MSTS 1 October 1949. She served in Korean waters 17 July 1953 to 1 January 1954. She was struck from the navy list 9 January 1969.

General William Mitchell TAP 114: (P2-S2-R1) [d. 11,828; 622'7" × 75'6"; 20.6 k; cpl. 507; troops 5,289; a. 4-5", 16-1.1", 20-20mm; Class General John Pope] Launched 31 October 1943, she was commissioned 19 January 1944. Transferred to the MSTS from the Naval Transportation Service October 1, 1949, she participated in the North Korean Aggression, Communist China Aggression, First UN Counter Offensive, and UN Summer–Fall Offensive campaigns.

General William Weigel TAP 119: (P2-S2-R1) [d. 11,828; 622'7" × 75'6"; 20.6 k; cpl. 507, troops 5,289; a. 4-5", 16-1.1", 20-20mm; Class General John Pope] She was launched 3 September 1944 and commissioned as the *General William Weigel* 6 January 1945. She was with the second echelon group at the Inchon Landing and participated in North Korean Aggression, Communist China Aggression, Communist China Spring Offensive, UN Summer–Fall Offensive, Second Korean Winter, Korean Defense Summer–Fall 1952 and Third Korean Winter campaigns. She earned seven battle stars.

James O'Hara TAP 90/179: (TC-3S-A1) [d. 8,600; 492 × 69'6"; 19 k; cpl. 538; troops 2,200; a. 1-5", 2-3"; 16-20mm] Laid for the Army by the Maritime Commission, launched 30 December 1941, delivered to the army 30 November 1942, she was acquired by the navy 15 April and commissioned 26 April 1943. Decommissioned 5 April 1946 and transferred to Army Transportation Service, she was reacquired 1 May 1950 for the MSTS. She participated in Korean waters from November 1950 to July 1954 and during the Communist China Aggression campaigns, receiving one battle star. She was struck 1 July 1961.

Lt. Raymond O. Beaudoin TAP 180: Hull 823. Launched 21 May 1945 and delivered 15 June 1945, originally *Marshall Victory*, she was transferred to the army in 1947 and then acquired by the MSTS 22 July 1950. She was placed in service during the Communist China Spring Offensive, UN Summer–Fall Offensive, Second Korean Winter, and Korean Defense Summer–Fall 1952 campaigns. She was awarded four battle stars.

Marine Adder TAP 193: (C4-S-AS) [d. 10,210; 523 × 72; 17 k; troops 3,674; Class Marine Adder] Launched 16 May 1945, placed in Maritime Commission reserves 1947, she was reacquired 23 July 1950 for the MSTS. She made seventeen voyages to Korea, participating during the Communist China Aggression, First UN Counter Offensive, Communist China Spring Offensive, UN Summer–Fall Offensive, Second Korean Winter, Korean Defense Summer–Fall 1952, Third Korean Winter, and Korea Summer–Fall 1953 campaigns, receiving eight battle stars. She entered the reserve fleet 8 June 1957 and was struck 6 June 1958.

Marine Carp TAP 199: (C4-S-AS) [d. 10,210; 523 × 72; 18 k; troops 3,451; Class Marine Adder] Launched 5 July 1945, placed in reserves in 1946, she was reactivated 17 March 1952 for the MSTS. She served in Korea from 30 June to 10 July 1953, and participated in the Korea Summer–Fall 1953 campaign. Struck 11 September 1958, she was sold 20 July 1967 and became *Green Spring*.

Marine Lynx TAP 194: (C4-S-AS) [d. 10,210; 523 × 72; 18 k; troops 3,451; Class Marine Adder] Launched 17 July 1945, she entered reserves in 1947 and was reactivated and assigned to the MSTS 23 July 1950 as noncommissioned ship with civilian crew. She served in Korean waters during the North Korean Aggression, First UN Counter Offensive, Communist China Spring Offensive, UN Summer–Fall Offensive, Second Korean Winter, Korean Defense

General William Weigel at Pusan, 1953

Marine Adder offloading troops at Pusan

Summer–Fall 1952, and Korea Summer–Fall 1953 campaigns, receiving seven battle stars. Stricken 1 May 1958, she was sold and became *Transcolumbia*.

Marine Phoenix TAP 195: (C4-S-AS) [d. 10,210; 523 × 72; 18 k; troops 3,451; Class Marine Adder] Launched 9 August 1944, placed in reserves in 1947, she was reacquired by the MSTS 21 July 1950, and sailed as noncommissioned ship with civilian crew. The *Marine Phoenix* served in Korean waters during the North Korean Aggression, First UN Counter Offensive, Communist China Spring Offensive, UN Summer–Fall Offensive, Second Korean Winter, Korean Defense Summer–Fall 1952, Third Korean Winter, and Korea Summer–Fall 1953 campaigns, receiving eight battle stars. She was struck in 1958 and sold 25 April 1967.

Marine Serpent TAP 202: (C4-S-AS) [d. 10,210; 523 × 72; 18 k; troops 3,451; Class Marine Adder] Launched 12 June 1945, taken by a private owner, she was placed in reserves in July 1947. Reacquired by the navy 8 May 1952, she was assigned to the MSTS as a noncommissioned ship with civilian crew. She served in Korean waters during the Korean Defense Summer–Fall 1952, Third Korean Winter, and Korea Summer–Fall 1953 campaigns. She also participated in the transportation of North Korean POWs at Cheju-de and Koje-do. She received three battle stars and was struck 17 August 1955.

Private Joe P. Martinez TAP 187: (VC-2S-AP2) [d. 15,199; 455'3" × 62'1"; 15.5 k; cpl. 96; troops 1,259; Class Boulder Victory] Laid as Maritime Commission hull 825, she was launched 29 May 1945 and converted to a troop ship. Transferred and renamed 1 March 1950, she participated in the Communist China Spring Offensive and UN Summer–Fall Offensive campaigns, receiving four battle stars. She was struck 6 November 1952.

Private Sadao S. Munemori TAP 190: (VC-2S-AP2) [d. 15,199; 455'3" × 62'1"; 15.5 k; cpl. 96; troops 1,259; Class Boulder Victory] Laid as *Wilson Victory* 6 July 1945, she was converted to a troop ship and transferred to the Army 21 August 1946. Renamed, she was delivered to MSTS 22 July 1950. Listed by Cagle as being involved in the second echelon movement at the Inchon Landing, she received four battle stars and was struck 6 November 1952.

Sgt. David C. Shanks TAP 180: (VC-2S-AP2) [d. 15,199; 455'3" × 62'1"; 15.5 k; cpl. 96; troops 1,259; Class Boulder Victory] She participated in the landing at Pohang and the defense of Pusan Perimeter, and served in Korean waters during the Communist China Aggression campaign.

Sgt. G. D. Keathley TAP C 117: (C1-M-AV1) [d. 6090 (f); 338'9" × 50'4"; 11.5 k; cpl. 48; troops 101; Class Jonah E. Kelley] Built on hull 2247, she was launched 7 December 1944 and commissioned February 1945. On 1 July 1950 she became USNS TACP 117, with a civilian crew. She served in Korean waters during most of the war and participated in nine of the ten campaigns: the North Korean Aggression, Inchon Landing, First UN Counter Offensive, Communist China Spring Offensive, UN Summer–Fall Offensive, Second Korean Winter, Korean Defense Summer–Fall 1952, Third Korean Winter, and Korea Summer–Fall 1953 campaigns. She received nine battle stars. Struck 24 October 1967, she was sold to the Republic of China 29 March 1972 and became *Ghu Hwa*.

Sgt. Howard E. Woodford TAP 191: (VC-2S-AP2) [d. 15,199; 455'3" × 62'1"; 15.5 k; cpl. 96; troops 1,259; Class Boulder Victory] Laid under Maritime Commission hull 286, she was assigned to the MSTS 22 July 1950 and served in Korean waters during the First UN Counter Offensive, Communist China Spring Offensive, UN Summer–Fall Offensive, Second Korean Winter, and Korean Defense Summer–Fall 1952 campaigns. She was sold 27 March 1972.

Sgt. Joseph E. Muller TAP C 118: (C1-M-AV1) [d. 6090 (f); 338'9" × 50'4"; 11.5 k; cpl. 48; troops 101; Class Jonah E. Kelley] Built on Maritime Commission hull 2485, launched 17 February 1945 as *Check Knot*, at the end of the war she was transferred to the Army Transportation Service (USAT) and renamed *Sgt. Joseph E. Muller*. Transferred to the MSTS in July 1950, she served in Korean waters during the North Korean Aggression, Communist China Aggression, First UN Counter Offensive, Communist China Spring Offensive, UN Summer–Fall Offensive, Second Korean Winter, Korean Defense Summer–Fall 1952, Third Korean Winter, and Korea Summer–Fall 1953 campaigns. She was struck 13 November 1969.

Sgt. Sylvester Antolak TAP 192: (VC-2S-AP2) [d. 15,199; 455'3" × 62'1"; 15.5 k; cpl. 96; troop 1,259; Class Boulder Victory] Laid as Maritime Commission hull 830 as *Stetson Victory*, launched 16 June and delivered on 18 July 1945, she was renamed 31 October 1947 and operated by the army. On 22 July 1950 she was transferred to the MSTS. She served in Korea during the North Korean Aggression, Communist China Aggression, First UN Counter Offensive, Communist China Spring Offensive, UN Summer–Fall Offensive, Second Korean Winter, and Korean Defense Summer–Fall 1952 campaigns. She was struck 6 November 1952 and sold in December 1971.

Repair ship (AR, ARG, ARV, ARVE, ARVH)

Ajax IV AR 6: [d. 8,975; 529'5" × 73'4"; 19.2 k; cpl. 1,121; a. 4-5"; Class Vulcan] The fourth *Ajax* was laid down 7 May 1941 and commissioned on 30 October 1943. During World War II she saw action in the Pacific. When war in Korea broke out, she saw several tours and was in Korean waters during the UN Summer–Fall Offensive, Second Korean Winter, Korean Defense Summer–Fall 1952, and Third Korean Winter campaigns. She was decommissioned in San Diego on 31 December 1986.

Aventinus ARVE 3: [d. 4,100; 328 × 50; 11.6 k; cpl. 245; a. 8-40mm, 12-20mm; Class Aventinus] Laid to be LST-1092, she was designated ARVE 3 on 8 December 1944. She was commissioned on 30 May 1945, joined the Pacific Fleet, and at the end of the war was decommissioned and put in reserve on 30 August 1946. Recommissioned 25 July 1950, she journeyed to Korea where she provided air repair service. She saw service in Korean waters from 26 December 1950 to 14 October 1951. She was decommissioned on 4 April 1952 and transferred to the government of Chile where it served as the *Aquila*. She was scuttled in August 1980 after running aground.

Delta II AK 29: [d. 8,975; 490'6" × 69'6"; 18 k; cpl. 903; a. 1-5", 4-3"; Class Delta] Built originally as *Hawaiian Packer*, she was acquired by the navy 4 June 1941 and commissioned 16 June of that year. On 1 July 1942 she was reclassified AR-9. During World War II she repaired craft near Algeria, Tunisia, and Palermo, Italy. Decommissioned 5 March 1947, she was recommissioned 1 November 1950 for service in Korea. She provided repair service to ships in the Pacific, operating in Korean waters during the Korean Defensive Summer–Fall 1952 campaign. During her last tour she served as flagship for the Blockading and Escort Force off Korea. She received one battle star. She was decommissioned and placed in reserve 1 December 1955.

Fabius ARVA 5: [d. 3,960; 328 × 50; 12 k; cpl. 245; a. 2-40 mm; Class Fabius] Launched 11 April 1945 and commissioned 7 June 1945, during World War II she repaired aircraft in the vicinity of Okinawa. After the war she was decommissioned and placed in reserves 30 August 1946. Recommissioned 28 July 1950, she sailed for Korea. She saw service in Korean waters during the Communist China Spring Offensive campaign, and received one battle star. She was decommissioned 4 April 1952.

Hector III AR 7: [d. 9,140; 529'5" × 73'4"; 19 k; cpl. 1,108; a. 4-5", 8-40mm, 8-20mm; Class Vulcan] A modified Liberty ship, she was commissioned 7 February 1944. During World War II she served in the Pacific where she repaired the twice torpedoed cruiser *Houston*. During the Korean War she alternated repair service along the Korean coast and Japan. She served in Korean waters during the North Korean Aggression campaign.

Hooper Island ARG 17: [d. 5.159; 441'6" × 56'11"; 12 k; cpl. 500; a. 1-5", 3-3", 4-40mm, 12-20mm, Class Luzon] The ex–Liberty ship *Bert McDowell*, she was launched 30 October 1944 and acquired and commissioned by the navy 13 July 1945. She was assigned to the Pacific where she provided repair service, completing her deployment in August 1947, and was decommissioned 24 January 1948. Recommissioned 12 April 1952, she made three deployments in support of the 7th Fleet, serving in Korean waters during the Third Korean Winter and the Korea Summer–Fall 1953 campaigns. She received one battle star. After the Korean War she served with ice-breaking operations and was decommissioned 15 July 1959. She was struck from the navy list 1 July 1960.

Kermit Roosevelt ARG 16: [d. 5,159; 441'6" × 56'11"; 12.5 k; cpl. 525; a. 1-5", 4-40mm, 12-20mm; Class Luzon] Originally laid as *Deal Island* but renamed *Kermit Roosevelt* 29

September 1944, she was acquired by the navy 21 October 1944 and commissioned 31 May 1945. She aided nationalist Chinese forces on the Chinese mainland. She made four deployments to the Far East near Sasebo, Japan; Wonsan; Hungnam and Pusan. She saw service in Korean waters during the North Korean Aggression, Communist China Aggression, and Korea Summer–Fall 1953 campaigns, receiving three battle stars. Decommissioned on 31 October 1959, on 25 August 1960 she was sold for scrap.

Laertes AR 20: [d. 5,801; 441'6" × 56'11"; 12.5; cpl. 525; a. 4-40mm, 12-20mm; Class Xanthus Class] Laid down as the *Dutiful* under a Maritime Commission contract, she was acquired by the navy and converted to a repair ship. She was commissioned 24 March 1945. During World War II she repaired ships damaged during the final phases of the war. She was decommissioned 15 January 1947, then recommissioned 19 December 1951 and deployed to the Far East, serving more than five months steaming off the coasts of Japan and Korea. She saw service in Korean waters during the Korean Defense Summer–Fall 1952 and Third Korean Winter campaigns, winning two battle stars. Decommissioned 26 February 1954, she entered the Pacific Reserve Fleet.

Luzon II ARG 2: [d. 4,023; 441'6" × 56'11"; 12 k; cpl. 525; a. 1-5", 3-3", 4-40mm, 12-20mm, Class Lassen] Originally laid as *Samuel Bowles* under a Maritime Commission contract, she was acquired by the navy, renamed *Luzon* and commissioned 12 October 1943. During World War II she served in the Pacific. She was decommissioned 24 June 1947 but, in response to the needs of the Korean War, recommissioned 20 September 1950. She provided repair service for ships of the 7th Fleet and saw service in Korean waters during the Korea Summer–Fall 1953 campaign, receiving one battle star. She was decommissioned 1 July 1960 and struck from the Naval Register on 1 September 1961.

8

TENDERS AND TUGS, RESCUE, REPAIR, AND SALVAGE

A ship is just a ship, but a tug is a home.
— Darian Cobb, sailor

These special service ships are lumped together because of their rescue characteristics, for these are the ships that took care of other ships and planes, the tugs that moved them when needed, as well as salvage and rescue ships. The ships considered are the destroyer tenders (AD), the salvage ship (ARS), the submarine tender (AS) the submarine rescue ship (ASR), fleet ocean tugs (ATF), auxiliary fleet tugs (ATA), and seaplane tenders (AVP).

Destroyer Tender (AD)

Destroyer tenders, designed to aid and repair destroyers at sea, did more than serve destroyers, of course, for the crew was primarily made up of technicians and repair specialists, and they were able to offer repair and replacement service to many ships. The first of the tenders was the Dixie-class ship *Prairie* (AD 15) commissioned in 1940. There were six destroyer tenders on duty during the Korean War. As was true of other tenders, the increased size and automation of modern destroyers, plus their increasing reliance on nuclear power, made the destroyer tender less valuable as time went on.

Bryce Canyon AD 36: [d. 14,900; 492 × 70; 18 k; cpl. 859; a. 1-5", 4-3"; 2 twin 40mm, 8 twin 20mm; Class Shenandoah] Launched 7 March 1946 and commissioned 15 September 1950, she reported to the Pacific Fleet. Beginning 12 April 1951, she spent the next seven months in Japanese waters repairing and servicing vessels. She made two additional trips to the Far East, the last in Korean waters. She received one battle star for her service there. She was decommissioned on 30 June 1981, the only ship in the United States Navy to have won five consecutive Gold "E" efficiency awards. She was struck from the navy register 30 June 1981.

Dixie II AD 14: [d. 16,500; 530 × 73'3"; 18 k; cpl. 1262; a. 4-5"; Class Dixie] Launched 27 May 1939 and commissioned 25 April 1940, she served with the Pacific Fleet during World

War II. She participated in Operation Crossroads, the atomic tests, and was in the Sasebo Channel when hostilities broke out in Korean. She was immediately sent to clear the mines at Chinnampo. She served as the flagship during the January 1951 amphibious feint at Kansong, and on 31 March 1952 as the flagship for Rear Admiral John E. Ginrich. She participated in the First UN Counter Offensive, Second Korean Winter, Korean Defense Summer–Fall 1952, Third Korean Winter, and Korea Summer–Fall 1953 campaigns. She was awarded five battle stars for Korean service.

Frontier AD 25: [d. 11,755; 492 × 69'6"; 18 k; cpl. 826; a. 1-5", 4-3"; Class Klondike] Launched 25 March 1945 and commissioned 2 March 1946, the *Frontier* was decommissioned 29 September 1947, but recommissioned for Korean service on 11 November 1952. She saw service in Korean waters during periods from 15 June 1952 until 20 December 1953. She was finally decommissioned 28 June 1968 and sold.

Hamul AD 20: [d. 14,900; 492 × 69'6"; 18 k; cpl. 857; a. 1-5", 4-3", 2 twin 40mm; Class Shenandoah] Launched May 1940 and commissioned 14 June 1942, she sailed as the *Sea Panther* and *Doctor Lykes*. During World War II she participated in the capture of U-505, the first U.S. capture of a ship on the high seas since 1815. She operated in Korean waters during the Third Korean Winter campaign. There was always some question about her name. Since all AKs are named after stars, it is assumed she was named after the star Hamal, by typographical error, though she continued with the name *Hamul* even after being converted to a destroyer tender. She was decommissioned 15 June and finally struck from the navy list on 1 July 1963.

Piedmont AD 17: [d. 14,037; 530'6" × 73'4"; 20 k; cpl. 1,181; a. 4-5", 8-40mm; Class Dixie] Launched 7 December 1941 and commissioned 5 January 1944, she served as a destroyer tender during World War II. She was in Japan when the Korean War began. She completed four tours in the Western Pacific, providing tender service to ships of the U.S., Canada, Colombia, New Zealand, South Korea and Thailand navies. The *Piedmont* operated in Korean waters during the North Korean Aggression, Second Korean Winter, Korean Defense Summer–Fall 1952, and Third Korean Winter campaigns. The *Piedmont* received four battle stars for Korean service. She later served during the Vietnam War. She was decommissioned 30 September 1982 and struck from the navy list on the same day. She was loaned to Turkey and then sold 6 August 1987.

Prairie II AD 15: [d. 16,500; 530'6" × 73'4"; 18 k; cpl. 1,698; a. 4-5", 4-40mm; Class Dixie] Launched as the second *Prairie* on 9 December 1939 and commissioned 5 August 1940, she entered the Atlantic theater during World War II. Late in the war she was transferred to the Pacific. When the North Koreans invaded she sailed to support UN forces from 2 February to 3 August 1951 and 6 April to 10 September 1952, and again from late August 1953 to 11 April 1954. She was decommissioned 26 March 1993.

Net Tenders AN

Naval net tenders are named after trees or old USN monitors. They are assigned to guard and maintain harbor nets. As station vessels they also preformed numerous duties associated with maintaining harbors, as maintaining moorings and buoys. They also served as harbor passenger boats.

Elder AN 20 (YN-15): [d. 560; 163'2" × 30'6"; 12 k; cpl. 48; a. 1-3"; Class Aloe] Launched 19 June 1941, she was placed in service in November 1941. The *Elder* was redesignated AN 20 on 20 January 1944. She served in the Pacific during World War II. The ship suffered a nearly destructive fire on 11 March 1950 but managed to survive. She served in Korean waters during periods between 6 May and 3 December 1951, providing net operations at Yokosuka, Japan. She was decommissioned 18 December 1959.

Etlah AN 79: [d. 785; 168'6" × 33'10"; 12 k; cpl. 46; a. 1-3"; Class Cohoes] Launched 16 December 1944 and commissioned 16 April 1945, the *Etlah* served with the task force conducting atomic weapons tests at Bikini in Operation Crossroads. Decommissioned on 14 March 1947, she was recommissioned 10 August 1950 and set sail for the Far East. She worked as net guard at Pusan and Cheju, Korea. She served in Korean waters during the Third Korean Winter and Korea Summer–Fall 1953 campaigns and received two battle stars. She was decommissioned 31 May 1960.

Landing Ship Repair (ARL)

During World War II when the U.S. Navy was building and using landing craft by the thousands, it acknowledged the necessity to provide repair and maintenance near the action. The existing repair ships were not well designed or equipped to deal with the small, wooden craft. A shallow-draft repair ship was needed, and the Auxiliary Repair Ship Light (Landing) was designed and produced from converted LSTs. Between 1943 and 1945, when conversions were done, the tank decks were divided to make specialized shops. A superstructure was also added on the main forward deck. Two cargo booms were added and an A-frame boom was added on the port side. The normal complement of about 250 men worked on deck and in engineering, communications, repair and supply. During the Korean War they serviced mostly landing craft.

Askari ARL 30: [d. 3,960; 328 × 50; 11.6 k; cpl. 253; a. 1-3", 8-40mm; Class Achelous] Launched 8 December 1944, she was commissioned 15 March 1945 as the LST 1131. After conversion she was recommissioned as the *Askari* on 23 July 1945. She participated in nuclear testing operations. She sailed for Korea in August 1950 where she participated in the Inchon Landing, and at Wonsan, Hungnam, and Pusan. She saw service in Korean waters during the North Korean Aggression, Communist China Aggression, and the First UN Counter Offensive campaigns, receiving four battle stars. She was decommissioned 21 March 1956, and recommissioned 13 August 1966 for service in Vietnam. On 1 September 1971 she was decommissioned again and loaned to the Indonesian navy. She was not struck from the navy list until February 1979. At this point she was sold to the Indonesian navy.

Atlas II ARL 7: [d. 3,960; 328 × 50; 11.6 k; cpl. 253; a. 1-3", 2-40mm, 2-20mm. Class Achelous] Laid as LST 231 and launched 19 October 1943, she was redesignated the *Atlas II* and commissioned 3 November 1943. She served in support of landing ships during the Normandy landing in Europe. She was decommissioned 13 September 1946, then recommissioned 1 June 1951 and sent to Korea. She participated in Korean waters from 2 December 1951 through 27 July 1954. She was decommissioned 13 April 1956, struck from the navy list 1 June 1972 and sold 18 September 1973.

Satyr ARL 23: [d. 3,960; 328 × 50; 11.6 k; cpl. 250; a. 1-3", 2-40mm and 2-20mm; Class Achelous] Launched 13 November 1944 and commissioned 27 November 1944 as the LST 852, she was converted to a landing craft repair ship (ARL 23) on 28 April 1945. She was decommissioned 28 December 1944 and recommissioned 28 April 1945 as the *Satyr*. She was reactivated 8 September 1950. She participated in activities near Pusan, and Sasebo, Japan.

She saw service in Korean waters during the Communist China Spring Offensive and the UN Summer–Fall Offensive campaigns, receiving two battle stars. She was decommissioned 17 April 1956 then called into service again in December 1966 for Vietnam. She was transferred to the South Vietnamese navy on 30 September 1971 and recommissioned as the VNS *Vinh Long*. With the fall of the South Vietnamese government, she served in the Philippine navy.

Sphinx ARL 24: [d. 2,130; 328 × 50; 11.2 k; cpl. 253; a. 1-3", 8-20mm; Class Achelous] Laid as LST 963 on 20 October 1944, she was redesignated the *Sphinx* and launched 18 November 1944. She was commissioned on 10 May 1945. Assigned to the Pacific Fleet during World War II, she participated in Operation Crossroads, the atomic testing. Declassified 26 May 1947, she was placed back in service on 3 November 1950. She saw service in Korean waters during the Second Korean Winter campaign. She earned one battle star for Korean service. Placed out of commission 31 January 1956, she was reactivated for Vietnam in January 1967. She was finally placed in reserves 30 September 1971.

Salvage Ship (ARS)

Rescue and salvage ships are designed to give immediate attention to combat ships that have received battle damage, or, if necessary, to tow them to safety for repair. They also provided rapid firefighting and pumping. During World War II twenty-two ARS were constructed (ARS 44–49 were cancelled) and they continued to provide service in both the Atlantic and Pacific fleets, in the Naval Reserve Force and in the Coast Guard until well into the 1990s.

Bolster ARS 38: [d. 1,497; 213 × 39; 15 k; cpl. 120; Class Yuma] Launched 23 December 1944, she was commissioned 1 May 1945. She saw service in Korean waters during the North Korean Aggression, Communist China Aggression, First UN Counter Offensive, Communist China Spring Offensive, Second Korean Winter, and Korean Defense Summer–Fall 1952 campaigns. Decommissioned 1 February 1994, she was struck from the navy list the same day.

Conserver ARS 39: [d. 1,441; 213'6" × 39; 15 k; cpl. 120; a. 2-40mm; Diver Class] She was launched 27 January and commissioned 9 June 1945, and she participated in Operation Crossroads, the atomic bomb tests. She saw service in Korean waters during the North Korean Aggression, Communist China Aggression, Inchon Landing, First UN Counter Offensive, UN Summer–Fall Offensive, Second Korean Winter, Third Korean Winter, and Korea Summer–Fall 1953 campaigns. She was awarded nine battle stars for service in Korea. She was decommissioned 1 April 1994 and struck from the navy list on that date.

Current ARS 22: [d. 1,950; 213'6" × 39; 13 k; cpl.120; a. 2-40mm; Class Diver] Launched 25 September 1943 and commissioned 14 June 1944, she was then decommissioned 9 February 1948, only to be recommissioned 10 October 1951 for Korean War service. She participated in the Second Korean Winter, Korean Defense Summer–Fall 1952, and Korea Summer–Fall 1953 campaigns. She was struck from the navy list 1 June 1973 and sunk 27 June 1975.

Deliver ARS 23: [d. 1,530; 213 × 39; 15 k; cpl. 120; a. 2-40 mm; Class Diver] Launched 25 September 1943 and commissioned 14 July 1944, she saw service in Korean waters during the UN Summer–Fall Offensive, Second Korean Winter, and Korea Summer–Fall 1953 campaigns. She was sold to the Republic of Korea navy on 1 August 1979.

Reclaimer ARS 42: [d. 2,160; 213'6" × 43; 16 k; cpl. 120; a. 4-40mm; Class Diver. This salvage ship was laid down 10 November 1944, launched 23 June 1945 and commissioned 20

December 1945. She operated during the Operation Crossroads atomic tests, and was decommissioned 23 June 1947. Recommissioned for service in Korea on 1 December 1950, she participated in the Communist China Spring Offensive, UN Summer–Fall Offensive, Second Korean Winter, Third Korean Winter, and Korea Summer–Fall 1953 campaigns. While there she towed burning ships, assisted in minesweeping at Wonsan Harbor, and towed the British hospital ship *Maine*. She operated in Korea through October 1953. She earned six battle stars for Korea. She was decommissioned 16 September 1994.

Safeguard ARS 25: [d. 1,630; 213'6" × 39; 15 k; cpl. 120; a. 4-40 mm; Class Diver] Launched 20 November 1953 and commissioned 30 September 1944, the *Safeguard* was decommissioned 12 December 1947 and then recommissioned 13 February 1952. She saw service in Korean waters during the Korean Defense Summer–Fall 1952 and the Third Korean Winter campaigns. She was struck from the navy list 6 August 1987 and sold to Turkey on the 18th of that month.

Seaplane Tender (AV) and Small Seaplane Tender (AVP)

In 1936 the first of the "bird boats" (AM minesweepers) were designated as small seaplane tenders with numbers from AVP 1–9. Prior to this time seaplanes had been attended to by minesweepers. During 1938 and 1939 several of the World War I "flush-deck and four-pipe" destroyers were reclassified as seaplane tenders. The program expanded again during World War II when, during 1940–41, the Navy built 44 Barnegat Class AVP, 28 of which were completed. The ships were widely used in support of aviation, and were often used for other missions. During the Korean War armament was provided for tenders. This usually meant the addition of two depth charge racks off the stern, one 3" battery, two 20mm single mounts, and occasionally two mousetrap depth-charge launchers on the forecastle.

Bering Strait WAVP-382: [d. 1,766; 310'9" × 41'2"; 18.2 k; cpl. 215; a. 1-5"; Class Barnegat] Launched 15 January and commissioned 19 July 1944, she was decommissioned 21 June 1946 and loaned to the United States Coast Guard. Identified as WAVP on 17 September 1948, she is not listed in *DANFS*, but is included in the Coast Guard listing as being eligible for the Korean Service Medal. Her designation was changed again, to WHEC, on 1 May 1966. Decommissioned in June 1968, she was transferred to the South Vietnam navy and renamed *Tran Quang Khai*.

Corson AVP 37: [d. 1,650; 319'9" × 41'1"; 18 k; cpl. 215; a. 2-5"; Class Barnegat] Launched 16 July 1944 and commissioned 3 December 1944, she tended planes in the Pacific. She was placed out of commission and in the reserves 21 June 1946. Recommissioned 13 February 1951, she participated in the western Pacific at Japan, Okinawa, and the Pescadores. She saw service during the Third Korean Winter. She was placed out of commission and in reserves on 9 March 1956. She was decommissioned in March 1956 and destroyed as a target in 1966.

Gardiners Bay AVP 39: [d. 2,592; 310'9" × 41'2"; 18.2 k; cpl. 215, a. 1-5", 8-40mm; Class Barnegat] Launched 2 December 1944 and commissioned 11 February 1945, she assisted in Japanese waters following World War II, and did four tours of service in Korean waters, including the North Korean Aggression, Communist China Aggression, First UN Counter Offensive, and Summer–Fall 1953 campaigns. She received four battle stars for Korea. She was decommissioned 1 February 1958 and transferred to Norway where she took the name *Haakon VII*.

Gresham WAVP 387/AGP-9/WAGW 387: [d. 2,530 loaded; 309'9" × 13'6"; 18.3 k.; cpl. 151; a. 1-5", 2 tt: Class Casco] Built as a seaplane tender by the navy, she was converted to a PT boat tender, named *Willoughby*, and was turned over to the Coast Guard after decommissioning 25 June 1946. Her name was struck from the navy list 19 July 1946. She was converted to a weather vessel and renamed *Gresham*. She served at a series of ocean stations in the Pacific and was eligible for the Korean Service Medal. She participated in the Vietnam War and later would carry Soviet Premier Nikita Khruschev on a tour of San Francisco Bay. She was decommissioned 25 April 1973 and sold for scrap in 1973.

Kenneth Whiting AV 14: [d. 8,510; 492 × 69'6"; 18.7 k; cpl. 1,077; a. 2-5", 12-40mm, 16-20mm; Class Whiting] Launched 15 December 1943, she served in the Pacific during World War II, then was decommissioned 29 May 1947. With the outbreak of war in Korea she was recommissioned 24 October 1951. She sailed for Far East duty 13 March 1952 and operated out of Iwakuni. She returned for another deployment during the final days of the war. The *Kenneth Whiting* served in Korean waters during periods between 29 March 1952 and 27 July 1954. The ship was again decommissioned on 30 September 1958, then was stricken on 1 July 1961 and sold for scrap.

Onslow AVP 48: [d. 2,800; 310'9" × 41'2"; 18.2 k; cpl. 367; a. 1-5", 8-40mm; Class Barnegat] Launched 20 September 1942 and commissioned 22 December 1942, the AVP served with Task Group 57.3 during World War II, and remained in the Pacific for the Asian occupation. She was decommissioned in June 1947. Reactivated in January 1951, she operated in Japan and Korea tending planes. The *Onslow* participated in Korean waters during the Korean Summer–Fall 1952 campaign. She was decommissioned 22 April 1960 and struck from the register on 1 June 1960. She was sold to the Philippine Presidents Line in October of that year. She was later hired by the navy to evacuate South Vietnamese refugees.

Pine Island AV 12: [d. 14,000 (f); 540'5" × 69'3"; 18 k; cpl. 684; 4-5", 3-40mm, 40 dual 40mm, 20-20mm; Class Currituck] Launched 26 February 1944 and commissioned 26 April 1945, she was quickly involved in the final period of World War II. After service in Japan she was decommissioned 1 May 1950 and recommissioned 7 October 1950. In Korean waters during periods from 31 December 1950 to 27 February 1954, she tended seaplanes that were flying missions over Korea. She was decommissioned 16 June 1967 and transferred to the National Defense Reserve Fleet.

Salisbury Sound AV 13: [d. 13,635 (f); 540'5" × 69'3"; 19.2 k; cpl. 684; a. 4-5", 20-40mm, 20-20mm; Class Barnegat] Launched 18 June 1944 and commissioned 26 November 1945, she was deployed in the western Pacific during portions of each year from then to 1966. She tended planes in Korea and the Taiwan Strait, and served in Korean waters during periods between 6 August 1950 to 23 February 1953. She was decommissioned 31 March 1967 and transferred to the Maritime Administration, entering the reserve fleet on 3 July 1968. She was sold on 7 February 1972.

Suisun AVP 53: [d. 2,592; 310'9" × 41'2"; 18.2 k; cpl. 367; a. 1-5", 8-40mm, 6-20mm; Class Barnegat] Launched 14 March 1943 and commissioned 13 September 1944, she served at Eniwetok, the Marshall Islands and the Mariana Islands. She deployed to the Far East from 12 February to 6 August 1951 and from 26 November 1951 to 25 May 1952, and saw service in Korean waters during the Second Korean Winter campaign. She received two battle stars for service in Korea. She was placed out of commission and in reserve 5 August 1955 and struck from the navy list on 1 April 1966. She was sunk as a target in October of the same year.

Submarine Tender (AS)

Since World War I, submarine tenders provided maintenance and logistic support for submarines. The vast distances in the Pacific made this service even more significant, and the crews, primarily technicians and repairmen, made it possible for the submarines to operate for longer periods of time. These tenders were able to supply just about everything needed, and if it was unavailable, to make most parts required. The facilities included pattern shops, machine shops, basic foundries, presses, welding machines, electronic and optical services, medical and dental facilities. As well, they carried the supplies and replacement parts for just about everything from toothpaste to periscope lenses. They were critical to the success during World War II, often becoming "mother ships," as well. At the end of World War II there were seventeen submarine tenders in operation, but all but four of these were retired through the reduction of naval forces. During the Korean War, two were brought back into service.

Florikan ASR 9: [d. 1,780; 251'4" × 42; 16.5 k; cpl. 102; a. 2-5"; Class Chanticleer] While listed as an ASR, much of her Korean service was as a tender (AS) and she is listed as a tender in several sources. Launched 14 June 1942, she was commissioned 5 September 1943. She served in Korean waters from 19 September 1951 until 26 September 1953. She was decommissioned 2 August 1991 and was struck from the navy list 3 September 1991.

Sperry AS 12: [d. 9,250; 530'7" × 73'4"; 15.4 k.; cpl. 1,307; a. 4-5"; Class Fulton] She was launched 17 December 1941 and commissioned 1 May 1942. During World War II she mainly served in Pacific waters and then remained active during the period between the wars. From 1951 to 1953 she saw service in Korea. In some sources the USS *Sperry* is confused with the *Charles S. Sperry*, a destroyer.

Submarine Rescue (ASR)

Submarine rescue ships served as surface support vessels for submarine rescue operations. They used the McCann rescue chamber, and supported divers in pressurized chambers. They also served as operational control ships during deep-sea salvage operations, and performed rescue, escort, fueling and tender service for submarines.

Chanticleer III ASR 7: [d. 1,780; 251'4" × 42; 16 k; cpl. 102; a. 2-3"; Class Chanticleer] *Chanticleer III* was launched 29 May 1942 and commissioned 20 November 1942. The ship served in the Pacific during World War II. She was in Korean waters during periods from 7 December 1950 to 27 July 1954. She was placed out of service 2 August 1991 and struck 3 September 1991.

Coucal ASR 8: [d. 1,780; 251'4" × 42; 16.5 k; cpl. 102; a. 2-5"; Class Chanticleer] Launched 29 May 1942 and commissioned 22 January 1943, she served submarines of the 7th Fleet, and operated in Pacific waters during World War II. She participated in Operation Crossroads. She served in the Far East during deployment in 1951–1953, during which she cruised the Korean coast in support and salvage duties. The ship was in Korean waters during periods from 17 April 1951 to 20 April 1953. She received one battle star for Korea. She was struck from the navy list 15 September 1977 and sunk as a target.

Greenlet ASR 10: [d. 2,042; 251'4" × 42; 15 k; cpl. 102; a. 2-3", 8-20mm, dc; Class Chanticleer] Laid down 15 October 1941 and commissioned 29 May 1943, she served at Pearl

Harbor and Midway during World War II. She was sent to Korea on 6 July 1950 and operated there for six months, stationed out of Yokosuka. She was transferred to the Turkish navy on 12 June 1970 (some official records say 1973).

Fleet Tug and Auxiliary Fleet Tug (AFT, AT, ATA)

The purpose of a fleet tug was deep-ocean towing and salvage operations. The tugs also towed target vessels for practice gunnery, with the target towed about a mile behind the ship. The crew consisted of at least five sailors qualified as divers, and beach gear which allowed her to create pulling advantages to free grounded vessels. The tug *Lipan* (AT 85) had the motto *Pauca Sed Fortissima* ("Small but Mighty") and that is a perfect description of the tugs that service the fleet. Loss of power, or damage that prevented movement, was fortunately not widespread, but when it happened the prime solution was to call on the oceangoing tug capable of pulling great weight even in the most difficult seas.

Abnaki ATF 96: [d. 1,240; 205 × 38'6"; 16.5 k; cpl. 85; a. 1-3", 2-40mm; Class Abnaki] Launched 22 April 1943 and commissioned 25 November 1943, the *Abnaki* operated in the Atlantic until transferred to Japanese waters. Following the war she remained in the Pacific, and after the outbreak of the Korean War she supported UN forces from July 1951 to February 1952. She participated during the Communist China Spring Offensive and the Second Korean Winter campaigns. She earned three battle stars for Korean service. Decommissioned 30 September 1978, she was transferred to Mexico and struck from the navy list the same day.

Apache IV ATF 67: [d. 1,675; 205 × 38'6"; 16.5 k; cpl. 85; a. 1-3", 12-.50 cal. mg; Class Abnaki] *Apache IV* was launched 8 May 1942 and commissioned 12 December 1942 after which she sailed as a part of Task Force 31 for the invasion of Bougainville, then later at Saipan, Guam, and Luzon. On 15 May 1944 she was redesignated a fleet ocean tug (AFT). She was decommissioned on 3 December 1946 but recalled on 20 July 1951. She arrived in Korea on 17 December and began operation near Wonsan Harbor. She operated in Korean waters during the Second Korean Winter and the Korean Defense Summer–Fall 1952 campaigns. She received two battle stars for service in Korea and went on to participate in the Vietnam conflict. She was decommissioned 27 February 1974 and struck from the navy list.

Arikara ATF 98: [d. 1,589; 205 × 38'6"; 16.5 k; cpl. 85; a. 1-3,", 2-40mm; Class Abnaki] Launched 22 June 1943 and commissioned 5 January 1944, she served in the Atlantic during World War II, participating in the maneuvering of the two "mulberries," the artificial harbors on the French coast. During the Korean War she saw service at Pusan, Wonsan, and Sasebo. In 1952 she was back in Korean waters at Wonsan, Cho Do, and Pusan. She saw service in Korean waters during the North Korean Aggression, Communist China Aggression, Inchon Landing, Second Korean Winter and Korean Defense Summer–Fall campaigns. She earned five battle stars. Later she served in Vietnam. She was decommissioned and transferred to Chile where she sailed under the name *Aldea*. She was decommissioned by the Chilean navy and sunk as a target in August 1992.

Chowanoc ATF 100: [d. 1,240; 206 × 38'6"; 16 k; cpl. 86; a. 1-3"; Class Cherokee] Launched 20 August 1943, she was commissioned 21 February 1944. During the close of World War II she operated in the Marshall Islands, and took part in the invasion of Leyte. She participated in the Operation Crossroads atomic test. During the Korean War she operated in Korean waters during the Korean Summer–Fall 1953 campaign. She received one battle star for Korean service. She was stricken 1 October 1977.

Chickasaw III ATF 83: [d. 1,240; 206 × 38'6"; 16 k; cpl. 86; a. 1-3"; Class Cherokee] Launched as the third *Chickawaw* on 23 July 1942, she was commissioned as an AT on 4 February 1943, after which she reported to service in the Pacific. On 15 May 1944 she was reclassified as ATF 83. She saw service in Korean waters during the Third Korean Winter and the Korea Summer–Fall 1953 campaigns. She received two battle stars for Korean service.

Cocopa ATF 101: [d. 1,240; 205 × 38'6"; 16 k; cpl. 85; a. 1-3"; Class Cherokee] Launched 5 October 1943 and commissioned 25 March 1944 as an AT, she was reclassified ATF 101 on 15 May 1944. During the close of World War II she operated in both the Atlantic and the Pacific. Later she ran between Hawaii and the Far East and was in Korean waters during the Korea Summer–Fall 1953 campaign. She received one battle star for Korean service. She was struck from the navy list 30 September 1978.

Hitchiti ATF 103: [d. 1,240; 205 × 38'6"; 16 k; cpl. 85; a. 1-3", 2-40mm; Class Cherokee] Decommissioned on 30 April 1948 after World War II service, she was recommissioned 3 January 1951. The *Hitchiti* operated in Korean waters during the Communist China Spring Offensive, UN Summer–Fall Offensive, and the Second Korean Winter campaigns. Sold to Mexico 1 September 1976, she was struck from the navy list 30 September 1978. There is some question about her Korean service but she is listed in *DANFS*.

Mataco ATF 86: [d. 1,240; 1,205 × 38'6"; 16 k; cpl. 97; a. 2-40mm, 2-20mm; Class Navajo] Laid 27 June 1942, she was commissioned 29 May 1943. She was redesignated ATF on 15 May 1944. She was in the Philippines when the Korean War began, and she performed combat salvage and air-sea rescue, beginning with the Inchon invasion. For fourteen months she supported the United Nations forces in Korea, serving in Korean waters during the North Korean Aggression, Communist China Aggression, and Korean Defense Summer–Fall 1952 campaigns. She received four battle stars for service in Korea. She later saw service during the Vietnam War.

Moctobi ATF 105/AT: [d. 1,240; 205 × 38'6"; 16.5 k; cpl. 85; a. 1-3", 2 twin 40mm, 2-20mm; Class Abnaki] Launched 25 March 1944, redesignated fleet ocean tug on 15 May 1944, she was commissioned 25 July 1944. Decommissioned 30 June 1948 and recommissioned 8 November 1950, she participated in the Communist China Spring Offensive and the UN Summer–Fall Offensive. She earned two battle stars for Korean service. She was decommissioned 30 September 1985, struck from the navy list 27 January 1992, and sold.

Quapaw ATF 110: [d. 1,646; 205 × 38'6"; 16 k; cpl. 85; a. 1-3", 4-40mm; Class Navajo] Launched 15 May 1943 and commissioned 6 May 1944, she was redesignated ATF 110 on 15 May 1944. During World War II she served in the Pacific. She was decommissioned 30 April 1948. Recommissioned on 5 December 1950, she headed for Korea where she provided service at Inchon from 30 April 1950 to 17 July 1951, and at Wonsan from 19 July through 3 August 1951. During 1952 and 1953 she operated in the areas of Cho Do and Tae Chong Do. She operated in Korean waters during the First UN Counter Offensive, Communist China Spring Offensive, UN Summer–Fall Offensive, Korean Defense Summer–Fall 1952, and the Korea Summer–Fall 1953 campaigns. She received five battle stars for the Korean service.

Takelma ATF 113: [d. 1,589; 205 × 38'6"; 16.6 k; cpl. 85; a. 1-3", 2-40mm; Class Abnaki] Launched 1 September 1943 and commissioned on 3 August 1944, she operated along the California coast until moving on to the Pacific where she towed vessels at Ulithi, Leyte, Hollandia, Subic Bay, and Milne Bay. In 1947 she towed target ships for atomic bomb testing. Following the outbreak of war in Korea she operated for a year at Subic Bay and in Japanese waters. On her second tour she operated at Sokcho, Pusan and Wonsan, Cho Do, and Yongyong Do. She participated in Korean waters during the Korean Defense Summer–Fall 1952 and Third Korean Winter campaigns. In January of 1953 she again entered the combat area, returning to Sasebo on 22 February. During the Vietnam War she was located at "Yankee Station." She received two battle stars for service in Korea. She was eventually traded to the Argentina navy and renamed *Castillo*.

Tawakoni ATF 114: [d .1,330; 205 × 38'6"; 16.5 k; cpl. 85; a. 1-3", 2-40mm. Class Abnaki] Launched 28 October 1943 and commissioned 16 September 1944, she operated in the Pacific, participating in the Iwo Jima campaign and at Okinawa. She remained in Pacific waters after the war and on 15 November 1950 she joined the Task Force 90 Amphibious Force, Far East, working near Inchon and Hungnam. She operated in Korean waters during the Communist China Aggression, First UN Counter Offensive, and Communist China Spring Offensive campaigns. She received three battle stars for service in Korea. She would later participate in the Vietnam War. She was struck from the navy list 1 June 1978 and sold to Taiwan.

Tawasa ATF 92: [d. 1,330; 205 × 38'6"; 16.5 k; cpl. 85; a. 1-3", 2-40mm; Class Bannock] Launched 22 February 1943 and commissioned 17 July 1943, she was assigned to Service Force, Pacific Fleet, and participated in campaigns at the Gilbert and Marshall islands, and in that area until the end of World War II. From 4 June 1952 until 1 March 1953 she supplied United Nations forces in Korea and operated near the ports of Cho Do, Sokcho, and Chinhae. She operated in Korean waters during the Korean Defense Summer–Fall 1952 and Third Korean Winter campaigns. She received two battle stars for Korea and went on to serve during the Vietnam War. She was decommissioned and removed from the navy list 1 April 1975.

Yuma II ATF 94: [d. 1,589; 205 × 38'6"; 16.5 k; cpl. 85; a. 1-3", 2-40mm; Class Navajo] Launched 17 July and commissioned 31 August 1943, she operated in the Pacific during World War II, participating at the Solomon and New Hebrides islands, and with the Western Islands Attack Group. When the Korean War broke out she performed missions in support of UN troops, and served during the UN Summer–Fall Offensive and the Second Korean Winter campaigns. She received two battle stars for Korea. She was decommissioned 11 March 1959 and placed on loan to Pakistan. She was struck from the navy list on 25 March 1959.

Auxiliary Fleet Tug (AT, ATA)

Cree AT 84: [d. 1,240; 205 × 38'6"; 16 k; cpl. 85; a. 1-3"; Class Cherokee] Launched 17 August 1942 and commissioned 28 March 1943, she was reclassified as an ATF in May 1944. She was involved in the Pacific during World War II, and with the arrival of the Korean War she participated in salvage, towing, and supporting the Inchon Landing. In Korean waters during the North Korean Aggression, Communist China Aggression, and the First UN Counter Offensive campaigns, she received three battle stars.

Keosanqua ATA 198: [d. 534; 143 × 34; 13 k; cpl. 48; a. 1-3", 2-20mm] Originally ATR 125, she was redesignated ATA 198 and launched 17 January 1945. She was commissioned 19 March 1945 and served in the Pacific during World War II. Renamed 16 July 1948, she participated in the UN Summer–Fall Offensive, Second Korean Winter, and Korean Defense Summer–Fall 1952 campaigns. She was transferred to Republic of Korea navy 1 February 1962 and renamed *Yong Mun*.

Lipan AT-85: [d. 1,675; 205.4 × 38'5"; 14 k; a. 1-3", twin 40mm and 20mm; Class

Navajo] Commissioned 29 April 1943 and designated ATF, fleet ocean tug on 15 May 1944, she served primarily in the Pacific during World War II. She served in Korean waters during the North Korean Aggression, Communist China Aggression, Inchon Landing, and Korea Summer–Fall 1953 campaigns. She was sunk as a target ship 22 January 1990.

Molala ATF 106: [d. 1,330; 205 × 38'6"; 16 k; cpl. 85; a. 1-3", 2-40mm, 2-20mm; Class Abnaki] Launched 23 December 1942 and commissioned 29 September 1943, she operated from the Marshall Islands, and supported the Iwo Jima invasion. She participated in Korean service during the Korean Defense Summer–Fall 1952, Third Korean Winter, and Korea Summer–Fall 1953 campaigns. She received three battle stars for service in Korea.

Munsee ATF 107: [d. 1,680; 205 × 39'3"; 16 k; cpl. 85; a. 1-3", 2-40mm; Class Abnaki] Launched 21 January 1943, she was deployed between Midway and the Marshall Islands. Redesignated ATF (from AT) 15 May 1944, she screened transports during the landings at Palaus. In Korean service between 17 August 1953 and 8 February 1954, she would later serve in Vietnam.

Sarsi AT-111:[d. 1,300; 205 × 38'6"; 16 k; cpl. 88; a. 1-3", 2-40mm, 2-20mm; Class Abnaki] Commissioned 24 June 1944, she served in the Aleutians during World War II. On 24 March 1952 she sailed for Korea, taking ammunition. She moored near Wonsan Harbor and performed towing, salvage, patrol, escort, buoy tender and transportation duties. During the next few months she operated between southeastern Korea and Kyushu. On the 27 August 1952 she was hit, probably by a floating mine, and despite the efforts of the crew, sank within twenty minutes. Four men were killed, the others escaped in the ship's whaleboat. The destroyers *Boyd* and minesweepers *Zeal* and *Competent* rescued the crew. Serving in Korean waters during the Second Korean Winter and the Korean Defense Summer–Fall 1952 campaigns, she earned two campaign stars.

Unadilla III ATA 182: [d. 860; 145 × 33; 14 k; cpl. 46; a. 1-3"; Class ATA-121] Launched 5 August and commissioned 16 October 1944, she supported the war effort in the Pacific until she was decommissioned 26 November 1946. She received the name *Unadilla* 15 June 1948 and was recommissioned 3 May 1951. She was twice employed in Korean waters, participating during the Second Korean Winter, Korean Defense Summer–Fall 1952, Third Korean Winter, and Summer–Fall 1953 campaigns. On her second tour she carried a medical unit to Ullong Do to combat a typhus outbreak. She received two battle stars, and a Korean Presidential Unit Citation. Decommissioned 2 July 1955 and struck 1 September 1961, she was disposed of between 1972 and 1975.

Ute AS 76: [d. 1,589; 205 × 38'6"; 16.2 k; cpl. 85; a. 1-3", 2-40mm; Class Navajo] Recommissioned in September 1951 after World War II service, she sailed for Korea in January 1952. She operated in Wonsan Harbor, laying buoys, participating in shore bombardments, and assuming salvage duties for several ships. She earned the name "Good Shoot Ute" from forces blockading the west coast. She also operated in Song Jin Harbor. Assigned picket duty as well, she provided mail and supplies, and delivered 20,000 gallons of fresh water. She spent four combat tours in Korea participating in the Second Korean Winter and Korean Defense Summer–Fall 1952 campaigns, receiving two battle stars. She served in Vietnam and then was struck from navy list October 1979.

Sea Plane Tender (AV) and Small Seaplane Tender (AVP)

Floyds Bay AVP 40: [d. 1,766; 310'9" × 41'2"; 18 k; cpl. 216; a. 1-6"; Class Barnegat] Launched 28 January 1945 and commissioned 25 May 1945, she was sent to the Pacific during World War II. She saw service in Korean waters during the Korean Defense Summer–Fall 1952 campaign and received one battle star. She was decommissioned 26 February 1960.

Gardiners Bay AVP 39: [d. 2,592; 310'9" × 41'2"; 18.2 k; cpl. 215; a. 1-5", 8-40mm: Class Barnegat] Launched 2 December 1944 and commissioned 11 February 1945, she saw considerable service during World War II. She departed San Diego 27 June 1950 for the first of four tours in support of the UN during the Korean War. In October 1950 she was at Chinnampo, servicing PMBs from the Far East Wing 6. She was tendered at Inchon and prepared fights over Chinnampo. She operated at Iwakuni, Tsushima Strait, and the Yellow Sea. Her second tour, 12 September 1951 to 9 April 1952, supported aviation patrols, and her third tour, 10 July 1952 to 26 January 1953, was spent at station Chinhae. She was decommissioned 1 February 1958 and transferred to Norway on 17 May 1958 where she served under the name *Haakon VIII*. She received four battle stars for service in Korea.

Jupiter AVS 8/AK 43/AV 58: [d. 5,994] A C-2 Cargo ship built as the *Santa Catalina*, she was acquired by the navy June 1941. Commissioned with a naval crew in August 1942 and named *Jupiter*, she served in the Pacific during World War II. She was classified AV 8 on 31 July 1945. Decommissioned May 1947 and recommissioned October 1950, she saw service in Korean waters during the First UN Counter Offensive, Communist China Spring Offensive, UN Summer–Fall Offensive, Second Korean Winter, Korean Defense Summer–Fall 1952, Third Korean Winter, and Korea Summer–Fall 1953 campaigns. Decommissioned again June 1964, she was transferred to the Maritime Administration in 1965 and sold for scrap in March 1971.

9

ATTACK TRANSPORTS

The wonder is always new that any man can be a sailor.
— Ralph Waldo Emerson

Attack transports were designed to travel to the site of an amphibious landing carrying both assault troops and their support equipment. They were designed to provide all that was necessary for the movement of large numbers of troops: bunks, chow, medical care and even some recreational facilities. They were large enough to carry an entire battalion of men and were capable of landing troops on the beachhead using their own landing craft. The ships were then prepared to stand offshore and in a position to evacuate troops, if necessary, or to onload casualties and prisoners of war.

During World War II several civilian passenger vessels were acquired and converted to meet the requirements of attack transports, with hull numbers in the AP series. It soon became obvious that these ships represented a separate category of craft, and they were redesignated, officially in February 1943, attack transports.

Attack cargo ships (AKA) and attack personnel transports (APA) differed from the cargo and personnel transport ships in that they were specially designed and maintained to participate in amphibious operations. Those ships with AKA and APA designations still on active commission 1 January 1969 were redesignated LPAs.

Attack Cargo Ships (AKA)

Achernar AKA 53: [d. 6,556; 469'2" × 63; 16.6 k; cpl. 429; a. 1-5", 8-40mm, 18-20mm; Class Andromeda] She was launched 3 December 1943 and commissioned 31 January 1944. Within a month of the opening of the Korean War, 14 July 1950, she headed out and operated in Korean waters during the North Korean Aggression, the Communist China Aggression, and the Inchon Landing campaigns. During this time she participated in moving 1st Marine Division from Inchon to Wonsan, and the 2nd Infantry division to Wonsan. She returned to the United States accompanying the damaged USS *Brush* and USS *Mansfield*. She received three battle stars for service in Korea. Placed out of commission on 1 July 1963, the *Achernar* was sold to Spain on 2 February 1965 and renamed *Castilla*, then was scrapped in 1982.

Algol AKA 54: [d. 6,556; 459'2" × 63; 16.5 k; cp. 429; a. 1-5", 8-40mm, 18-20mm. Class Andromeda] Originally commissioned as the *James Baines*, she was launched 17 February 1943, transferred to the navy in November 1943, and in December 1943 converted into an auxiliary cargo attack vessel. She was renamed *Algol*. Inactivated on 26 November 1947, she was reactivated on 18 February 1948. Nicknamed the "Steaming Demon," she participated in the invasions of Inchon and Wonsan, and the Chinnampo evacuation on 4 December 1950. She saw service in Korean waters during the North Korean Aggression, Communist China Aggression, First UN Counter Offensive, Communist China Spring Offensive, and Korean Defense Summer–Fall 1952 campaigns. She received five battle stars. Placed out of commission on 2 January 1958, she was sunk as an artificial reef in New Jersey's Shark River. L. Ron Hubbard, the founder of Scientology, was an officer on the *Algol*.

Alshain TAKA 55: [d. 6,556 light; 459'3" × 63; 16.5 k; cpl. 336; a. 1-5", 4-40mm, 18-20mm; Class Andromeda] Launched 26 January 1944, she was commissioned on 1 April 1944 after being acquired by the navy. She was assigned to the Naval Transportation Service in 1946, and then to the Military Sea Transportation Service, where she was redesignated TAKA 55 on 1 October 1949. She operated in Korean waters during the North Korean Aggression, Communist China Aggression, and Inchon Landing campaigns. She qualified for three battle stars for Korea. The *Alshain* was decommissioned 14 January 1957 and struck from the navy list 1 July 1960. She was scrapped in 1978.

Andromeda AKA: [d. 6,556 light; 459'3" × 63; 16.5 k; cpl. 336; a. 1-5", 4-40mm, 18-20mm; Class Andromeda] Launched 22 December 1942 as an AK, she was then redesignated AKA 15 and commissioned 2 April 1953. During World War II she served in both Atlantic and Pacific waters. During the Korean War she participated in the First UN Counter Offensive, Communist China Spring Offensive, Second Korean Winter, and Third Korean Winter campaigns. She won five battle stars. Decommissioned 1 May 1956, she was struck 1 July 1960 and sold 12 March 1971.

Bellatrix AKA 3/AK 20 (C2-T2): [d. 8,045; 459'3" × 63; 16.5 k; cpl. 369; a. 1-5", 4-3"; Class Bellatrix] The ex–*Raven* was launched 15 August 1941 and commissioned 17 February 1942, and then reclassified 1 February 1943 as an AKA. She took part in the Guadalcanal invasion. She was decommissioned 1 April 1946 and returned to the Maritime Commission. She was reacquired 27 August 1951 and recommissioned 16 May 1952. She operated in Korean waters during the Korean Defense Summer–Fall 1952 campaign. She received one battle star. She was decommissioned 3 June 1965.

Chara AKA 58: [d. 6,556; 459'2" × 63; 16 k; cpl. 247; 1-5", 4-twin 40mm, 18-single 20mm; Class Achernar] She was launched 15 March 1944 and commissioned 25 June 1944, and saw service during World War II. Called to Korea, she participated in the evacuation of Hungnam and Wonsan, and during her second tour she operated in the Wonsan-Songjin bomb-line triangle. She took part in the relocation of POWs from Koje do. She saw service in Korean waters during the North Korean Aggression, Communist China Aggression, First UN Counter Offensive, UN Summer–Fall Offensive, Second Korean Winter, Korean Defense Summer–Fall 1952, and Third Korean Winter campaigns, winning seven battle stars. She was placed out of commission on 21 April 1957.

Diphda TAKA 59: [d. 6,737; 459'2" × 63; 16 k.; cpl. 429; a. 1-5"; Class Achernar] She was commissioned 7 July 1944. During the Second World War she took part in the invasion of Okinawa. When the Korean War broke out she was assigned to Service Force Pacific, and made an emergency delivery of ammunition to Pusan. During an extended tour she carried ammunition to combat units and ships at sea. She participated in Korean waters during the

North Korean Aggression, Communist China Aggression, First UN Counter Offensive, Communist China Spring Offensive, UN Summer–Fall Offensive, and 1952 Korean Defense Summer–Fall campaigns. From 5 February to 11 November 1952 she served with the Military Sea Transportation Service, and received six Korean battle stars. The *Diphda* was placed out of commission 11 May 1956.

Faribault AKA 179: [d. 2,474; 338'6" × 50; 12 k; cpl. 85; a 1-3"; Class Alamosa] Launched 24 February 1945 and commissioned 20 April 1945, she served in the Pacific in the support of the occupation of Japan. She was decommissioned 10 July 1946. Reacquired 16 May 1947, she was recommissioned 26 June 1947 and assigned to the Pacific Fleet. Between 7 November 1952 and 22 July 1953 she served in Korean waters, participating in the Korean Defense Summer–Fall 1952, Third Korean Winter and Korea Summer–Fall 1953 campaigns. She received four battle stars for Korean service.

Kukui WAK 186/AK 174: [d. 5,650; 338'9" × 50'4"; 10 k; cpl. 112; no a.; Class C1-M-AV1] Launched in the spring of 1945, she was acquired by the navy and commissioned *Colquitt* (AK 174) on 22 September 1945. She was permanently assigned to the Coast Guard and named *Kukui* (WAK-186). She was decommissioned 1 March 1972 and turned over to the navy which in turn gave her to the Philippine navy.

Leo TAKA 60: [d. 6,556 light; 459'3" × 63; 16.5 k; cpl. 336; a. 1-5", 4-40mm, 18-20mm; Class Andromeda] Launched 29 July 1944, the *Leo* was acquired by the navy and commissioned AKA 60 on 30 August 1944. The *Leo* was assigned to the Naval Transportation Service in 1946, and to the Military Sea Transportation Service on 1 October 1949. She saw service in Korean waters during the First UN Counter Offensive, the Communist China Spring Offensive, the UN Summer–Fall Offensive, the Second Korean Winter, and the Third Korean Winter campaigns. She received five battle stars for Korean service. She was decommissioned 11 February 1955, struck from the navy list 1 June 1960, and then finally scrapped in 1976.

Mathews AKA 96: [d. 6,761; 459'2" × 63; 16.5 k; cpl. 247; a. 1-5", 8-40mm; Class Andromeda] Commissioned 5 March 1945, she was immediately assigned to the Pacific where she operated, eventually ferrying occupation troops to Korea. She was decommissioned 4 April 1947 but reacquired by the navy in 1951. While in Korea she transported prisoners of war. She operated in Korean waters in periods between 25 July and 5 December 1953 and her crew qualified for the Korean Service Medal. She later operated in the Vietnam War. She was decommissioned 31 October 1968, struck from navy list 1 November 1968 and sold for scrap the following year.

Merrick AKA 97: Hull 219 [d. 6,761; 459'3" × 63; 16.5 k; cpl. 247; a. 1-5", 4-3"; Class Andromeda] Built originally on a Maritime Commission contract and launched 28 January 1945, she was acquired by the navy and commissioned 31 March 1945. During World War II she delivered occupation troops, and took part in Operation Highjump, America's Antarctic expedition, establishing Little America IV base camp. She was decommissioned 25 June 1946, then recommissioned 19 January 1952 for service in Korea. She served in Korean waters in periods between 2 July 1952 to 16 November 1953. She served in Operation Big Switch, carrying more that 6,400 prisoners from Koje Do and Choju Do to Inchon. She later served in Vietnam. She was reclassified LKA 97 on 1 January 1969, and struck from the navy list 1 September 1976. She was scrapped in 1980.

Montague AKA 98: [d. 6,761; 459'2" × 63; 16.5 k; cpl. 474; a. 1-5", 8-40mm, 18-20mm; Class Andromeda] Launched 11 February 1945 and commissioned on 13 April, she operated in Korean waters during the North Korean Aggression, the Communist China Aggression, the First UN Counter Offensive, and the Second Korean Winter campaigns, receiving four battle stars. Decommissioned 22 November 1955, she was transferred to the Maritime Administration 29 January 1960.

Oberon AKA 14: [d. 7,391; 459'3" × 63; 16.5 k; cpl. 494; a. 1-5", 4-40mm, 18-20mm; Class Libra] Launched 18 March 1942, she was commissioned on 15 June 1942, the same day she was acquired by the navy. During World War II she served both in the Atlantic and Pacific. In 1 October 1949 she became an ammunition replenishment transport for the Korean conflict. She served two tours of duty in Korean waters during the First UN Counter Offensive, the Communist China Spring Offensive, the UN Summer–Fall Offensive, the Second Korean Winter, and the Korean Defense Summer–Fall 1952 campaigns. She received five battle stars. She was decommissioned 27 June 1955 and struck from the navy list 1 July 1960.

Oglethorpe AKA 100: [d. 6,761; 459'2" × 63; 16.5 k; cpl. 425; a. 1-5", 8-40mm; Class Andromeda] Launched 15 April 1945, she was commissioned 6 June 1945. In an urgent need to land the First Cavalry Division at Pohang, the *Oglethorpe* was rushed into Yokosuka and equipped with prefabricated boat skids, towing bridles, and boat slings. She operated in Korean waters during the North Korean Aggression and the Inchon Landing campaigns, receiving two battle stars. She was struck from the navy list 1 November 1969.

Seminole AKA 104: [d. 8,635; 459'2" × 63; 16.5 k; cpl. 425; a. 1-5", 4-40mm, 18-20mm; Class Tolland] Launched 28 December 1944, she was acquired by the U.S. Navy, converted to AKA, and commissioned 8 March 1945. Too late for much action in World War II, she operated in the Korean War during the North Korean Aggression, Communist China Aggression, Inchon Landing, and First UN Counter Offensive campaigns. She received six battle stars for Korea. Redesignated LKA 104 in January 1969, she was decommissioned 23 December 1970 and struck from the Naval Register 1 September 1976. She was sold for scrap 1 December 1977.

Skagit AKA 105: [d. 6,556; 459'3" × 63; 16.5 k; cpl. 336; a. 1-5", 4-40mm, 18-20mm; Class Andromeda] This Andromeda-class ship was launched 18 November 1944 and commissioned on 2 May 1944, after which she saw World War II service. Decommissioned 30 June 1949, she was placed in reserve at Mare Island Naval Yard 30 June 1948. Recalled into active service on 26 August 1950, the *Skagit* was on hand to participate in the evacuation of troops from Inchon if needed. She also participated in movement of POWs from Koje Do. She received two battle stars for Korea and later saw some Vietnam service. The ship's designation was changed 1 July 1969 to amphibious cargo ship (LKA) and she was decommissioned and struck from the navy list on 1 July 1969.

Sussex II AK 213: [d. 7,125; 338'6" × 50; 11 k; cpl. 85; a. 1-3", 8-20mm; Class Alamosa] This attack transport was laid 3 October 1944 and commissioned in 1945. She was operated by the U.S. Coast Guard. The second *Sussex* was put into the reserve fleet 23 May 1946. She was recommissioned 27 May 1947, and from August 1951 to January 1952 operated in the Korean War zone moving supplies and ammunition to Pusan, Suyong, and Inchon. After the war, on 5 December 1959, she was decommissioned and sold for scrap. The USS *Sussex* received three battle stars for service in Korea.

Thuban AKA 19: [d. 6,556; 459'3" × 63; 16.5 k; cpl. 247; a. 1-5", 4-40mm, 18-20mm; Class Andromeda] Launched 26 April 1943, she was commissioned 10 June 1943 and assigned to the Asiatic-Pacific Theater where she participated in the Gilbert Islands, Marshall Islands, Leyte and Luzon operations. Assigned to the Naval Transportation Service in 1946 and then the Military Sea Transportation Service on 1 October (TAKA-19), she saw service in the Korean War. Operating in Korean waters during the North Korean Aggression, the Communist China

Aggression and the Inchon Landing campaigns, she received three battle stars. Decommissioned in October 1967, she was redesignated LKA 19 in January 1969 and removed from the navy list the following January. She was disposed of 27 September 1984, her fate unknown.

Titania TAKA 13/AK-55: [d. 13,910; 459'3" × 63; 16.5 k; cpl. 267; a. 1-5", 8-40mm, 18-20mm; Class Arcturus] Launched 28 February 1942 and commissioned 27 May 1942, she was reclassified AKA 13 on 1 February 1943. During World War II she took part in the Bougainville, Mariana, Luzon and Borneo operations. After the war she was assigned to Naval Transportation Service in 1946, and then to the MSTS on 1 October 1949. Called into service for the emergency landing of the First Cavalry Division at Pohang, she was converted at Yokosuka with prefabricated boat skids, towing bridles, and boat slings. During the Korean War she participated in the Korean waters during the North Korean Aggression, Communist China Aggression, Communist China Spring Offensive, UN Summer–Fall Offensive, Second Korean Winter, and Korean Defense Summer–Fall 1952 campaigns. She received seven battle stars. Decommissioned 10 July 7 1955 she was struck 2 July 1961 and scrapped in 1974.

Union AKA 106: [d. 8,635 light; 459'3" × 63; 16.5 k; cpl. 395; a. 1-5", 4-40mm, 16-20mm; Class Tolland] Laid as the *North Carolina*, she was renamed *Union* and launched 23 November 1944. Commissioned 25 April 1945, she was too late for extended service during World War II. She took part in amphibious operations off Kodiak and Whittier, Alaska. When the Korean War broke out she headed for Yokosuka, and transported troops and equipment to Pohang, Korea. She participated in the Second Korean Winter and the Korean Defense Summer–Fall 1952 campaigns. On 14 July 1953 she sailed for her fifth cruise where she moved prisoners from Koje do to Inchon. She won two battle stars for Korea and later served in the Vietnam War. Redesignated LKA 106 on 1 January 1969, she was decommissioned 5 June 1970, struck from the naval list 1 January 1976, and sold for scrap in September 1977.

Uvalde AKA 88: [d. 6,556; 459'3" × 63; 16.5 k; cpl. 366; a. 1-5", 8-40mm, 18-20mm; Class Andromeda] Laid down 27 March 1944 as a Maritime Commission contract, she was commissioned on 18 August 1944, then participated in the Lingayen Gulf and Mindoro landings during World War II. The former *Wild Pigeon*, she operated in Korean waters during the Communist China Aggression, the Second Korean Winter, and the Korea Summer–Fall 1953 campaigns. She was decommissioned 26 June 1957, and struck from the Naval Register. She received three battle stars for her Korean service. She was recommissioned briefly during the 1960s and finally sold for scrap in 1969.

Virgo AKA 20: [d. 13,910; 459'3" × 63; 16.5 k; cpl. 473; a. 1-5", 4-3"; Class Andromeda] The 13,910-ton Andromeda-class attack cargo ship was launched 4 June 1943 and commissioned 16 July 1943. She made four combat tours to Korea, carrying passengers, supplies, and ammunition. She saw service in Korean waters during the North Korean Aggression, Inchon Landing, First UN Counter Offensive, Communist China Spring Offensive, UN Summer–Fall Offensive, Second Korean Winter, Korean Defense Summer–Fall 1952, Third Korean Winter, and Korea Summer–Fall 1953 campaigns. She was decommissioned in April 1961, but recalled for Vietnam and converted to ammunition carrier (AE-30). Decommissioned once again on February 1971, she was sold for scrap. The *Virgo* was the ship on which the author of *Mister Roberts* served.

Warrick AKA 89: [d. 6,556; 459'3" × 63; 16.5 k; cpl. 336; a. 1-5", 4-40mm, 18-20mm; Class Andromeda] Launched 29 May 1944 and commissioned 30 August 1944, she participated in the Luzon and Iwo Jima operations during World War II. During the Korean War she operated in Korean waters during the North Korean Aggression and the Second Korean Winter campaigns. She received two battle stars. She was decommissioned 3 December 1957 and was struck from the navy list 1 July 1961. Reacquired by the Navy for use as a target on 20 April 1977, she was torpedoed by *Trigger* on 28 May 1977.

Washburn AKA 108: [d. 8,635; 459'3" × 63; 16.5 k; cpl. 425; a. 1-5", 4-40mm, 16-20mm; Class Andromeda] Launched 18 December 1944, she was acquired by the navy and commissioned 17 May 1945. During the Korean war she participated in the North Korean Aggression, the Communist China Aggression, the Inchon Landing, the UN Summer–Fall Offensive, and the Korea Summer–Fall 1953 campaigns. She received five battle stars for Korea. She later participated in the Vietnam War. Redesignated LKA 108 on 1 January 1969, she was decommissioned 16 May 1970, struck from the navy list 1 October 1976 and scrapped in 1980.

Whiteside AKA 90: [d. 6,556; 459'3" × 63; 16.5 k; cpl. 274; a. 1-5", 4-40mm, 18-20mm; Class Andromeda] Launched 12 June 1944 and commissioned 11 September 1944, she participated in Korean waters during the North Korean Aggression, the Communist China Aggression, and the Korean Defense Summer–Fall 1952 campaigns. She earned two battle stars for Korea. She was decommissioned 30 June 1958 and struck from the navy list, only to be reactivated for use as a target. It was in this capacity that she was sunk in 1971.

Winston AKA 94/LKA 94: [d. 6,556; 459'3" × 63; 16.5 k; cpl. 336; a. 1-5", 4-40mm, 18-20mm; Class Andromeda] Launched 30 November 1944 and commissioned 19 January 1945, the *Winston* participated in the Korean War during the North Korean Aggression, Communist China Aggression, First UN Counter Offensive, Communist China Spring Offensive, Third Korean Winter, and Korea Summer–Fall 1953 campaigns. She earned six battle stars. Decommissioned 1 February 1957, she was recommissioned 24 November 1961 and served during the Vietnam War. She was redesignated LKA 94 on 1 January 1969 and placed out of commission in November of that year, then struck from the navy list 1 September 1976.

Yancey AKA 93: [d. 6,556; 459'3" × 63; 16.5 k; cpl. 336; a. 1-5", 4-40mm, 18-20mm; Class Andromeda] Launched 8 July 1944 and commissioned 11 October 1944, she served during World War II where she participated in the Iwo Jima and Okinawa campaigns. During the Korean War she operated in Korean waters during the North Korean Aggression and the First UN Counter Offensive. She earned three battle stars for Korean service. She was decommissioned in December 1957, then recommissioned 17 November 1961 and redesignated LKA 93 on 1 January 1969. Decommissioned 20 January 1971, she was struck from the navy list 1 January 1997 and sunk to be used as an artificial reef off Moorehead City, North Carolina.

Attack Transport (APA)

In reaction to the needs of World War II, the navy acquired a large number of civilian passenger ships and large freighters. These were converted into transports and given AP hull numbers. Some were equipped with boat davits to enable the handling of landing craft. When the number of these ships passed a hundred it was decided to give them a separate category and they were identified as attack transports (APA) and numbers assigned to 58 in commission or under construction. It was not until February 1943, however, that this was accomplished. The further conversion of Maritime Commission ships moved the list of APA to 247 (14 were to be cancelled prior to completion: 181–186, 240–247). Finally 248 and 249, converted Mariner-class freighters, were added. The last of these fine ships was decommissioned in 1980 and sold. This designation now is considered extinct.

Perhaps the best known of this class was the USS *Horace A. Bass* (APD 124) known as the "Ghost of the Korean Coast" because of its clandestine activities. Her crew had refined the APD to mean "Any Purpose Designated." She conducted a series of missions for the Central Intelligence Agency, Eighth Army G-3 Miscellaneous (Guerrilla) Section, and for Commander Task Force 95, which included destroying railway tracks and tunnels, and capturing North Korean transportation workers for intelligence purposes. She landed guerrilla troops for raids, ambushes, and demolitions in places like Chongjin, Yong Do and Tanchon, landing her men in rubber boats taken in to 200 feet from the target. Prior to the landing at Inchon, the *Bass* took Underwater Demolition Team (UDT) members in to test the tide and flat-beach gradients. Later she was engaged in debarking UDT personnel for mine-sweeping duties at Wonsan and Chinnampo. During this time Commander Lavrakas and the boat officers each received the Bronze Star.

Drawing from the best sources it appears that the following ships participated during the Korean War. They represented several classes, including Haskell and Bayfield.

Bayfield APA 33: [d. 8,100; 492 × 69'6"; 18.4 k; cpl. 575; a. 12-5", 4-40mm, 12-20mm. Class Bayfield] Launched 15 February 1943 and acquired by the navy in June 1943, she was converted to an amphibious warfare ship and commissioned in November 1943 with a Coast Guard crew. She was the flagship for the Utah Beach landing. In 1945 she landed Marines on Iwo Jima and took part in the Okinawa invasion. In the mid–1950s she was brought back for the Korean War, and saw service in Korean waters during the North Korean Aggression, Communist China Aggression, First UN Counter Offensive, Second Korean Winter, and Korean Defense Summer–Fall 1952 campaigns. She took part in the Kojo amphibious deception. She later served in Vietnam. She was decommissioned and sold for scrap in September 1969.

Bexar APA 237: [d. 6,873; 455 × 62; 19 k; cpl. 533; a. 1-5", 4 twin 40mm, 10 single 20mm; Class Haskell] Launched 25 July 1945 and commissioned 9 October 1945, she participated in Operation Crossroads, the atomic tests. She took part during the North Korean Aggression, Communist China Aggression, and the Second Korean Winter campaigns. In August 1950 she took Marines from Japan and then was involved in the Inchon and Wonsan landings, and later evacuations from Inchon and Chinnampo. She served as flagship for Operation Big Switch. She received three battle stars for her time in Korea. In 1960 she became the first US amphibious vessel to circle the globe in one continuous voyage, logging 27,828 miles in 84 days. She later served during the Vietnam War. Officially decommissioned on 15 December 1969, she was transferred to the mothball fleet.

Calvert II APA 32/ AP 65: [d. 8,100; 492 × 69'6"; 16 k; cpl. 523; a. 1-5", 2-2"; Class Crescent City] Launched 22 May 1942, transferred to the navy, and redesignated APA 32, she was commissioned 1 October 1942. During World War she participated in the Sicily campaign. In 1943 she headed for the Pacific where she operated in the Marianas. She was placed out of commission 26 February 1947. Recalled for the Korean War, she was recommissioned 18 October 1950, and she served two tours in the Far East. She operated in Korean waters during the Korean Defense Summer–Fall 1952 and Third Korean Winter campaigns. She received two battle stars for Korea. She later served in the Vietnam War.

Cavalier APA 37: [d. 8,100; 492 × 69'6"; 18 k; cpl. 523; a. 2-5"; Class Bayfield] Began as an AP (82) launched 15 May 1943, and reclassified APA 37 on 1 February 1943, she was acquired by the navy 19 July 1943 and commissioned 15 January 1944. She was named after a county in North Dakota. APA 37 was in Japanese waters when the Korean War broke out. She took part in the Pohang Landing 18 July 1950, the Inchon Landing 15 September 1950, and later, 14 July 1951, laden with Marines, headed for Pusan. She carried the 45th Division to Inchon. She saw service in Korean waters during the North Korean Aggression, UN Summer–Fall Offensive, and Second Korean Winter campaigns, and won four battle stars.

Deuel APA 160: [d. 6,720; 455 × 62; 17 k; cpl. 536; a. 1-5"; Class Haskell] This Haskell-class attack transport named for Harry P. Deuel and Deuel County in South Dakota was launched 4 September 1944 and commissioned 23 October 1950. She was decommissioned 17 May 1946 and then recommissioned on 23 October 1950. While not listed in *DANFS*, the official listings for the Korean Service Medal suggest she served from 10 to 16 September 1953. She was decommissioned 27 June 1956.

George Clymer APA 27: [d. 11,058; 489 × 69'6"; 18.4 k; cpl. 512; a. 1-5", 4-3", 8-20mm, 4-.50 cal. mg; Class Arthur Middleton] Laid down as the *African Planet* under a Maritime Commission contract, she was launched 27 September 1941 and commissioned 15 June 1942. Acquired from the Maritime Commission and named *George Clymer* 9 January 1942, she was commissioned the same date. During World War II she was the first attack transport to participate in both Mediterranean and Pacific waters. Known as the Lucky George, she participated in the assault on Okinawa. During the Korean War she took part in beach operations at Pusan, Inchon, Wonsan and Hungnam. She received seven battle stars. She later saw service in Vietnam.

Henrico APA 45: [d. 8,100; 492 × 69'6"; 16 k; cpl. 67 officers, 1,425 enlisted; a. 2-5", 8-40mm; Class Bayfield] Named for Henrico County, Virginia, the former *Sea Darter* was launched 12 November 1942, converted to an attack transport, and recommissioned on 26 November 1943. It was active during World War II, took part in Operation Magic Carpet, the return of GI after World War II, and in Operation Crossroads, the atomic tests. When the Korean War broke out, the *Henrico* loaded on 12 July 1950 and took units of the 5th Marines to Pusan. She participated in the landing at Inchon and Wonsan. She moved to Hungnam to withdraw the 3rd Infantry Division and elements of the Republic of Korea First Army Corps. After an overhaul she returned to Korean service on 16 October 1951, landing troops at Sok-Cho-Ri. She was involved in the 45th Infantry Division/1st Cavalry Division rotation, and the removal of the 21st Infantry Division from Yokohama to Inchon. After a visit to Pearl Harbor she returned to Korea where she took part in Operation Big Switch. She served during the Cuban alert and the Vietnam War.

Lenawee APA 195: [d. 6,720; 455 × 62; 17.2 k; cpl. 536; 1,562 troops; a. 1-5", 12-40mm; Class Haskell] The *Lenawee* served in three wars and was present at the surrender of Japan. Laid as a Maritime Commission vessel, she was launched 22 May 1944 and acquired for the navy and commissioned on 11 October 1944. She received two battle stars for World War II. She was decommissioned 3 August 1946 and recommissioned from the Pacific Reserve Fleet on 30 September 1950 and made her first voyage 22 March 1951. She carried 12 LCVP, 4 LCM, and 3 LCPL. She saw service in Korean waters during the Communist China Spring Offensive, UN Summer–Fall Offensive, and Korea Summer–Fall 1953 campaigns, receiving three battle stars. After later serving in Vietnam, she was decommissioned and struck 30 June 1968. Final disposition unknown.

Leon APA 48: (C3-S-A2) [d. 8,100; 492 × 69'6"; cpl. 571; 1,266 troops; a. 2-5", 4-40mm, 18-20mm; Class Bayfield] Planned as the *Sea Dolphin* (AP 93), renamed 3 October 1942, she was launched 19 June 1943 and commissioned 11 September 1943. In *Awards* but not on all lists.

Logan APA 196: [d. 14,387; 455 × 62; 17.7 k; cpl. 692; a. 1-5", 12-40mm, Class Haskell] Launched 27 May 1944 and commissioned 14 October 1944, she is not listed in most sources but apparently was in Korea during the Korean Defense Summer–Fall 1952 campaign.

Magoffin APA 199: [d. 10,680; 455 × 62; 17.2 k; cpl. 528; a. 1-5", 12-40mm; Class Haskell] Launched 4 October 1944 and commissioned 25 October of the same year, she served in the Pacific during World War II. Decommissioned 14 August 1946, and recommissioned 4 October 1950, she participated in Korea during the Communist China Spring Offensive and Korean Defense Summer–Fall 1952 campaigns, receiving two battle stars. She was decommissioned 10 April 1968 and redesignated LPA 100 on 1 January 1963.

Menard APA 201: [d. 6,873; 455 × 62; 19 k; cpl. 536; a. 1-5", 4 twin 40mm; 10 single 20mm; Class Haskell] Originally laid on a Maritime Commission contract, she was launched on 11 October 1944, and acquired by the navy and commissioned 31 October 1944. She saw service during World War II and earned one battle star. Decommissioned 14 June 1948, she was recommissioned 2 December 1950. The *Menard* sailed for Korean in 1951, and operated supplying vital stores for three years. She saw service in Korean waters during the Communist China Spring Offensive, UN Summer–Fall Offensive, and Korean Defense Summer–Fall 1952 campaigns. She also saw service during the Vietnam War. She was decommissioned 18 October and struck from the navy list on 1 September 1961.

Menifee APA 202: (UCL-S-AP5) [d. 6,873; 455 × 62; 17 k; cpl. 567; a. 1-5", 12-40mm; Class Haskell] Launched 15 October 1944 and commissioned 3 February 1945, she was recommissioned 2 December 1950 and served in Korea transporting troops from April 1951 to March 1952, and from August 1953 to April 1954.

Montrose APA 212: [14,387; 455 × 62; 18 k; cpl. 692; a. 1-5", 12-40mm; Class Haskell] Launched 13 September 1944 under an MC contract, and acquired by the navy and commissioned 2 November 1944, she received one battle star for World War II. She was decommissioned 26 October 1946 and then recommissioned for Korean service 12 September 1950. She saw service in Korean waters during the First UN Counter Offensive, Communist China Spring Offensive, and UN Summer–Fall Offensive campaigns. She received three battle stars. Her designation was changed on 1 January 1969 to amphibious transport LPA 212. She later served in Vietnam. She was decommissioned and struck from the Naval Register 2 November 1969.

Mountrail APA 213: [d. 14,837; 455 × 62; 17.7 k; cpl. 567; a. 1-5", 12-40mm; Class Haskell] Launched 20 September 1944, she was commissioned 16 November 1944 and saw service during World War II in the Pacific. She was decommissioned 12 July 1946, then recommissioned 9 September 1950 and sailed that December carrying men to the Far East. She participated in the Kojo amphibious deception and saw service in Korean waters during the First UN Counter Offensive, Communist China Spring Offensive, and Korean Defense Summer–Fall 1952 campaigns. She received three battle stars. She was decommissioned 1 October 1955, then returned to service 22 November 1961 in the Atlantic Fleet.

Noble II APA 218: [d. 10,500; 455'3" × 63'4"; 18 k; cpl. 536; a. 1-5", 12-40mm; 24 landing craft; Class Haskell] She was laid down as MCV 566 on 20 July 1944, launched 18 October 1944 as a modified Victory ship, and then was acquired by navy and commissioned 27 November 1944. She was undergoing overhaul when war broke out. When the Korean War began she arrived in time to participate during the North Korean Aggression, Communist China Aggression, Inchon Landing, First UN Counter Offensive, UN Summer–Fall Offensive, and Second Korean Winter campaigns. She was transferred to Spain in December 1964.

Okanogan APA 220: [d. 6,873; 455 × 62; 18 k; cpl. 536; a. 1-5"; 4 twin 40mm; 10 single 20mm; Class Haskell] With her mission to carry and disembark with her own landing craft and a full battalion of troops, and to evacuate troops, she was laid 19 August 1944 as a Maritime Commission type. Acquired by the navy and commissioned 3 December 1944, she joined the Pacific fleet at the outbreak of the Korean War, loaded part of the 1st Marine

Division and landed them at Inchon. She also participated in the assault of Wonsan and served as flagship in demonstration amphibious landings at Kojo. APA 220 saw service in Korean waters during the North Korean Aggression, Communist China Aggression, First UN Counter Offensive, Communist China Spring Offensive, Second Korean Winter, and Korean Defense Summer–Fall 1952 campaigns. Later she also served in Vietnam. On 1 January 1969 her designation was changed to amphibious transport (LPA-220) and she was decommissioned and struck from the Naval Register on 1 June 1973.

Pickaway APA 222: [d. 14,837; 455 × 62; 18 k; cpl. 536; a. 1-5", 18-40mm; Class Haskell] Launched 5 November 1944, she was converted into an APA and commissioned 12 December 1944. She participated in the Pacific. On 15 September 1950 she participated in the Inchon Landing, and in time landed troops on most of the Korean beachheads. She saw service in Korean waters during the North Korean Aggression, UN Summer–Fall Offensive, Second Korean Winter, Korean Defense Summer–Fall 1952, Third Korean Winter, and Korea Summer–Fall 1953 campaigns. She received six battle stars. Later she would serve in Vietnam.

President Jackson TAPA 18: [d. 16,000; 491'10" × 69'6"; 18 k; cpl. 513; a. 1-5", 4-3", 6-40mm; Class President Jackson] *President Jackson* could transport 1,388 troops. Launched 7 June 1940 and commissioned 16 January 1942, she sailed for the Pacific. On 1 February 1943 she was redesignated APA 18 and served in both Japanese and Chinese waters. Acquired by MSTS on 22 October 1949, during the Korean War she participated in the Inchon Landing, and saw service in Korean waters during the North Korean Aggression, Communist China Aggression, and Korean Defense Summer–Fall 1952 campaigns. She received three battle stars for Korea. She was struck from the navy list and transferred to the Maritime Commission 1 October 1958.

Renville APA 227: [d. 14,837; 455 × 62; 18 k; cpl. 533; a. 1-5", 12-40mm, 26-20mm; Class Boulder Victory] She was laid 19 August 1944, launched 25 October 1944, and commissioned 15 November 1944. Decommissioned 30 June 1949, she was recommissioned 5 January 1952 for service in Korea. She shuttled troops between Japan, Pusan and Inchon and saw service in Korean waters during the Third Korean Winter and Korea Summer–Fall 1953 campaigns, receiving two battle stars. Transferred to the Maritime Administration 23 April 1968, the *Renville* played a role in Otto Preminger's film *In Harm's Way*.

Sandoval APA/LPA 194: [d. 6,873; 455 × 62; 19 k; cpl. 536; a. 1-5"; 4 twin 40mm; 10 single 20mm; Class Haskell] Laid 16 May 1944 as a Maritime Commission vessel, she was launched 2 September 1944. Commissioned on a loan charter on 7 October 1944, she saw significant service during World War II, including the Iwo Jima and Okinawa campaigns. Decommissioned 19 July 1946, she was called back and recommissioned 22 September 1951. She saw service in Korean waters during the Second Korean Winter and Korean Defense Summer–Fall 1952 campaigns. She participated in the movement of troops to Koje Do in an effort to quell riots there. She received two battle stars for Korean service. She was taken off the navy list on 1 September 1961 but was later recalled during the Cuban Missile Crisis. On 14 August 1968 she was redesignated amphibious transport LPA 194, returned to the Maritime Administration, and then struck from the Naval Register 1 December 1976.

Talladega APA 208: [d. 12,460; 466 × 62; 17.7; cpl. 659, 1,662 troops, a. 1-6", 12-40mm; Class Haskell] Launched 17 August 1944 and commissioned 31 October 1944, she operated in the Pacific. She was decommissioned 27 December 1946, and recommissioned 8 December 1951. She loaded men and equipment of the 1st Cavalry Division for Korea, and served in Korean waters during the Third Korean Winter and the Korea Summer–Fall 1953 campaigns. She received two battle stars. She later served in the Vietnam War.

Telfair APA 210: (VC2-S-AP5) [d. 14,837; 455 × 62; 17.7 k; cpl. 532; 1,562 troops;

Class Haskell] Laid down 30 May 1944 as a Marine Commission vessel and launched 30 August 1944, she was acquired by the navy and commissioned 31 Oct 1944. She was deactivated on 20 July 1946 but restored to service in 1950. She saw extensive service in Korean, moving men and supplies between Sasebo, Japan, and Inchon and Chinnampo. She served in Korean waters during the First UN Counter Offensive, the Communist China Spring Offensive, the Third Korean Winter, and the Korea Summer–Fall 1953 campaigns, earning three battle stars. The *Telfair* was decommissioned 29 February 1958 but was rescued on 1 July 1960 and went on to serve again. Decommissioned for the third time 31 October 1968, she was struck from the navy list next day. On 1 January 1969 she was redesignated as amphibious transport LPA 210, and she was sold for scrap 26 May 1969.

Thomas Jefferson APA 30: [d. 11,760; 492 × 69'6"; 18.4 k; cpl. 593; 1,382 troops; a. 4-3", 4-40mm; Class President Jackson] Laid as *President Garfield*, launched 20 November 1940 and commissioned 31 August 1942, she was redesignated as ATA 30 on 1 February 1943. Transferred on 1 October 1949 to the MSTS, she saw service in Korean waters during the North Korean Aggression, the Communist China Aggression, the First UN Counter Offensive, the Communist China Spring Offensive, and the UN Summer–Fall Offensive campaigns. She received four battle stars. She was struck 1 October 1958 and sold 1 March 1973 for scrap.

Fast Transport (APD)

The ships that the Navy called high speed transports (APD) served in a variety of roles during the Korean War. Built during World War II, they had the hull of a destroyer escort and the superstructure needed for troop transport. They could launch and recover light vehicles and equipment, as well as four 36-foot landing boats. Most of them were armed with eight 20mm cannon located in four mounts and aimed by the gunners. In Korea they saw considerable service in the transportation and support of raiding parties.

Begor APD 127: [d. 1,450; 306 × 36'10"; 24 k; cpl. 256; a. 1-5"; Class Crosley] Laid originally as DE 711, she was reclassified APD 127 on 17 July 1944, launched 25 May 1944 and commissioned 14 March 1945. Assigned to the Pacific fleet, she took part in the occupation of Japan. During the Korean war she served two tours, and was involved in the Hungnam evacuation and the landing of clandestine operatives behind enemy lines. She served in Korean waters during the Communist China Aggression, the First UN Counter Offensive, the Communist China Spring Offensive, the Third Korean Winter, and the Korea Summer–Fall 1953 campaigns. Apparently sold for scrap, she sank after a collision at sea in 1966.

Diachenko APD 123: [d. 1,450; 306 × 36'10"; 24 k; cpl. 256; a. 1-5"; Class Crosley] Named after Alex Maxwell Diachenko who had served on the *Eberie* DD 430 in March 1943, she was commissioned 8 December 1944. She sailed 30 June 1950, and supported UN forces, carrying underwater demolition teams, making beach surveys and conducting reconnaissance. In her second tour of duty in Korea, 10 March to 5 December 1952, she carried UDT and was involved in the bombardment and blockade of the coast from Wonsan to Chongjin. She saw service in Korean waters during the North Korean Aggression, the Communist China Aggression, the Inchon Landing, the First UN Counter Offensive, the Second Korean Winter, and the Korean Defense Summer–Fall campaigns. She received six battle stars for Korea. Later she served as flagship during "Passage to Freedom," carrying refugees from North Vietnam. The *Diachenko* was decommissioned 30 June 1959.

Horace A. Bass APD 124: [d. 1,400; 306 × 37; 23.6 k; troops 163; 4 LCUP landing craft; a. 9-3", 3 twin 40mm, 6-20mm, 2 dcr; Class Crosley] This Buckley-class ship was named after Horace Ancel Bass Jr. who was awarded the Navy Cross for action in 1942. She was launched 15 August 1944 and commissioned in December 1944. She sailed 14 July 1950 to join fleet units off Korea, arriving 2 August with marines. Underwater demolition teams and marine reconnaissance units were assigned to her, and she moved on the east coast of North Korea to carry out raids on communist supply lines, making three successful raids between 11 and 17 August. She was involved in placing raiding parties, reconnoitered possible landing beaches, took part in the Inchon invasion and the clearing of Sonsan, and spent three months on beach-survey duty. On a second tour, she returned to Korea 24 September 1951 and resumed bombardment and raiding duties. On her third tour, which started 15 July 1953, she served as the flagship of the Amphibious Control Squadron. She saw service in Korean waters during the North Korean Aggression, First UN Counter Offensive, UN Summer–Fall Offensive, Second Korean Winter and Korean Defense Summer–Fall 1952 campaigns, receiving six battle stars and the Navy Unit Commendation. She was decommissioned 9 February 1959.

Joseph Wantuck APD 125: [d. 1,650; 306 × 37; 23.6 k; cpl. 204; a. 1-5", 6-40mm, 6-20mm, dc; Class Crosley] Named after Private John Wantuck who had been awarded the Navy Cross posthumously, the *Joseph Wantuck* was in Hong Kong when war broke out. She saw service in Korean waters during the North Korean Aggression, Communist China Aggression, UN Summer–Fall Offensive, Second Korean Winter, Third Korean Winter, and Korea Summer–Fall 1953 campaigns. She was also involved in landing units at Inchon. She executed a series of raids with the Royal Marine Commandoes near Wonsan. The ship received five battle stars and the Korean Presidential Unit Citation for service in the Korean War. Struck from the navy list on 4 March 1958, she was sold for scrap.

Walter B. Cobb APD 106: [d. 1,650; 306 × 37; 23.6 k; cpl. 203; a. 1-5", 6-40mm, 6-20mm; Class Crosley] Launched 23 of February 1944, she was commissioned 25 April 1945 after being reclassified an APD. She was involved in the preparation for a landing on Japan when the war ended. Decommissioned on 29 March 1946, she remained in reserve until 6 February 1951 when she was recommissioned for the Korean War. She was in Korea during the spring of 1954 and the summer of 1955, making her barely eligible for the Korean Service Medal.

Weiss APD 135: [d. 1,450; 306 × 36'10"; 23 k; cpl. 214; a. 1-5", 6-40mm, 6-20mm, 2 dt; Class Crosley] Launched 15 February 1945, she was commissioned 7 July 1945 as one of the most versatile of all amphibious ships. She was assigned to the Atlantic fleet. She was decommissioned 2 May 1949, but with the outbreak of hostilities she was taken out of mothballs and arrived in Korean waters on 3 May 1951. She spent most of her first tour in bombardment activities and with underwater demolition teams. On her second tour she participated in Operation Fishnet. The *Weiss* served in Korean waters during the UN Summer–Fall Offensive, Korean Defense Summer–Fall 1952, and Third Korean Winter campaigns. On March 2 1958 she was placed out of commission again. On 20 October 1962 she went back into commission. She was reclassified as LPR (Landing Personnel and Reconnaissance) 1 January 1969 and decommissioned a year later. She was stricken 15 September 1974 and sold for scrap.

10

MINESWEEPERS

The main lesson of the Wonsan operation is that no so-called subsidiary branch of the naval service, such as mine warfare, should ever be neglected or relegated to a minor role in the future.
— Vice Admiral C. Turner Joy

The motto of the minesweepers is "where the fleet goes, we've already been." This was certainly no idle boast when it came to Korea. Deliberately sailing into an area filled with mines meant that every movement included the possibility of setting off one of the very weapons being hunted. It is with some irony that the submarine mine, an American invention, would be used with such efficiency during the war in Korea. First invented in 1776 by David Bushnell, an American, it was little more than a watertight wooden keg loaded with gunpowder that could be hung from a float and which he called a torpedo. Even though the effort to destroy a fleet of British warships anchored in the Delaware River failed, the mine as a concept of cheap defense was fully engaged. Used in a relatively large scale during the American Civil War, particularly by the Confederates, mines are estimated to have sunk 27 Union vessels. The truth of the mine was that it was a cheap defensive weapon that could also be offensive, advantageous to smaller or less-financed causes.

Still called torpedoes, they were in abundance when Admiral Farragut purportedly issued his famous command "Damn the torpedoes, Captain Drayton, go ahead." The naval mine was an effective weapon against the Kaiser during World War I, and used as a defensive barrier along the coasts from Scotland to Norway. During World War II the United States was required to invest a massive expenditure of men and money to establish means of combating mines which had proven their effectiveness — an estimated 1,316 Axis ships and 1,118 Allied ships were lost due to sea mines. Over 12,000 mines were laid against Japan's shipping routes, forcing her into more narrowly defined courses open to submarine attacks. These same mines created a major problem when they had to be cleared after the war.

At the close of World War II, the Pacific minesweeper fleet alone consisted of more than 500 ships and 33,000 officers and enlisted troops. Within five years, however, the minesweeping force for the entire navy had been reduced to 21 small sweepers, two divisions of destroyer sweepers and two divisions of minesweepers. It is also true that the navy had not maintained its interest in the sea mine as perhaps it should have.

Shortly after the end of the war in the Pacific, training in mine warfare had pretty much been halted, the belief being that most naval officers could gear up for this work when and if it was needed. The destroyer minesweepers developed during the war were used primarily in antisubmarine work, and naval ships no longer carried the paravanes used to protect the vessel against moored (contact) mines. The process to lessen the metal ship's vulnerability to magnetic mines, called degaussing, was no longer generally in use. Sonars that could easily be modified to aid in the detection of mines had not been provided to most minesweepers.

When the Korean War broke out, the Far East minesweeping force consisted of four 180-foot steel-hulled ships and six wooden auxiliary sweepers. In 1947 Admiral Chester Nimitz had been required to discontinue his mine warfare command in the Pacific. By the time war began again only three officers in the Pacific fleet command had mine warfare experience.

What the fleet was up against was a variety of mines that had been constructed in the millions during World War II and that retained their potency. The most common was the buoyant contact mine anchored to the sea bottom, waiting a distance below the water's surface, ready to explode when hit by a ship. A large portion of the mines in Korea were of this type. There were also acoustic mines set off by the engine sounds made by a passing ship. Perhaps the most difficult to deal with were the magnetic mines, bottom-dwellers, that were set off by the electrical field cause by a passing ship.

Mines were easy to sow. They could be, and were, slipped off the side of a ship, ejected through the torpedo tubes of a submarine, dropped from planes, or, as was the case for many of the mines in Wonsan Harbor, simply floated down the coast. Even Mother Nature joined in — on more than one occasion typhoons broke mines loose from their moorings and allowed them to float free over large territories.

While the extent to which this is true remains to be seen, a good many mines and their placement was in the hands of the Soviet Union. According to Arnold S. Lott in *Most Dangerous Sea* (1959), the Soviets not only trained North Koreans in the use of mines, but were

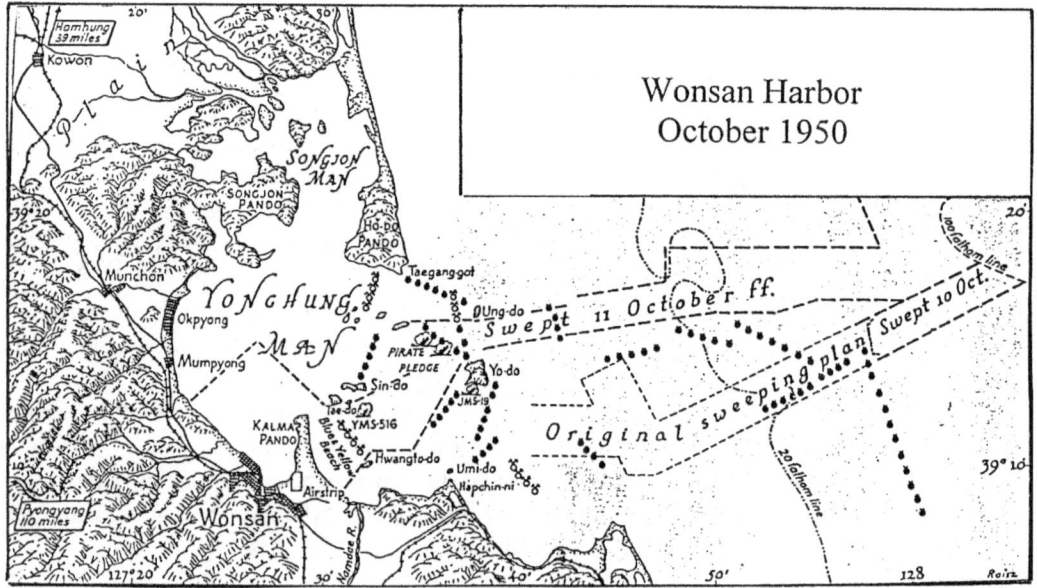

Map of Wonsan Harbor

10. Minesweepers

actually involved in supervising the assembly and laying of magnetic mines. They also held schools for North Koreans in the assembly and sowing of magnetic mines.

Perhaps the first positive mine sighting occurred on 4 September 1950, southwest of Chinnampo, but for largely unexplained reasons the problem did not seem to register. The *McKean* spotted mines in the water near Chinnampo. On 10 September 1950 the crew of PC 703 of the Republic of Korean Navy caught the enemy sowing mines in the water near Inchon. However, on 26 September the destroyer *Brush*, patrolling off Tanchon, hit a mine, causing considerable damage and the loss of 13 lives. From then on the problem increased. On 28 September the Republic of Korea sweeper YMS 509 hit a mine, killing 26, and two days later the *Mansfield* sailing near Changjon lost most of her bow to a mine that also wounded 28 sailors. On 1 October 1950, near Yongdok, the AMS *Magpie* was sunk, losing 21 of her 23-man crew. The next day the ROK YMS 504 was mined at Mokpo. Fortunately the invasion force at Inchon in September 1950 encountered only a few mines, and most located were still on the beach. Those still in the channel were destroyed by gunfire from destroyers. The navy also had to deal with floating mines which had been launched to take advantage of the southerly currents. It was a floater that hit the destroyer *Walke* and inflicted serious damage and killed 25.

The primary method for clearing mines was for the sweeper to tow a device known as a paravane. This torpedo-shaped float was pulled away from the ship towing it, so that moored mines were snagged and deflected away. The mine which came to the surface was then exploded or sunk by cannon fire. When the fighting began in Korea, seven Admirable-class minesweepers were recalled into active service. What was needed, because of the large number of magnetic mines, were wooden sweeper ships with keel, hull and decks made of wood, mostly of northern red oak. Only the essentials of machinery, equipment and fittings were metal, in order to produce the lowest magnetic field possible.

Sweeping was a constant task, and area sweeps were conducted over and over again as new minefields were sown to replenished those destroyed. However, since Wonsan, the size of the force increased and they had learned some significant lessons. Technological improvements had been made, and the well-coordinated teams of patrol planes, helicopters, and even underwater demolition teams made the job easier. The LST 799 had been converted to a minesweeper tender and helicopter base. The work was difficult, uncomfortable and dangerous, and the problem was not eliminated. On 2 February 1951 the AMS *Partridge* hit a mine and sunk.

Sweeping a minefield was dangerous service. Deliberately heading into a minefield was bad enough, but the nature of the business was such that the duty generally took the sweeper to within range of the enemy's short batteries. It was particularly risky for the AMS, the wood-hulled minesweepers that were often refurbished YMS ships from World War II.

The sweepers were in action almost from the beginning. First priority was the east coast location at Pohang-dong where the sweepers were followed, three days later, by 36 assault ships and the 1st Cavalry Division had to clear a landing spot. The 1st was scheduled to land on 18 of July and the sweepers had only three days to clear the area. At it turned out there were no mines encountered at Pohang-dong. This sent an inaccurate message about the communists' intentions. It became necessary to clear and maintain the harbor at Pusan as well, and once again it was fortunate that no mines were located. The channels in and out of Pusan were about the only lifeline the UN had during the early months of the war.

There was a great deal of pride wrapped up in the sign that appeared welcoming the marines as they finally landed on 26 October 1950, at Wonsan: "The Beach is All Yours Through the Courtesy of Mine Squadron III." It was not an idle boast. The mine war in Korea was an extensive and highly significant one. At Wonsan Harbor alone, the power of the massive, even nuclear-armed navy of the most powerful military nation in the world was held in check for more than a week by a communist minefield. At this point, the communists, without putting a single ship into harm's way, had managed to sink five U.S. ships, two Republic of Korea ships, and damage numerous others. During the first two years of the war all of the UN naval vessels that were sunk, and 70 percent of the casualties received by the navy, were the result of mines. The minesweeping force took the brunt of this. While the men on the minesweepers made up less than 2 percent of the UN naval forces in Korea, they accounted for over 20 percent of the naval casualties. Ten navy ships were awarded the Presidential Unit Citation during the Korean War; all ten were minesweepers.

In the United States Navy, minesweepers are named after birds, and their larger counterpart, the destroyer sweepers, are named after heroes. There is confusion as to the number of minesweepers that were active during the Korean conflict. *Jane's Fighting Ships* lists forty-one and *American Gunboats and Minesweepers* lists fifty-four. *The Dictionary of American Naval Vessels* and the listing of awards for the navy and marines also offer different totals. In February 1955 these minesweepers were reclassified as minesweeper fleet, steel hull (MSF) and the government began to sell and scrap them.

The minesweepers that served during the Korean War are listed below. In those cases where there is some question about their service, it is noted. In general the wooden AMS, known as "chicks," were really refurbished YMS-type ships from the World War II period. They typically carried a complement of three officers and four enlisted men.

Destroyer Types

Commander Cagle describes the DMS as "neither fish nor fowl. It is neither a good destroyer nor a good minesweeper, too large, too costly, and too hard to maneuver as a minesweeper, too little fire power as a destroyer."*

Carmick DMS 33/DD 493: [d. 1,630; 348'3" × 36'1"; 37.4 k; cpl. 276; a. 5-5", 6-20mm, 10 tt, 2 dc; Class Gleaves] Launched 8 March 1942 and commissioned 28 December 1942, the *Carmick* was named after David Carmick who led the marines on board the USS *Constitution*. She served during World War II, including the operations on D-Day. On 23 June 1945 she was converted to a high-speed minesweeper and reclassified DMS 33. The sweeper entered Korean waters, operating with Task Force 95 out of Yokosuka, and patrolled off both coasts of Korea, providing fire-support and minesweeping operations. From 29 October to 3 December 1950 she penetrated the harbor at Chinnampo to sweep mines. During her second tour of duty beginning in 1952 she patrolled off Yang Do Island and provided cover for minesweeping operations through February 1953. She saw service in Korean waters during the Communist China Aggression, First UN Counter Offensive, UN Summer–Fall Offensive, Second Korean Winter, and Korean Defense Summer–Fall 1952 campaigns. For these actions she earned the Navy Unit Commendation and received five battle stars. The *Carmick* was placed out of service on 13 February 1954.

Doyle DMS 34/ DD 494: [d. 1,620; 348'4" × 36'1"; 35 k; cpl. 208; a. 4-5", 5-21" tt; Class Gleaves] Launched 17 March 1942, she was commissioned 27 January 1943. She saw service in operations at Wonsan, Hungnam, and Suwon and participated in the North Korean

---

* Malcom W. Cagle and Frank A. Mason. *The Sea War in Korea.* Annapolis, MD: Naval Institute Press, 1957.

Aggression, Communist China Aggression, First UN Counter Offensive, UN Summer–Fall Offensive, Second Korean Winter, and Korean Defense Summer–Fall 1952 campaigns. She received six battle stars for Korea.

Endicott DMS 35: [d. 1,630; 348'4" × 36'1"; 34.7 k; cpl. 208; a. 5-5", 5-21" tt, 6 dcp, 2 dct; Class Bristol] Launched 5 April 1942 and commissioned 25 February 1943 as DD 495, she was ordered to the Atlantic fleet on convoy duty. She was reclassified as DMS 35 on 30 May 1945. Toward the end of the war she was designated flagship of the Task Force 52 sweeping group, and operated in the Yellow Sea. In June 1950 she headed for Korea where she screened carriers *Badoeng Strait* (CVE 116) and *Sicily* (CVE 118), and escorted Korean LSTs in a feint attack against Chang Sa Dong. After an overhaul she departed for her second tour in Korea where she joined in shore bombardment and patrol. In 1953 she provided gun support for minesweepers operating in Korea. She was decommissioned 17 August 1954 and reclassified DD 495 on 15 July 1955. The *Endicott* suffered several hits during her service. Minor damage resulted from two hits from shore batteries at Songjin, North Korea, 4 February 1952. There were no casualties. Nor was anyone hurt when she suffered insignificant damage after being hit by shore battery at Chongjin, North Korea, on 7 April 1952. The *Endicott* also suffered minor damage after receiving one hit from the shore battery at Songjin, North Korea on 19 April 1952. There were no casualties. She participated in the North Korean Aggression, Communist China Aggression, First UN Counter Offensive, UN Summer–Fall Offensive, Second Korean Winter, Korean Defense Summer–Fall 1952, Third Korean Winter, and Korea Summer–Fall 1953 campaign.

Thompson DMS 38: [d. 2,500; 348'3" × 36'1"; 37.4 k; cpl. 276; a. 4-5", 4-40mm, 5-21" tt; Class Gleaves] Launched 15 July 1942 and commissioned 10 July 1943, she served on convoy duty and was a participant in the D-Day landing. On 30 May 1945 she was reclassified as a fast minesweeper DMS 38. She arrived in Korea in time to be involved in the sweeping of Chinnampo, to serve in harbor control at Inchon and Wonsan, and operate as the screen for the USS *Missouri* (BB 63) and *Manchester* (CL 83) while they conducted shore bombardment duties. She was involved in the bombardment of Kyoto Wan, and in junk busting. She participated in the North Korean Aggression, Communist China Aggression, First UN Counter Offensive, Communist China Spring Offensive, UN Summer–Fall Offensive, Korean Defense Summer–Fall 1952, and Third Korean Winter campaigns. She was badly damaged 14 June 1951 after being hit by shore batteries at Songjin, North Korea. Three men were killed and four wounded. Later she suffered minor damage at Songjin, North Korea, with 13 casualties on 20 August 1952, and was hit once out of the 89 rounds fired at her at Wonsan 20 November 1852. She won seven battle stars and the Navy Unit Commendation. She was decommissioned 18 March 1954.

AMS Types

Chatterer AMA 40 /AM 123: [d. 890; 221'2" × 32; 18 k; cpl. 105; a. 1-3", 2-40mm; Class Auk] She was originally built as YMS 415 and was commissioned in October 1944 after which she was assigned to the Pacific war, operating primarily off Okinawa. She remained in Japan as a minesweeper after the war. On 11 May 1947 she was reclassified as a motor minesweeper and renamed *Chatterer* AMS 40. Stationed in Japan when the Korean War broke out, she joined the efforts to clear enemy minefields. She participated in the defense of the Pusan Perimeter and in the North Korean Aggression, Communist China Aggression, Inchon

Landing, First UN Counter Offensive, Communist China Spring Offensive, UN Summer–Fall Offensive, Second Korean Winter, Korean Defense Summer–Fall 1952, Third Korean Winter, Korea, and Summer–Fall 1953 campaigns. In February 1955 she was redesignated MSC (O) 40 and the following April loaned to Japan and renamed *Yurishima*. She was returned to the U.S. Navy in 1967 and sold for scrap in September 1969.

Condor AMS 5: [d. 270; 136 × 32; cpl. 32; a. 1-3", 2-20 mm; Class YMS] Originally named YMS 192, she was a 270-ton auxiliary motor minesweeper. She was launched 5 December 1942 and commissioned on 13 June 1943. She served along the East Coast and in the Caribbean until the end of the war in 1945. She was reclassified 18 February 1947 as a motor minesweeper AMS, and was renamed *Condor*. She was recommissioned in November 1950 for service in the Korean War and provided sweeping and patrol service off Korea and Japan. She participated in the Communist China Spring Offensive, UN Summer–Fall Offensive, Second Korean Winter, Korean Defense Summer–Fall 1952, Third Korean Winter and Korea Summer–Fall 1953 campaigns. In February 1955 she was loaned to Japan and renamed *Ujishima*. She was sunk as a target in August 1968.

Curlew IV AMS 8: [d. 270; 136 × 32; cpl. 32; a. 1-3", 2-20 mm; Class YMS] Originally YMS 218, she was launched 23 December 1942 and commissioned 23 June 1943. She served in the Asiatic-Pacific during World War II. She was placed out of commission in 1947. On 17 February 1947 she was reclassified as a motor minesweeper and renamed *Curlew* AMS 8. Recommissioned in June 1949, she was sent to the Pacific to support the Korean conflict and was in the active zone performing mine clearance and blockade support. She participated in the Communist China Aggression, First UN Counter Offensive, Communist China Spring Offensive, UN Summer–Fall Offensive, Second Korean Winter, Korean Defense Summer–Fall 1952, Third Korean Winter, and Korea Summer–Fall 1953 campaigns. She remained in Korea after the war ended. On 8 February 1955 she was again redesignated, this time as MSC (O), and transferred to Korea in January 1956. She was renamed *Kum Hwa* and was discarded sometime in 1977.

Firecrest AMS 10: [d. 270; 136 × 32; cpl. 32; a. 1-3", 2-20 mm; Class YMS] Originally YMS 231, she was launched 3 April 1943 and commissioned 6 August 1943. Following service in World War II she was reclassified AMS on 17 February 1947. During her Korean service she was hit several times while conducting her sweeps. AMS 10 received minor damage near Kalma Gak Point, just east of Wonsan, when the 75mm shell that hit her did not explode but pushed through the plywood deck and out the side. She also suffered minor damage after being hit by shore battery at Hungnam, North Korea. There were no casualties from this attack on 5 October 1951, nor were there on 30 May 1952 when the *Firecrest* took fire from machine guns. She participated in the Communist China Aggression, First UN Counter Offensive, Communist China Spring Offensive, UN Summer–Fall Offensive, Second Korean Winter, Korean Defensive Summer–Fall 1952, Third Korean Winter, and Korea Summer–Fall 1953 campaigns. She was transferred to Japan 15 March 1955 and named *Eta Jima*.

Gull II AMS 16: [d. 270; 136 × 25; 14 k; cpl. 34; Class Auk] Launched 14 October 1943, the Auk-class USS *Gull II* was commissioned 28 February 1944 as YMS 324. She swept for enemy mines at Peleliu and continued sweeping there and at Ulithi. She remained in the Pacific until the end of the war. Redesignated *Gull* AMS 16 on 18 February 1947, she conducted peacetime training until arriving at Chinnampo, Korea, in support of a British Royal Marine commando raid, 15 June 1951. The *Gull* suffered minor damage from one hit after receiving 60 rounds at a range of 5,400–10,000 yards while at Pkg 2, suffering 2 casualties, 16 March 1953. She was awarded the Navy Unit Citation. On 1 August 1954 she was redesignated AMCU 46 and underwent conversion, after which she was again redesignated as minehunter MHC 6 on 7 February 1955. She was decommissioned 14 January 1958 and disposed of March 1959. She earned nine battle stars for service in Korea.

Heron II AMS 18: [d. 215; 136 × 24'6"; 13 k; a. 1-3", 2-20mm] This ship was once the YMS 369 and during World War II served in the Pacific. She was mothballed, reclassified AMS 18 on 7 February 1947, and then recommissioned 15 July 1949 as an AMS. While in Korea she was hit from fire at Kalma Gak Point, just east of the city of Wonsan. The hit was above the waterline and no one was hurt. She was also hit on 10 September 1951 by shore battery near Wonsan. There were no casualties. She participated in the Communist China Aggression, First UN Counter Offensive, Communist China Spring Offensive, UN Summer–Fall Offensive, Second Korean Winter, Korean Defense Summer–Fall 1952, Third Korean Winter and Korea Summer–Fall 1953 campaigns, and received eight battle stars. Reclassified MSC (O) 18 on 17 February 1955, she was decommissioned 21 May 1967.

Kite II AMS 22/ YMS 374: [d. 270; 136 × 25; 15 k; cpl. 32; a. 1-3", 2-20mm, dcp] Launched as YMS 374 on 17 February 1944, she was commissioned 31 May 1944. She took part in the Iwo Jima invasion and then was in the Marianas until the end of the war. She supported the occupation of Korea and Japan. In February 1947 she was redesignated a motor minesweeper AMS, renamed *Kite*, and then decommissioned. Recommissioned in May 1949, she went to the Western Pacific, and with the outbreak of war was active off Pusan, and participated at the Inchon and Wonsan operations. The *Kite* was hit on 19 November 1952 by fire from a shore battery at Wonsan. The result was the destruction of one of its small boats and five casualties. She saw service in Korean waters during the North Korean Aggression, Communist China Aggression, First UN Counter Offensive, Communist China Spring Offensive, UN Summer–Fall Offensive, Second Korean Winter, Korean Defense Summer–Fall 1952, Third Korean Winter, and Korea Summer–Fall 1953 campaigns. She remained in Korea until the end of the war. She was redesignated MSC (O) on 22 February 1955, transferred to the Republic of Korea in 1956, and renamed *Kim Po*. She was discarded in 1977.

Magpie II AMS 25: [d. 300; 136 × 24'6"; 14 k; cpl. 33; a. 1-3", 2-20mm, 4 dct, 2 dcp] Laid down as a YMS-100-class ship, she was renamed YMS 400 and then on 17 February 1947 renamed *Magpie* and reclassified as AMS 25. She was based at Guam and operating out of Apra Harbor when the war broke out. She began sweeping duties in September 1950. The *Magpie* struck a mine two miles off Ch'uksan on 29 September 1950. It blew the channel house off and the ship sank. It took the lives of 21 of the 33-man crew, including her commanding officer Lieutenant Junior Grade Warren R. Person. She received one battle star for her Korean service. She was struck from the navy list on 20 October 1950. She saw service in Korean waters during the North Korean Aggression campaign.

Merganser II AMS 26: [d. 272; 136 × 25'4"; 15 k; cpl. 34; a. 1-3", 4-20 mm, 2 dct, 2 dcp; Class YMS 1] Launched 29 January 1944, she was commissioned November 1944 as YMS 417. She spent the next half a dozen years in the Pacific until redesignated a motor minesweeper (AMS) in February 1947 and renamed the *Merganser*. She began operations in the Far East, supporting efforts off Wonsan. She served as the mother ship for seven minesweepers between 1952 and 1954. In Korea she participated in the North Korean Aggression, Communist China Aggression, First UN Counter Offensive, Communist China Spring Offensive, UN Summer–Fall Offensive, Second Korean Winter, Korean Defense Summer–Fall 1952, Third Korean Winter, and Korea Summer–Fall 1953 campaigns. In February 1954 she was converted to a coastal mine hunter and redesignated AMCU, then changed to HMC in February 1955. She was decommissioned in April 1958 and sold in May 1960.

Mockingbird II AMS 27: [d. 270; 136 × 24'6"; 15 k; cpl. 34 ; Class YMS 410] Originally launched on 23 May 1944 as a YMS-410-class auxiliary motor minesweeper (sometimes identified as YMS 419), she was commissioned 18 November 1944. In February 1947 she was redesignated a motor minesweeper (AMS) and renamed *Mockingbird*. She was in the Far East when war broke out, and she began sweeping in July 1950, working in operations at Pohang, Inchon, Wonsan and Hungnam during the last half of that year. She became the flagship of MinDiv 31, which allowed her to be the first to penetrate minefields and channels through November of 1950. She conducted cleanup sweeps from the 39th Parallel to Pohang. She continued to operate, alternating between the east and west coast of Korea, in check sweeps until the end of the war. She participated in the North Korean Aggression, Communist China Aggression, Inchon Landing, First UN Counter Offensive, Communist China Spring Offensive, UN Summer–Fall Offensive, Second Korean Winter, Korean Defense Summer–Fall 1952, Third Korean Winter, and Korea Summer–Fall 1953 campaigns. She received ten battle stars for her service in Korea. Following the end of the war she remained on patrol. During this time she was redesignated as MSC (O27). On 6 January 1956 she was decommissioned and transferred to the Republic of Korea where she served as the *Kochang*. She was discarded in 1977.

Osprey III AMS 28: [d. 270; 136 × 24'6"; 15 k; cpl. 34; a. 1-3", 2-20mm, dcs; Class YMS 410] Originally YMS 422 during World War II, she was an auxiliary motor minesweeper commissioned in September 1944. In February 1947 she was redesignated a motor minesweeper (AMS) and renamed *Osprey*. The *Osprey* was involved in operations at Pohang, Inchon and Wonsan, and continued in sweeping operations until the end of the war. The *Osprey* suffered considerable damage after being hit by shore battery off Wonsan, North Korea, on 29 October 1951. There was one casualty. She was also hit by fire from the shore battery at Songjin, North Korea, on 24 April 1952. There were no casualties that time. She was also hit by shore batteries at Kojo, North Korea, where she took four casualties on 14 October 1952. She served in Korean waters during North Korean Aggression, Communist China Aggression, Inchon Landing, First UN Counter Offensive, Communist China Spring Offensive, UN Summer–Fall Offensive, Second Korean Winter, Korean Defense Summer–Fall 1952, Third Korean Winter, and Korea Summer–Fall 1953 campaigns, for which she received ten battle stars. On 28 February 1955 she was redesignated as MSC (O) and the next month loaned to the Japanese Maritime Self-Defense Force where she was renamed the *Yakushima*. She remained under Japanese command until 1969.

Partridge AMS 31: [d. 350; 136 × 24'6"; 12 k; cpl. 50; a. 1-3", 2-20mm; Class YMS 186] Launched 22 April 1945 and commissioned 25 July 1945, she was reclassified AMS 31 on 18 February 1947. She participated in the North Korean Aggression, Communist China Aggression, Inchon Landing, and First UN Counter Offensive campaigns. On 2 February 1951 she struck a mine while operating in Wonsan Harbor, and sunk, killing eight and wounding six. She was struck from the navy list on 27 February 1951.

Pelican II AMS 32: [d. 350; 136 × 24'6"; 12 k; cpl. 50; a. 1-3"; Class YMS 441] The *Pelican II* was launched 13 November 1943 and commissioned 21 February 1945. She participated in minesweeping operations with the 3rd Fleet. In February 1947, while at Guam, she was redesignated *Pelican* and classified AMS 342. After the war she was outfitted with experimental gear at the Eniwetok atomic tests. At the start of the Korean War, refitted with her minesweeping gear, she was deployed to Korea where she participated in numerous minesweeping operations, including the sweep of Chinnampo. She participated in the North Korean Aggression, Communist China Aggression, First UN Counter Offensive, Communist China

Spring Offensive, UN Summer–Fall Offensive, Second Korean Winter, Korean Defense Summer–Fall 1952, Third Korean Winter, and Korea Summer–Fall 1953 campaigns. She remained in the Far East until 1955. She was redesignated as MSC (O) 32 and loaned to Japan on 16 April 1955 where she became the *Ogishima*. Returned to the navy in April 1968, she was struck on 1 May 1968.

Pirate AMS 275: [d. 850; 184'6" × 33; 15 k; cpl. 104; a. 1-3"; Class Admirable] She was launched 16 December 1943. The second sweeper named *Pirate*, she was commissioned 12 June 1944. She served with naval forces in the Pacific during World War II and was decommissioned on 6 November 1946. She was moved to the Service Force Pacific fleet in December 1947 for deployment to Japanese waters in a caretaker capacity, and thus was in the area when the war broke out. She was recommissioned 14 August 1950. She saw service off the northern coast of Formosa. She served with Mine Division 32 in the sweep of Wonsan Harbor. During the sweep, a helicopter counted 27 mines in *Pirate*'s path. After several days of service the sweeper struck a mine on 12 October 1950; her main deck broken in two, she sunk in about five minutes. Twelve died and one went missing. The *Endicott* and *Incredible* picked up the survivors. Diving teams were unable to salvage much, and the sweeper was destroyed. She saw service in Korean waters during the North Korean Aggression campaign and received the Presidential Unit Citation.

Swallow III AMS 36: [d. 272; 136 × 24'6"; cpl. 33; a. 1-3"; Class YMS] Laid as PCS 1416, redesignated YMS 461, she was launched 8 January 1944 and commissioned 22 January 1944. She served in the Pacific during World War II. On 18 February 1947 she was named *Swallow* and designated AMS 36. She spent nine years in the Far East. She participated in the sweep of Chinnampo. On 25 May 1952 the *Swallow* suffered slight damage after three hits from shore battery at Songjin, North Korea. There were no casualties. On 7 February 1955 she was redesignated MSC (O) 36. Decommissioned 16 April 1955, she was loaned to Japan. On 1 May 1968 she was returned to the United States and struck. She was sold for scrap.

Waxbill AMS 39: [d. 890; 221'1" × 32'2"; 18 k; cpl. 107; a. 1-3", 4-40mm, 8-20mm; Class Auk] The *Waxbill* was launched 29 December 1944, commissioned 21 August 1945, and converted 18 February 1947. This ship was unique for a sweeper in that it had experimental sonar gear. Instead of sound, the pulse produced a picture on a screen. She was decommissioned, then recommissioned in reserves 1 September 1950, and fully commissioned 25 September 1950. In Korea she served in waters around Pusan, Kyoshin Tan and To Jang Po. In May 1952 the *Waxbill* reported that it had swept for 28 straight nights without a break. On the night of 20 August 1952 the *Waxbill* scraped her bottom on a rocky reef off Chin Cho, in Haeju Wan, Korea, on the west coast north of Inchon. It destroyed the sonar, and damaged one screw and the drive shaft, but she limped back to Sasebo, Japan, where she was repaired. She took part in the decoy invasion at Kojo, Korea, in October 1952. For four years she operated in Japanese and Korean waters. She earned six battle stars. She was struck from the navy list 1 November 1959.

AM Types

Chief AM 315/ MSF0 315: [d. 890; 221'2" × 32'2"; 18 k; cpl. 105; a. 1-3"; Class Auk] This Auk-class minesweeper was commissioned October 1943. After service in the Marianas and Okinawa she was decommissioned in March 1947. She was recommissioned February 1952 and deployed to the Far East in 1952–53 and 1953–54. She saw service in Korean waters during the Korean Defense Summer–Fall 1952 and Third Korean Winter campaigns, for which she received two battle stars. She was decommissioned November 1954 and in February 1955 was reclassified as a fleet minesweeper, MSF 315. She was sold to Mexico in February 1973 and renamed *Jesus Gonzalas Otraga*.

Competent AM 316: [d. 890; 221'2" × 32'2"; 18 k; cpl. 105; a. 1-3"; Class Auk] Launched as the *Amehia* 30 January 1943, she was retained by the navy and commissioned 10 November 1943 as the minesweeper *Competent*. She was decommissioned 30 January 1947 and recommissioned 29 February 1952. She participated in the Korean Defense Summer–Fall 1952 and Third Korean Winter campaigns. She suffered superficial damage and lost her sweep gear after being hit by shrapnel from a near miss fired by a shore battery on 27 August 1952. There were no casualties. She received two battle stars. She was decommissioned and placed in reserves 15 April 1955.

Defense AM 317: [d. 890; 221'2" × 32'2"; 18 k; cpl. 105; a. 1-3"; Class Auk] Launched 18 February 1943, she was commissioned in January 1944. The minesweeper served in the Pacific during World War II, participating in the Iwo Jima and Okinawa campaigns. She was decommissioned in May 1946. Recommissioned in February 1952 in response to the Korean War, she served two tours of duty in 1952–1953 and 1953–1954. During this time she was near the Wonsan-Chongjin-Songjin area. She participated in the Korean Defense Summer–Fall 1952 and Third Korean Winter campaigns, for which she received two battle stars. Reclassified MSF 317 on 7 February 1955, she was decommissioned in April 1955. She was transferred to Mexico in 1973 and renamed *Manuel Doblado*.

Devastator AM 318: [d. 890; 221'2" × 32'2"; 18 k; cpl. 105; a. 1-3"; Class Auk] Commissioned January 1944, she served in the Pacific until the end of World War II, participating in the invasions of Iwo Jima and Okinawa. She was decommissioned in January 1947. Recommissioned in February 1952, she was twice deployed to Korea from 8 July 1952 to 5 February 1953 and from October 1953 to 2 June 1954. In 1952–53 she engaged in minesweeping and participated in the Korean Defense Summer–Fall 1952 and Third Korean Winter campaigns. In February 1955 she was reclassified MSF 318. She received two battle stars. She was decommissioned again 15 April of 1956 and transferred to Mexico in 1973, renamed *Sebastian Lerdo de Tejada*.

Dextrous AM 341: [d. 890 tons; 221'2" × 32'2"; cpl. 105; a. 1-3"] Launched 17 June 1943 and commissioned 8 September 1943, she was assigned to the Atlantic and then in November 1945 sailed for the Pacific. She was decommissioned 5 June 1946. Recommissioned 1 December 1950, she made her first Far Eastern cruise from 3 March 1951 to 28 February 1952. While in Korea she swept on both coasts. She returned for a second cruise 1 December 1952 to 3 July 1953. The *Dextrous* was hit on 11 August 1951 and superficially damaged by shore batteries coming from Wonsan. One man was killed and three wounded. She also suffered minor damage after being hit by a shore battery at Wonsan, North Korea, on 23 November 1951. There were no casualties then. A third hit, also from Wonsan, North Korea, damaged the *Dextrous* on 11 January 1952. She suffered minor damage and there were three casualties that time. Participating in the Communist China Spring Offensive, UN Summer–Fall Offensive, Second Korean Winter, Third Korean Winter, and Korea Summer–Fall 1953 campaigns, she received five battle stars for service in Korea. She was reclassified MSF 341 on 7 February 1955, then placed out of commission and in reserve 31 October 1956.

Gladiator II AM 319: [d. 890; 221'2" × 32; 18 k; a. 1-3"; Class Auk] She was launched 7 May 1943 and commissioned 25 February 1944. During World War II she participated in the battle for Okinawa. The *Gladiator* was decommissioned 4 October 1946. She was recommissioned 29 February 1952 and deployed to Korea to assume mine-sweeping duties off Wonsan, Inchon, and Hungnam where she remained into March 1953. Placed in the reserve fleet in March 1955, she was redesignated an MSF and remained in mothballs until 1973 when she was transferred to Mexico where she served under the name *Santos Delgollado*.

Impeccable AM 320: [d. 890; 221'2" × 32; 18 k; cpl. 195; a. 1-3", 2-40mm, 2 dct, 2 dcp; Class Auk] Launched 21 May 1943 as BAM 7, she was commissioned 24 April 1944. She was decommissioned 27 May 1947 and recommissioned for the Korean War on 12 March 1953. In Korea she served in the waters around Wonsan and during the Kojo feint. She participated in the Korean Defense Summer–Fall 1952 and Third Korean Winter campaigns. She received two battle stars. Decommissioned 14 October 1955, she was placed in the Pacific Reserve Fleet.

Incredible AM 249: [d. 530; 189'6" × 33; 15 k; cpl. 104; a. 1-3", 4-40mm, 6-20mm, 2-.50 cal, 2 dct, 3 dcp; Class Admirable] Launched 21 November 1942, she was commissioned 17 April 1943. Placed out of commission 28 November 1947, she was recommissioned 14 August 1950. She served with Mine Division 32 and participated in action during the engagements at Wonsan Harbor, during which the *Pirate* and *Pledge* were sunk. She suffered total engine failure. She participated in the North Korean Aggression, Communist China Aggression, First UN Counter Offensive, and Communist China Spring Offensive campaigns. She received four battle stars. Reclassified MSF on 7 February 1955 she was decommissioned 1 December 1959, dropped from the Naval Register 1 December 1959 and sold 8 August 1960.

Mainstay AM 261: [d. 530; 184'6" × 33; 14 k; cpl. 104; a. 1-3", 4-40mm; Class Admirable] Launched 31 July 1943 and commissioned 24 April 1944, she joined Mine Division 32 and operated in the Mediterranean. As the World War ended she moved toward the Pacific where she operated near Japan and north of Formosa. She was decommissioned 6 November 1946 and entered the Pacific Reserve Fleet. She was placed in service from 28 November 1947 until 16 April 1948 in the Far East. Recommissioned 1 March 1949, she was assigned to Mine Squadron 3, and operated off Kyushu. She was decommissioned 10 January 1950. Recommissioned 12 December 1950, she began coastal sweeps in support of the Blockading and Escort Force. She supported rescue operation after *Partridge* AMS 31 was struck off Sokcho. She operated off Wonsan. After operation along the California coast she was again deployed to the Far East 6 August 1953 and patrolled off South Korea. She participated in the Communist China Aggression, First UN Counter Offensive, Communist China Spring Offensive, and the UN Summer–Fall Offensive campaigns. She was decommissioned 21 September 1954 and reclassified MSFG 261. Her name was struck on 1 December 1959 and she was sold for scrap. She received four battle stars for Korea.

Murrelet AM 372: [d. 890; 221'1" × 32'2"; 18 k; cpl. 107; a. 1-3", 4-40mm, 8-20mm, Class Auk] Launched 29 December 1944, she was commissioned 21 August 1945. Too late for service in World War II, she was decommissioned 20 June 1946 and then recommissioned 28 October 1950 for service in Korea. AM 372 received slight damage after being hit by shore battery at Songjin, North Korea, on 26 May 1952. There were no casualties. During her service in Korea she won five battle stars. Reclassified MSF 372 on 7 February 1955, she was decommissioned 14 March 1957 and struck from the navy list 1 December 1964. She was transferred to the Philippine navy and served as the *Rizal*.

Pledge AM 277: [d. 945; 184'6" × 33; 15 k; cpl. 104; a. 1-3", 2-40mm, 6-20mm, 2 dct, 2 dcp; Class Admirable] Launched 23 December 1943 and commissioned 29 July 1944, she reported to the Atlantic fleet during World War II and then was assigned to the Pacific. She was decommissioned 6 November 1946 and recommissioned 28 November 1947 for service in Japan. Reduced in commission 10 January 1950, she was recalled to work in the Korean War. The steel-hulled sweeper served in Mine Division 32. She struck a mine at Wonsan, North Korea, on 12 October 1950 and sunk in about an hour. Shore batteries opened fire on the survivors. Unable to salvage her, diving teams destroyed the *Pledge*. She participated in the North Korean Aggression and Inchon Landing campaigns. She received a Presidential Unit Citation for service in Korea.

Ptarmigan AM 376: [d. 850; 221'2" × 32'2"; 18 k; cpl. 117; a. 1-3", 2-40mm; Class Auk] Launched 15 July 1944 and commissioned 15 January 1945, she operated clearing mines off Japan, and was decommissioned 3 June 1946. She was recommissioned again 28 October 1950 and was in Korea by June 1951. She destroyed mines at Hungnam, Chonjin, and Chaho, and patrolled the Korean coast to prevent sampans from laying mines. She was back in Korea in 1953 and operated off Hungnam, Inchon, Pusan, and Choto Island. She received four battle stars for Korean Service. She served post-war mining duties until 7 February 1955 when she was reclassified as MSF 376. She was decommissioned 17 May 1957 and struck from the Naval Vessel Register 1 July 1963. She was transferred afterward to the Republic of Korea.

Redhead AMS 34: [d. 320 tons; 136 × 24'6"; 15 k; cpl. 32; a. 1-3", 2-20mm, 2 dpc; Class YMS] Originally YMS 44S, she was laid 21 October 1943 and commissioned 15 December 1944. She served on the west coast and then engaged in combat duty at Okinawa, Guam, and the Ryukyus. Serving in Japanese waters until 1950, she headed for Korea on 12 July 1950 and served as a unit of Mine Division 31 during 1950 and 1951. She swept with "O" type gear as a mine-destruction vessel and gear retriever. She received the Presidential Unit Citation for service from 11–24 October. Later, still on tour, she steamed the acoustic hammerbox and "open and closed jigs," and conducted air-sea rescue and night patrols. Through the end of 1953 she continued night identification patrol duties off Wonsan, Po Hang, Cho To and Daengyong Do. She participated in the Communist China Spring Offensive, UN Summer–Fall Offensive, Second Korean Winter, Korean Defense Summer–Fall 1952, Third Korean Winter, and Korea Summer–Fall 1953 campaigns, earning ten battle stars in Korea. On 1 September 1954 she was reclassified minehunter AMCU 48. She was decommissioned 6 December 1957 and placed in reserve.

Redstart AM 378: [d. 890; 221'1" × 32'2"; 18 k; cpl. 117; a. 1-3", 2-40mm, 8-20mm, 2dct, 4 dcp; Class Auk] This sweeper was commissioned 4 April 1945 and she was on the West Coast when the war ended. She continued minesweeping duties in the Pacific, returning April 1946. She was decommissioned 26 November 1946. Recommissioned 1 December 1950, she arrived in Wonsan and started minesweeping while the shore bombardment was in process. The *Redstart* suffered minor damage after being hit by shore battery at Wonsan, North Korea, on 10 September 1951, but suffered no casualties. She operated off California most of 1952, then on 1 December 1952 left for seven-month deployment off the Korean coast. She set a record for the Korean War with 81 mines swept. She participated in the Communist China Spring Offensive, UN Summer–Fall Offensive, Second Korean Winter, Third Korean Winter, and Korea Summer–Fall 1953 campaigns. On 1 March 1955 she was redesignated MSF 378. She was decommissioned 15 March 1956 and transferred to Nationalist China where she served an escort vessel. She received five battle stars for her Korean service. In some reports she is listed as an AMS.

Ruddy AM 380: [d. 890 tons; 221'2" × 32'2"; 18 k; cpl. 105; a. 1-3", 2-40mm, 2 dct, 5 dcp; Class Auk] Launched 29 October 1944 and commissioned 28 April 1945, she provided sweeping and courier service, and supervised YMS operations. She took part in Operation

Crossroads in July 1946, the atomic tests, and was decommissioned 15 January 1947. Recommissioned 12 March 1952, she swept off Wonsan and transported POWs to Yo Do. She saw service in Korean waters during the Third Korean Winter and Korea Summer–Fall 1953 campaigns. She was inactivated and decommissioned on 31 August 1956, and was then transferred to the government of Peru. She earned two battle stars for her service in Korea.

Shoveler AM 382: [d. 890; 221'2" × 32'2"; 18.1 k; cpl. 117; a. 1-3", 2-40mm, dc; Class Auk] Launched 10 December 1944 and commissioned 22 May 1945, she was assigned to the Pacific during World War II and was decommissioned and put into reserve on 5 November 1946. She was recommissioned 24 July 1951 and assigned to Mine Squadron 5. She arrived in Sasebo on 20 May 1952 and began sweeping at Wonsan. She operated in that general area for more than four months. In addition to sweeping, she destroyed nine sampans with gunfire, and bombarded the coasts. Following the Korean War she operated first on the coasts of Korea, Sasebo, and Keelung, Taiwan, as well as on the west coast of the United States. She served during the Korean Defensive Summer–Fall 1952 campaign, after which she was reclassified to MSF 382 on 7 February 1955. She was placed in reserve 28 September 1956 and loaned to Peru. She received one battle star for service in Korea.

Surfbird AM 890: [d. 890; 221'2" × 32'2"; 18 k; cpl. 117; a. 1-3" 2-40mm; Class Auk] The *Surfbird* was the last of the Auk-class minesweepers to serve in the Navy. Launched on 31 August 1944 and commissioned 25 November 1944, she served at Okinawa, Retto, Eniwetok, Guam and Ulithi. She was decommissioned 5 June 1946. She was recommissioned 12 March 1952 and began to sweep between Wonsan and Hungnam. She served in Korea during the Third Korean Winter and Korea Summer–Fall 1953 campaigns. In February 1955 her designation was changed from AM to MSF. On 15 June 1957 she received degaussing equipment and redesignated as ADG 383, working in Japan, Korea, the Republic of China, the Philippines and the Republic of South Vietnam. She was decommissioned on 18 December 1970 and attached to the Pacific Reserve Fleet. She received two battle stars.

Swift AM 122: [d. 890; 221'2" × 32; 18 k; cpl. 105; a. 1-3", 2-40mm; Class Auk] Launched 5 December 1942 and commissioned 29 December 1943, she was assigned Atlantic convoy duty during World War II until transferred to the Pacific. She was decommissioned 4 June 1946 and then recommissioned 17 April 1951. The *Swift* received superficial damage on 29 May 1953 from a single hit after receiving thirty rounds of 75mm fire from a shore battery at Walsa-ri, North Korea. There was a single casualty. She served in Korea during the Third Korean Winter and Korea Summer–Fall 1953 campaigns. She was reclassified MSF 122 (flat bottom, steel) on 7 February 1955 and decommissioned 13 December 1955. She was struck from the navy list 1 July 1972 and sold for scrap.

Symbol AM 123: [d. 890; 221'2" × 32; 18 k; cpl. 105; a. 1-3", 2-40mm; Class Auk] Launched 2 July 1942, this Auk-class sweeper was commissioned on 10 December 1942. During the war she operated between North African and Italian ports. She took part in the invasion of southern France and swept near Golfe de Juan and off Cannes. Then, transferred to the Pacific, she swept from Okinawa to Japanese home waters. She was decommissioned 21 May 1946. Placed in commission again, the minesweeper operated in Korean waters in 1952 from 7 to 25 February, 17 March to 20 April, 7 May to 9 June, and 29 June to 39 July, operating around Wonsan Harbor. She conducted a second tour of duty in Korea from 29 May to 18 June 1953, and 29 September to 20 October 1953. She served in the Second Korean Winter, Korean Defense Summer–Fall 1952, and Third Korean Winter campaigns. She received minor damage in the vicinity of the bridge after an air burst and near misses from shore battery at Songjin, North Korea, suffering 13 casualties, 20 August 1952. There months later, on 20 November 1952, she was hit by one shell after 89 rounds had been fired from a shore battery at Wonsan. There was one casualty. She saw service in Korean waters during the Second Korean Winter, Korean Defense Summer–Fall 1952, and Korea Summer–Fall 1953 campaigns. She received two battle stars and the Navy Unit Commendation for service in Korea. On 27 July 1956 she was decommissioned. Struck from the navy list on 1 July 1972, she was sold for scrap.

Toucan AM 387: [d. 890; 221'1" × 32'2"; 18 k; cpl. 117; a. 1-3", 2-40mm; Class Auk] Launched 15 September 1944 and commissioned 25 November 1944, she swept the waters around the Ryukyus and then, as the war ended, participated in the general defensive sweep. She was decommissioned and put in the reserves 1 July 1946. Brought back for the Korean War, she was recommissioned 27 October 1950. She commenced Korean War operations on 21 February 1952 and operated off the coast of Wonsan. Her duty was to disrupt the North Korean fishing trade, and in service she took thirteen prisoners, destroyed three sampans and damaged twenty-two more. She returned for a second tour in the summer of 1953. She saw service in Korean waters during the Second Korean Winter, Korean Defense Summer–Fall 1952, and Korea Summer–Fall 1953 campaigns, for which she received two battle stars. In February 1955 she was redesignated MSF 387. She was withdrawn from the reserve fleet for conversion and transfer to the Republic of China on 22 December 1964.

Waxwing AM 389: [d. 890; 221'1" × 32'2"; 18.1 k; cpl. 117; a. 1-3", 2-40mm; Class Auk] This Auk-class sweeper was launched on 10 March 1945; she was commissioned on 6 August 1945, just as World War II ended. She spent a good deal of the post-war period cleaning out minefields that were still hazards to shipping. She was decommissioned on 12 May 1947 and placed in the Pacific Reserve Fleet. Following the North Korean invasion she was recommissioned 19 March 1952, and late in the year, and in 1953, she conducted minesweeping activities in Korea. After the end of the war she conducted local operations, and in 1955 she was redesignated MSF, a fleet minesweeper. After being scheduled for inactivation by May 1957, she was transferred to the Nationalist Chinese navy 14 October 1965, where she served as *Chu Yung* (PCE-67)

Zeal AM 131: [d. 890; 221'1" × 32; 18.1 k; cpl. 105; a. 1-3", 2-40mm, 2-20mm; Class Auk] The Auk-class *Zeal* was launched 15 September 1942 and commissioned 9 July 1943. During World War II she escorted convoys between the islands of the southwestern Pacific, and conducted antisubmarine patrols near the New Hebrides and Marshall Islands. She took part on the last campaign, the assault on Okinawa, where she served on radar picket stations. Following World War II she did sweeping operations around Japan and the East China Sea. Placed out of commission on 4 June 1946, she remained inactive until 19 December 1952 when she was recommissioned. When the war broke out in Korea she took part in minesweeping operations near Wonsan, Hungnam, and Chongjin. She participated in the rescue of twenty-six crew members of the *Sarsi* after the tug had hit a mine. She remained in Korea until the fall of 1952 after which she operated on the west coast of the United States. She earned one battle star for the Korean War. Redesignated MSF 131, she conducted training operations. She was decommissioned in 1956. Her name was struck on 1 December 1966 and she was sunk as a target on 9 January 1967.

YMS

While primarily unnamed, or unrecorded, the wooden-hull YMS auxiliary-motor minesweeper played a significant role both in World War II and Korea. Often ignored by both the public and historians because of the fact that they were identified by number rather than name (it is assumed), they nevertheless were excellent craft. When they entered service in the Korean War they were designated AMS. The first craft was completed in March 1942 and after that a total of 481 ships were built at a variety of shipyards. The basic YMS had a displacement of 270 tons, dimensions of 136 × 24'6", a speed of 13 knots, and a complement of 4 officers and 29 crew members, and was armed with 1-3", 2-20mm, 2 depth charge tracks and 2 depth charge projectors. They operated with two 500-horsepower diesel engines. The difference between vessels was basically cosmetic. YMS 1-134 had two stacks, YMS 135-445 and 480-481 had one stack, and YMS 446-479 had no stack. The last of this type of ship, the MSCO 54 (originally YMS 359) was struck from the navy list in 1969.

11

Merchant Marines

*I don't know what the hell this logistics is that Marshall is always talking about, but
I want some of it.*
— Fleet Admiral E. J. King, to a staff officer in 1942

In February 1950, Secretary of Defense Louis A. Johnson expressed the belief that if the United States found itself facing a military emergency it would be handicapped by a serious shortage of shipping. The best preparation to avoid this would be a pool of allied potentials. This pool would be established by a combination of four different alternatives: the Merchant Marine, the Military Sea Transportation Service, the National Defense Reserve Fleet, and the U. S. Maritime Administration reserve. Two of these provided vessels and two fed vessels into the system as needed.

A few months later, when war broke out on the Korean peninsula, the system was put to the test. It suddenly became necessary to establish and then maintain a 5,000-mile-long Pacific pipeline. To meet the immediate needs of men and supplies, the Military Sea Transportation System (MSTS) moved into action and, along with commercial ships of the merchant marine and Japanese time-charter ships, began shipments at once. The first act was to order the USAT *Sergeant George D. Keathley*, a coastal transport, and the USNS *Cardinal O'Connell*, a cargo ship, to transport much-needed ammunition to Pusan. From 5 to 8 July 1950 the Navy found it necessary to activate two gasoline tankers, seven auxiliary ships that headed north from the Marianas, six transports from Pearl Harbor, and seven from the west coast of the United States. The unit, identified as Service Squadron Three, consisted of two destroyer tenders, two reefers, three cargo ships, three fleet oilers, two gasoline tankers, two repair ships, five fleet tugs and a dock landing ship.

From this beginning there soon was a bridge of ships forming across the Pacific to carry the necessary goods of war to Japan and then on to Korea. The key to this bridge was the United States commercial shipping fleet. Beginning with six ships under charter, it reached a command of 255 ships as the program peaked. During the war more than 85 percent of the cargo shipped to Korea by sea was delivered by commercial carriers. One hundred thirty Victory ships, already famous from prolonged service during World War II, were released and reactivated from the National Defense Reserve Fleet and crewed by civil service merchant mariners. Some were assigned, or chartered, by the MSTS. These ships not only carried supplies, they also served as naval auxiliaries. During the invasion of Inchon in September 1950, 13 USNS cargo ships, 28 chartered American and 34 Japanese-crewed merchant ships, participated.

The Maritime Administration (MARAD)

MARAD was not a Navy facility but rather a government agency, under the Department of Transportation (DOT), which was responsible for promoting and maintaining a merchant marine for both commerce and defense. It replaced the U.S. Maritime Commission, established 29 June 1936. The Commission was abolished 24 May 1950.

The Merchant Marine

The Military Sea Transportation Service was neither designed to provide all the shipping needs of the military command, nor was it able to do so. While the MSTS carried a good portion of the immediate needs of the military, it had to rely on a large armada of contracted vessels to meet the logistical demands required in equipping, supplying and replenishing the vast UN army in the field. It was the power of this expanded transportation element that made it possible for the United States to supply the tremendous tonnage needed for fighting a modern war. Those called on for this service are identified as the Merchant Marine. Just what the Merchant Marine consists of remains something of a mystery to most Americans.

Francis Thronson, in an article entitled "Merchant Marines and Lower Case Letters" provides an answer to America's poor understanding of the role of this vast fleet, by suggesting the problem lies in the fact "that there is no there there." What he meant by this is a lack of solidarity among this rather dismembered collection of vessels. It is not possible to write a letter to the Merchant Marine headquarters; there is no building, there is no administrator, admiral or CEO in charge. There is no phone number nor address for the "U.S. Merchant Marines." As Thronson points out, it is not even correct to capitalize the name, for it is not a proper noun. Nevertheless, it is capitalized in this volume out of respect. To seek the location of the Merchant Marine is like seeking an address for the airline industry. The Merchant Marine is an amalgamation of privately owned merchant shipping companies that, in time of need, rally to the cause. Nevertheless the Merchant Marine has a long and historic tradition, having supplied American forces through many of its wars, and having written for itself an epic of duty, endurance, and courage during World War II. As the United States once again faced the difficulties of fighting, thousands of miles from home, the nation turned to this loose amalgamation of merchant ships and their crews.

Month after month during the Korean War, the demand for supplies, equipment, and repair put a steady pressure on the logistics and support functions of the navy. Relying a great deal on the vessels and facilities developed during World War II, hundreds of thousands of tons of necessities were supplied across the Pacific. A good many merchant ships took part in the landing at Inchon and Wonsan, and participated in the Hungnam redeployment. Following the end of the Korean War, President Truman gave the American Merchant Marine a "well done" acknowledgment for its outstanding support of the United Nations Command. He noted that the supreme effort had meant that the logistics necessary to contain the communist aggression had not diminished the Merchant Marine ability to move goods necessary to maintain the nation's economy. During 1950–1953, there was a worldwide shortage of ships, with over 600 used to deliver coal to Northern Europe and grain to China. Despite the demands of the Korean War, Truman's concern that the American people have both "guns and butter" during the Korean War was accomplished.

Unlike its service during World War II, the Merchant Marine did not face long and dangerous voyages, usually in convoy, in the face of enemy submarines and surface raiders. So, despite the fact that they were often in "harm's way" and suffered several accidents in their activity, there were no direct losses of merchant ships during the Korean War. On one occasion the Merchant Marine did lose a ship to the enemy, not by combat, but by actions of the crew. The American captain and chief engineer of the SS *Kimball R. Smith* were aboard the "Baltic Coaster"-class ship that had been loaned to the South Koreans. While aboard the ship, the crew mutinied and took the ship to a North Korean port where the two officers were interned, but later released. The SS *Kimball R. Smith* was used by the North Koreans during the war.

The records of most of these ships are difficult if not impossible to locate. The best source for participation, listing ships on the basis of their eligibility for the Korean Service Medal, is the *Navy and Marine Corps Awards Manual* (U.S. Navy, 1956) referred to throughout this text as *Awards*. Even with this aid it is difficult to assign particulars to many of the individual ships. Hard as it is to believe, some seem to have simply disappeared from any official accounting. Over the years, as they have aged, many of the Victory and Liberty ships created for World War II and used during the Korean War became too expensive to operate, and they have been sold for scrap to reap the value of their metal. Five ships have been located that serve as floating museums. They are the *Jeremiah O'Brien, John W. Brown, American Victory, Red Oak Victory*, and *Victory Lane*. In a few cases ships are documented as having participated in the Korean War, but for some reason are not listed in *Awards*. They are included here when evidence appears to support it, and a source is given.

Those serving with the Merchant Marine are presented in alphabetical order, followed by what information is available. The hull number is the Maritime Commission (MCV) hull number. The first Victory ship was named SS *United Victory*, and the next thirty-four were named for the Allied nations that participated in World War II. The next 218 were named for American cities, the next 154 for educational institutions, and the rest named miscellaneously.

A wide variety of ships were in service, though most were either Liberty ships or Victory ships built during World War II. Unlike the Liberty ships, there was only one significant conversion among Victory ships. Early in 1945, under the authority of the War Shipping Administration, ninety-seven were converted to troopships, and manned by crews through commercial steamship companies. The first of these, *Central Falls Victory*, was converted on 23 April 1945. The conversion included berthing, galleys, messes, toilets, showers, medical facilities, and common rooms. Additional lifeboats and floats were included. These ships had the capacity to carry approximately 1,597 troops.

The Liberty ship was the popular name for the EC2 (Emergency Construction) contracted by the Maritime Commission and nicknamed "ugly duckling" by President Franklin Delano Roosevelt. The first of the 2,751 ships built was launched on 27 September 1941. A standardized and mass-produced vessel, it required 250,000 parts which were made throughout the nation and then welded together. It took about seventy days to complete a ship, at a cost of less than two million dollars. These ships were 441 feet long and 56 feet wide, and had a speed of about 11 knots. They could carry more than 9,000 tons of cargo, with more lashed to the deck. These ships were named after important and deceased Americans. Any organization that was able to raise two million dollars in war bonds could suggest a name for a Liberty ship, a practice which explains some of the more unusual names.

At the end of World War II, the Maritime Commission reported that the *Stanley R. Fisher* was the last of the Liberty ships. Actually sixteen other ships were laid and delivered after the *Stanley R. Fisher*, and the *Albert H. Boe* was the last to be delivered. Frank Lane's *Ships for Victory* (1951) lists 2,708 as being built, but that is considerably more than the 2,580 claimed by the Maritime Commission. The American Bureau of Shipping, as reported by John Gorley Bunker in *Liberty Ships: The Ugly Ducklings of World War II*, states that 2,751 Liberty ships were built. Those built as Victory ships are designated V (Victory) C (Cargo). The numeral 2 indicates a length between 400 and 450 feet. The VC2-AP2 had a light displacement of 4,420, were 455'3" × 62, and had a speed of 17 knots. The VC2-AP 5 (primarily attack transports) had a displacement of 6,700, and were 436'6" × 62, with a speed of 17 knots. The VC3 had a higher horsepower (8,500 rather than 6,000) and a displacement of 8,236, with a length of 492 × 69'6" and a speed of 16.5 knots. The VC1-M had a light tonnage of 2,382, was 338'8" × 50, and had a horsepower of 1,700 and a speed of 11 knots. Victory ships were armed with one 5" gun on the stern, a 3" gun on the bow, and eight 20mm guns.

Note: Ships with crafted designations, such as an oiler, are listed with their designated groupings.

Aberdeen Victory: (VC2-S-AP3) Hull 110. Delivered 22 June 1944 for the WSA, she was transferred to the navy 26 July 1951 as the *Altair* (AK 257), then in 1953 identified as AKS 32. Decommissioned in 1969, she was transferred to the Maritime Administration 1 September and scrapped in 1974. Listed in Cagle and *Awards* but not by the Merchant Marine Association.

Acorn Knot: (VC1-M. AV1) Completed and launched as *Alexander R. Nininger, Jr.*

Adelphia Victory: (VC2-S-AP 2) Hull 60. Built 2 June 1945 for the WSA, she made nine trips to the Korean theater between 1 October 1951 and 18 July 1953. She was scrapped in 1993.

Admiral Dewey: Made three trips between 4 July 1953 and 14 October 1953.

Adrian Victory: (VC2-S-AP 3) Hull 164. Built 26 January 1945 for the WSA, she was renamed *Hawaiian Traveler*, *Joseph*, *Olga*, *Battle Creek*, and *St. Joan*. She made a trip to Korea between 28 September and 5 October 1950.

Afoundia: This merchant ship is listed in *Awards* and by the Merchant Marine Association, but there are no other indications of service.

African: This merchant ship is listed in *Awards* and by the Merchant Marine Association, but there are no other indication of service.

African Glade: Built in 1944 as the *Ann McKim*, she was sold in 1947 and renamed the *African Glade*. She was in Korean waters from 29 October to 5 November 1953.

African Grove: Built in 1944, the ex–*Gauntlet* was purchased in 1947 by the Maritime Administration. In Korean waters from 25 to 31 August 1953, she was scrapped in 1969.

African Moon: Built in 1947, she was in Korean waters 13 to 17 August 1953. Sold in 1973, she was renamed *Moon*.

African Patriot: Built in 1944 as the *Argonaut*, in 1947 she was purchased for the Maritime Administration and named *African Patriot*. She made four trips to the Korean theater from 18 September 1950 to 16 May 1951. Laid up in 1963, she was scrapped in 1971.

African Pilgrim: Built in 1944 as the *Archer*, she was purchased in 1947 by the

Maritime Administration and renamed *African Pilgrim*. She made four trips from 18 September 1950 to 9 February 1951. Laid up 1963, she was scrapped 1974.

African Pilot: Built in 1944 as the *Mandarin*, in 1947 she was sold to the Maritime Administration and renamed the *African Pilot*. She participated in delivering the 7th Division during the Inchon Landing and the Hungnam redeployment and made five trips from 8 October 1950 to 6 July 1953. She was laid up in 1963 and scrapped in 1974.

African Rainbow: This merchant built in 1946 participated in delivering the 7th Division during the Inchon Landing and was involved in the Hungnam redeployment. She made three trips between 23 August 1950 and 10 March 1951. In 1971 she was sold and renamed *Rainbow*. She was scrapped in 1993.

African Star II: This merchant built in 1942 was sold to a private corporation and renamed *African Star*. She made two trips, between 2 March 1952 and 28 December 1952. Scrapped in 1973, she is not listed in *Awards*, but Cagle records her as being at Inchon.

Alamo Victory: (VC2-S- AP 3) Hull 42. Launched 1 August 1944 by the WSA, she was later renamed *Victoria*, and sold in 1971. Not in *Awards* but listed in Cagle, she is sometimes listed as Hull 745.

Alaskan: See *Midland Victory*.

Albion Victory: (VC2-S-AP 2) Hull 624. Launched 5 January 1945 and delivered to the WSA on 3 November 1945, she made nine trips between 12 June 1951 and 26 April 1953. She was scrapped in 1994.

Alfred Victory: (VC2-S-AP 5) Hull 745. Launched 11 April 1945 for the WSA, she made six trips to the Korean theater between 22 February 1951 and 23 March 1953. She was scrapped in 1988.

Allegheny Victory: (VC2-S-AP 2) Hull 762. Launched 9 June 1945 for the WSA, she made nine trips between 6 March 1951 and 11 July 1953. She was scrapped in 1993.

Alma Victory: (VC2-S-AP 3) Hull 692. Launched 1 July 1945 for the WSA, she participated in the Hungnam Korea Redeployment. She made eight trips between 26 September 1950 and 21 November 1951. She was scrapped in 1971.

Amarillo Victory: (VC2-S-AP 2) Hull 801. Launched 1 July 1945 for the WSA, she aided in the support of the Marshall Plan. Put in reserves in 1947, she was withdrawn to carry military supplies to forces in the Korean War. She made eleven trips between 23 June 1951 and 22 July 1952. She also carried supplies during the Vietnam War. She was scrapped in 1995.

American: This merchant ship made seven trips to Korean waters from 14 May 1952 until 27 July 1954.

American Attorney: Hull 642. Launched as *Attleboro Victory* on 16 April 1945, she was sold in 1948 and renamed *American Attorney*. She participated in the Inchon Landing and the Hungnam redeployment. She made three trips into the Korean theater between 3 September and 21 November 1950.

American Eagle: Hull 3063: Built in October 1944 as the *Edward L. Logan* by the WSA, in 1947 she was sold and renamed *American Eagle*. She was in the Korean theater from 18 to 26 March 1951. She was abandoned in 1967.

American Press: (C1-B) This merchant ship was in the Korean theater from 8 October to 3 November 1950.

American Veteran: A merchant ship that participated in the Hungnam redeployment, she was in Korean waters from 4 October to 5 November 1950.

American Victory: (VC2-S-AP 2) Hull 792. Launched on 24 May 1945 for the WSA,

Dry-cargo ship with destroyer escort viewed from unidentified carrier

she was decommissioned, and then brought out of mothballs in 1951 for service in Korea. She made nine trips from 28 August 1951 until 18 November 1953. She would later serve in Vietnam. She was preserved as a museum ship in Tampa, Florida.

Amerocean: This merchant ship was in the Korean theater from 24 July to 5 August 1953.

Amersea: Hull 1843. Built December 1943 as the *Frank R. Stockton*, in 1951 she was sold and renamed *Amersea*. She made three trips into the Korean theater from 1 July to 8 November 1953. She was scrapped in 1968.

Amos G. Throop: Hull 676. Launched 26 November 1942, she made five trips in Korean waters from 14 January to 15 October 1953. Scrapped in 1968.

Ampac Idaho: This merchant ship built in July 1943 as the *Howard T. Ricketts* was sold and renamed *Ampac Idaho* in 1951. She made four trips into the Korean theater between 20 February and 28 November 1953. Scrapped 1967.

Ampac Nevada: She made five trips into Korean waters between 20 December 1953 and 31 October 1953.

Ampac Oregon: Hull 571. A Liberty ship completed February 1942 as *Henry Villard*, renamed in 1951, she made seven trips between 12 March and 25 August 1953. In 1956 renamed *Marine Progress*, she was scrapped in 1963.

Angus Glenn (Canadian ship): She made eight trips from 4 January to 21 May 1954.

Angus McDonald: Hull 2944. This Liberty ship was launched 12 July 1945. She was in Korean waters 15 to 16 April 1952. Scrapped 1969.

Anne Butler: Built January 1945 as *Frank E. Spencer* for the WSA, sold and renamed in 1951, she made four trips from 14 February to 8 December 1953. Scrapped 1968.

Annie C.: She made four trips into the Korean theater from 7 April to 18 September 1953.

Annioc: She was in Korean waters from 8 to 22 April 1954.

Anniston Victory: (VC2-S-AP 2) Hull 584. This freighter, launched 26 January 1945, was in the Korean theater from 24 to 30 May 1953. Scrapped 1985.

Apollo: Built February 1945 for the WSA, she was named *Neptune* in 1951, and then renamed again in 1952 as *Apollo*. She made three trips to the Korean theater.

Arcadia Victory: (VC2-S-AP 3) Hull 41. Delivered 3 September 1944 as a freighter, she made eight trips into the Korean theater from 24 October 1950 to 20 March 1952. She was struck 13 June 1973.

Argovan (Canadian ship): She was in Korean waters 14 to 23 December 1950, participating in the Hungnam redeployment.

Arizpa: This merchant ship made sixteen trips into the Korean theater between 14 September 1950 and 17 January 1954.

Asbury Victory: (VC2-S-AP 2) Hull 764. Launched 16 July 1945, she made twelve trips into Korean waters from 2 October 1950 to 20 August 1953. Placed on Ready Standby (ROS) in 1970, she was scrapped in 1991.

Atlantic Water: Hull 2963. Built 1944 as the *Richard J. Hopkins* for the WSA, she was sold and renamed in 1951. She made four trips between 17 February and 30 May 1953. She sank on 2 March 1964.

Atlanticus: Hull 1724. This Liberty ship built as the *Jeremiah M. Daily* was sold and renamed in 1948. She made five appearances in the Korean theater between 8 January and 8 October 1953. Scrapped 1962.

Audrey II: She made two appearances in the Korean theater between 3 September and 19 December 1953.

Augustine Daly: Hull 2264. This Liberty ship was built 17 February 1944. She was in Korean waters five times between 6 April and 22 July 1952.

B. T. Irvine: Hull 2067. A Liberty ship laid 31 July 1943 and launched 19 August 1943, she participated in Korean waters four times between 31 March and 7 July 1952. She was sold in 1963 and converted to a crane barge.

Badger Mariner: This merchant ship made two appearances in Korean waters between 3 December 1953 and 27 March 1954.

Barbara Fritchie: Hull 1827. This Liberty ship was launched 19 November 1943, sold to private owners in 1947 and served in Korean waters twice between 14 June 1953 and 7 January 1964. She was scrapped in 1969.

Barbara Lykes: This merchant ship was in Korean waters twice between 8 October and 9 November 1950.

Barenfels (foreign flag ship): She made six trips between 19 January and 15 July 1953.

Barnard Victory: (VC2-S-AP 2) Hull 742. Launched 31 May 1944, she made three appearances in Korean water between 18 September 1951 and 5 February 1953.

Barney Krishbaum: Hull 2348. This Liberty ship (a boxed aircraft transport) was laid 15 February 1945 and launched 30 May 1945 on a Maritime Commission contract. In Korean waters eleven times between 8 April 1952 and 4 June 1953, she was scrapped in 1975.

Bartlesville Victory: (VC2-S-AP 2) Hull 476. Launched 13 January 1945, she served as The *Wingless Victory* and the *Kathlena*. She was in Korean waters on ten occasions between 13 March 1951 and 20 June 1953. She was scrapped October 1971.

Baton Rouge Victory: (VC2-S-AP 2) Hull 846. Launched 22 August 1945 for the WSA, she made eight visits to Korean waters between 3 January 1951 and 28 March 1952. She was scrapped 1967.

Baylor Victory: (VC2-S-AP 2) Hull 772. Launched 6 March 1945 for the WSA, she made ten trips into Korean waters between 10 February 1951 and 8 May 1953. She was scrapped in 1970.

Beatrice Victory: (VC2-S-AP 2) Hull 580. Launched 27 December 1944 for the WSA, she was in the Korean theater twice between 25 February and 1 April 1952. She was scrapped in 1993.

Beauregard: This merchant ship made five trips into Korean waters between 3 October 1952 and 16 November 1953.

Beaver Victory: (VC2-S-AP 2) Hull 774. Launched 14 May 1945 for the WSA, she participated in the Inchon Landing and the Hungnam redeployment. She made fourteen visits into Korean waters between 4 September 1950 and 7 May 1953. She was scrapped in 1985.

Bedford Victory: (VC2-S-AP2) Hull 540. Delivered 11 November 1944 as a freighter for the U.S. Navy (AK 231), in 1946 she transferred to the USMC. She participated in the Hungnam redeployment and made seven trips into Korean waters between 9 December 1950 and 26 March 1953. She was scrapped in 1973.

Belgium Victory: (VC2-5-AP 3) Hull 92. Built in 1944 for the WSA, she participated in the Inchon Landing and the Hungnam redeployment. She made nine trips to Korean waters between 24 September 1950 and 5 December 1951. She was scrapped in 1993.

Belocean (Norwegian ship): She made fifty-six visits in Korean waters from 22 October 1950 to 19 April 1954, and participated in the Hungnam redeployment.

Beloit Victory: (VC2-S-AP 3) Hull 111. Launched 3 June 1944, she made eighteen visits to the Korean theater between 4 November 1950 and 14 September 1953. She was scrapped in April 1969.

Benjamin Hawkins: Hull 913. This Liberty ship was launched 7 September 1942 and made five trips into the Korean theater between 25 October 1951 and 23 October 1953. She was scrapped in 1973.

Berea Victory: (VC2-S-AP 2) Hull 734. Launched 3 March 1945, she made four trips into Korean waters between 19 August 1951 and 5 February 1953. Scrapped 1993.

Bessemer Victory: (VC2-S-AP 2) Hull 806. Launched 26 July 1945 for the Wartime Shipping Administration, she participated in the Inchon Landing and the Hungnam redeployment. She made sixteen trips into Korean waters between 24 September 1950 and 24 July 1953. She was scrapped in 1991.

Bet Jeanne (Norwegian ship): She participated in the Hungnam redeployment.

Binghampton Victory: (VC2-S-AP3) Hull 698. Launched 28 July 1945, she made five trips into Korean waters between 22 October 1950 and 28 February 1953. Scrapped 1970.

Black Eagle: see *Midland Victory*.

Bloomington Victory: (VC2-S-AP 2) Hull 805. Launched 21 July 1945 for the WSA, she made ten trips into Korean waters between 8 December 1951 and 6 August 1953. She was scrapped in 1972.

Blue Cross State: This merchant ship made ten visits to the Korean theater between 21 May 1951 and 26 December 1951.

Bluefield Victory: (VC2-S-AP 3) Hull 16. Launched 9 May 1944 for the WSA, she was in Korean waters from 5 to 20 November 1950. In 1969 she was renamed *Columbia Wolf*, then scrapped the same year.

Blue Island Victory: (VC2-S-AP 2) Hull 621. Launched 28 September 1944 as a troop transport, she made five trips into Korean waters between 5 June 1951 and 4 August 1952. Scrapped 1972.

Blue Star: Hull 2874. This Liberty ship was built September 1944 as *Frank Walsh* for the WSA. In 1951 she was sold and renamed *Blue Star*. She made sixteen trips into Korean waters between 3 May 1951 and 20 September 1953. In 1954 she was renamed *Melody* and she was scrapped in 1966.

Booker T. Washington: Hull 648. This Liberty ship was launched 29 September 1944 and sailed with all African-American officers aboard. She was sold to private owners in 1947. She served in Korean waters 6 July to 8 August 1952. She was scrapped in 1965.

Boulder Victory: (VC2-S-AP 2) Hull 536. Launched 31 August 1944 as AK 227 for the U.S. Navy, in 1946 she was transferred to the Maritime Commission. She was in Korean waters between 18 and 21 September 1953. She was scrapped in 1987.

Bowdoin Victory: (VC2-S-AP 2) Hull 588. Launched 24 February 1945 by the WSA, she made four trips into Korean waters between 28 January 1951 and 31 January 1952. She was scrapped in 1984.

Boy: She made five trips into Korean waters between 30 August 1952 and 14 October 1953.

Brainerd Victory: (VC2-S-AP 3) Hull 875. Launched 24 October 1945 for the WSA, she made two trips into the Korean theater between 23 September 1950 and 24 January 1951. She sank in 1964. Some sources identify her as the last Victory ship built.

Brazil Victory: (VC2-S-AP 3) Hull 8. Launched in 1944, she made ten trips into Korean waters between 1 January 1951 and 8 February 1952. Scrapped in 1992.

Brigham Victory: (VC2-S-AP 2) Hull 589. Launched 4 January 1945 for the WSA, she shot down a plane near Okinawa in 1945. She was in Korean waters from 1 to 12 June 1953. She was scrapped 1987.

Bright Star: She was in Korean waters from 27 May to 14 June 1953.

Britain Victory: (VC2-S-AP 3) Hull 88. Launched 4 February 1945, a freighter built for the WSA, she made thirteen trips into Korean waters between 22 April 1951 and 5 August 1953. She was scrapped in 1987.

Buckeye Mariner: She recorded two trips into Korean waters between 10 April and 21 June 1953.

Bucknell Victory: (VC2-S-AP 2) Hull 728. A freighter launched 10 February 1945, she made ten trips to the Korean theater between 13 March 1951 and 20 July 1953. She was scrapped December 1993.

Bucyrus Victory: (VC2-S-AP 2) Hull 543. Delivered 29 November 1944 as AK 234 for the Navy, in 1946 she was transferred to the Maritime Commission and named. She was scrapped in 1969.

Burbank Victory: (VC2-S-AP 2) Hull 721. Launched 28 January 1945 for the WSA, she made eleven trips into Korean waters between 23 April 1951 and 26 May 1953. She was scrapped in 1986.

Burco Trader: She recorded eight trips into Korean waters between 20 July 1952 and 18 May 1963.

C.C.N.Y. Victory: (VC2-S-AP 2) Hull 834. Launched 23 June 1945 for the WSA, she made twelve trips into Korean waters between 25 May 1951 and 20 April 1953. She was scrapped in 1994.

California: See *Drew Victory*.

California Bear: See *Paducah Victory*.

Californian: Listed in *Awards*, she served in Korean waters four times between 30 May 1953 and 10 March 1954.

Canada Mail: She participated in the Hungnam redeployment and operated in Korean waters 20 October to 27 December 1950.

Canton Victory: (VC2-S-AP 2) Hull 765. Launched as a freighter on 20 June 1945 for the WSA, she made seven trips into Korean waters between 27 November 1950 and 2 July 1953. She was scrapped in 1989.

Cape Comfort: (C1-A) She made three trips into Korean waters between 11 May and 7 July 1952.

Cape Elizabeth: (C1-B) She made two trips into Korean waters between 15 May and 4 July 1953.

Cape Saunders: She made two trips into Korean waters between 9 June to 23 August 1952.

Capt. N. B. Palmer: Hull 1903. Launched 2 November 1943 as *Albert J. Berres* for the WSA, in 1950 she was renamed *Nikoklis*, and in 1952 *N. B. Palmer*. Wrecked in 1952, she was finally scrapped in 1962.

Carleton Victory: (VC2-S-AP 2) Hull 738. Launched 17 March 1945, she made twelve trips into Korean waters between 13 December 1950 and 3 June 1953. She was scrapped 1992.

Carroll Victory: (VC2-S-AP 3) Hull 27. Launched 26 June 1944, she made four trips into Korean waters between 23 January 1952 and 20 April 1953. Scrapped 1993.

Carter Braxton: See *Hoosier State*.

Catawba Victory: (VC2-S-AP 2) Hull 706. This freighter was launched 6 June 1945 and made nine trips to the Korean theater between 27 June 1951 and 12 August 1953. She was scrapped 2005.

Catherine Goulandris: Hull 2268. A Liberty ship launched April 1944 as the *Henry Adams*, she was sold and renamed in 1949. She was in Korean waters six times between 5 August 1952 and 23 July 1953. Scrapped 1968.

Cecil N. Bean: Hull 2457. Launched 6 March 1944, sold to private owners 1949, she made five visits into Korean waters between 12 January 1951 and 27 April 1953. She was scrapped 1967.

Central Victory: (VC2-S-AQP 2) Hull 736. Built in April 1945 for the WSA, she made five trips into the Korean theater between 18 May 1951 and 31 August 1953. She was scrapped 1993.

Chain Trader: Hull 2995. A Liberty ship launched February 1945 as *Leonardo L. Romero* for the WSA, she was sold and renamed in 1951. She made four trips into Korean waters between 5 July and 8 November 1953. Scrapped 1970.

Charles Lykes: She was in Korean waters three times between 29 August and 5 November 1950 and participated in the Inchon invasion.

Charles M. Conrad: Hull 403. A Liberty ship laid 7 October 1942 and launched 14 November 1942, she was in the Korean theater between 20 May and 7 June 1953. She was scrapped in 1963.

Charles McNary: Hull 2974. A Liberty ship launched 16 November 1944 and sold to private owners in 1947, she was in Korean waters 19 February to 9 March 1952. She was scrapped in 1968.

Charles Winsor: She sailed with Korean flag and crew but with an American captain and navigator.

China Victory: (VC2-S-AP 3) Hull 1. Launched 26 January 1944 for the WSA, she was in Korean waters twice between 26 September and 9 November 1950. Also named the *P & T Leader* (1951), *Smith Leader* (1962), *Transnorthern* (1965), and *Buckeye Victory* (1969), she was scrapped in 1972.

Choctaw Victory: See *Dartmouth Victory*.

Christain: Launched May 1944 as the *William Sproule*, in 1951 she was sold and renamed. She made ten trips into Korean waters between 31 May and 29 December 1951. Scrapped 1963.

Christine: Laid February 1944 as the *Harry Kirby* for the WSA, she was renamed in 1949. She made three trips into Korean waters between 14 July and 7 October 953. Scrapped 1969.

Christos M.: She made five trips to the Korean theater between 26 September 1952 and 26 January 1953.

Citrus Packer: She participated in the Hungnam redeployment and made thirteen trips into Korean waters between 27 September 1950 and 16 February 1952.

City of Alma: She made twelve trips into Korean waters between 11 September and 9 July 1954.

Clarksburg Victory: (VC2-S-AP 2) Hull 888. A Liberty ship launched 15 September 1944 for the WSA, she participated in the Hungnam redeployment and made five trips into the Korean theater between 21 December 1950 and 10 September 1953. Scrapped 1974.

Clarksville Victory: (VC2-S-AP 2) Hull 629. Launched 30 January 1945 for the WSA, she made two trips into Korean waters between 22 May and 19 July 1953. She was scrapped 1974.

Clearwater Victory: (VC2-S-AP 2) Hull 583. Launched 20 January 1945 for the WSA, she was in Korean waters 6 to 15 June 1952. The freighter was scrapped in 1973.

Clove Hitch: She completed thirty-two trips into the Korean theater between 15 February 1952 and 29 January 1954.

Clovis Victory: (VC2-S-AP 3) Hull 32. Launched 13 July 1944, she made ten trips into Korean waters between 8 January 1951 and 26 November 1952. She was scrapped 1972.

Coastal Sentry: (C1-M-AV1) Completed for the navy in 1943 as the *Somerset* (AK 205), she was renamed the *Coastal Sentry* and made thirty-nine trips into Korean waters between 2 March 1952 and 15 January 1954.

Codington: (C1-M-AV1) Completed for the navy as AK 173, she made thirty-eight trips into Korean waters between 6 March 1952 and 27 July 1954.

Coe Victory: (VC2-S-AP 3) Hull 189. Launched 3 May 1945, she served in Korea 11 October to 14 November 1950. Scrapped 1969.

Coeur d'Alene Victory: (VC2-S-AP 3) Hull 153. Launched 15 September 1945 as APA 145 for the U.S. Navy, in 1946 she was transferred to the Maritime Commission. She made two trips in Korean waters between 12 December 1950 and 14 January 1951. She was scrapped in 1974.

Coffeyville Victory: See *Mormacelm*.

Colgate Victory: (VC2-S-AP 3) Hull 170. She was launched 10 February 1945. During her service she also sailed under the names *Hongkong Transport*, *Oregon Victory*, and *Ridgefield Victory*. She was in Korean waters four times between 20 October 1953 and 29 May 1954. Scrapped 1969.

Columbia Trader: (VC2-S-AP 2) Hull 101. She made two trips between 22 June 1953 and 18 September 1954.

Compass: She served in the Korean theater between 27 September and 14 October 1953.

Constitution State: See *Skagway Victory*.

Cooper Union Victory: See *Green Harbor*.

Coral Sea: She made two trips to Korea between 5 December 1950 and 18 January 1951.

Cornell Victory: (VC2-S-AP 2) Hull 778. Launched 30 May 1945 for the WSA, she made fifteen trips in the Korean theater between 20 December 1950 and 15 September 1953. She participated in the Hungnam redeployment. She was scrapped in 1994.

Cornhusker Mariner: She made three trips to Korean between 17 February 1953 and 6 July 1953. Grounded while at Pusan in 1952, she had to be pulled off by the ARS *Current*.

Cotton Mariner: Hull 926. This Liberty ship was laid 28 September 1942, and according to Cagle she participated in the Hungnam redeployment, but *Awards* lists her as being in Korea in October 1953. Scrapped 1960.

Cotton State: See *Spartanburg Victory*.

Council Bluffs Victory: (VC2-S-AP 2) Hull 890. Launched 27 September for the WSA, she made nine trips to Korean waters between 4 October 19540 and 3 February 1952. She was scrapped in 1994.

Creighton Victory: (VC2-S-AP 3) Hull 178. Launched 21 March 1945 for the WSA, she made seven trips to Korea between 6 January 1951 and 3 April 1952. She was scrapped 1984.

Cuba Victory: (VC2-S-AP 3) Hull 530. Launched 27 June 1944 for the WSA, she was in the Korean theater five times between 16 November 1950 and 17 July 1953. She was damaged in 1968 during the Vietnam War, and scrapped 1985.

Dartmouth Victory: (VC2-S-AP 3) Hull 169: Launched 15 March 1945 as the *President Arthur*, she served under the names *Dartmouth Victory* and *Choctaw Victory*, making fifteen trips to Korea between 26 November 1950 and 14 October 1952. She participated in the Hungnam redeployment.

David B. Johnson: Hull 1511. This Liberty ship was launched 23 November 1943. She was scrapped in 1968.

David Dudley Field: Hull 470. This Liberty ship, launched 24 March 1943, was in Korean waters twice between 19 March and 9 May 1952. She was scrapped in 1970.

Del Aires: She was in Korean waters twice between 26 April 1953 and 20 January 1954.

Del Alba: She was in Korean waters three times from 3 September 1950 to 20 January 1951, and participated in the Hungnam redeployment.

Denise: She was in the Korean theater nine times between 8 October 1950 and 15 November 1953 and participated in the Hungnam redeployment.

DePauw Victory: (VC2-S-AP 2) Hull 727. Launched 7 February 1944 for the WSA, she was in Korean waters three times between 13 December 1950 and 25 August 1951. She was scrapped 1989.

Diamond Mariner: (C4-5-1A) Hull 493. She was in Korean waters from 4–14 March 1954. Sold to Spain in 1980.

Digby County: She was in Korean waters from 21 to 29 October 1950.

Ditto: Hull 1596. This Liberty ship was built in March 1943 as *Hall J. Kelley* for the WSA. In 1949 she was sold and renamed. She was in the Korean theater eleven times from 6 November 1950 and 39 December 1953. Scrapped 1968.

Dolly Turman: She made two trips to Korean waters in September and November of 1950, and participated in the Inchon invasion.

Dorothy Stevenson: Hull 1734. This Liberty ship was laid September 1943 as *George W. Kendall*. In 1948 she was renamed *Dorothy Stevenson*. She was Korean waters twice between 10 July and 7 September 1953. Scrapped 1967.

Drew Victory: (VC2-S-AP3) Hull 691. Launched 17 June 1945, in 1949 she was renamed the *California*. She made four trips into Korean waters between 4 November 1950 and 5 April 1951, and participated in the Hungnam redeployment. Scrapped 1973.

Drury Victory: (VC2-S-AP 2) Hull 761. Launched 6 June 1945 for the WSA, she was in Korean waters four times between 4 October 1950 and 24 July 1853. She was scrapped 1985.

Dudley H. Thomas: Hull 2341. This Liberty ship (a boxed air craft transport) was launched 8 February 1945. She was in Korean waters three times between 15 March and 15 June 1953. In 1953 she was redesignated the *Interpreter* (YAGR 14). Scrapped 1974.

Duke Victory: (VC2-S-AP 2) Hull 731. Launched 21 February 1945 for the WSA, she was in Korean waters nine times between 9 January 1951 and 29 June 1953. She was scrapped 1985.

Durango Victory: (VC2-S-AP 2) Hull 549. Launched 16 December 1945 for the WSA. She was in Korean waters four times between 14 August 1951 and 12 March 1952. She was scrapped in 1995.

Earlham Victory: (VC2-S-AP 2) Hull 763. Launched 13 June 1945 for the WSA, she was in Korean waters four times between 28 October 1951 and 30 March 1952. She was scrapped 2005.

East Point Victory: (VC2-S-AP 2) Hull 645. Launched 26 March 1945 for the WSA the freighter was in Korean waters seven times between 23 March 1951 and 15 March 1953. She was scrapped in 1971.

Edison Mariner: A Liberty ship built in 1945 by the WSA, in 1947 she was sold and renamed. She was in Korean waters eleven times between 2 July 1952 and 15 January 1955. She sank in 1966.

Edwin Markhan: Hull 284. A Liberty ship laid 18 February 1942 and launched 5 May 1942 for the Army Transportation Service, she was in Korean waters twice between 20 March and 23 April 1952. She was scrapped 1965.

Eileen: She was in Korean waters three times between 5 October 1950 and 9 August 1950.

Elby: She sailed in Korean waters twice between 19 March and 26 April 1951.

Elko Victory: (VC2-S-AP 2) Hull 548. Launched 8 December 1944, she served in Korean waters three times between 15 October 1950 and 5 November 1951. She was scrapped in 1994.

Elly: She was in Korean waters 6 to 13 December 1950 and participated in the Hungnam redeployment.

Elmira Viceroy: (VC2-S-AP 3) Hull 105. Launched 12 May 1944 for the WSA, she was in the Korean theater in May 1953. She was scrapped in 1993.

Empire Marshall (British ship): She was in Korean waters sixteen times between 11 April 1951 and 26 June 1952. She participated in the Inchon invasion and the Hungnam redeployment.

Empire State Mariner: She was in Korean waters 7 to 18 July 1954.

Empire Viceroy: She was in Korean waters fourteen times between 11 July 1951 and 10 August 1952.

Empire Wallace: Operated under British charter, she participated in the Inchon invasion and the Hungnam redeployment. She was in Korean waters thirty-nine times between 31 August 1950 and 3 July 1954.

Enid Victory: (VC2-S-AP 2) Hull 712. Launched 27 June 1945 for the WSA, she was in Korean waters six times between 24 November 1950 and 24 March 1952, and participated in the Hungnam redeployment. She was scrapped in 1993.

Escanaba Victory: (VC2-S-AP 3) Hull 112. Completed June 1944 for WSA, she was laid as *Regulus* (AF 57). She went aground July 1971 and was scrapped 1972. This ship is often confused with the *Escambia*.

Ethiopia Victory: (VC2-S-AP 3) Hull 526. Launched 20 April 1944, she served in Korean waters twelve times between 22 December 1950 and 1 June 1953. Renamed *Victoria* (TAK 281) for the U.S. Navy in 1965, she was scrapped in 1987.

Eugenie: She served in the Korean theater three times between 15 June and 15 October 1953.

Evergreen Star: The ex–*William Frederic Kraft* was at Pusan in 1952. Not listed in *Awards*.

Exmouth Victory: She operated in Korean waters four times between 6 October and 25 December 1950. She participated in the Hungnam redeployment.

Fairhope: She served in Korean waters three times from 24 August 1952 to 7 January 1953.

Federal Voyager: She served in Korean waters six times between 18 December 1953 and 4 May 1954.

Ferdinand Westfall: Hull 2186. This Liberty ship was in Korean waters four times between 24 April 1952 and 11 July 1952. She was scrapped in 1967.

Flora C.: Built in June 1944 as *Edward P. Ripley* for the WSA. She was renamed *Flora C* in 1949, and in 1956 as *Arthur Fribourg*. She served in Korean waters seven times between 27 July 1952 and 18 May 1953. Scrapped as *Dorothy* in 1968.

Frederic C. Collins: This Liberty ship built in December 1944 for the WSA was renamed in 1949. She sailed in Korean waters thirteen times between 19 June 1951 and 6 September 1953. After 1958 she had a variety of names. Scrapped in 1968, she is listed in *Awards*.

Frederick Brouchard: Hull 3076. This Liberty ship launched 11 November 1944 made four trips into Korean waters between 16 January and 21 April 1952. She was scrapped in 1961.

Frederick E. Williamson: Hull 2334. This Liberty ship launched 23 December 1944 served in the Korean theater six times between 21 May 1952 and 17 August 1953. She was transferred to the U.S. Navy in 1970 and scuttled with excess ammunition that same year.

Free State Mariner: The *Mariner* made five trips into Korean waters between 31 March and 23 December 1953.

Fribourg Trader: She made nine trips into Korean waters between 27 September 1952 and 25 November 1953.

Frontenac Victory: (VC2-S-AP 2) Hull 625. Launched February 1945 for the WSA, she served in Korean waters eleven times between 12 February 1951 and 20 November 1952. In 1967 renamed *Oceanic Ondine*, she was scrapped in 1995.

Frostburg Victory: (VC2-S-AP 2) Hull 622. Launched 20 January 1945, she was scrapped in 1971.

Furman Victory: (VC2-S-AP 3) Hull 174. Launched 6 March 1945 by the WSA, she served in Korean waters eleven times between 30 September 1950 and 2 July 1953. In 1963 she was renamed *Furman* (TAK 280) by the U.S. Navy.

Gainesville Victory: (VC2-S-AP 3) Hull 22. Launched 9 June 1944, she participated in the Hungnam redeployment, and was in Korean waters eighteen times between 30 October 1950 and 26 July 1953. Scrapped 1993.

General George Patton: Hull 1012. A Liberty ship built in July 1943 for the WSA as the *George M. Cohen*, she was renamed in 1952. Scrapped 1969.

George A. Lawson: Hull 3097. A Liberty ship laid 18 December 1944 and launched 21 February 1945, she was sold to private owners in 1947. She was in Korean waters three times from 3 April to 23 October 1953. She was sunk in 1964.

George Eastman: Hull 110. This Liberty ship was launched 20 April 1943. Assigned to the U.S. Navy in 1952, she was in Korean waters 9 to 22 March 1952. Scrapped in 1977.

George F. Duval: This Liberty ship was built in 1945 as *Frede Joyce* for the WSA. In 1951 she was renamed, and she served in Korean waters twice between 21 June and 26 August 1953. Scrapped in 1961.

George M. Culucundis: She was built in July 1943 as the *Louis Marshall*. In 1953 she was renamed the *Sea Wizard*. The ship sank in 1954.

Golden City: She served in Korean waters from 30 December 1950 to 1 January 1951.

Golden Mariner: She was in Korean waters from 3 March to 4 August 1954.

Great Falls Victory: (VC2-S-AP 2) Hull 717. Launched 14 July 1945 for the WSA, she served in Korean waters four times between 17 February 1951 and 3 April 1952. She was scrapped 1988.

Greece Victory: (VC2-S-AP 3) Hull 2. Launched 3 February 1944 by the WSA, she served nine times in Korean waters between 5 October 1950 and 14 April 1954. She was scrapped in 1972.

Greeley Victory: (VC2-S-AP 2) Hull 714. Launched 4 July 1945 by the WSA, she made nine trips into Korean waters between 26 February 1950 and 16 June 1952. She was scrapped in 1989.

Green Bay Victory: (VC2-S-AP 3) Hull 159. Launched 1945 (AK 237), she was one of the first ships to Okinawa, and later served eleven times in Korean waters between 24 September 1950 and 5 July 1953. She was transferred to the Maritime Commission in 1975, and was scrapped in 1985.

Green Harbor: (VC2-S-AP 2) Hull 783. Launched 19 April 1945 as the *Cooper Union*, she served in Korea from 4 October to 13 November 1950. Renamed *Green Harbor*, she made two trips in Korean waters between 9 March and 4 May 1951. Scrapped 1970.

Green Star: She was in the Korean theater seven times between 25 January and 29 October 1953.

Green Valley: Hull 72. Launched 8 May 1945, originally under the name *Ouachita Victory*, she was renamed in 1949. She served in Korean waters four times between 12 October 1950 and 16 March 1951, and participated in the Hungnam redeployment. She was scrapped in 1970.

Gretna Victory: (VC2-S-AP 2) Hull 722. Launched 14 February 1945 for the WSA, the ship was in Korean waters eight times between 14 March 1951 and 29 June 1953. She was scrapped in 1988.

Grinnell Victory: (VC2-S-AP 2) Hull 729. Launched 14 February 1945 for the WSA, she was in Korean waters five times between 22 August 1951 and 21 May 1953. She was scrapped in 1985.

Groton Trails: In Korean waters eleven times between 21 November 1950 and 10 February 1952, she participated in the Hungnam redeployment.

Gulf Water: She was in Korean waters from 10 to 21 July 1953.

Halalua Victory: (VC2-S-AP 2) Hull 581. Launched 9 January 1945 for the WSA, after service during World War II she served in Korean waters twice between 25 May and 23 September 1953, and was scrapped in 1993.

Hamilton Victory: (VC2-S-AP 2) Hull 707. Launched 15 June 1945 for the WSA, the ship was in Korean waters twice between 25 May and 24 September 1953. She was scrapped in 1993.

Hannibal Victory: (VC2-S-AP 2) Hull 579. Launched 21 December 1944 for the WSA, she made five trips into Korean waters between 8 September 1951 and 21 March 1952. She was scrapped in 2006.

Harold D. Whitehead: Hull 2980. This Liberty ship launched 7 December 1944 was sold to private owners in 1947. She was in Korean waters twice between 1 August and 19 November 1953. She was scrapped in 1969.

Harold L. Winslow: Hull 1807. This Liberty ship launched 16 October 1943 was in Korean waters twice between 20 March and 10 May 1952. She was sold to private owners in 1964 and converted to a floating warehouse.

Harold T. Andrews: Hull 1544. This Liberty ship launched 28 December 1943 was sold to private owners in 1947, served in Korea, and was scrapped in 1967.

Harpoon: A Liberty ship built April 1943 by WSA, in 1950 she was sold and renamed. In Korean waters four times between 29 July and 24 October 1953, in 1954 she was renamed *Centaur*. She was scrapped in 1963.

Harvard Victory: (VC2-S-AP 2) Hull 724. Launched 27 January 1945 for the WSA, she served in Korean waters seven times between 17 September 1951 and 26 July 1953. She was scrapped in 1993.

Hattiesburg Victory: (VC2-S-AP 2). Hull 809. Launched 14 August 1945 for the WSA, she saw limited service in Korea. She is considered to still be in reserves.

Hawaii Bear: See *Kelso Victory*.

Hawaiian: She made three trips into Korean waters between 26 February 1952 and 11 August 1953.

Hawkeye Mariner: She made three trips into Korean waters between 28 April and 24 June 1954.

Helen Lykes: She was in the Korean theater three times between 8 October 1950 and 2 January 1951, and participated in the Hungnam redeployment.

Helen Stevenson: Built December 1943 as *Nicholas Longworth* for the WSA, in 1948 she was renamed. Later she served in Korean waters twice between 15 September 1952 and 7 March 1954. In 1957 she was renamed *Elderfields* and she was scrapped in 1966.

Hendry D. Lindsley: (VC2-S-AP 5) Hull 26. She was in Korean waters twice between 26 April and 4 June 1952.

Heywood Broun: Hull 1780. This Liberty ship launched 6 September 1943 was sold to a private owner in 1947. She made seven trips into Korean waters between 23 June 1952 and 6 September 1953. She was scrapped in 1969.

Hibbing Victory: (VC2-S-AP 3) Hull 113. Launched 10 June 1944 for the WSA, she was in Korean waters between 9 and 24 July 1951. In 1952 she was renamed *Denebola* (AF 56) for service with the U.S. Navy. The reefer was scrapped in 1976.

High Point Victory: (VC2-S-AP 2) Hull 851. Launched 6 September 1945 for the WSA, she served in Korean waters from 16 to 29 June 1953. She was scrapped in 1973.

Hobart Victory: (VC2-S-AP 2) Hull 705. Launched 25 May 1945 by the WSA she was in Korean waters eleven times between 15 October 1951 and 28 July 1953. She was scrapped in 1993.

Holy Star: She made six trips in to Korean waters between 7 February and 18 October 1953.

Honda Knot: (C1-M-AV1) She made thirty-three visits to Korean waters between 15 February 1952 and 27 November 1953.

Hongkong Transport: See *Colgate Victory*.

Hoosier Mariner: She was in Korean waters twice between 30 August 1953 and 11 March 1954.

Hoosier State: Hull 22. Temporarily known as the *Carter Braxton*, this Liberty ship was in Korean waters four times between 17 March and 6 December 1951.

Hope Victory: (VC2-S-AP 2) Hull 751. Launched on 2 May 1945 for the WSA, the *Hope Victory* made six trips into Korean waters between 15 February 1951 and 21 April 1952. She was scrapped in 1990.

Hunter Victory: (VC2-S-AP 2) Hull 754. Launched 12 May 1945 for the WSA, she was in Korean waters eight times between 26 October 1950 and 23 April 1952. She participated in the Hungnam redeployment. Scrapped in 1988.

Hurricane: She served in Korean waters twice between 2 May and 10 June 1954.

Ike: The former *Sea Daring* served in Korean waters twice between 28 July and 15 October 1953.

Iran Victory: (VC2-S-AP 3) Hull 527. Launched on 25 May 1944, she served in Korean waters twelve times between 27 February 1951 and 17 March 1953. Transferred to the Maritime Commission in 1950 as *Iran Victory*, she was scrapped in 1970.

Irene Star: Laid June 1943 as *J. D. Ross*, in 1949 she was renamed and then served in Korean waters five times between 14 December 1951 and 6 October 1953. She was sunk in 1966.

Isaac Van Zandt: Hull 2431. This Liberty ship launched 18 March 1944 was sold to private owners in 1947. She was in Korean waters three times between 22 March and 12 June 1952. She was scuttled with obsolete ammunition in 1966.

Israel Putnam: Hull 12. This Liberty ship launched 13 September 1942 served briefly in Korea, and was scrapped in 1965.

James B. Weaver: Hull 732. Launched 23 March 1943, for the Army Transportation Service, she was in Korean waters from 5 to 23 May 1952. She was scrapped in 1965.

James H. Couper: Hull 1063. Launched 1 October 1943, this Liberty ship served briefly in the Korean theater. She was scrapped in 1965.

James H. Price: Hull 2889. Laid 28 October 1944 and launched 5 December 1944, this Liberty ship served briefly in Korea, and was scrapped in 1964.

James McHenry: Hull 1030. This Liberty ship launched 4 March 1943 was in Korean waters four times between 17 May and 28 August 1952. She was scrapped in 1970.

Jefferson City Victory: (VC2-S-AP 3) Hull 165. Launched 1945 for the WSA, in 1949 she was sold to Victory Carrier Inc. She was in Korean waters six times between 28 September 1950 and 29 May 1953. She was scrapped in 1973.

Jelandside: She was in Korean waters from 20 October to 13 November 1950.

Jericho Victory: (VC2-S-AP 2) Hull 67. Launched on 6 December 1945, she was in Korean waters seven times between 4 October 1951 and 1 August 1953. She was renamed *Thunderbird* in 1961, renamed *North River* in 1970, and scrapped in 1971.

John B. Whidden: She is reported to have been in Korean waters with a Korean crew and American captain, engineer and radio officer on board. Not listed in *Awards*.

John Ball: Hull 2527. This Liberty ship launched 17 November 1943 served in Korean waters four times between 20 April and 22 August 1952, and was scrapped in 1965.

John C.: She served in Korean waters four times between 20 April and 22 August 1952.

John H. B. Latrobe: Hull 52. This Liberty ship launched 13 July 1942 served in Korean waters 17 to 27 March 1952. She was scrapped in 1969.

John H. Marion: Hull 1895. This Liberty ship launched 17 October 1943 and sold to private owners in 1947 served in Korean waters five times between 21 November 1950 and 14 December 1951. She was scrapped in 1967.

John Hanson: Hull 2677. Launched 21 September 1944, sold to private owners in 1947, she served in Korean waters twice between 10 November 1950 and 13 January 1951, and participated in the Hungnam redeployment. A U.S. Army Transport, it was scrapped in 1965.

John Howland: Hull 958. A Liberty ship launched 19 March 1943 for the WSA and the Army Transportation Service was sold to private owners in 1947, and was in Korean waters seven times between 17 December 1952 and 20 September 1953. She was scrapped in 1968.

John Kulkundis: Listed by the navy as being in Korean waters, it is not in *Awards*.

John Lyras: (British ship) She was in Korean waters three times between 1 December 1950 and 2 February 1951, and participated in the Hungnam redeployment.

John Paul Jones: Hull 67. This Liberty ship launched 3 December 1941 was in Korean waters twice between 16 August and 1 October 1953. She was scrapped in 1970.

John T. McMillan: Hull 1575. This Liberty ship launched 15 June 1943 was in Korean waters from 8 to 9 March 1952. She was scrapped in 1970.

John W. McKay: Hull 1570. This Liberty ship launched 6 June 1943 was in Korean waters 1 to 24 March 1952. She was scrapped in 1969.

John W. Powell: Hull 1022. This Liberty ship launched 28 June 1943 and delivered 28 July 1943 to the USAT was sold to private owners in 1947. She was in the Korean theater during the war. She was scrapped in 1967.

Joliet Victory: (VC2-S-AP 3) Hull 114. Launched 14 June 1944 as a freighter, she served in Korean waters seven times between 22 September 1950 and 23 July 1953. She was scrapped in 1977.

Joplin Victory: (VC2-S-AP 3) Hull 12. Launched 25 April 1944, she made ten visits to Korean waters between 11 August 1950 to 7 April 1953. She was scrapped in 1994.

Jose Marti: Hull 1017. A Liberty ship launched 16 July 1943 by the WSA, she was sold to private owners in 1947, and was in Korean waters six times between 25 September 1952 and 7 March 1054. She was scrapped in 1966.

Joseph Feuer: Built in 1944 as *Charles A. McCue* for the WSA, in 1947 she was sold and renamed. She was renamed again in 1942 as the *Ocean Leader*. Altogether she was in Korean waters four times between 6 March and 23 November 1953. She was scrapped after dragging her anchor in 1965.

Joseph Lee: Hull 3078. This Liberty ship launched 3 December 1944 was in Korean waters three times between 26 April and 22 October 1922. She was scrapped in 1964.

Joseph Priestley: Hull 1675. A Liberty ship launched 17 June 1945, she was scrapped in 1973.

Joshua Slocum: Hull 3082. A Liberty ship launched 17 December 1944, she was in Korean waters three times between 31 March and 4 July 1952. She was scrapped in 1965.

Jumper Hitch: (C1-M-AV1) She was in the Korean theater forty-six times between 31 March 1952 and 25 July 1954.

Katharine B. Sherwood: Hull 2813. This Liberty ship launched 26 September 1944 served in Korean waters twice between 29 May and 26 June 1952. She was scrapped in 1966.

Kelso Victory: (VC2-S-AP 3) Hull 157. Launched on 30 December 1945, she was in the Korean theater twice between 16 November 1950 and 4 January 1951. In 1951 she was renamed *Hawaii Bear*; in 1962, *Smith Caper*; in 1965, *Caper*; and in 1972 *Oriental Destiny*. Scrapped in 1976. She participated in the Hungnam redeployment.

Kenneth Stevenson: She served in Korean waters four times between 20 June and September 1951.

Kenyon Victory: (VC2-S-AP 2) Hull 795. Launched 5 June 1945 for the WSA, between 5 September 1950 and 7 June 1952 she made ten visits to the Korean theater, and participated in the Hungnam redeployment. She was scrapped in 1985.

Kern: (Cross listed as *Kern Hills*) She made 103 visits to Korean waters between 18 January 1952 and 25 June 1954.

Keystone Mariner: (C1-51A) This ship was launched in 1952 and was in Korean waters twice between 23 September and 5 December 1950.

Kimball R. Smith: Not officially in the Korean theater during the war, she was in Korean waters in 1949 before hostilities began, and she was taken by her Korean crew who defected to North Korea.

Knox Victory: (VC2-S-AP 3) Hull 184. Launched on 13 April 1945 for the WSA, she went on to make nine trips into Korean waters between 19 October 1950 and 15 September 1952. In 1960 the Navy renamed her *Huntsville* (TAGN-7). Scrapped 1975.

Lafayette Victory: (VC2-S-AP 2) Hull 752. Launched 5 May 1945 for the WSA, she made eight visits to Korean waters between 23 October 1950 and 4 December 1951. She participated in the Hungnam redeployment. She was scrapped in 1988.

Lafitte: She served in Korean waters from 28 September to 7 October 1954.

Lahaina Victory: (VC2-S-AP 2) Hull 601. Launched 18 January by the Maritime Commission, she was in Korean waters 28 August to 15 September 1951. She was scrapped in 1993.

Lake Minnewanka: She made six trips into Korean waters between 24 December 1953 and 17 April 1954.

Lake Pennask: She was in Korean waters from 31 July to 16 August 1951.

Lakeland Victory: (VC2-S-AP 2) Hull 718. Launched 18 July 1945, she had nine visits to Korean waters between 1 October 1950 and 4 June 1952. She was scrapped in 1968.

Lakeside (foreign-flag ship): She was in Korean waters from 31 July to 10 August 1951.

Lakewood Victory: (VC2-S-AP 2) Hull 545. Launched 17 November 1944 (AK 236), completed in 1946 for the Maritime Commission, she made six trips into Korean waters between 15 October 1950 and 23 June 1953, and was scrapped in 1993.

Lane Victory: (VC2-S-AP 2) Hull 794. Launched 31 May 1945, sold in 1946 to American President Line, she went in reserves in 1948, and then was reactivated in 1950 for Korea. She made eight trips into Korean waters between 19 November 1950 and 24 June 1953. She participated in the Hungnam redeployment and she was pulled into service to evacuate Korean civilians and UN personnel at Wonsan. Placed in reserves, she was reactivated in 1966 for Vietnam, then reserved again in 1971. Since 1988 she has been a museum ship available for tours.

Laredo Victory: (VC2-S-AP 2/APA 125) Hull 723. Launched 24 January 1945, she made six trips into Korean waters between 13 September 1951 and 24 June 1953, and was scrapped in 1988.

Lawrence Victory: (VC2-S-AP 3) Hull 185. Launched in 17 April 1945 for the WSA, she made fourteen trips into Korean waters between 2 October 1950 and 7 April 1953. She was scrapped in 1986.

Letitia Lykes: She was in Korean waters twice between 16 September and 27 December 1950 and participated in the Hungnam redeployment.

Lewis H. Emery, Jr.: Hull 1806. This Liberty ship was launched 15 October 1943, sold to private owners in 1947, served briefly in the Korean theater, and was scrapped in 1968.

Liberty Bell: Laid in February 1945 as *Francis A. Retka* for the WSA, in 1951 she was renamed, and she made nine trips into Korean waters between 2 August 1952 and 1 April 1953. She went aground and was lost in 1965.

Liberty Flag: Laid January 1945 as *Ezra Meech* for the WSA, in 1951 she was renamed, then went on to make eleven trips into Korean waters between 29 June 1952 and 23 July 1953.

In 1958 she was renamed *Pacific Carrier*. Scrapped in 1967.

Lilica: She was in the Korean theater from 15 to 22 March 1951.

Linfield Victory: (VC2-S-AP 3) Hull 689. Launched 7 June 1945 for the WSA, she was in Korean waters 8 to 10 August 1950, and was scrapped in 1986.

Lipari: This Liberty ship was laid June 1943 as *Edward L. Grant* for the WSA. In 1951 renamed *Lipari*, she was in Korean waters for four trips between 13 March and 12 December 1953. In 1954 renamed *Santa Rosa*, she was scrapped in 1964.

Loma Victory: (VC2-S-AP 3) Hull 156. Launched 27 December 1945 for the WSA, then placed in reserves, she was reactivated for the Korean War. She made thirteen visits to Korean waters between 27 October 1950 and 7 October 1953. She was sold to Taiwan and scrapped in 1988.

Lone Star Mariner: She made four trips into Korean waters between 14 February 1953 and 9 March 1954.

Longview Victory: (VC2-S-AP 3) Hull 147. Launched 30 November 1944, she made three voyages into Korean waters between 5 September and 1 November 1950. She was scrapped in 1974.

Loyola Victory: (VC2-S-AP 2) Hull 739. Launched 21 March 1945 by the WSA, she made seven trips into Korean waters between 5 November 1950 and 30 June 1953. She was scrapped in 1994.

Lucille Bloomfield: Hull 1002. A Liberty ship laid June 1943 as *Edward L. Grant*, she was in Korean waters for two trips between 23 July and 29 August 1953.

Lumber Carrier: She was in Korean waters from 12–22 December 1953.

Lumberman (foreign flag ship): She served in Korean waters from 16 to 28 March 1952.

Luxembourg Victory: (VC2-S-AP 3) Hull 90. Launched 28 February 1944, she participated in the Inchon invasion.

Lynn Victory: (VC2-S-AP 2) Hull 847. Launched 15 August 1945 for the WSA, she made two trips into Korean waters between 12 October to 15 November 1950. She was scrapped in 1993.

M. E. Comerford: Hull 2390. This Liberty ship launched 12 December 1944 served in Korean waters four times between 3 May and 12 July 1952. She was scrapped in 1970.

Macalester Victory: (VC2-S-AP 3) Hull 188. Launched 28 April 1945, she served briefly in Korean waters. In 1963 she was renamed *Windsor Victory*, and she was scrapped in 1973.

Madaket: She was in the Korean theater on seven visits between 5 October 1950 and 1 April 1951, and participated in the Hungnam redeployment.

Malden Victory: (VC2-S-AP 2) Hull 607. Built in 1944 for the WSA, she was in the Korean theater seven times between 19 September 1950 and 27 June 1953. She was scrapped in 1993.

Manderson Victory: (VC2-S-AP 2) Hull 539. Launched 23 September 1944 as the AK 230 by U.S. Navy, she was in the Korean theater on eight occasions between 16 December 1950 and 19 May 1953, participated in the Hungnam redeployment, and was scrapped in 1993.

Mankato Victory: (VC2-S-AP 3) Hull 872. Launched 29 August 1945 for the WSA, she made eight visits to Korean waters between 10 January 1951 and 7 September 1953. Scrapped in 1973.

Marine Snapper: She was in Korean waters from 15–19 November 1950.

Mariner: The *Mariner* was in Korean waters twice between 20 June and 17 August 1953.

Marquette Victory: (VC2-S-AP 2) Hull 753. Launched 9 May 1944, she was in the Korean theater twelve times between 10 October 1950 and 29 February 1953. She was scrapped in 1972.

Marshfield Victory: (VC2-S-AP 3) Hull 106. Launched 15 May 1944, she served in Korean waters four times between 29 September 1952 and 3 June 1953.

Martin Behrmen: Hull 2827. A Liberty ship, she made four trips into Korean waters between 17 November 1951 and 4 February 1952.

Marven: She was in Korean waters four times between 2 February and 26 October 1953.

Mary Adams: This Liberty ship was laid in January 1945 for the WSA. In 1951 she was renamed, and went on to make five trips from 24 August 1952 to 8 October 1953. She was scrapped in 1969.

Massillon Victory: (VC2-S-AP 2) Hull 578. Launched 16 December 1944 for the WSA (AK 232, U.S. Navy), in 1946 she was transferred to the Maritime Commission. She was in Korean waters four times between 20 December 1951 and 13 December 1952. She was scrapped in 1994.

Mayfield Victory: (VC2-S-AP 2) Hull 541. Launched 1944, she was in Korean waters five times between 10 November 1951 and 17 December 1952. She was scrapped in 1994.

Meredith Victory: (VC2-S-AP 2) Hull 799. Launched 23 June 1945, she was in Korean waters eight times between 6 October 1950 and 13 April 1952, and participated in the Hungnam redeployment. She was scrapped in 1985.

Meridian Victory: (VC2-S-AP 3) Hull 24. Launched 20 June 1944 for the WSA, she was in Korean waters nine times between 1 October 1950 and 15 August 1953. She ran aground at Suyong, South Korea, in February 1952. She was scrapped in 1985.

Michael J. Goulandris: Hull 2616. A Liberty ship laid in April 1944 as *Lawrence Brengle*, in 1948 she was renamed. Then she served in Korean waters six times between 22 December 1950 and 26 January 1953. She was scrapped in 1967.

Michael Moran: Hull 3050. This Liberty ship was laid 28 June, launched 16 August 1944 and scrapped in 1958.

Midland Victory: (VC2-S-AP 3) Hull 690. Laid as the *Black Eagle*, then renamed the *Alaskan*, she was launched for the Maritime Commission on 12 June 1952. As the *Midland Victory* she was in Korean waters between 27 and 29 September 1950. Scrapped 1970.

Minot Victory: (VC2-S-AP 3) Hull 149. She was launched in 1945 and scrapped in 1985.

Mohawk: Hull 198. A Liberty ship laid in June 1944 as the *James Fenimore Cooper*, she was renamed in 1951 and was in Korean waters six times between 20 August 1952 and 7 February 1953. She was scrapped in 1961.

Mohican: She sailed in Korean waters four times between 1 March 1953 and 2 February 1954.

Monroe Victory: (VC2-S-AP 2) Hull 79. Launched 24 January 1945, she served in Korean waters ten times between 13 February 1951 and 16 January 1953. She was scrapped in 1974.

Morgantown Victory: (VC2-S-AP 2) Hull 632. Launched 5 February 1945, she served in the Korean theater seven times between 13 December 1950 and 2 September 1950. She participated in the Hungnam redeployment. She was scrapped in 1984.

Mormacdale: (C1-A) She served in Korean waters twice between 21 October and 10 November 1950.

Mormacelm: (VC2-S-AP 3) Hull 695. Lunched 5 July 1945 as *Coffeyville Victory*, in 1947 she became *Mormacelm*. She participated in the Korean theater 27 September to 4 October 1954. She was scrapped in 1970.

Mormacmar: She was in Korean waters three times between 18 September 1953 and 13

March 1954.

Mormacmoon: In Korean waters twelve times between 9 September 1950 and 3 May 1954, she participated in the Hungnam redeployment.

Mormacpine: She made seven trips to Korean waters between 17 September and 2 August 1953.

Mormacport: In the Korean theater six times between 21 September 1950 and 26 September 1953, she participated in the Second Echelon Movement Group at the Inchon invasion.

Mormacrio: She was in Korean waters five times between 24 October 1952 and 24 December 1953.

Mormacson: She was in the Korean theater on 5 and 6 August 1950.

Mormacspruce: See *Muncie Victory*.

Mormactide: She was in Korean waters seven times between 26 November 1952 and 12 June 1954.

Mormacwave: She served in the Korean theater five times between 8 September 1952 and 12 February 1954.

Morning Light: She served in Korean waters twice between 2 January and 2 June 1954.

Mother M. L.: Originally the *Alfred E. Smith*, she was launched in January 1945. In 1949 she was renamed. She made two trips to Korean waters between 21 April and 28 May 1953. In 1955 renamed *Captain Lyras*, and in 1957 renamed *Ocean Chief*, she was sold in 1965.

Mountain Mariner: She served in Korean waters from 27 August to 16 September 1953.

Muhlenberg Victory: (VC2-S-AP 2) Hull 837. Launched 12 July as a troop transport for the WSA, she served in Korean waters six times between 18 October 1951 to 15 April 1952. She was scrapped in 1993.

Muncie Victory: Hull 576. Launched 7 December 1944, in 1959 she became *Green Island*. Scrapped 1971. She is not listed in *Awards*.

Nashua Victory: (VC2-S-AP 2) Hull 843. Launched 6 August 1945 for the WSA. Made two visits to Korean between 10 June and 27 July 1953. It was scrapped in 1984.

Nat Brown (foreign flag ship): Listed by Merchant Marines as being in Korea, but is not on all lists.

Nathaniel B. Palmer: Hull 1903 (Tanker). This Liberty ship launched 2 November 1943 as the *Caribou* was sold to private owners in 1947. She participated in the Hungnam redeployment. She is listed by Cagle but not in *Awards*. The ship was wrecked in 1952 and scrapped in 1962.

Nathaniel Crosley: Hull 2078. This Liberty ship laid 19 August 1943 served briefly in Korea. She was scrapped in 1950.

Navajo Victory: (VC2-S-AP 3) Hull 15. Launched 2 May 1944. She made twelve visits to Korean waters between 12 August 1950 and 9 September 1953. It was scrapped in 1985.

Neptune: See *Apollo*.

Netherlands Victory: See *Pelican State*.

Nevadan: (C1-S-A1) She was in the Korean theater three times from 30 December 1952 to 20 October 1953.

New Rochelle Victory: (VC2-S-AP 2) Hull 850. Launched 5 September 1945 by the WSA, she was in Korean waters three times between 6 June and 10 September 1953. She was scrapped in 1972.

New World Victory: (VC2-S-AP 2) Hull 759. Launched 30 May 1945 for the WSA, she made fourteen visits to Korean waters between 4 October 1950 and 28 July 1952. The ship was scrapped in 1972.

New Zealand Victory: (VC2-S-AP 3) Hull 6. Launched 20 March 1944 for the Navy as AK 233, she was in Korean waters eight times between 15 November 1950 and 3 January 1953. She participated in the Hungnam redeployment. In 1967 she was renamed *Halcyon Tiger* and in 1971 the *Palona*. Scrapped in 1973.

Newaden: She was in Korean waters from 1 to 4 September 1952.

Newcastle Victory: (VC2-S-AP 2) Hull 542. Launched 17 October 1944 for the WSA and transferred to the Maritime Commission in 1946 as an ammunition carrier, she served in Korea. In 1955 she was sold to United Fruit Company and she was scrapped in 1992.

Niagara Victory: See *Ocean Victory*.

Niantic Victory: (VC2-S-AP 3) Hull 100. Launched 25 April 1944, she made seven visits to Korean waters between 26 February 1951 and 12 June 1953. She was acquired by the MSTS and renamed *Watertown* in 1960 (TAGM 6). She was scrapped in 1974.

Nicholas C. H.: She was in Korean waters 5–24 July 1953.

Nigel: Hull 2845. A Liberty ship laid May 1945 as *Lawrence J. Gallagher*, in 1951 she was renamed *Nigel*, and then made five trips in Korean waters between 27 December 1952 and 28 December 1953. She was scrapped in 1966.

Noon Day: She made nine trips into Korean waters between 26 September 1950 and 6 March 1952.

Norcuba: Between 3 June 1951 and 11 September 1953 she was in Korean waters six Times, and participated in the Hungnam redeployment.

North Heaven: She was in Korean waters four times between 24 April and 27 December 1953.

North Light: Laid March 1943 as *George Sharswoo* for the WSA, in 1950 she was renamed. She served in Korean waters seven times between 19 November 1950 and 30 November 1953. She was scrapped in 1962.

North Pilot: Formerly the *Westchester*, she was in Korean waters twice between 23 July and 17 November 1953.

North Platte Victory: (VC2-S-AP 2) Hull 807. Launched 3 August 1945 for the WSA, she visited Korean waters three times between 18 September 1952 and 4 June 1953, and was scrapped in 1984.

North Sky: Hull 2173. This Liberty ship was laid October 1943 as *George K. Fitch* for the WSA, renamed in 1948, and served in Korean waters seven times between 15 October 1952 and 19 October 1953. She was scrapped in 1968.

Northport: She served twice in Korean waters between 13 August and 9 October 1953. Not listed in *Awards*.

Norwalk Victory: (VC2-S-AP 3) Hull 696. Launched 10 July 1945 for the WSA, she was laid up in 1946 and then released for the Korean War. She was in Korean waters eight times between 30 September 1950 and 23 February 1952. She was recommissioned in 1963 (TAK 279), and scrapped in 1994.

Norwich Victory: (VC2-S-AP 2) Hull 769. Launched 24 February 1945 for the WSA, she was in Korean waters seven times between 23 January 1952 and 26 March 1953. She went aground in 1969 and was scrapped later that year.

Nutmeg Mariner: She was in Korean waters 1–6 November 1953.

Oberlin Victory: (VC2-S-AP 2) Hull 592. Launched 21 March 1945 for the WSA, she was in the Korean theater nine times between 22 March 1951 and 19 June 1953. She was scrapped in 1988.

Ocala Victory: (VC2-S-AP 2) Hull 619. Launched 19 December 1945 for the WSA, she was in Korean waters ten times between 24 September 1950 and 4 June 1953. She participated at the Hungnam Redeployment and was scrapped in 1992.

Occidental Victory: (VC2-S-AP 2) Hull 784. Launched 23 April 1945 for the WSA, she was in Korea 17 September to 3 October 1951 and scrapped in 2006.

Ocean Betty: Hull 1711 A Liberty ship laid June 1943 as *Thomas M. Cooley* for the WSA, in 1953 she was renamed *Ocean Betty*. She was in Korean waters from 12–21 February 1954. In 1955 she was renamed *Ocean Rose*. She was scrapped in 1967.

Ocean Lotte: She made twelve trips into Korean waters between 10 October 1952 to 30 July 1954.

Ocean Navigator: This Liberty ship was laid November 1943 as *James A. Lane*. In 1949 renamed, the ship was in Korea twice between 3 March and 22 April 1953. Scrapped in 1957.

Ocean Seaman: Hull 2235. A Liberty ship launched February 1944 as *Allen C. Balch*, in 1951 she was renamed and made four trips into Korean waters between 4 April and 16 October 1953.

Ocean Skipper: A Liberty ship laid January 1944 for the WSA, she was in Korean waters three times between 9 May 1953 and 8 August 1953. Scrapped in 1967.

Ocean Star: Hull 3052. This Liberty ship was laid September 1944 as *Galen L. Stone*. In 1950 the name was changed, and she was in Korean waters five times between 16 February and 2 June 1953.

Ocean Victory: (VC2-S-AP 2) Hull 791. Launched 19 May 1945 as *Niagara Victory*, she was renamed *Ocean Victory* in 1951 and served in Korean waters twice between 25 May and 7 June 1954. Scrapped in 1970.

Ocean Villa: She served in Korean waters four times from 11 January to 18 December 1953.

Oceanic: A Liberty ship laid July 1944 as *Jasper F. Cropsey*, in 1949 she was renamed. She was in Korean waters three times from 30 January to 11 September 1953. Scrapped in 1967.

Ocklawaha: (T2 SE A2) Hull 20. Launched 6 September 1943 and completed March 1944, she made six trips into Korean waters between 8 December 1950 and 23 July 1953.

Old Colony Mariner: She sailed in Korean waters four times between 17 January 1953 and 24 January 1954.

Old Dominion Mariner: She made four trips into Korean waters between 24 December 1952 and 7 January 1954.

Old Dominion State: She was in the Korean theater on nine occasions between 5 August 1951 and 14 March 1952.

Olympic Pioneer: This ship made ten trips into Korean waters between 27 March 1951 and 17 July 1952.

Omega: She served in Korean waters 7–21 July 1952.

Ontonagon: Hull 18. Launched September 1944 for WSA, she made fifty-two trips into the Korean theater between 1 January 1952 to 7 June 1954. She was scrapped in September 1965.

Oregon Trader: She was in Korean waters seven times between 16 May 1951 and 10 December 1954.

Oregonian: Hull 2631. A Liberty ship laid May 1944 as the *James D. Trask* for WSA, she made nine visits to Korean waters between 21 July 1952 to 12 August 1953. Not listed in *Awards*.

Oshkosh Victory: (VC2-S-AP 2) Hull 808. Launched 9 August 1945 for WSA, she was in Korean waters 5–11 November 1950. Scrapped in 1992.

Ouachita Victory: See *Green Valley*.

P & T Explorer: She made seven trips in Korean waters between 22 October 1950 and

28 December 1952.

P & T Navigator: She was in Korean waters twice between 24 September and 22 February 1953, and participated in the Inchon invasion.

P & T Pathfinder: She was in Korean waters twice between 28 December 1953 and 1 February 1954.

Pacific Victory: (VC2-S-AP 2) Hull 800. Launched 28 June 1945 for the WSA, she was in Korean waters twice between 7 November 1951 and 27 March 1952. She was scrapped in 1989.

Paducah Victory: (VC2-S-AP 3) Hull 168. Launched 9 February 1945 for the WSA and renamed *California Bear* in 1951, she was in Korean waters three times between 17 September 1950 and 15 January 1951, and participated in the second echelon at the Inchon Landing, and in the Hungnam redeployment. Renamed the *Golden Noon* in 1970, she was scrapped in 1971.

Pan American Victory: (VC2-S-AP 2) Hull 746. Launched 14 April 1945 for the WSA, she served in Korean waters twice between 4 September 1951 and 12 March 1952. She remains in reserves, used for parts.

Park Benjamin: Hull 3008. A Liberty ship laid 19 March 1944, she made four trips to Korean waters between 26 March 1952 and 24 January 1953. Scrapped in 1959.

Pegor: She made three trips in Korean waters between 15 February and 13 June 1953.

Pelegia: See *Sea World*.

Pelican Mariner: She made four trips in to Korean waters between 27 March and 4 August 1954.

Pelican State: (VC2-S-AP3) Hull 91. Launched 6 March 1944 as *Netherlands Victory*, in 1949 she was renamed *Pelican State*. Renamed *Silver Robin* in 1969 and *Pacrobin* in 1970, she was scrapped 1971.

Petaluma: Hull 2647. A Liberty ship launched 28 November 1945 for the Maritime Commission, she made thirty-one trips into Korean waters between 22 January 1952 and 27

Deck cranes on a dry-cargo ship at sea

June 1954. She disappeared 2 February 1982.

Peter Del II (foreign flag ship): She was in the Korean theater thirty-nine times between 18 June 1952 and 3 May 1954.

Pierre Victory: (VC2-S-A P 3) Hull 150. Launched 6 December 1944 for WSA, she was in Korean waters 6–9 November 1950. In 1967 renamed *Columbia Eagle*, in 1971 she was hijacked to Cambodia. Scrapped 1994.

Pine Tree Mariner: She made four trips to Korean waters between 11 May 1953 and 15 January 1954.

Pioneer Dale: Listed by Merchant Marine Association as being in Korea, she is not in *Awards*.

Plymouth Victory:(VC2-S-AP 3) Hull 99. Launched 20 April 1944 for WSA, she made eleven trips into Korean waters from 9 June 1951 to 23 June 1953. In 1969 she was renamed *Cortez*; in1971, *Evelyn*. Scrapped 1972.

Portland Tender: She was in Korean waters six times between 24 November 1950 and 10 February 1954.

Prairie Mariner: She was in the Korean theater three times between 17 July 1954 and 13 September 1954.

Pratt Victory: (VC2-S-AP 2) Hull 782. Launched 14 April 1944, she was selected as a part of the Guinea Pig Squadron at the close of World War II, designed to locate mines in Japanese waters by automated ships. She participated in the Korean War. Scrapped in 1971, she is not listed in *Awards*.

President Harrison: (C3-S-A2) Built in 1943, she served in Korean waters from 8–21 October 1950.

Princeton Victory: (VC2-S-AP 2) Hull 587. Launched 19 February 1945 for the WSA, she served in Korean waters five times between 20 May 1951 and 12 March 1952. She was scrapped in 1989.

Provo Victory: (VC2-S-AP 2) Hull 537. Launched 9 September 1944 by the WSA, she participated in the Hungnam redeployment. She was scrapped in 1984.

Purdue Victory: (VC2-S-AP 2) Hull 740. Launched 9 September 1945 for the WSA, completed for the navy as AK 228, she made nine trips to Korean waters between 15 May 1951 and 26 February 1952. She was scrapped in 1992.

Purple Star: She made four trips to Korean waters between 14 March and 11 October 1953.

Queens Victory: (VC2-S-AP 2) Hull 789. Launched 12 May1945 for the War Shipping Administration she made seven trips to Korea between 12 January and 28 March 1952.

Ragnor Naess: See *Sea Pender*.

Red Oak Victory: (VC2-S-AP 2) Hull 544. Built in 9 November 1944 by the WSA, she served in Korea delivering military cargo, making ten trips into the Korean theater between 10 February 1951 and 24 January 1953. Currently the *Red Oak Victory*, she is a ship museum at Richmond, California.

Reef Knot: (C1-M-AV1) She made thirty-two trips to Korean waters between 21 November 1952 and 20 June 1953.

Rheinholt (Norwegian ship): Not listed in *Awards*. This appears to be a ship that evacuated more than 700 Americans and dependents from Inchon at the beginning of the war.

Rice Victory: (VC2-S-AP 2) Hull 797. Launched 16 June 1945 for the War Shipping Administration, she served in Korean waters seven times between 5 September 1951 and 15 April 1952. She was placed in reserve, and then scrapped in 1989.

Richard H. Davis: Hull 1630. This Liberty ship served in Korean waters five times between 1 April 1950 and 26 July 1953.

Rider Victory: (VC2-S-AP 2) Hull 777. Launched 26 May 1945, she was in Korean waters fifteen times between 13 December 1950 and 25 October 1953 and participated in the Hungnam redeployment. She remains in reserves.

Rincon (Hills): Listed with both names, she made forty-one trips in Korean waters between 1 February 1952 and 23 July 1954.

Robert B. Forbes: Hull 3056. A Liberty ship launched 18 September 1944, she was in Korean waters five times between 2 April and 4 June 1952. She was scrapped in 1965.

Robert G. Ingersoll: Hull 1855. This Liberty ship built in June 1943 and assigned to the Army Transportation Service and participated in Korean waters three times between 16 February and 11 April 1952.

Robin Goodfellow: She made four trips to Korean waters between 20 September 1950 and 6 February 1953, and participated in the Inchon invasion;

Robin Gray: She was in Korean waters four times between 24 October 1950 and 28 September 1954, and participated in the Hungnam redeployment.

Robin Hood: Served in Korean waters four times between 30 September 1965 and 17 October 1952. She participated in the Hungnam redeployment.

Robin Kirk: She was in Korean waters four times between 20 August and 27 December 1950, and participated in the Inchon Landing and the Hungnam redeployment.

Robin Mowbray: She was in Korean waters from 8–29 July 1953.

Robin Trent: She made six trips to Korean waters between 1 September 1950 and 11 March 1951, and participated in the Inchon invasion.

Rock Springs Victory: (VC2-S-AP 3) Hull 160. Launched 12 January1945, she was in Korean waters four times between 27 November 1952 and 3 September 1953. Her name was changed in 1963 to *Seneca*, in 1965 to *Express Buffalo*, and in 1966 to *American Pride*. She was scrapped in 1970.

Rose Knot: She was in Korean waters twenty times between 23 November 1952 and 4 December 1953.

Rutgers Victory: (VC2-S-AP 2) Hull 82. Launched 2 February 1945 by the WSA, she was in Korean waters five times between 26 February 1951 and 5 November 1952. She was scrapped in 1985.

Sailor's Splice: (C1-M-AV1) She made two trips to Korean waters between 21 February and 12 March 1952.

St. Augustine Victory: (VC2-S-AP 2) Hull 849. Launched 7 September 1945 by the WSA, she made thirteen trips to Korean waters between 8 September 1950 and 18 March 1952. She participated in the Hungnam redeployment, and was scrapped in 1993.

San Mateo Victory: (VC2-S-AP 2) Hull 713. Launched 30 June 1945 for the WSA, she served in Korean waters seven times between 2 December 1950 and 4 April 1954. She was scrapped in 1994.

Santa Clara Victory: (VC2-S-AP 2) Hull 773. Launched 9 March 1945 for the WSA, she was in Korean waters thirteen times between 14 October 1950 and 12 April 1953. She was scrapped in 1985.

Santa Venetia: She served in Korean waters five times between 23 February and 21 September 1953.

Sapulpa Victory: (VC2-S-AP 3) Hull 14. Launched 29 April 1944, she made nine trips to Korean waters between 2 February 1951 and 25 June 1953. Her name was changed to *Halcyon Panther* in 1963. Struck 1972.

Saxon: Hull 2476. A Liberty ship laid May 1949 as *George E. Merrick*, in 1951 she was renamed. She was in the Korean theater five times between 1 March and 19 October 1953. She was scrapped in 1972.

Schuyler: (C1-M-AV1) Completed for the navy as AK 209, she was in Korean waters forty-five times between 31 March 1952 to 7 October 1954.

Schuyler Otis Bland: (C1-S-1X1) She was in Korean waters four times between 2 January and 27 December 1953. Sold 15 August 1979.

Sea Bon: She made six visits to Korean waters between 24 August 1952 and 29 September 1953.

Sea Champion: A Liberty ship laid March 1944 as *Sea Champion*, she made eight trips to Korea between 14 November 1952 and 5 October 1953. Scrapped 1966.

Sea Cliff: Hull 3104. A Liberty ship laid March 1945 as *Donald H. Holland*, in 1952 she was renamed *Sea Cliff*, and she made seven visits to Korean waters between 6 February 1953 and 16 January 1954. She was renamed *Ike* in 1963. She was abandoned 28 November 1962.

Sea Comet II: Hull 2511. This Liberty ship was laid December 1944 as *Walter M. Christiansen*. Renamed in 1951, she was in Korean waters five times between 9 July 1953 and 17 April 1954. She was scrapped in 1967.

Sea Coral: Hull 3148. This Liberty ship was laid September 1945 as *Ora Ellis*, a boxed aircraft transport. Renamed in 1951, she then made nine trips to Korean waters between 8 September 1951 and 4 December 1953. She sank in 1960.

Sea Coronet: Hull 2642. This Liberty ship was laid June 1944 as *Chung Tung*, launched as the *William Hodson*, and its name was changed again in 1951. She served in Korean waters six times between 23 November 1952 to 29 September 1953. In 1964 she was converted to a container ship.

Sea Daring: Laid March 1945 as *Donald E. Holland*, in 1952 she was renamed. She made six visits to Korean waters between 20 July 1952 to 21 February 1953. See also *Ike*.

Sea Faith: Hull 2762. This Liberty ship was laid March 1944 as *Henry M. Stephen*. In 1951 she was renamed, and then made three visits to Korean waters between 4 May and 17 July 1953. She was scrapped in 1967.

Sea Fort: She made six visits to Korean waters between 3 March to 10 November 1953.

Sea Garden: Hull 2562. This Liberty ship was in Korean waters eight times between 10 August 1952 and 26 November 1953.

Sea Gate: A Liberty ship laid February 1944 as *Horatio Allen*, in 1952 she was renamed. She then made two trips to Korean waters between 13 August 1953 and 13 January 1954. She was scrapped in 1956.

Sea Glamor: She was in Korean waters three times between 21 June and 18 October 1953.

Sea Glider: She made three trips to Korean waters between 30 June and 29 November 1953.

Sea Globe: She made three trips to Korean waters between 8 October and 27 December 1952.

Sea Herald: Hull 1973. A Liberty ship laid May 1945 as *Kemp P. Battle*, in 1947 she was purchased and renamed *Governor Graves*, then in 1952 renamed *Sea Herald*. She made five trips to Korean waters between 6 November 1952 and 27 July 1953.

Sea Leader: She made eleven trips to Korean waters between 6 May and 15 July 1953.

Sea Legend: She was in Korean waters twelve times between 5 June 1951 to 1 November 1953.

Sea Life: She was in Korean waters six times between 5 October 1952 and 23 July 1953.

Sea Manor: She made three visits to Korean waters between 7 September 1952 and 16

January 1953.

Sea Merchant: A Liberty ship laid January 1945 for the Wartime Shipping Administration as the *Seaton*, in 1951 she was renamed. She was in the Korean theater twice between 2 August 1952 and 3 January 1953. Scrapped in 1966.

Sea Merit: Hull 2033. Formerly the *Simon Benson*, this Liberty ship laid 30 May 1943 was sold to a private corporation in 1947 and renamed. She made four trips to Korean waters between 13 March and 8 November 1953. Scrapped 1968.

Sea Monitor: She made eighteen trips to Korean waters between 5 May 1951 and 15 April 1954.

Sea Mystery: She was in the Korean theater five times from 9 February to 13 June 1953.

Sea Pender: She made four trips to Korean waters between 4 September and 14 July 1952. Later known as *Ragnor Naess*.

Sea Ranger: Hull 1931. A Liberty ship laid in January 1944 as *J. C. W. Beckham* and launched as *Raccoon*, in 1951 she was renamed. She served in Korean waters 19 January to 11 February 1953. She was scrapped in 1968.

Sea Splendor: In the Korean theater ten times between 15 September 1950 and 23 July 1954, she participated in the Hungnam redeployment.

Sea Star: Hull 2992. This Liberty ship was laid February 1945 as *Wallace M. Tyler*. Renamed in 1951, she made six trips to Korean waters between 13 August 1952 and 31 August 1953. She was scrapped in 1966.

Sea Victory: She served in Korean waters seven times between 2 August 1952 and 10 July 1953.

Sea Wind: A Liberty ship laid December 1944 for the WSA, she was renamed in 1949 and saw service in Korean waters three times between 22 November 1950 and 8 August 1953. She participated in the Hungnam redeployment.

Sea World: She made five trips to Korean waters between 11 August 1952 and 3 January 1953. Later known as *Pelegia*.

Seaborne: See *Selma Victory*.

Selma Victory: (VC2-S-AP 3) Hull 23. Originally *Seaborne*, launched 16 June 1944 for the WSA, she was in Korean waters six times between 26 September 1950 and 3 October 1954. She was scrapped in 1994.

Seton Hall Victory: (VC2-S-AP 3) Hull 686. Launched 22 May 1945, she served in Korean waters seven times between 29 November 1950 and 3 June 1954. She was renamed *Wheeling* (TAGM 8) in 1964. Stricken from the navy list in 1990, she is believed sunk as a target.

Sharon Victory: (VC2-S-AP 3) Hull 29. Launched 28 June 1944, she made ten trips to Korean waters between 26 February 1951 and 25 July 1953. She was scrapped in 1988.

Shinecock Bay: Hull 2882. A Liberty ship laid November 1944 as *Milton Foreman*, she was renamed in 1951 and then made two trips to Korean waters between 10 September and 10 October 1953. She was scrapped in 1965.

Simmons Victory: (VC2-S-AP 3) Hull 182. Launched 6 April 1945 by the WSA, she made nine trips to Korean waters between 18 November 1950 and 23 December 1952. She was renamed *Liberty* (AG 168) in 1964. Attacked by the Israeli air force on 8 June 1967, she was scrapped in 1974.

Sioux Falls Victory: (VC2-S-AP 2) Hull 70. Launched 19 December 1944 by the WSA, she made nine trips to Korean waters between 20 April 1951 and 4 April 1952. She was scrapped in 2006.

Skagway Victory: (VC2-S-AP 3) Hull 685. Launched 19 May 1945, named *President Buchanan* in 1948, and then renamed *Constitution* in 1949. She was in Korea waters from 5–31 January 1951 as *Skagway Victory*. Scrapped 1970.

South Bend Victory: (VC2-S-AP 3/AGS 21) Hull 694. Launched 30 June 1945 by the WSA, she made eight trips to Korean waters between 2 April 1951 and 21 April 1953. Renamed *Bowditch* in 1957, she was scrapped in 1988.

Southwestern Victory: (VC2-S-AP 2) Hull 786. Launched 30 April 1945 for the WSA, she made five trips to Korean waters between 24 August 1951 and 3 October 1953. She was scrapped in 1999.

Southwind: She participated in the Inchon invasion and the Hungnam Redeployment.

Spartanburg Victory: (VC2-S-AP 2) Hull 845. Launched 9 August 1945, she was renamed *Cotton State* in 1957. She made four trips to the Korean theater between 24 September 1950 and 18 February 1951. Scrapped 1970.

Stathes Yamaglias: Hull 2454. Laid March 1944 as *George A. Marr*, in 1947 she was renamed. Renamed again in 1951, to *Ania*, she was abandoned 8 February 1964.

Stock Star: She served in Korean waters from 9–11 September 1952. ***Sue Lykes***: This Liberty ship was laid as the *Tornado* and completed as *Sue Lykes*. She was in Korean waters from 4 October to 19 November 1950.

Sunion: She was in Korean waters twice between 23 June and 19 October 1953.

Susquehanna: (T1-MT-M1) Hull 16. Built in June 1948, she made thirty-two trips to Korean waters between 3 January 1952 and 15 October 1953.

Swarthmore Victory: (VC2-S-AP 2) Hull 737. Launched 14 May 1945 by the WSA, she made eleven trips to Korean waters between 16 September 1950 and 20 February 1952. She was scrapped in 1988.

Sword Knot: (C1-M-AV1) She made forty-six trips to Korean waters between 26 Feb-

Boxed aircraft transport at Wonsan Harbor

ruary 1952 and 27 July 1954.

Tabitha Brown: Hull 0582. A Liberty ship laid August 1944 and renamed in 1949, she participated in Korean waters from 7–16 March 1952. Scrapped 1967.

Taddei: Hull 848. Launched 23 August 1945, she was in Korean waters in 1953. She was scrapped in 1976.

Taineron: In Korean waters three times between 7 November 1950 and 4 January 1951, she participated in the Hungnam redeployment.

Tallulah: (VC2-S-AP 2). Redesignated AO 50 (T2-SE-A1), she was launched as *Valley Forge* in July 1952 and completed as the *Tallulah*. She was in Korean waters fifteen times between 25 March 1952 and 17 August 1953.

Tar Heel Mariner: She was in Korean waters twice between 25 July and 28 October 1953.

Texas: She served in Korean waters four times between 21 May to 30 December 1953.

Thunderbird: See *Jericho Victory*.

Timber Hitch: Hull 2315. She served in Korean waters forty-seven times between 20 March 1952 and 20 July 1954.

Towanda Victory: (VC2-S-AP 2) Hull 611. Launched 11 November 1944, she was in Korean waters five times between 13 December 1950 and 3 April 1952. Participated in the Hungnam redeployment. Scrapped in 1974.

Transamerican: Hull 2329. This Liberty ship was laid November 1944 as *Charles H. Marshall*. In 1949 she was renamed, and she served in Korean waters three times between 28 July and 6 December 1953. She was scrapped in 1972.

Transatlantic: Hull 2391. A Liberty ship laid December 1944 as *Felix Riesenberg*, in 1951 she was sold and renamed. She served in Korean waters twice between 23 July and 31 December 1953. She was scrapped in 1972.

Transoceanic: Hull 2366. A Liberty ship laid July 1944 as *James W. Cannon*, in 1951 she was sold and renamed. She served in Korean waters seven times between 22 August 1952 and 18 December 1953. She was scrapped in 1963.

Transpacific: A Liberty ship that was laid May 1944 for the WSA, in 1951 she was sold and renamed. She was in Korean waters four times between 9 July and 2 November 1953. Scrapped in 1968.

Transunion: Hull 2893. A Liberty ship laid January 1945 as *Mack Bruton Bryan*, in 1951 she was sold and renamed. She served in Korean waters twice between 13 February 1953 and 14 March 1954. She was scrapped in 1967.

Trinity Victory: (VC2-S-AP 2) Hull 747. Launched 18 April 1945, she served in Korean waters twice between 4 July 1951 and 28 September 1953. She was scrapped in 1972.

Trojan Trader: Hull 2988. A Liberty ship laid in February 1945 as *Clifford E. Ashby*, in 1951 she was sold and renamed *Penconic Bay*. Again in 1952 she was renamed, this time *Trojan Trader*. She served in Korean waters twice between 14 July and 18 November 1953. She served under several names and was scrapped in 1969.

Tucson Victory: (VC2-S-AP 2) Hull 803. Launched 13 July 1945 by the WSA, she was in Korean waters six times between 3 June 1952 and 9 July 1953. She was scrapped in 1994.

Tulane Victory: (VC2-S-AP 2) Hull 593. Launched 28 March 1945 by the WSA, she was in Korean waters ten times between 11 April 1951 and 25 June 1953. She was scrapped in 1992.

Tuskegee Victory: (VC2-S-AP 3/AGS 22) Hull 682. Launched 8 May 1945 by the WSA, she was in Korean waters five times between 5 September 1951 and 2 February 1953. She was renamed *Dutton* (AGS 22, U.S. Navy) in 1957, and scrapped in 2006.

Twin Falls Victory: (VC2-S-AP 3) Hull 167. Launched 6 February 1945 by the WSA, she served in Korean waters fifteen times between 24 September 1950 and 9 May 1953. She participated in the Inchon invasion and the Hungnam redeployment. Redesignated TAGM 11 in 1962, she was struck in 1970. Reactivated as the *John W. Brown II* in 1972, she was scrapped in 1983.

USO: Hull 1811. This Liberty ship was laid 29 September 1943 and launched 21 October 1943. Sold to a private firm in 1947, she served in Korean waters four times between 2 January and 3 August 1953. She was scrapped in 1967.

Union Victory: (VC2-S-AP 3) Hull 683. Launched 11 May 1945, she was in Korean waters eight times between 7 October 1950 and 27 March 1953. She participated in the Hungnam redeployment. Renamed *Perseus* (TAF 64), a reefer ship, in 1962, she was scrapped in 1973.

Valdosta Victory: (VC2-S-AP 2) Hull 617. Launched 11 December 1944 by the WSA, she was in Korean waters ten times between 3 December 1950 and 29 March 1952. She was scrapped in 1984.

Vanderbilt Victory: (VC2-S-AP 2) Hull 781. Launched 11 April 1945 by the WSA, she was in Korean waters 20–24 May 1952. She was scrapped in 1993.

Vercharmain (foreign flag ship): She was in Korean waters eighteen times between 29 July 1953 and 24 July 1954.

Virginia City Victory: (VC2-S-AP 2) Hull 597. Launched 31 December 1944, built by the WSA, she was in Korean waters thirteen times between 25 December 1950 and 13 October 1953, and participated in the Hungnam redeployment. She was scrapped in 1971.

Volunteer Mariner: She was in Korean waters 13–14 November 1953.

Wabash Victory: (VC2-S-AP 2) Hull 796. Launched 9 June 1945, renamed *Pvt. Francis X. McGraw* by the Army Transportation Service in 1947, she was reactivated into the Navy as MST AK 22 (TAK 24) in 1950, and was in Korean waters twenty times between 28 July 1952 and 25 July 1954. She was scrapped in 1974.

Wacosta: She was in Korean waters twice between 23 August 1950 and 25 January 1951, and participated in the Hungnam redeployment.

Wake Forest Victory: (VC2-S-AP 2) Hull 594. Launched 31 March 1945, she was in Korean waters eight times between 15 August 1950 and 15 September 1953, and scrapped in 1973.

Walter F. Perry: Hull 3131. This Liberty ship was launched as a boxed aircraft transport on 26 September 1945. Scrapped 1972.

Waltham Victory: (VC2-S-AP 2) Hull 720. Launched 1945, she was in Korean waters four times between 12 September 1951 and 7 February 1953. She was scrapped in 1972.

Walton (foreign flag ship): She was in Korean waters five times between 1 February and 16 May 1954.

Warrior: She was in Korean waters twice between 13 April and 21 June 1953.

Warwick Victory: (VC2-S-AP 2) Hull 887. Launched 1945, she was in Korean waters six times between 29 November 1951 and 9 June 1952. She was renamed U.S. *Navigator* in 1966 and scrapped in 1971.

Wellesley Victory: (VC2-S-AP 3) Hull 117 (also listed under 177). Launched 16 March 1945 by the WSA, she was in Korean waters eight times between 13 February 1951 and 29 October 1953, and participated in the Hungnam redeployment. Scrapped in 1971.

Wesleyan Victory: (VC2-S-AP 2) Hull 589. Launched 28 February 1945 by WSA, she was in Korean waters seven times between 27 October 1950 and 26 June 1953, participating in the Hungnam redeployment. She was scrapped in 1971.

West Lynn Victory: (VC2-S-AP 3) Hull 155. Launched 22 December 1945 by the WSA, she was in Korean waters thirteen times between 16 October 1950 and 16 May 1952. She was scrapped in 1972.

Westchester: (T2-SE-A1) A Liberty ship laid June 1944, in 1951 she was acquired by the Maritime Commission in 1953. She was in Korean waters three times between 5 February 1953 and 15 March 1953. She was renamed *North Pilot* later in 1953 and scrapped as the *Korthi* in 1968.

Western Ocean: She was in Korean waters eleven times between 24 December 1951 and 7 December 1953.

Western Rancher: She served in Korean waters three times between 8 July 1953 and 22 September 1953.

Western Trader: Launched April 1943 as *William Thorton*, in 1951 she was sold and renamed *Western Trader*. She was in Korean waters from 28 July to 24 August 1953. She was scrapped in 1968.

Westport Victory: She was in Korean waters three times 28 April 1953 and 2 September 1953.

William Clagett: Hull 2687. This Liberty ship launched 23 May 1944 for the Army Transportation Service. Sold to private owners in 1968.

William Coddington: Hull 1457. A Liberty ship, launched 27 November 1942 for the Army Transportation Service, she was in Korean waters three times between 10 April and 14 July 1952. She was scrapped in 1967.

William Eaton: Hull 667. This Liberty ship launched 7 November 1942 was wrecked in 1952.

William F. Lester (foreign flag ship): Not on all lists.

William H. Carruth: Hull 1902. A Liberty ship launched 5 February 1943, she was in Korean waters five times between 6 October 1951 and 7 February 1952. She was sold to private owners 1968.

William H. Wilmer: Hull 959. A Liberty ship launched 25 March 1943, she was in Korean waters seven times between 15 November 1952 and 1 November 1953. She was scrapped in 1965.

William L. McLean: Hull 2890. A Liberty ship launched 13 December 1944, she was in Korean waters three times from 1 April to 31 May 1952. She was scrapped in 1964.

Wolverine Mariner: She was in Korean waters twice between 20 January and 22 April 1954.

Woodstock Victory: (VC2-S-AP 2) Hull 604. Launched 23 September 1944 by the WSA, she was in Korean waters six times between 29 January 1951 and 25 April 1952. She was scrapped in 1984.

Xavier Victory: (VC2-S-AP 2) Hull 590. Launched 7 March 1945 by the WSA, she was in Korean waters five times between 2 May 1951 and 20 May 1952. She was scrapped in 1984.

Yale Victory: See *Archer T. Gammon*, TAP 243.

Yankee Pioneer: This Liberty ship was laid January 1944 as *Mason Weems*. In 1948 she was renamed and in 1949 converted to a dry cargo carrier. She visited Korean waters four times between 2 September 1950 and 10 March 1951. Late in 1951 she was renamed *W. L. McCormick*.

Yugoslavia Victory: (VC2-S-AP 3) Hull 98. Launched 15 April 1944, she was in Korean waters six times between 3 February 1951 and 29 January 1953. She was renamed *Fairisle* in

12

OTHER SHIPS IN ACTION

A good navy is not a provocation for war, but is the surest guarantee of peace.
— Theodore Roosevelt

It would be impossible to include all of the vessels that were involved in the Korean War, particularly the auxiliary ones. The geography of Korea, with its long coastline, required the ability to move around the inlets, harbors, and shallows. This led to the adaptation of some of the national crafts as well as bringing into play a wide variety of American craft. Many of the "work boats" of the navy, as well as those of some of the other services, plied their trade in and around Korea inconspicuously and with little recording, but doing important work. Few of the dozens of such crafts can be mentioned here. Keep in mind that serving the UN troops in Korea were punts, pinnaces, longboats, barges, lighters, gigs, wiggle boats, power barges, launches, junks, sampans, whale boats, rubber boats, water ships, klepper canoes, tenders, generating ships, degaussing ships, crane ships, cable ships, and generating ships, among others. Both the Democratic People's Republic of Korea and the Republic of Korea used a vast number of junks and sampans. Designed for transportation, shipping, fishing, even for living, many of these were quickly adapted to military needs and incorporated in services ranging from delivering troops to sowing sea mines. Most of these boats left little or no record.

The Army's Navy

While the Army Transportation Service was disbanded and its ships transferred to the Military Sea Transportation Services prior to the Korean War, the Army still maintained some ships and a few of these were in Korea. Widely diversified, they fell into groups distinguished by their hull markings: FP (freight and passenger), FS (freight and supplies), FA (cargo vessel, used primarily by the Army Air Corps), F (steel cargo boat) and Y (Tanker). While the records for these ships and their service in Korea are difficult, if not impossible, to locate, they left behind some evidence of their participation. There is an excellent photograph of FS 525 and FS 291 lying side by side at anchor in Wonsan. They have been identified as 114-foot interisland freighters built in World War II for the army. During World War II they were crewed primarily by Coast Guard members, but in Korea seem to have been crewed by army personnel.

Barges and Lighters

Lighter is the name used for the broad, flat-bottomed boats used in transporting cargo between a ship and the shore. The difference between a lighter and a barge tends to be its use rather than design. The term barge is usually reserved for those craft that made long-distance hauls while lighter referred to a shorter haul. One hundred twenty-three Japanese barges were contracted for use first at Pusan, and then ordered to their destination at Inchon. The crews of 28 of the barges, on learning they were heading for an invasion, returned to Japan. The remaining 92, in company with a mother ship and a repair ship, were escorted to Inchon by a Korean Navy tug and a minesweeper. There were both "dumb" (motorless) and powered barges involved.

CIA Vessels

All of the Central Intelligence Agency's early activities were processed through a front organization, the Joint Advisory Commission, Korea (JACK), that operated out of Tonnae, a small village located near Pusan. The CIA, then under the direction of General Walter Bedell Smith, operated through authority of the National Security Council which sanctioned

U.S. Army transports FS 525 and 291 at Pusan

a wide range of covert operations, from psychological warfare to execution of raids. The group was primarily trained for prisoner snatches, ship-launched and supported ambushes, and the destruction of North Korean coastal railway tracks, tunnels, and bridges. Their primary platform was a destroyer transport (APD) with shallow drafts to enable them to get close to shore. The main vessels were the USS *Wantuck* and the *Horace A. Bass*. They were equipped with four 36-foot Landing Craft Vehicle, Personnel (LCVP) which they launched and then used to tow the guerrilla-laden boats to shore. Recovery was accomplished by the same means, rubber boats paddled out to a pickup point, and then linked for a tow back to the APD. These smaller vessels were often accompanied by a command boat. The PR-3 got a lot of use in this capacity. Though not required, liaison was maintained with CCRAK, Combined Command for Reconnaissance Activities, Korea.

Crash Rescue Boats: The Air Force's Navy

During the Korean War the U.S. Air Force maintained a series of rescue stations. The first mission was to rescue downed pilots or others adrift on the sea. The Kunsan Harbor station was manned by the 22nd Crash Rescue Boat Squadron (CRBS) of the Far East Air Force (FEAF). This unit, like the rest, operated pretty much on its own, and there was little interaction between them and other air force personnel. Those involved operated on temporary duty from other assignments. Their job was to support rescue operations in the area, and to provide refueling for spook missions in the north. Each unit was assigned responsibility for particular air locations. In each case the "headquarters" for the mission was different, but for the 22nd it consisted of a Quonset hut built on a flat-deck steel barge. The ships and men were in a constant rotation process because there were no locations or facilities, without returning to Japan, for the boats to be repaired or maintained. It was anticipated that eventually crash rescue boats would be housed in six or seven locations, but there were not enough boats to accomplish this.

A second mission was less humanitarian and more clandestine. One of the reasons there is so little available about these units is the unorthodox nature of their mission and organization, that is, there was no clearly defined structure of command and responsibility. But, to some extent the dearth must be blamed on the generally unpublicized nature of clandestine missions.

For most headquarters persons, the idea of a craft operating 200 to 400 miles from shore, supported by men living onboard for extended periods of time on the open sea, and commanded by an NCO, was incomprehensible. But this was the case. With a normal crew of 8–10 men, including an engine room man, a medical technician, a radio operator and a cook, and generally in the command of an E-5 or E-6, they used hand-pumped fresh-water systems and alcohol stoves for cooking. None had refrigeration.

There were two basic types of boats used, 63' and 85' crash boats. Each station tried to maintain two 63' boats and one 85' boat, but they rarely had such equipment. The craft were identified as the R-1 and R-2. The boats were very small and uncomfortable. There was only a pitifully inadequate system of small gasoline heaters in the below-deck compartments, fed by high-octane oil. The crews were authorized to wear navy dungarees and Dixie-cup hats, but in most cases these had to be purchased at the expense of the sailor. Some personnel wore blue USAF baseball caps.

The boats were often under fire. Jim Jarvis, commander of R-1-667, reported that his boat was periodically attacked by North Korean patrol boats in the open sea.

The 63' boats were generally restricted to duties in the south, and were not authorized to move into North Korean waters. They did not carry enough water for showers and shaving, just 500 gallons for cooking and for the water jackets on the engines. There was no heating system on board.

The 85' boats were generally equipped with a Quad 50 forward, two 50-caliber machine guns in mid-turrets, and a 20mm gun in the rear.

Some of the 85' boats off Pyongyang-do were used to transport clandestine agents into and out of North Korea. There is little written material available about these units, both because of the unorthodox nature of their mission and organization, and because of the limited knowledge available about the crash boats themselves. Two books address the topics briefly. One is *Apollo's Warriors: United States Air Forces Special Operations during the Korean War*, by Mike Hass, a retired Air Force colonel. Also, Earl McCandlish, the skipper of one of the boats, wrote a book called *Crash Boat*. Some limited information is offered by official sources.

Distillery Ship (AW)

The only distillery ship that was known to be in operation in Korea was the *Pasig II*.

Pasig II AW 3: (T2-SE-A2) [d. 22,350; 523 × 68; 15 k; cpl. 259; a. 1-5", 4-40mm, 8-20mm; Class Pasig] This was the second Pasig, and was laid down 18 May 1944, redesignated AW-3 on 28 August 1944, and commissioned 11 December 1944. During World War II she supplied fresh water to units of the Allied navies in the western Pacific. Decommissioned in February 1947, she was recommissioned 15 March 1951. For thirty-seven continuous months her 120,000-gallon/day process provided fresh water for UN forces operating in Korea and Japan. She saw service in Korean waters during the Communist China Spring Offensive, UN Summer–Fall Offensive, Second Korean Winter, and Korea Summer–Fall 1953 campaigns. She was awarded six battle stars for her service in Korea.

Degaussing Ship (ADG)

Degaussing is the means by which unwanted magnetic fields on ships can be cancelled or reduced. A large steel warship is a good deal like a magnet with a field surrounding it. As it moves through the water it adds to, or detracts from the Earth's magnetic field, and it can distort magnetic images used for weapons control or any of a series of compass devices. The degaussing ship is designed to cancel the field by running a current through coils wound in specific locations within the hull.

Ampere ADG-11: [d. 640; 184'6" × 33; 14 k; cpl. 68; a. 1-3", 4-20mm; Class Admirable] Launched 12 August 1944 and commissioned 15 August 1945, she was stricken 1 July 1961 and sold the next year.

Lodestone ADG-8: [d. 640; 184'6" × 33; 14 k; cpl. 65; a. 1-3"; Class YDG-8] Launched 27 May 1943 and commissioned 10 June 1944, she was decommissioned May 1946 and reactivated 1 November 1947. Cagle lists her as being in Korea.

The Gig

Most gigs were small boats attached to naval ships and used primarily as the captain's taxi. Generally smaller and lighter than the longboat, the gig was originally crewed by four oarsmen and a coxswain. Presumably built on the Whitehall Rowboat model, it had a high, wine-glass transom, a full keep, and somewhat rounded sides, with the gunwales nearly straight from bow to stern. It was not very seaworthy and so was used primarily in harbors. The Cornish pilot gig was larger than the Captain's gig, and was primarily used in the transportation of pilots to and from ships entering harbor.

Junk

While not an official vessel of the U.S. Navy, there were a good many junks used by the UN during the Korean War. There were numerous junks owned by South Koreans that were incorporated into duty, but more than that, captured North Korean junks became a vessel of choice for a good many clandestine activities. While some junks were as long as 495 feet, and seemed as though they might have sailed to the New World in earlier centuries, most were a wee 40' to 60' in length, with a beam about a third of the length, flat-bottomed, with a high stern, square bow, and two or three masts. The hull was divided by a series of bulkheads that ran both lengthwise and crosswise, providing a compartmentalized hull that resisted sinking. There are few records of their use, but in the report of Operation Sea Dragon, in April 1953, several captured junks are identified. The 6006th Air Intelligence Support Squadron (AISS) operated continually with captured North Korean junks, and in September 1952, according to Wolfpack reports, they lost three motorized and ten sail junks due to heavy storms.

Klepper Canoe

A naval special forces team, the United Kingdom Special Boat Squadron, a branch of the Royal Marines, had been created to attack the enemy using small waterborne craft, mini-subs, and swimming insertions. Most of their raids were accomplished using the two-person Klepper canoe. This special force, which had been developed during World War II for clandestine marine operations, was called back into service during the Korean War. In Korea they operated on the North Korean coast where they gathered intelligence, and destroyed railways and installations. As a part of the UN forces that were performing raids along the North Korean coast, they often used their signature two-man canoes, departing from a submarine like the USS *Perch*. For a clandestine approach to an enemy coastline there appeared to be few better vessels than the collapsible Klepper. It was a part of the training for those entering this command that they be able to paddle a Klepper thirty miles, and carry them on their backs cross-country for ten miles.

PT Boat

As far as can be determined, there were no U.S. or UN motor torpedo boats (PT) serving in Korea, other than the three or four that had been transferred to the Republic of Korea

Navy. (See UN Vessels, ROK, PT 809, 810, 811, 812.) The Commander of Naval Forces in the Far East requested PTs for use in his command, but the request was apparently never filled.

Rubber Boat

The term "rubber boat" takes in a wide variety of craft. Most of these were skips, as in the case of the USS *Perch*'s skip, but other types were used. In response to need, a provisional Raider Company was organized on 5 July 1950. The unit, called the GHQ 1st Raider Company (Provisional), was later to be redesignated the 8227th Army Unit. On 7 September 1950 the Special Activities Group (SAG) was organized and the raiders became one of its units. They saw their first action on 12 September 1950 when the HMS *Whitesands Bay* landed them. Their second action was at Inchon where the mission required them to land by rubber boat. The mission was cancelled because it was determined that rubber boats could not handle the tide currents in the area.

The unit was disbanded in April 1951 when the Department of the Army deactivated all Ranger units. But the use of rubber boats increased. The operating procedure for landing special clandestine teams had been well worked out. An APD would halt several thousand yards off the target beach at night. LCPR were launched, and tows engaged to guerrilla-laden boats. About 500 yards from shore, the tow would be released and the raiders would start paddling their boats until about 250 yards from the shore. There, swimmer scouts would be sent out to reconnoiter the target, and then, if an all clear was given, the guerrillas paddled in. The evacuation was a reversal of this process. While being towed, about all that could be seen of the low shadow of the boats was a phosphorescent wake on the surface of the sea.

Sampan

"Sampan" comes from the Cantonese word for "three planks," and labels a flat-bottomed wooden boat from twelve to fifteen feet long, often with a small shelter at one end. They are traditionally propelled by an oar, but some were motorized. They were used primarily for quick movement within a harbor.

Lighthouse Tender (WAGL)

The U.S. Lighthouse Service is one of the oldest agencies in the federal government. It was merged with the U.S. Coast Guard in 1939. The transition involved more than 5,000 personnel and a fleet of 64 vessels called lighthouse tenders. The tenders were designed for general duty consisting primarily of providing and servicing navigational aids, and in support of lighthouses and lightships. They were built with adequate deck space and derricks for dealing with buoys, and were designed with a rather shallow draft and twin screws. Stability and a low freeboard was a necessity. The tenders were manned by full-time civilian crews that became members of the Coast Guard. They were usually named after flora and were classified as WAGL. In 1965 this identification changed to WLB for oceangoing vessels and WLR for those in coastal service. Two served in Korea.

12. Other Ships in Action

Top: Small junk/sampan at Wonsan Harbor. Bottom: Sampans at Pusan unload.

Ironwood WAGL 297: [d. 1,025; 180 × 37; 13 k; a. 1-3"; Class Mesquite] This buoy tender was launched 16 March 1943. The *Ironwood* was the last U.S. ship still on active duty at the time of the 50th anniversary of those serving in the Korean War theater. She served as a loran station support vessel for navigation stations in the Pacific between 19 November 1951 and 2 May 1954. She had fifty-seven years in continuous service. Decommissioned 6 October 2000.

Planetree WAGL 307: [d. 1,025; 180 × 37; 13 k; a. 1-3"; Class Mesquite] Launched 20 March 1943 and commissioned 4 November 1943, this 180-foot buoy tender carried a complement of six officers and seventy-one enlisted men. She was out of commission from 1947 to 1949. In service in Korean waters from 15 May to 27 July 1954, she was retired 19 March 1999.

Net Tender (AN)

Butternut AN 9: [d. 700; 151'8" × 30'6"; 14 k; cpl. 40; a. 1-3"; Class Aloe] Launched 10 May 1941, she was commissioned 13 May 1942. During World War II she tended nets in the New Hebrides and Solomon Islands, and later at Leyte and the Philippine Islands. Following repairs at Pearl Harbor she sailed to Sasebo, Japan. She was in Korean waters 27 December 1950 to 7 July 1951. She was decommissioned 18 June 1969 and stricken on 1 July 1971.

Catalpa II AN-5: [d. 560; 163'2" × 30'6"; 12 k; cpl. 48; a. 1-3"; Class Aloe] The second ship with this name, she was launched as YN-5 and commissioned 22 May 1942. She served in South Pacific bases during World War II. She was decommissioned and placed in reserves 21 October 1946. Recommissioned 7 August 1950, she sailed to the Far East where she was in Korean waters from 29 March 1953 to 27 July 1954. She was placed out of commission on 7 October 1955.

Elder AN 20 (YN 15): [d. 560; 163'2" × 30'6"; 12 k; cpl. 48; a. 1-3"; Class Aloe] Launched 19 June 1941 and placed in service 12 November 1941, she was redesignated as AN 20 on 20 January 1944. During World War II she served in the Pacific. Scheduled for service in the Far East, she was badly damaged by an engine fire in 1950. After repairs, she operated at Yokosuka, Japan, a key base for the Korean War. She was decommissioned 18 December 1959.

Mulberry AN 27: [d. 805; 163'2" × 30'6"; 12.5 k; cpl. 48; a. 1-3", 3-20mm, 1-Ygun; Class Aloe] Originally designated Y 22, she was launched 26 May 1941, commissioned 19 December 1942, and reclassified AN 27 effective 20 January 1944. She supported military activities in Alaskan and Aleutian waters during World War II and after. She then moved to net tending at Sasebo and Yokosuka Harbors. She served in Korean waters during the Korea Summer–Fall 1953 campaign and received one battle star. She was decommissioned 11 April 1960 and was then transferred on loan to Ecuador in November 1965 where she served as *Orion*.

Whaleboat

For more than two centuries the whaleboat has been the navy's most common method for transporting troops from ship to shore. Named after the design which had been used by New England whale hunters, the whaleboat is one of the most widespread and active boats in the navy. In World War II however, the whaleboat took on a more tactical use, and they were engaged in special operations to infiltrate behind enemy lines, to transport prisoners, and rescue downed pilots and wounded sailors. The standard shipboard whaleboat that was available for use during the Korean War was a leftover from World War II, the wooden, motor whaleboat. The boats saw considerable service in special operations along the coast of Korea, as well as daily work transporting personnel and as lifeboats. Typically they were 26' × 7'5", Mark II (Magnetic), with a capacity of twenty-two persons. They displaced 8,850 pounds. Of the thousands of these boats made, few remain intact.

Sometimes the ship of last resort, whaleboats were often called upon for tight evacuations. When there was some concern that a delay in sweeping might not allow ships to reach Chongha in time for a necessary evacuation of troops, Admiral Hartman prepared an evacuation plan designed to take troops on rafts towed by whaleboats. Fortunately, four LSTs arrived in time. Other uses were found as well. One of the blockade techniques was to use a ship's whaleboat for the detection of targets along the coastline. The whaleboat would lie close to a designated beach area, waiting, watching, and listening for trains, maintaining communication with the parent ship by walkie-talkie. A second use for was fire-direction for the mother ship's guns. A third was the capture of enemy sampans and junks.

Wiggle Boat

A small wooden craft with one sail and a single sculling oar was used for movement around the harbors of Korea. These were known as wiggle boats.

13

ALLIED NATIONS

You eat the Queen's salt, and you obey the Queen's Regulations.
—General Sir Anthony Farrar-Hockley

The Korean War was fought under the flag of the United Nations and executed by the United Nations Command. Perhaps this cooperation was nowhere more apparent than among the naval forces. During the war more than 100 warships, from a wide variety of nations, participated in the combat mission. In addition there were numerous other ships, from hospital ships to oilers, that also served. Arriving quickly and staying throughout the course of the war, these ships, large and small, played a significant role.

However, it is worth noting that the number of nations involved provoked some unusual difficulties, from the difference in weapons and ammunition, to the cultural distinctions of the diets they required. The fact that so many nations were able to work so well together is a tribute to all those involved. While it is estimated that forty-nine nations and a good number of private corporations provided aid and supplies, the nine countries provided war ships and auxiliaries that fit into the scope of this book. These nations participated in the battle, took casualties, and reimbursed the United States for the logistical support they received.

Was it possible for a common, or at least understood, series of signals and phraseology to be developed? The solutions, and there were many, were found in persistence and ingenuity. So much so that Rear Admiral George C. Dyer, commander of CTF-95 would say: "Without any reservation, the association of all these navies together has not only been a very cordial and profitable one but "there had been no major difficulty."

Australia

Within four days of the beginning of the Korean War, the Australian government committed fighting ships to the UN effort. On 30 June 1951 the government committed its ships that were in Japanese waters to Commander, U.S. Naval Forces, Far East (ComNavFE). During the war these ships included the carrier HMAS *Sydney*, and the destroyers *Anzac, Arunta, Warramunge,* and *Tobruk*. As well, Australia supplied four frigates deployed in patrolling, engaging shore batteries, providing gunfire support, screening for carriers, support for island hopping, and clandestine raids. The Australians suffered 191 casualties out of a total of 4,507 officers and men who served in the war. The frigates were as follows:

HMAS *Condamine* K 698: [d. 1,537; 301 × 36'5"; 19 k; cpl. 175; a. 4-4", 3-40mm, 8-20mm, dct.; Modified Bay Class] She was launched 4 November 1944 and commissioned 22 February 1946. She served in Korean waters from 4 July 1952 to 10 April 1953. She was paid off 1955 and sold 21 September 1961.

HMAS *Culgoa* K408: [d. 1,537; 301 × 36'5"; 19 k; cpl. 175; a. 4-4", 3-40mm, 8-20mm, dct.; Modified Bay Class] The ex–*MacQuarie* was built in 1944 and commissioned 1 April 1947. Records indicate that she was in Korean waters from 14 March to 2 November 1951. She was sold 15 February 1972.

HMAS *Murchison* K442: [d. 1,537; 301 × 36'5"; 19 k; cpl. 175; a. 4-4", 3-40mm, 8-20mm, dct.; Modified Bay Class] She was launched 31 October 1944 and commissioned 17 December 1945. She served in Korean waters between 9 May 1951 to 17 February 1952. Paid off January 1956 and sold 21 September 1961.

HMAS *Shoalhaven* K535: [d. 1,537; 301 × 36'5"; 19 k; cpl. 175; a. 4-4", 3-40mm, 8-20mm, dct.; Modified Bay Class] Launched 14 December 1944 and commissioned 2 May 1946, she served in Korean waters from 27 June to 22 September 1950. Paid off 19 December 1955, she was sold January 1962.

New Australia: [d. 22,424; 579 × 76; 19 k; cpl. 456; troop capacity 700] Launched 17 March 1931, originally the *Monarch of Bermuda*, she caught fire 24 May 1947. Renamed in 1949 and operated by the Ministry of Transport, she was charted by the government to take troops to Korea and bring them home from Korea in 1952.

Canada

At the time war broke out in Korea, Canada was in no position to send troops. The Canadian army was small and unprepared for any expanded assignment, and the Royal Canadian Air Force was basically a transport service. Only the navy was in a position to help. On 12 July 1950, three Canadian destroyers sailed for Korean waters where they remained on a rotation basis until the end of the war. They maintained blockades, engaged shore batteries, and took part in the landings at Inchon and the famed "truck busting" club on the east coast. When the war ended, 3,621 officers and men serving in eight ships had participated in the Korean effort.

In addition, the Canadian merchant marine supplied twelve ships for Korean service. The Canadian Merchant Marines is not an official organization, and veterans were denied benefits given to members of the armed forces. A belated compensation was provided in 1990. The names of the Canadian ships have not been isolated here, but are identified in chapter 11 as foreign flag ships.

Colombia (Armada da la Republica de Colombia)

The Colombian units were the only Latin American representatives aiding the UN cause. They provided an infantry regiment and the following frigates.

ARC *Almirante Brion*: [d. 1,430; 303'5" × 37'5"; 20 k; cpl. 147; a. 3-3", dcr] The former USS *Burlington* was built in 1944. She operated in Korean waters from June 1953 to April 1954.

ARC *Almirante Padilla*: [d. 1,430; 303'5" × 37'5"; 20 k; cpl. 147; a. 3-3", dcr] The former USS *Groton* was built in 1944, and carried out coastal duty in Korea from May 1951 until February 1952. She was assigned to the special mission of moving ROK agents from Yodo Island to Songjin.

ARC *Captain Tono*: [d. 1,430; 303'5" × 37'5"; 20 k; cpl. 147; a. 3-3", dcr] The former USS *Bisbee* was built in 1944. She participated in Korean War activity from April 1952 to January 1953.

Denmark

Denmark's contribution to the UN cause was the ship *Jutlandia*, an 8,500-ton cargo vessel built in 1937. The *Jutlandia* had been trapped in Danish waters during World War II. Officially it was a civilian ship under UN command, and sailing under the Red Cross. The hospital and crew were Danish personnel. She could achieve 15 to 17 knots. The ship had room for 350 patients, and included dental clinics, X-ray facilities, and three operating rooms. She had a crew of 105. Launched in 1939 and commissioned in November 1934, she became a hospital ship 23 January 1951. She sailed from Copenhagen in September 1950 and arrived in Pusan in October. After her first tour she had a helicopter deck installed. She was anchored at Inchon during her second tour. She was in Korean service from 7 March 1951 to 24 July 1951, 29 September 1951 to 27 March 1952, and 20 September 1952 until 16 October 1953. She returned to Denmark in October 1953, was restored as a cargo passenger vessel, and was sold. Commemoration stamps were issued by Denmark and the Republic of Korea. The *Jutlandia* missed the chance at considerable publicity. General Ridgway, when suggesting the opening of armistice negotiations with North Korea and China, recommended that the first meeting be held on the Danish hospital ship. The communists rejected the hospital ship, and instead suggested the old capital city of Kaesong, South Korea, where the meetings were finally held.

France

FMS *La Grandiere* 731: [d. 1,969; 340 × 41'8"; 15'5 k; cpl. 133-194; a. 3-5.5", 4-40mm and 11-20mm] Despite being heavily involved in Indochina, the French provided a token participant by sending the frigate *La Grandiere*. The former *Ville D'Ys* was completed in 1939 as a First Class Sloop (Minelaying). She arrived on 29 July 1950. She was immediately engaged in transport and escort missions between Japan and Pusan. The crew of the *La Grandiere* were awarded the Korean Service Medal.

Great Britain

On 29 June, just four days after the outbreak of war, the British Admiralty put the Royal Navy units, which were in Japanese waters, under the command of ComNavFE. The 32

Hospital Ship *Jutlandia*

warships of the Royal Navy included five carriers, six cruisers, seven destroyers, and fourteen frigates, as well as numerous supply and fleet vessels. A combination of 17,000 officers and men of the Royal Navy and Royal Marines served aboard. The sloops and frigates fell into three classes. Bay Class: displacement 1,600; 307'5" × 38'5"; 19 k; cpl. 157; a. 5-4"AA, 6-40mm, 2-20mm. Black Swan Class: displacement 1,350 standard; 285 × 38; 20 k; cpl. 180-192; a. 6-4", 4-2 pounder (pdr) pompons, later added 4-8 20mm and 40mm Begfors AA guns. Loch Class: displacement 1,600; 307'5" × 38'5"; 19 k; cpl. 160; a. 2-4", 2-40mm. Sloops and frigates are listed here.

HMS *Alacrity*: A modified Black Swan frigate, she was launched 1 September 1944 and commissioned in 1945. She was assigned to Task Force 96.8, was involved in blockade efforts, and went on to serve in Korea from June 1950 until February 1952. She was scrapped in 1962.

HMS *Alert IX*: A modified Loch-class frigate, laid in 1944 as the *Loch Scamadale*, renamed *Dundrum* and launched July 1945, she was converted 1 October 1945 to a dispatch vessel. She arrived in Korea on 3 August 1950, served as a dispatch vessel to the Commander in Chief and, until the arrival of the *Ladybird*, as the headquarters ship. She was in Korean waters from August 1950 to October 1951, during which she steamed a reported 5,000 miles. Broken up 31 October 1971.

HMS *Amethyst*: She was launched 7 May 1943. The ship was famous for an incident when it was attacked by the communist People's Liberation Army. The sloop exchanged fire on 20 April 1949 with Chinese communist shore batteries along the Yangtze River, with a loss of forty-four men. She later took part in the Chinnampo mine sweep, participated in

Cho Do and Sok To duels with shore batteries, and served in Korea from February 1951 to June 1952.

HMS *Blackswan*: Primarily a sloop, she was a specialized convoy-defense vessel that exchanged speed for longer range. Built in 1939, she was assigned to Task Force 96.8, took part in the first blockade efforts and supplied gunfire support at Inchon. She served from June 1950 to November 1951.

HMS *Cardigan Bay*: A Bay-class frigate, she was the ex–*Loch Laxford*. Launched 30 November 1944, she saw service in Korean waters from November 1950 until July 1953. On 20 July 1951 she was involved in the efforts to recover a crashed MiG-15 that was in the sea near Hanchon.

HMS *Crane*: Launched 9 November 1942, she was a modified Black-Swan-class ship. She participated in the early bombardment off Ho Do. She received a long-range hit that caused minor damage but no casualties. She served in Korea from March 1952 until July 1953, and was involved in the evacuation of islands which, under the armistice agreement, would remain in North Korean hands. She later served in the Suez affair, and was scrapped in 1965.

HMS *Hart*: This modified Black Swan frigate was launched 7 July 1943, commissioned 12 December 1943, and sold to German Federal Republic in 1958. She took part in the first blockade assignments in Korea, and was later assigned to Task Force 96.8. She served in Korean waters from June 1950 until March 1951 when she returned to the United Kingdom.

HMS *Ladybird*: [d. 3,400; 295 × 45] The first *Ladybird* was attacked by Japan on 12 December 1937 as it was upriver from the USS *Panay*. It was later sunk off Tobruk in 1944. *Ladybird II* was the ex–*Wusueh*, an ex-commercial Yangtze Patrol ferry. She was purchased in August 1950 to replace the HMS *Altert*. She served as flagship for Rear Admiral Scott-Moncrieff, and was in Korea from September 1950 to April 1953. She was returned to its owner in 1953.

HMS *Maine*: [d. 7,500; 429'5" × 52] The HMS *Maine* was provided by Great Britain and it was for some time the only ship available for the evacuation of wounded from Korea. Formerly an Italian cruise ship and temporarily the Royal Yacht, she had been taken from the Italians on 14 February 1941 and was employed as a transport during World War II. When war broke out she was in Kobe, Japan, and quickly arrived in Korea where she served until February 1952. She had a second tour from May 1952 until June 1953. During the course of the war she treated more than 2,115 U.S. casualties, conducted 1,006 surgeries, and made eight voyages of evacuation. Poorly ventilated and barely adequate, she was replaced by more modern ships as quickly as possible.

HMS *Modeste*: This modified Black-Swan frigate arrived in the Korean theater in May 1953 and joined the inshore bombardment line at Amgak and off Chinnampo. She served in Korean waters from then until July 1953. She later served in the Suez affair.

HMS *Morecambe Bay* F 624: A Bay-class frigate previously named *Loch Heilen*, she was built in 1944, served in Korean waters, participated in the Kusan Port attacks, and was eventually sold to Portugal in 1961.

HMS *Mounts Bay*: A Bay-class frigate previously named *Loch Kilbirnie*, she was launched 8 June 1945 and commissioned 11 April 1946. She was involved with the Advanced Screening Group at Wolmi-do, and as the protective screen at Inchon. During this time she dropped depth charges on a reported enemy submarine. She participated in the Wonsan "Day of Bombardment" in July of 1951, and saw service in Korean waters August 1950 until June 1953. She was hit by North Korean shore batteries five times, and received a fatality and casualties. Later she served on the approaches to Amgak and Chinnampo. She was sold to Portugal on 9 May 1961 and named *Vasco da Gama*.

HMS *Opossum* F 33: A modified Black-Swan frigate built in 1944 and transferred to the reserve fleet 30 November 1949, she was activated and served in Korean waters between December 1952 and April 1953. She was involved in the bombardment of Haeju and Sunwido, and in the recovery of a downed MiG-15 in the waters north of Hanchon. She was scrapped in 1962.

HMS *St. Brides Bay*: A Bay-class frigate, previously a Loch-class frigate named *Loch Achilty*, she was launched 16 January 1945 and commissioned 15 June 1945. She was too late to take part in World War II but served in Korean waters from December 1950 until June 1953. She was hit by shore fire, though no casualties were reported. Scrapped 3 September 1962.

HMS *Sparrow*: Launched 18 February 1946 as a modified Black-Swan frigate, the *Sparrow* served in Korea from December 1952 until June 1953. She was involved in bombardment groups where she received a hit that caused minor damage but no casualties.

HMS *Telemachus* P-321: [d. 1,080; 275 × 9; 15 k; cpl. 68; a. 1-4", 2 mg and aa; 10-21" tt with 16 torpedoes; "T" Class group] Launched 19 June 1943 and commissioned 25 October 1943, this submarine sank a Japanese freighter in July 1944. She was in Korea, assigned to Group Three. Broken up and scrapped 1 August 1961.

HMS *Tyne IV*: [d. 11,000 tons; 623 × 66; 17 k; cpl. 520; a. 8 dp 4.5 and 8 quad 2 pounders; Class Hecla] The *Tyne* was a destroyer depot ship as well as a headquarters ship. Launched 28 February 1940 and commissioned 28 February 1941, she served as the depot ship for the Far East Station. She provided maintenance to weapons and machinery, as well as radio and ASDIC antisubmarine detection. She also had accommodations for Commonwealth Naval Forces. Among other things she could produce 25,000 pounds of freshly baked bread per day.

HMS *Unicorn*: [d. 14,750; cpl. 1200; a. 8-4" twin aa, 4-4", 20-10 mm and 20mm] This large British ship looked like an aircraft carrier but was more completely an aircraft repair facility. Commissioned in 1943, she could hold up to seventy aircraft and was an example of a one-ship class. Her responsibly was to carry replacement aircraft and transport cargo. She first carried the 1st Battalion Middlesex Regiment from Hong Kong to Pusan. During the Korean War she steamed 130,000 nautical miles, spent 500 days at sea, handled 600 airplanes, and 6,000 passengers. While usually stationed on the coast of Japan, she moved into Korean waters on several occasions and once, in 1953, fired her four-inch guns against targets in North Korea.

HMS *Whitesand Bay* F 633: A Bay-class frigate previously named *Loch Lubnaig*, she was launched 16 December 1944 and commissioned 30 July 1945. She served in Korean waters from August 1950 until July 1953. She expended over a thousand 4" shells in a fifteen-day bombardment of traffic along the coastal railway of North Korea. On 17 April 1951 she had her aerials shot away but was otherwise undamaged. She was scrapped in 13 February 1956.

OILERS

Great Britain provided much of her own supply, particularly oil for her ships. The diesel-powered RFA Ranger class tankers generally displaced 3,500 tons and had a speed of 12 knots. The funnel was fitted on the port side, and they were equipped with a derrick at the beam for fueling at sea. They could carry 2,600 tons of fuel oil, 550 tons of diesel and 90 tons of gasoline, and drums of lubricating fluid on their deck. These ships flew the Blue Ensign which identified them as partly civilian and partly military in terms of crew. The civilians were members of the merchant navy who operated under naval discipline. Some of the ships carried a small amount of armaments, usually 20mm or 7.62mm guns.

RFA *Abbeydale* A109: [d. 17,200; 481'5" × 62; 11.5 k; cpl. 40] This was a Dale-class Type 2 auxiliary fleet tanker launched 28 December 1936.

RFA *Birchol* A127: [d. 2,670; 232 × 39; 11 k; cpl. 26] An OL Class oiler launched 19 February 1946, this coastal tanker was sold to Belgium 1969.

RFA *Brown Ranger* A169: [d. 3,313; 365'8" × 47; 12 k] Built in 1940, she was a fleet support tanker of the Royal Fleet Auxiliary, powered by Harland and Wolff engines, launched 12 December 1940. The Ranger-class tanker could carry 2,600 tons of fuel oil, 550 tons of diesel and 90 tons of gasoline. They were designed with a derrick and a 9-ton barge which could be used to refuel Royal Air Force flying boats. Few if any of these flying boats were ever carried, and the space was used to carry drums of lubricating oil. During the early months she ferried oil from Sasebo and served as a station tanker.

RFA *Choysang*: [d. 1,923; 282 × 44] The ex–*Empire Witham* and *Aeolus*, the ship was taken as a prize in Kiel in May 1945 by the Royal Navy. It was later called into Korean War service. She deployed from Hong Kong, serving primarily as a temporary armament-stores-issuing ship.

RFA *Eaglesdale* A104: [d. 17,200; 481'5" × 62; 11.5 k; cpl. 40] Previously the *Empire Metal Service*, the *Eaglesdale* was a Dale-class, Type 1 oiler, launched 18 November 1944. She was scrapped in 1959.

RFA *Echodale* A170: [d. 17,200; 481'5" × 62; 11.5 k; cpl. 40] A Dale-class, Type 1 fleet tanker built in 1941, she was scrapped in 1961.

RFA *Green Ranger* A152: [d. 3,417; 355'8" × 47; 12 k] This Ranger-class tanker could carry 2,600 tons of fuel oil, 550 tons of diesel and 90 tons of gasoline. Launched 21 August 1941, she was designed with a derrick and a 9-ton barge which could be used to refuel Royal Air Force flying boats. (See RFA *Brown Ranger*.) Like the *Brown Ranger*, during the early months she ferried oil from Sasebo and served as a station tanker.

RFA *Oakol* A300: [d. 2,670, 232 × 39; 11 k; cpl. 26] Launched 28 August 1946, this OL-class oiler was sold to Belgium in 1969. The so-called Wave Liberators had a different bridging system. The *Wave Baron*, *Wave Chief*, *Wave Commander*, *Wave Conqueror*, *Wave Duke* and *Wave Laird* were powered with Metrovick-geared turbines; the others had Parson-geared engines. The dimensions for the Wave-class tankers had a displacement of 8,200 (cap. 16,650); were 465' × 64'; and traveled at 15 knots.

RFA *Wave Baron* A242: Originally named *Empire Flodden*, she was launched 19 February 1946. She served in Korea and was broken up at Bilbao in 1972.

RFA *Wave Chief* A265: Originally laid as the *Empire Edgehill* by Harland and Wolff, she was launched April 1946 as a fleet tanker. Renamed *Wave Chief* on completion in August 1946, she was the first oiler available, and brought in fuel from Singapore. In one routine period she provided sixty-six replacements at sea of fuel (including aviation fuel) taken on by ships of the Royal Navy, and the navies of Canada, Australia, New Zealand, the United States and the Netherlands. She was scrapped at Inverkeithing in 1974.

RFA *Wave Conqueror*: Built in 1943 as the *Empire Law*, she was launched 27 November 1943, and sold 1960.

RFA *Wave Knight* A249: Originally the *Empire Naseby*, she was launched 22 October 1945.

RFA *Wave Laird* A 119: Launched 3 April 1946 as the *Empire Dunbar*.

RFA *Wave Monarch*: Launched 6 July 1944.

RFA *Wave Premier*: Launched 27 June 1946, she was a fleet support tanker. On 9 June 1951 she pumped contaminated aviation fuel to the HMS *Glory*, causing her recall.

RFA *Wave Prince* A207: Originally the *Empire Herald*, launched 27 July 1945 as a fleet support tanker, she was scrapped in 1971.

RFA *Wave Regent* A 486: Launched 18 March 1945, she served as an ammo supply ship.

RFA *Wave Sovereign* A211: A fleet support tanker, she was launched 20 November 1945.

Supply and Troop Ships

Fort Charlotte A 236: [d. 9,788; 424'3" × 57; 11 k] Launched in 1944, she entered RFA service in 1950. She operated in Korean waters, and was one of the first bringing supplies from Hong Kong, some 1,600 miles distant, delivering everything but fresh vegetables. She served primarily as a stores-issuing ship. She was sold in 1967.

Fort Langley A 230: [d. 9,788; 424'3" × 57; 11 k] Built in 1945 as a merchant fleet auxiliary, she served in Korea primarily as an armament-stores carrier. Eventually she was equipped with a helicopter pad. She was returned to the Canadian government in 1970 and sold for scrap.

Fort Rosalie A 186: [d. 9,788; 424'3" × 57; 11 k] Built in 1944, she was the best known of the fleet auxiliaries. She operated in Korean waters for more than 18 months and supplied most of the ammunition used by Commonwealth ships, a total of some 9,000 tons of bombs and ammunition. She was sold for scrap 1972.

Fort Sandusky A 316: [d. 9,788; 424'3" × 57; 11 k] She served in Korean waters as an armament-stores carrier. Sold for scrap in 1972.

HMT *Devonshire*: This ship was used to transport Australian troops, leaving Sydney for Korea in 1952. She was scrapped in 1963.

HMT *Empire Fowey*: [d. 19,047; 605 × 74] Built in 1936 as the *Empire Jewel*, she served as a passenger liner, was seized by the Allies in 1943 and converted to a troop transport. She returned the Glosters to Southampton in 1951.

HMT *Empire Halladale*: [d. 13,589; 13 k; capacity 1886 passengers] Formerly the *Antonio Delfino*, this troopship served from October 1952 to May 1953, making at least two trips to the Far East. Built in 1921, she sailed briefly as the *Sierra Nevada*, and in 1940 as a naval accommodation ship at Kiel. In November 1945 she was transferred to the Ministry of War Transport, and renamed *Empire Halladale*. She made two trips to Korea between October 1952 and March 1953 to disembark UK and Commonwealth troops at Pusan. Laid up in October 1955, she was sold for scrap the next year.

HMT *Empire Longford*: Completed in 1912 as the *Dimboola*, she was renamed *Hong Kong* in 1935, and *Empire Longford* in 1951.

HMT *Empire Pride*: [d. 9,248; 473 × 64] Completed 1941. After serving in Korea she was converted to cargo ship in 1954.

HMT *Empire Trooper*: [d. 14,106; 500 × 64; cpl. 1922] This transport was built in Hamburg in 1920 as the *Cap Norte*. She was captured by the HMS *Belfast* in 1940. Reestablished as the *Empire Trooper*, she was used as a troopship and transported the Devonshire troops to Korea. She was scrapped in 1955.

HMT *Empire Windrush*: [d. 13,882; 500 × 65'7", 14 k; troop accommodation 2,428] Built in 1930 as the *Monte Rosa*, she was used as a troopship during World War II. In 1944 she was briefly refitted as a hospital ship, and was used as an accommodation ship for the damaged battleship *Tirpitz*. In 1946, repaired and refitted as a troopship, she was renamed *Empire Windrush*, and managed for the Ministry of War Transport. She made 13 round-trip voyages to the Far East. She sank after an engine-room fire in 1954.

RASC *Frederick Clover* LST: [d. 4,820; 346 × 54; 13.6 k; cpl. 104; a. 4 (twin) 20mm DPAA, and 2-20mm DP AA] This Royal Army Service Corp ship, under the command of the Royal Navy, was the ex–L3001 and was completed in 1945.

RASC *Maxwell Brander* LST: [d. 4,820; 346 × 54; 13.6 k; cpl. 104; a. 4 (twin) 20mm DPAA, and 2-20mm DP AA] This Royal Army Service Corp ship, under the command of the Royal Navy, was the ex–L3024, and was completed in 1945. She carried elements of New Zealand's ground forces from Japan to Korea.

RASCV *Charles Macleod* LST: [d. 4,820; 346 × 54; 13.6 k; cpl. 104; a. 4 (twin) 20mm DPAA, and 2-20mm DP AA] This Royal Army Service Corp ship, under the command of the Royal Navy, was the ex–L3021 and was completed in 1945.

RASCV *Reginald Kerr* LST: [d. 4,820; 346 × 54; 13.6 k; cpl. 104; a. 4 (twin) 20mm DPAA, and 2-20mm DP AA] This Royal Army Service Corp ship, under the command of the Royal Navy, was the ex–L3009 and was completed in 1945.

Japan

The Japanese, albeit still under occupation, made a significant contribution to the outcome of the war. It came through the U.S. Navy via the Shipping Control Administration Japan (SCAJAP), operating under Commander Naval Forces Far East. For the first few days of the war, the SCAJAP ships, former U.S. Navy Landing Ships, Tank (LST), transported vastly necessary men, weapons, and equipment across the waters to Korea. The thirty-eight LSTs the Japanese made available were essential to the Pusan Perimeter defense, and amounted to about 60% of the amphibious vessels available for Inchon. Japanese minesweepers under Admiral Takeo Okubo were deeply involved in the clearing of Wonsan, North Korea.

On 2 October 1950 Admiral Burke requested the use of Japanese minesweepers. These were not Japanese war surplus, but rather ships of the Japanese Maritime Safety Agency that had been involved in sweeping the Inland Sea since the end of the war. Four days later the JMSA (Japanese Maritime Defense Force after the end of World War II) authorized twenty minesweepers, four patrol boats as mother ships, and one other ship to deal with the growing threat of magnetic mines. Some went to the Korean coast, ten or twelve to Wonsan.

Fentriss Maru: A time-chartered SCAJAP ship, she was engaged in the Hungnam redeployment.

Malay Maru #2: A SCAJAP time-chartered ship, she was engaged in the Hungnam redeployment in December 1950.

Senzan Maru: A SCAJAP time-chartered ship loaded with 50,000 bags of flour, she missed the channel at Hungnam and hit a mine. Though eight feet down at the forward, she was saved.

Shinano Maru: A SCAJAP time-chartered ship, she was engaged in the Hungnam redeployment in December 1950 when she served as the mother ship for the 1,200 Japanese who served the port facilities.

Tobato Maru: A time-chartered SCAJAP ship, she was engaged in the Hungnam redeployment in December 1950.

Yon Yama Maru: A time-chartered SCAJAP ship, she was engaged in the Hungnam redeployment in December 1950.

There were several types of Japanese minesweepers involved. The AMC was an auxiliary motor minesweeper. The JMS were Japanese-built sweepers, somewhat smaller than the American AMS. The YMS were motor minesweepers that had been left behind in Japanese waters following World War II to carry out sweeping operations of Japanese ports. During the period between the wars, many of them had been sold or loaned, and had taken on other assignments. Two Japanese minesweepers suffered destruction. The JMS 305 was sunk by mistake by UN fire on 29 June 1950, leading to the widespread belief that a Russian cruiser was sailing in the Samchok area. The JMS 306 struck a mine off the coast of Chinnampo on 6 May 1951 and sank.

The Netherlands: (Koninklijke Marine)

Six ships and a total of 1,360 men of the Netherlands served in Korea as a part of the U.S. 7th Fleet. Officially the ships were labeled HNLMS (Haar Nederlandse Majesteit Schip/ Her Netherlands Majesty's Ship). Three were destroyers — the HRMS *Eversten*, *Van Galen*, and *Poet Heim*— and outside our discussion. Three of them were frigates. (See below.) Two Netherlands sailors died while in service in Korea.

HNLMS *Dubois*: [d. 1,525; 308 × 36'8"; 21 k; a. 3-3", 21" tt, 1 twin 40mm, 8-20mm, 8K projectors] This frigate was previously the USS *O'Neill* (DE 188). Launched 14 February 1943 and commissioned 6 December 1943, she was decommissioned 2 May 1946 and transferred to the Netherlands on 23 October 1950. She served in Korea from May 1953 to October 1953. Returned in 1967, she was scrapped in 1968.

HNLMS *Johan Maurits van Nassau*: [d. 1,463; 301 × 36'5"; 29 k; cpl. 120 ; a. 2-4", 7-20mm] Previously the HMS *Ribble*, she was launched 23 April 1943 and commissioned 25 June 1943. She served in Korean waters from January to November 1953. She was awarded the Presidential Unit Citation (ROK).

HNLMS *Van Zijll*: [d. 1,240; 306 × 36'7"; 21 k; cpl. 216; a. 3-3", 8-40mm, 10-20mm; 8 dcp, 2 dct; Class Cannon] This frigate was previously the USS *Stern* (DE 187). Launched 31 October 1943 and commissioned 3 January 1951, she was sold to the Netherlands 1 March 1951. She served in Korean waters from October 1954 to January 1955. Returned to the United States in December 1967, she is not listed in Crocker.

New Zealand

One of the first nations to offer naval assistance to the United Nations, New Zealand dispatched two frigates from Auckland on 3 July 1950. In addition to their ground forces, New Zealand committed six RN Loch-class frigates. From then on, six frigates and more than 1,300 men served in the UN Command, with two ships always on station in Korea.

HMNZA *Hawea*: [d. 1,435; 307'5" × 38'7"; 18 k; cpl. 114; a. 1-4", 4-2 pounders, 6-20mm] The former *Loch Eck*, she was built in 1944, and served in Korean waters from March 1951 to 1 January 1952, and August 1952 to 30 August 1953.

HMNZA *Kaniere*: [d. 1,435; 307'5" × 38'7"; 18 k; cpl. 114; a. 1-4", 4-2 pounders, 6-20mm] The former *Loch Achray* was built in 1945, and served in Korea from 2 March 1953 until the armistice.

HMNZA *Pukaki*: [d. 1,435; 307'5" × 38'7"; 18 k; cpl. 114; a. 1-4", 4-2 pounders, 6-20mm] The former *Loch Achanalt* and *Naver*, she was built in 1944. She served in Korean waters 3 July 1950 to December 1950, and was with the Advanced Screening Group that was responsible for Wolmi-do during the Inchon landing.

HMNZA *Rotoiti*: [d. 1,435; 307'5" × 38'7"; 18 k; cpl. 114; a. 1-4", 4-2 pounders, 6-20mm] The former *Loch Katrine* was built in 1944, and served in Korean waters from 7 October 1950 to 21 November 1951, and 7 January 1952 to March 1953.

HMNZA *Taupo*: [d. 1,435; 307'5" × 38'7"; 18 k; cpl. 114; a. 1-4", 4-2 pounders, 6-20mm] The former *Loch Shin*, she served in Korean waters from 29 August 1951 to 21 October 1952.

HMNZA *Tutira*: [d. 1,435; 307'5" × 38'7"; 18 k; cpl. 114; a. 1-4", 4-2 pounders, 6-20mm] The former *Loch Morlich*, she was built in 1944. She was in Korean waters from 3 July 1950 to 3 December 1950, and operated with the U.S. Navy screening force for the Inchon Landing. The sole New Zealand naval casualty occurred during *Tutira*'s participation on one of the shore islands. She served in Korean waters July 1950 until May 1951.

HMS *Ormonde*: This passenger ship that had carried troops during World War II (and had suffered a mutiny on board because of the conditions) was selected to carry the New Zealand Expeditionary Force to Japan.

HMS *Wahine*: A troopship scheduled to take New Zealand troop to Korea, she was shipwrecked in January 1952.

Thailand

One of the first to respond to the United Nations resolution, Thailand provided a regimental combat team of 4,000 men, an air transportation squadron, and five vessels.

HMTS *Bangpakong*: [d. 1,060; 203'2" × 33; 16 k; cpl. 101; a. 7-20mm, 1-4"] The former *Burnet*, she served in Korean waters from November 1950 until February 1952.

HMTS *Prasae*: [d. 1,060; 203'3" × 33; 16 k; cp. 101; a. 1-4" DPAA, and 7-20mm DPAA, 6 dct] The *Royal Prasae* (ex–*Sind* and ex–*Betuny*) patrol frigate was completed in 1943. In Korea from November 1950 until 7 January 1951, she was lost while on patrol of the east coast of Korea. She went aground during a snowstorm in an area behind enemy lines, and when it was determined that she could not be broken loose, the U.S. Navy frigate *Gallup* (PF-47) was transferred to Thailand as a replacement. It was also named *Prasae*. (See below.)

HMTS *Prasae II*: [d. 1,430; 304 × 37'5"; 20 k; cpl. 180; a. 10-40mm and 6-20mm] The second *Prasae*, previously the USS *Gallup*, was built in 1944. She served in Korean waters from December 1951 until January 1955.

HMTS *Sichang*: [d. 815; 160 × 28; 16 k; cpl. 30; a. 2-20mm] A naval transport ship, she served in Korean waters from November 1950 until 15 July 1951. She arrived carrying elements of the 21st Royal Thai Army Regiment.

HMTS *Tachin*: [d. 1,430; 304 × 37'5"; 20 k; cpl. 180; a.10-40mm, 6-20mm] Formerly the *Glendale*, this patrol frigate was in Korea from December 1951 to January 1955.

Republic of Korea

The navy of the Republic of Korea was new, small, and not very experienced, but it was deeply involved in the defense of the country. In fact the only essential naval surface battle during the war was fought by the ROKN. When war broke out the Republic of Korea Navy consisted of 6,956 men and 71 naval vessels, most so small as to remain unidentified. They had been concentrated along the southern and western coasts and were unable to prevent the initial landings of North Korean troops as far south as Samchok. On the other hand, they were able to destroy or deter other raids attempted. On 2 July, the ROKN's Naval Base Detachment at Pohang wiped out a North Korean landing force.

Lacking a centralized command, they assumed operation control under Commander Michael J. Luosey as Deputy Commander, Naval Forces. When Admiral Sohn returned to South Korea with his newly acquired submarine chasers, the ROK Navy stepped up its operations. During the war they worked in the clearing of mines as well as running mine-checks, raided enemy-held islands, landed special forces, fired on inshore targets, maintained the coastal blockade in inland waters, landed guerrilla parties, conducted coastal raids, and assisted the United Nations in the movement of men and equipment and the transportation of refugees.

In 1948 several ships were transferred to the newly formed Republic of Korea Navy. These included eighteen minesweepers (YMS), eleven former Japanese mine sweepers (JMS), two minelayers (LML), an oiler, and two sub chasers. In November 1950 the ROKN received two more Tacoma-class patrol frigates, and three more in 1951–52.

While there is not enough information to list the LSTs involved, the presence of Japanese-owned and crewed LST was highly significant to the naval plans. Most of them were old, dirty, and just plain worn out. A good many did not have the power in their winches to pull heavy loads. Of the thirty-nine available through SCAJAP, only sixteen were capable of carrying troops. The others, converted during July 1950, were dirty and in poor condition.

Apnok PF 62: [d. 1,430 (l); 303'1" × 37'6"; 20 k; cpl. 190; a. 3-3", 2 twin 40-mm, 9-20 mm, 8 Y gun projectors, 2 dcr] Originally the US Navy frigate *Rockford* (PF-48), she was commissioned May 1944, loaned to the USSR in 1945, returned in 1949, and then in October 1950 loaned to the ROK Navy. On 15 April 1951 she fought off an enemy air attack in the Yellow Sea while downing an enemy plane. In May 1952 she was damaged in a collision. She was returned to the United States in September 1952, and was replaced by the *Imchin*. Removed from the navy list in May 1953, she was sunk as a target that year.

Chiri San PC 704: [d. 284; 173'8" × 23; 21 k; cpl. 65; a. 1-3", 1-40mm, 5-20mm, 2 dct, 2 dcr, 2 Y guns] Built as USS PC 810, she was launched 11 December 1945 and commissioned 3 April 1945. Decommissioned in February 1946 and in storage until May of that year, she was transferred to the ROK Navy in 1950. She was en route to Korea when the war broke out. She was sunk after striking a mine on 25 December 1951, while working off Wonsan, North Korea.

Han La San PC 705: She was the U.S. PC 485, then leased to the ROK Navy where she became *Han La San*.

Imchin, Frigate PC 66: [d. 1,430 (l); 303'1" × 37'6"; 20 k; cpl. 190; a. 3-3", 2 twin 40-mm, 9-20 mm, 8 Y gun projectors, 2 dcr] Formerly the USS *Sausalito*, this 1430-ton Tacoma-class frigate was commissioned in March 1944 with a Coast Guard crew. Loaned to the USSR and then recommissioned, she served in harbor contact at Hungnam. In June 1952 she transferred to ROK to replace the frigate *Apnok*. She served in coastal waters for the remainder of the war.

Kang Hwa Man: She was LSSL 91 and leased to ROK Navy where she became *Kang Hwa Man* LSSL 108.

Kum Kang San PC 702: [d. 284; 173'8" × 23; 21 k; a. 1-3", 1-40mm, 5-20mm, 2 dct, 2 Y guns, 2 dcr] Commissioned 3 August 1944, this was the former USS PC 799, transferred to the ROK Navy in October 1950. Ably suited for inshore service, she provided valuable service in support of larger ships. According to the Naval Historical Center she was the former PC 810, but photographs of the ship show the number 799 on her stern. She was involved, along with PC 703, in the sinking of twelve enemy ammunition-carrying sampans west of Inchon. In August 1950 she led Operation Lee, landing a guerilla force on Tokchok Island, then later at Yonghong Island in efforts to divert the enemy from the landing at Inchon. She remained in Korean service until 1960.

Munsan LST: [d. 1,225; 318 × 50; 12 k; cpl. 111; carried 2 LCVP] Launched 7 August 1943 and commissioned 22 September 1943, she took part in the capture of Saipan and Tinian. Decommissioned 7 January 1946, the former U.S. LST 120 was transferred to the Republic of Korea in February 1947. She is described by the Naval Historical Center as a merchant ship. She was involved in a raid on enemy territory north of Pohang in September 1950 when she was damaged after broaching the serf. After efforts to pull her out failed, she was lost.

Myo Hyang San PC 706: She was the U.S. PC 600 and was leased to ROK Navy where she became *Myo Hyang San*.

Nae Tong PF 65: [d. 1264; 303'11" × 37'6"; 20 k; cpl. 190; a. 2-2", 2-40mm, 9-20mm, hh, 8 Y guns] Launched as the *Hoquiam* (PF 5) 10 April 1943 by the MC and commissioned 8 May 1944, she was transferred to Russia on 16 August 1945. Returned in November 1949 and recommissioned 27 September 1950. On 7 May 1951 she was damaged by gunfire. Decommissioned 8 October 1951 and leased to the ROK, she received five battle stars. Scrapped 1973.

PF 61: Cagle lists the ROK PF 61 as sweeping mines off the coast of Chinnampo, but there is no record in *Awards*.

PF 62: Cagle lists the ROK PF 62 as sweeping mines off the coast of Chinnampo, but there is no record in *Awards*.

Pak Tu San PC 701: [d. 280; 173'8" × 23; 18 k; cpl. 65, a. 1-3"] Originally the USS PC 823, built in 1944, she was purchased by subscription by the ROK Navy in 1950. Originally identified as the PC 810, photographic evidence suggests it was the former PC 799, called *Ensign Whitehead*. She was the first major vessel of the Korean navy. The first night of the war she made contact with a North Korean freighter and sank her. Her crew boarded and sank a large sailing vessel. She remained in service until 1960.

Sam Kak San PC 703: [d. 280; 173'8" × 23; 18 k; cpl. 65; a. 1-3"] Originally the USS PC 802, she was built in 1945 and transferred to the ROK Navy in 1950. Involved with PC 702 in the destruction of twelve enemy sampans carrying ammunition to their troops near Inchon, she also carried Lieutenant Clark (USN) to his clandestine reconnaissance of Inchon from Yong-hong-do Island. She remained in service until 1960.

Tae Dong PF 63: [d. 1,264; 303'1" × 37'6"; 20 k; cpl. 190; a. 3-3", 4-40mm, 9-20mm, hh, 8 Y guns] Originally the USS *Tacoma* (PF 3), she was launched 7 July 1943, commissioned 6 November 1943, decommissioned 16 August 1945, and recommissioned again on 1 December 1945. Transferred to the USSR 16 August 1945, she was returned 16 October of the same year and leased to the ROK Navy on 9 October 1951. She was decommissioned 28 February 1973.

YMS 301: Listed in Cagle as participating in the Inchon Landing, 15 September 1950.

YMS 302: Listed in Cagle as participating in the Inchon Landing, 15 September 1950.

YMS 303: Listed in Cagle as participating in the Inchon Landing, 15 September 1950.

YMS 306: Listed in Cagle as participating in the Inchon Landing, 15 September 1950, and the sweep of Chinnampo in late October 1950. Later lost to enemy action.

YMS 307: Listed in Cagle as participating in the Inchon Landing, 15 September 1950.

YMS 501: Listed in Cagle as participating in the Inchon Landing, 15 September 1950 and the sweeps at Chinnampo's "cigarette" route in May 1951.

YMS 502: Listed in Cagle as participating in the Inchon Landing, 15 September 1950. Involved in the sweep of Chinnampo in late October 1950.

YMS 503: Cagle lists her at the Inchon Landing, 15 September 1950, and at the sweep of Chinnampo in late October, where she was the first to enter the harbor.

YMS 504: The YMS 504 was responsible for sinking or damaging fourteen of fifteen small sailboats encountered. She was severely damaged when her propeller caused a mine explosion, and then two sympathetic explosions. Five men were hurt.

YMS 509: Listed in Cagle, she struck a mine on 28 September 1950 which knocked off the bow of the ship but left her afloat.

YMS 510: She participated in the Inchon Landing, 15 September 1950. She was slightly damaged by fire from enemy shore batteries near Songjin, Cagle says.

YMS 511: Listed in Cagle as participating in the Inchon landing, 15 September 1950.

YMS 512: This old American minesweeper met and sank a 100-ton motorboat and one of 70 tons, which resulted in the drowning of numerous enemy soldiers. Listed in Cagle as participating in the Inchon Landing, 15 September 1950.

YMS 513: She destroyed a trio of communist supply vessels near Chulpo on 2 July 1951, then repeated the action by destroying three more off Chulpo. She was involved in the sweep of Chinnampo in late October 1950.

YMS 514: Listed in Cagle who reports that in the early days of the war she met and sank two large motorboats near Chindo, and badly damaged another.

YMS 515: Cagle situates her at the Inchon Landing, 15 September 1950, and the sweep checks at Chinnampo's "cigarette" route during May of 1951.

YMS 516: On 18 October 1950, working with minesweepers at Wonsan, the previous U.S. YMS 148 struck a magnetic mine while sweeping the invasion beaches, and nearly vaporized. More than half her crew died in the event.

YMS 518: A former American minesweeper, she was involved in the early patrol of Pusan Harbor. She is listed in Cagle as having been at the Inchon Landing, 15 September 1950, and involved in sweeping exercises at Chinnampo.

Yung Huang Man: She was LSSL 77 and leased to ROK Navy where she became *Yung Huang Man*, LSSL 107.

14

ANALYSIS OF THE OTHER SHIPS

While the Navy's role in the war has gone unpublicized for the most part, it is sufficient to know that, but for the Navy, the war in Korea would come to a sudden halt.
—Admiral C. Turner Joy, 1952

Perhaps the best way to sum up the role of the navy, and that of the smaller and auxiliary ships, is to point out that they did what they were asked, they did it well, and they did it with courage and efficiency. In the years following the war many have raised questions about the success of some of the particular tactics and strategies pursued during the war, but it would a harsh critic indeed who would deny that the navy fulfilled the missions it was given.

In our consideration of the navy's participation in the Korean War we must acknowledge that it was hampered from the beginning. During the interwar period, the service had been stripped of nearly 90 percent of its fleet and personnel, and had been involved in a bitter dispute which had, sorely disturbed it. As the war broke out in Korea, the Far East Naval Force consisted of only twenty-nine officers to meet the new and compelling demands.

Yet the scene was to change dramatically. Within forty-eight hours, operational control of 7th Fleet was transferred and in the next few weeks and months numerous American and UN ships came on line. Eventually the UN forces were formed into four separate task forces — the carrier force (TF 77), the Blockade and Escort Force (TF 95), Naval Forces Japan (TF 96) and Amphibious Force (TF 90) — which carried out the war effort. This was a United Nations response that even included Japan, a nation under foreign occupation and officially still at war with the Allied powers.

From the beginning, the primary role of the U.S. Navy in Korea was to support the United Nations in preventing a disaster in the Far East. The fact that neither the Democratic People's Republic of Korea, the People's Republic of China, nor the Soviet Union invested significant naval forces in the war, speaks for itself. There is no way to know the extent to which the presence of U.S. Navy submarines and planes, constantly on patrol along the coasts of Korea, prevented the Soviet Union from engaging its own naval forces. But, the constant maintenance meant that if such a move was made, the United Nations would be forewarned.

Superiority at sea, and to a major extent control of the sky, was a significant part of the effort which prevented the communists from sweeping over Korea.* This was accomplished with very little bloodshed. And, other than the early delays caused by the communist mining of harbors and ports, it went primarily unchallenged.

Also, the navy was involved in the effort to prevent the outbreak from becoming World War III, while at the same time preventing expansion of the Communist Chinese/nationalist Chinese conflict over Formosa. Standing in the middle, they worked to prevent any sort of Chinese communist attack on Formosa and to disrupt any plans nationalist Chinese leader Chiang Kai-shek might envision for an attack on the Chinese mainland. Recent documents released by the old Soviet Union, and made available through translation by Katharine Weathersby and others, have been very instructive. Among other things, these documents support the idea that the quick reaction of naval forces and the show of force in the Taiwan Straits were both instrumental in preventing the People's Republic of China from carrying out a long-planned invasion of Taiwan. Such an attack, at that time, would have had the potential of greatly widening the war.

These Soviet documents also provide evidence that the deployment of the U.S. Seventh Fleet, as well as land-based bombers, played a significant part in Joseph Stalin's decision not to honor his earlier pledge to provide the Communist Chinese forces with early Soviet air support.

The other roles played by the navy were well conducted, though postwar analysis has raised some serious questions about the outcome, not challenging the role of the navy, but the larger policies concerning the conduct of war.

It is certainly true that the navy interdiction strategy temporarily slowed the military advance of communism. The navy, unopposed at sea, turned their gigantic guns toward the shore, firing on enemy highways and troops in an effort to halt the flow of supplies. The Chinese and North Koreans had the ability to repair bridges, railroads, highways just as quickly as they could be destroyed. The interdiction program was a failure, reported 7th Fleet Commander, Vice Admiral J. J. Clark. "It did not interdict. The communists got the supplies through; and for the kind of a way they were fighting, they not only kept their battle lines supplied, they had enough surplus to spare that at the end of the war they could even launch an offensive."†

Bombardment set for the destruction of enemy property, and to curtail its ability to conduct the war, must also be seen as successful. While the air force and naval air arms soon found it difficult to locate new and important targets, the bombardment force was rather continuously involved in the destruction of enemy troops and equipment. When the war ended, the navy had dropped countless numbers of rockets and ordnance, as well as tons of bombs.

In totally pragmatic terms, the transportation and supply function — the primary role of most of the ships considered in this study — was successfully completed by the navy and the allied Merchant Marine. Six of every seven men who fought in Korea were transported by sea. The same was true for most of the equipment they needed and the supplies they used. Essential to any victory, and certainly to maintaining the war in Korea, was the efficient

---

*On 6 December 1950 Admiral Joy communicated an unconfirmed report that the Soviet Air Force was preparing an air attack on both Japan and Formosa in conjunction with the Chinese ground action in Korea. While nothing came of it, plans were made in preparation for such a Soviet attack. Message 070756Z NCC 9823, 7 December 1950, COMNAVFE to OM7FLT.

†Steve Leiver, "Navy Proved to be Dominant at Sea," *Stars and Stripes*.

delivery of "beans, bullets and black oil." In this case the delivery line was more than 5,000 miles in length, and the demand it sought to meet was created by more than twenty-seven different nations. Without the naval aspect of this supply, the replenishment systems, as well as the maintenance of Japanese bases close to the combat area, the UN successes would have been impossible. What was available to address this issue was primarily the legacy of World War II. Many of these vessels had been wisely maintained, albeit in reserve, for just such an emergency. After several months the supply, maintenance, and replenishment of the forces in Korea became somewhat routine, but it never became easy. The massive demands resulted from the almost continuous — as against the spasmodic operations of World War II — and the never-ending demands for ammunition and equipment. The volume of materials sent to Korea some months exceeded that being sent to the Pacific during World War II.

During the Korean War an estimated 31.5 million tons of supplies and equipment were shipped to the Far East, more than 95 percent of these by ship. Also, 80 percent of this cargo was shipped by privately owned merchant ships and by Military Sea Transportation Service ships, crewed by American citizen sailors.

In support of this effort it is important to note the role of the Merchant Marine crews, and the men and women of the Coast Guard. From their early involvement in the development of a Korean Coast Guard, through their rescue work, weather reporting, and air traffic control at sea, the Coast Guard was involved in this effort.

Naval Intelligence

As far as can be determined, the definitive work on military intelligence during the Korean War has not yet been written. For many, considering the war in Korea, it can only be said that the lack of proper intelligence was a vital concern. Few of America's intelligence-gathering bodies, neither the CIA nor the Armed Forces, were able to provide what might have been considered even adequate intelligence. The reasons for this were many. It must be pointed out that small-unit intelligence groups seemed to be far more efficient than the larger ones. Shortly after the war, an intelligence team from the Commander-in-Chief, Pacific Fleet (CINCPACFLT), a high-ranking naval group that was given the job of evaluating U.S. naval intelligence, returned with a harsh analysis, noting particularly that many of those involved had been out of the service for some time prior to the recall.

Cost to the Navy

The control of the sea, the delivery and replenishment of supplies, the transportation of the troops, and clearing of mines were not without considerable cost. During the war, five ships were sunk in action. Those sunk include the USS *Magpie*, *Pirate*, *Pledge*, *Partridge*, and *Sarsi*. In addition, eighty-seven others were damaged as the result of enemy action. Of the 5,720,000 Americans who served in and around the war in Korea, more than 265,000 navy personnel were involved. Of this number 475 seamen were killed in action and another 4,043 sailors died from injury or disease as a result of their service. Yet another 1,576 were wounded in action.

In looking back on the naval contribution, Eighth Army Commander, General Van Fleet, had this to say about the navy:

"We could not have existed in Korea without the Navy. The sea blockade was so complete that it was taken for granted. And at the same time the enemy could not supply himself by water. Naval gunfire on both east and west coasts added to his burden; and had the Eighth Army wished to go on the offensive, naval gunfire on the flanks would have made it much easier. Freedom from enemy air and naval attack left us free to operate in the open."*

Conclusion

Now, after more than half a century, Korea remains a mystery and a danger. North Korea has one of the largest armies in the world, including a significant air force and navy. It maintains an offensive posture and most certainly has at least some weapons of mass destruction. There is always the possibility — and it is one current policy planners must constantly consider — that the Democratic People's Republic of Korea will once again launch a massive land attack against the South. This awareness had kept a good many forces, military and economic, at hand, and preparations have been made for deployment and/or evacuation.

While the Cold War has ended, the vital problem of relations between North and South Korea has not yet been resolved; in fact, it has never adequately been addressed. Until it is, the chances of peaceful coexistence between both Koreas are not great. That problem, of course, is the quest for unification, the underlying dream of many a Korean, North or South.

---

*Cagle cites this as the result of a personal conversation. In Cagle and Manson, *The Sea War in Korea*, 492.

BIBLIOGRAPHY

Primary Sources

"CIA Analysis of North Korean Invasion," Intelligence Memorandum no. 302 (July 8, 1950).

"Deck Long Section," Ships History Branch, Naval Historical Center, Operational Archives Branch, Naval Historical Center.

Douglas, A. H. "The Fleet Service Forces and the Logistics Organization in Command Area," Staff Presentation, Naval War College, 10 November 1994. Historical Collection. Naval War College, Newport, R.I.

Oral History, Admiral Arleigh A. Burke, Retired. Oral History Department, U. S. Naval Institute, Annapolis, Maryland, Volume 1, 1979.

Records of the Reserve Fleet, Operational Archives Branch, Naval Historical Center, Washington, D. C. (The activities of the reserve fleets from 1947 through 1960 are available at the Ships Material Readiness Division, Reserve Fleet Ship Branch, Sub-Group Atlantic and Pacific Reserve Fleets, Records of Chief of Naval Operations, OP 432. It is located at Operational Archives Branch, Naval Historical Center, 805 Kidder Breese Street SE, Washington Navy Yard, DC 20374–5060.)

Report: Commander UN Blockading and Escort Force to Commander, Seventh Fleet, series 0031, subject: "Review of Operations and Comments on the United Nations Blockading Escort Force (TF 95) from 28 March 1951 to 9 January 1952," 30 January 1952, Post-January 1946 Action Rep Files, in Andrade, "History of Naval Special Warfare."

U.S. Navy Bureau of Ships. Boats of the United States Navy (NAVSHIPS 250–452). Washington, D.C.: The Bureau, 1960. Includes statistics and drawings of dinghies, punts, wherries, motor launches, whaleboats, work boats, mine-sweeping launches, mine-diving tenders, and torpedo retrievers; line-handling, rescue, utility, plane-rearming, plan-personnel, reconnaissance, picket, buoy, personnel, plane-service aircraft-refueling, noise-measuring underwater-ordnance-research, rounding, bomb-target, and distribution-box boats; inflatable life boards; landing boats; and mat boats.

"US Navy, Korean War: Chronology of U. S. Pacific Fleet Operations, June-December 1950." In United States Naval Vessels: The Official U.S. Navy Reference Manual. Washington, D.C.: Naval Historical Center, 28 June 1950.

Resources Available on the Internet

AmTracs of World War II and the Korean War: www.amtrac.org/2atmc/tracs/gen1.asp
Landing Craft Infantry, National Association: www.usski.com/html/aboutlci.html

LSTs of the United States Navy: www.multied.com/NAVY/patrol/30.html
Maritime Digital Encyclopedia: www.biblio.org/maritime/media
National Defense Reserve Fleet: www.fas.org/man/dod-101/sys/ship/ndrf.htm
Naval Historical Center: http://www.history.navy.mil/index.html
U.S. Maritime Administration: www.marad.dot.gov
U.S Maritime Commission C1 and C1-m Type Ships: www.usmm.org/c1ships.html
U.S. LSM-LSMR Association: lsm/smr.org
The Patrol Fleet: Forgotten Ships: PC Patrol Craft of World War II. www.astralpublishing.com/patrolcraft.html

Journals and Periodicals

The following journals provided a significant amount of information, published since June of 1950:

Alligator Alley
The American Neptune
The Journal of Strategic Studies
MAST Magazine
Naval War College Review
Parameters
Proceedings, Center for the Study of the Korean War

Proceedings, United States Naval Institution
Prologue
Royal United Service Institution Journal
Seawaves Magazine
Surface Warfare
Transportation Corps

Secondary Sources

Aber, John W. "The Navy and the Merchant Marine: A Critical Coalition," *Proceedings of the United States Naval Institute*, v. 96 no. 3 (March 1970): 40–44.
"Activity of the Republic of Korea Navy," in *The History of the United Nations Forces in the Korean War, Vol. 1,* Ministry of National Defense, Republic of Korea, 1972.
Alden, John D. *The Fleet Submarine in the U.S. Navy.* Annapolis, MD: Naval Institute Press, 1979.
Alligator Alley no. 45 (October 2001): 21.
Alexander, Joseph. *Fleet Operations in a Mobile War: September 1950-June 1951.* Washington D.C.: Naval Historical Center, 2001.
Allard, Dean C. "Interservice Differences in the United States, 1945–1950: A Naval Perspective," *Aerospace Power Journal* (Winter 1989).
Barlow, Jeffrey G. *Revolt of the Admirals: The Fight for Naval Aviation, 1945–1950.* Washington: Naval Historical Center, 1994.
Barger, Melvin D. *Large Slow Target: A History of the Landing Ship*, volume 1. Oxford, UK: Osprey Press, 1986.
Bauer, K. Jack and Stephen S. Roberts. *Register of Ships of the U.S. Navy, 1775–1990: Major Combatants.* New York: Greenwood Press, 1991.
Baer, George. *One Hundred Years of Sea Power: The U.S. Navy, 1890–1990.* Stanford, CA: Stanford University Press, 1994.
Black, William M. and Dale A. Hueber. "Army Watercraft Operations in Southwest Asia," *Transportation Corps* (September 1991): 10–14.
Blanton, Stephen Dwight. "A Study of the United States Navy's Minesweeping Efforts in the Korean War." Master's Thesis, Texas Tech University, 1993.
Bouwer, Norman J. *The International Register of Historic Ships.* London: Chatham Publishing, 1999.
"British Commonwealth Naval Operations During the Korean War," *Royal United Service Institution Journal*, 1 no. 96 (May 1951): 250–255; 2, no. 96 (November 1951): 606–616; 3, no. 97 (May 1952): 241–248.
Brown, M. R. "Convoy Operations in World War II," *Military Review* (September 1947): 52–57.
Bunker, John Gorley *Liberty Ships: The Ugly Ducklings of World War II.* Annapolis, MD: Naval Institute Press, 1972.
Bykofsky, Joseph and Harold Larson. *The Transportation Corps: Operations Overseas.* Washington, D.C.: Office of the Chief of Military History, 1957.
Cagle, Malcom. "Inchon: The Analysis of a Gamble," *Proceedings of the United States Naval Institute* 80, no. 1 (January 1954): 47–51.

Cagle, Malcom W. and Frank A. Mason. *The Sea War in Korea*. Annapolis, MD: Naval Institute Press, 1957.
Cagle, Malcom W. and Frank A. Mason. "Wonson: The Battle of the Mines," Naval Institute *Proceedings* 83, no. 6 (June 1957): 598–611.
Callaghan, William M. "Military Sea Transportation Service," *Naval War College Review* 5, no. 5 (January 1953) 31–57.
Carter, Worral Reed. *Beans, Bullets, and Black Oil*. Washington, D.C.: Department of the Navy, 1953.
Charles, Roland W. *Troopships of World War II*. Washington D. C.: Army Transportation Association, 1974.
Christley, J. L. *United States Naval Submarine Force Information Book*. Marblehead, MA: Graphic Enterprises of Marblehead, 1999.
Coletta, Paola E. "The United States Navy and Defense Unification, 1947–1950: The Navy," *Prologue* 7 (Spring 1975): 6–17.
Cracknell, William H. Jr. "The Role of the U.S. Navy in Inshore Waters," *Naval War College Review,* 21 no. 3 (November 1968): 65–87.
Crocker, M. P. *West Coast Support Group*. Latheronwaeer, Scotland: Whittles Publishing, 2003.
Croizat, Victor A. *Across the Reef: The Amphibious Tracked Vehicles at War*. London: Arms and Armour, 1989.
Danley, Mark H. "Colombian Navy in the Korean War, 1950–1953," *The American Neptune* 58 (1998): 243–261.
Danzik, Wayne. "Coalition Forces in the Korean War," *Naval War College Review*. 47, 25–39.
Danzik, Wayne. "Participation of Coalition Forces in the Korean War." Naval War College student paper. Document number M-U 41662 D199p. Newport, RI, 1994.
De La Pedrava, Rene. *A Historical Dictionary of the Merchant Marine and Shipping Industry: Since the Introduction of Steam*. Westport, CT: Greenwood, 1994.
Dictionary of American Naval Fighting Ships, volumes 1–8. Washington, D.C.: Navy History Division, Navy Department. (1959–1991).
Edwards, Harry W. "A Naval Lesson of the Korean Conflict," *Proceedings of the United States Naval Institute* 80 no.12 (1954): 1137–1140.
Edwards, Paul M. *The Inchon Landing, Korea, 1950: An Annotated Bibliography*. Westport, CT.: Greenwood Press, 1994.
Evans, J. M. "Special Operations Officers: A Small Yet Vital Force," *Surface Warfare* 21, no. 1 (January/February 1996): 8–10.
"Expeditionary Warfare: Maneuver From the Sea," *Surface Warfare* 19 (July/August 1994): 26–33.
Fane, Francis D. *The Naked Warriors*. New York: Appleton, 1956.
Farrar-Hockley, Anthony. *The British Part in the Korean War: A Distant Obligation*, volume 1. London: His Majesty's Stationery Office, 1990.
Fehrenbach, T. R. *This Kind of War: A Study in Unpreparedness*. New York: Macmillan, 1963.
Field, James A. *History of the United States Naval Operations: Korea*. Washington: Government Printing Office, 1962.
"Five Years of Service to the Service," *MSTS Magazine* (October 1954).
Franklin, Bruce Hampton. *The Buckley-Class Destroyer Escorts*. London: Chatham, 1999.
Friedman, Norman. *The Postwar Naval Revolution*. Annapolis, MD: Naval Institute Press, 1986.
_____. *U.S. Amphibious Ships and Craft: An Illustrated Design History*. Annapolis, MD: Naval Institute Press, 2002.
_____. *U.S. Small Combatants, Including PT Boats, Subchasers, and the Brown Water Navy: An Illustrated Design History*. Annapolis, MD: Naval Institute Press, 1987.
_____. *U.S. Submarines Since 1945: An Illustrated Design History*. Annapolis, MD: Naval Institute Press, 1995.
Gardiner, Robert, ed. *Conway's All the World's Fighting Ships, 1922–1946*. New York: Mayflower Books, 1980.
Gilbert, Bill. *Ship of Miracles: 14,000 Lives and One Miraculous Voyage*. Chicago: Triumph Books, 2000.
Goldman, Kenneth H. *USS Charles Carroll, APA 28: An Amphibious History of World War II*. Victoria, BC: Trafford Publishing, 2005.
Goulden, Joseph C. *Korea: The Untold Story*. New York: Times Books, 1982.
Gregory, Billy. "Operational Analysis of United States Submarine Deployment in the Korean War," Naval War College student paper. Document number M-U-41662 B599o.
Griffin, Harry K. "The Navy in Korean Waters," *Army Information Digest* 6 no. 12 (1951): 12–22.
Grover, David H. *U.S. Army Ships and Watercraft of World War II*. Annapolis, MD: Naval Institute Press, 1987.
Growden, Gordon A. *Freighters and Tankers of the U.S. Merchant Marines*. New York: Putnam's, 1954.
Haas, Michael E. *Apollo's Warriors: United States Air Force Special Operations During the Korean War*. Maxwell Air Force Base, Alabama: Air University Press, 1997.

_____. *In the Devil's Shadow: UN Special Operations During the Korean War.* Annapolis, MD: Naval Institute Press, 2000.

Habesch, David *The Army's Navy: British Military Vessels and Their History Since Henry VIII.* London: Chatham Publishing, 2001.

Hartmann, Gregory. *Weapons that Wait.* Annapolis, MD: Naval Institute Press, 1979.

Heefner, Wilson A. "Inch'on Landing," *Military Review* 75, no. 2 (March-April 1995): 65–77.

Heine, Irwin M. *The United States Merchant Marine: A National Asset.* Washington: National Maritime Council, 1976.

Holder, Frank. *Raiders of the China Coast: CIA Covert Operations During the Korean War.* Annapolis, MD: Naval Institute Press, 1999.

A Hundred Years of the U.S. Navy Submarine Force: A Century of Achievements. Naval Submarine League, n.d.

Huston, James A. *Guns and Butter, Powder and Rice: U.S. Army Logistics in the Korean War.* London: Associated University Presses, 1989.

Illsley, Rolf F. *LSM-LSM(R): Landing Ship Medium Amphibious Forces.* Paducah, Kentucky: Turner Publishing, 1994.

Illsley, Rolf F. *LSM-LSM(R): WWII Amphibious Forces.* Paducah, Kentucky: Turner Publishing.

Jaffee, Walter. *The Liberty Ship: From A.B. Hammon to Zona Gale.* Palo Alto, CA: Glencannon Press, 2004.

Jaffee, Walter. *The Victory Ship: From Aberdeen to Zanesville Victory.* Palo Alto, CA: Glencannon Press, 2006.

Karig, Walter, Malcolm W. Cagle, and Frank A. Manson. *Battle Report: The War in Korea.* New York: Rinehart, 1952.

Keighley, Larry. "Four Dead Three Wounded." *Saturday Evening Post* 223, no. 17 (1950): 32–33, 157.

Key, William G. "Combat Cargo Korea 1950–1951," *Pegasus* (November 1951) 5–6.

Kim, Sang Mo. "The Implication of the Sea War in Korea." *Naval War College Review* 20 (Summer 1967): 105–139.

King, Benjamin. "Never Enough: The Use of Lighters in U.S. Military Operations." *Transportation Corps* (April 1993): 26–29.

Kinney, Commander Sheldon. "All Quiet at Wonsan," *Proceedings of the United States Naval Institute* (1954): 859.

Kludas, Arnold. *Great Passenger Ships of World, Volume 4.* Wellington: Patrick Stephens, 1977, 90–141.

Krass, Henry. "From the Sea in 1950: Lessons for the 21st Century from Operation Chromite." Naval War College student paper. Document number M-U-41612 K91f.

Kutta, Timothy J., Don Greer, and Perry Manley. *DUKW in Action.* Carrollton, TX: Squadron/Signal Publications, 1996.

Land, Emory S. *The United States Merchant Marine at War.* Washington, D.C.: Naval Institute Press, 1946.

Lenton, H. T. *American Gun Boats and Minesweepers.* New York: Arco Publishing, 1974.

Lott, Arnold. *Most Dangerous Sea: A History of Mine Warfare and an Account of US Navy Mine War Operations in World War II and Korea.* Annapolis: Naval Institute Press, 1959.

Macdermott, Brian. *Ships Without Names: The Story of the Royal Navy's Tank Landing Ships of World War Two.* London: Arms and Armour, 1993.

Macpherson, Ken, and John Burgess. *The Ships of Canada's Naval Forces, 1910–1985.* Toronto: Collins, 1985.

Marriott, Leo. *Royal Navy Frigates since 1945.* London: Ian Allen, 1990.

Massman, Emory A. *Hospital Ships of World War II: An Illustrated History.* Jefferson, NC: McFarland, 1999.

"MATS Compiling Impressive Record," *National Defense Transportation Journal* 6 (September-October 1952): 52.

McCandlish, Earl. *Crash Boat.* Monticelo, Iowa: Tallships Books, 2000.

McFarland, Keith D. "The Revolt of the Admirals," *Parameters* 11 (June 1981): 53–63.

McGibbon, Ian. *New Zealand and the Korean War.* Auckland: Oxford University Press, 1996. Two volumes.

Melia, Tamara Moser. *"Damn the Torpedoes": A Short History of the U.S. Naval Mine Countermeasures, 1977–1991.* Washington: Naval Historical Center, 1991.

"The Merchant Marine Goes to War in Korea." *Seafarers Log* (September 1950).

Mercogliano, Salvatore R. "Military Sealift Command Ships of the Line," www.usmm.org/msts/line.html.

"Military Sea Transportation Service," *Proceedings of the United States Naval Institute* 77 no. 12 (December 1951): 1327–1336.

Miller, Marvin O., ed. *Underway Replenishment of Naval Ships.* Hueneme, CA: Naval Surface Warfare Center, 1992.

Miralda, Edward. *The U.S. Navy in the Korean War.* Annapolis, MD: Naval Institute Press, 2007.

Montross, Lynn and Nicholas A. Conzona. "Large Sedentary Targets on Red Beach." *Marine Corps Gazette* 44 (September 1960): 44–50.

Mooney, James L. *Dictionary of American Naval Fighting Ships.* Washington: Naval Historical Center, 1959–1981. Madison, WI: Nautical Books, 1975.

Musgrove, H.E. *U.S. Naval Ships Data Arranged by Hull Classification.*
Omori, Frances. *Quiet Heroes: Navy Nurses of the Korean War, Far East Command, 1950–1953.* Saint Paul, MN: Smith House Press, 2001.
"'Operation Sea Dragon' Minesweepers." *VFW Magazine,* 2 April 2002. (The operation took place in April 1953.)
Paine, Lincoln P. *Ships of the World: An Historical Encyclopedia.* Boston: Houghton Mifflin, 1997.
Phillips, Richard B. "The Siege of Wonsan," *Army Information Digest* 8 no. 11 (1953): 39–47.
Polmar, Norman. "The Name Game," *Proceedings of the United States Naval Institute* (June 1998).
Prince, Stephen. "The Contribution of the Royal Navy to the Korean War," *Journal of Strategic Studies* 17 (June 1994): 94–120.
Rottman, Gordon. *Korean War Order of Battle.* Westport, CT: Praeger, 2002.
Rottman, Gordon and Tony Bryan. *Landing Ships, Tank (LST) 1912–2002.* Oxford, UK: Osprey Publishing, 2005.
Rougeron, Camillo. "Some Lessons of the War in Korea," *Proceedings of the United States Naval Institute* 79, no. 6 (June 1953): 634–643.
Russell, Richard A. *Project HULA: Secret Soviet-American Cooperation in the War Against Japan.* Washington, D.C.: Naval Historical Center, 1997.
Sawyer, Leonard A. *Liberty Ships: The History of the "Emergency" Type Cargo Ships Constructed in the United States During the Second World War.* Cambridge, MD: Cornell Maritime, 1970.
Sawyer, Leonard A. *Victory Ships and Tankers: The History of the 'Victory' Type Cargo Ship and the Tankers Built in the United States of America During World War II.* Cambridge, MD: Cornell Maritime Press, 1974.
Sawyer, L. A. and W. H. Mitchell. *From America to United States.* London: World Ship Society 1979.
Scarborough, Franklin. "Life Was Tense on Minesweepers," *Salisbury Post* (February 12, 2001).
Scheina, Robert L. *United States Coast Guard Cutters and Craft, 1946–1990.* Annapolis, MD: Naval Institute Press, 1990.
_____. *United States Coast Guard Cutters and Craft of World War* II. Annapolis, MD: Naval Institute Press, 1982.
Schratz, Paul R. "The Admirals' Revolt," *Proceedings of the United States Naval Institute* 112 (February 1986): 70.
_____. *Submarine Commander: A Story of World War II and Korea.* Lexington, KY: University Press of Kentucky, 1988.
Scott-Moncrieff, A. K. "Navy Operations in Korean Waters," *Royal United Service Institution Journal* 98 (May 1953): 218–227.
"Ships of the Army," *Army Ordnance* (January/February 1945): 241–48.
Sigel, Clinton H. "The Reserve Fleet," *Proceedings of the United States Naval Institute* 77, no. 7 (July 1951): 681–689.
Straham, Jerry. *Andrew Jackson Higgins and the Boats that Won World War II.* Baton Rouge: Louisiana State University Press, 1998.
Thompson, Julian *The Lifeblood of War: Logistics in Armed Conflict.* London: Brassey's, 1991.
Thorgrimsson, Thor, and E. C. Russell. *Canadian Naval Operations in Korean Waters, 1950–1955.* Ottawa: Naval Historical Section, Canadian Forces Headquarters, Dept. of National Defense, 1966.
Tubak, Gary. "Where the Fleet Goes, We Go First," *VFW Magazine* (April 2002): 1–4.
Tucker, Spencer C., ed. *Encyclopedia of the Korean War: A Political, Social and Military History.* Santa Barbara, CA: ABC-CLIO, 2000.
United States Naval Hospital Ships. A Naval Historical Foundation Publication, n.d. Utz, Curtis A. *Assault from the Sea: The Amphibious Landing at Inchon.* Washington: Naval Historical Center, 1994.
Veigele, William J. *PC: Patrol Craft in World War II.* Santa Barbara, CA: Astral Publishing, 1998.
Walkowiak, Thomas. *Destroyer Escorts of World War II.* Missoula, MN: Pictorial Histories Publishing, 1987.
Watson, Bruce W. *The Changing Face of the World's Navies: 1945 to Present.* New York: Brassey's, 1991.
Wildenburg, Thomas. *Gray Steel and Black Oil: Fast Tankers and Replenishment at Sea in the US Navy, 1912–1992.* Annapolis, MD: Naval Institute Press, 1996.
Witt, Linda, Judith Bellafaire, Britta Granrud, and Mary Jo Binker. *A Defense Weapon Known to Be of Value: Servicewomen of the Korean War Era.* Hanover, NH:University Press of New England, 2005.
Witter, Robert E. *Small Boats and Large Slow Targets.* Missoula, MN: Pictorial Histories Publishing, 1998.
Young, Victor. *Merchant Ships of World War II: A Post War Album.* Market Drayton, England: Shipping Book, 1996.
Zaloga, Steven, Terry Hadler, and Michael Badrocke. *Amtracs: US Amphibious Assault Vehicles.* Oxford, UK: Osprey Publishing, 1999.
Zaloga, Steven. *Armor of the Pacific War.* Oxford, UK: Osprey Publishing, 1983.

Index

Abandoned 193
Abbeydale, REA 214
Aberdeen Victory, US 169
Abnaki, AFT 134, 135 136, 137
Achelous, class 129, 130
Achernar, AKA 139, 140
Acheson, Dean 3
Acorn Knot, US 169
Adak, Alaska 101
Adelphia Victory, US 169
ADG 202
ADJ-383 163
Admirable, class 153, 159, 161
Admiral C.F. Hughes see *General Edwin D. Patrick*
Admiral Dewey, US 169
Admiral E.W. Eberle see *General Simon B. Bunkner*
Admiral H.T. Mayo see *General Nelson M. Walker*
Admiral W.L. Capps see *General Hugh J. Gaffey*
Admiral W.S. Benson see *General Daniel L. Sultan*; *General Nelson M. Walker*
Admiral W.S. Sims see *General W.O. Darby*
Adria, class 97
Adrian Victory, US 169
Advanced Screening Group 218
Adventinus, class 125
AE-14 see *Firedrake*
Aeolus RFA see *Choysang*
AF-11 see *Polaris*
AF-29 see *Graffias*
AF-31 see *Arequipa*
AF-33 see *Karin*
AF-38 see *Merapi*
AF-48 see *Alstede*
AF-49 see *Zelima*
AF-54 see *Pictor*
AF-55 see *Aludra*

AF-58 see *Escanaba Victory*
Afoundia, US 169
African, US 169
African American 174
African Glade, US 169
African Grove, US 169
African Moon, US 169
African Patriot, US 169
African Pilgrim, US 169
African Pilot, US 170
African Planet see *George Clymer*
African Rainbow, US 170
African Star II, US 170
AG-9 see *Ryder*
AG-138 see *Ryder*
AG-141 see *Whidbey*
AG-146 see *Electron*
AH (hospital ship) 34
Aiken Victory, TAP 114
Air Intelligence Support Squadron AISS, 6006th 203
Air-Naval Gunfire Liaison Company (ANGLICO) 18
Ajak IV, AR 125
AK 128
AK-8 see *Brute II*
AK-22 see *Wabash Victory*
AK-227 see *Boulder Victory*
AK-230 see *Mandersosn Victory* ZZspelling
AK-231 see *Bedford Victory*
AK-233 see *New Zealand Victory*
AKA 126, 142
AKA 22, 28, 126, 142
AKA-59 see *Diphda*
AKA-60 see *Leo*
AKA-95 see *Yancy*
AKL 100
AKS 102
AKS-30 see *League Island*
AKS-32 169
AKS-47 see *Election*

AKV 100
Alacrity, HMS 8, 18, 211
Alamo, US 89
Alamo Victory, US 170
Alamosa Class 101, 141
Alaska 50, 52, 67, 101, 07, 206
Alaskan, US 61, 186; see also *Midland Victory*
Albacore, US 63
Albert J. Berres see *Capt. N.B. Palmer*
Albion Victory, US 170
Albuquerque, PF 50
Alert IX, HMS 211, 212
Aleutians 51, 52, 137, 206
Alexander, Joseph 4
Alexander R. Nininger. US 169
Alfred E. Smith see *Mother M.L. Alfred Victory*, US 170
Algeria 125
Algol, AKA 140
Allegheny Victory, US 170
Allen C. Balch see *Ocean Seaman*
Allies 8, 28, 42, 151, 168
Alligator 93
Alligator Alley 76, 77, 92
Alma Victory, US 170
Almirante Brion, ARC 210
Almirante Padilla, ARC 210
Almond, Gen. Edward Mallory 58
Aloe, class 128, 206
Alsbain, TAKA 140
Alstede, AF 96, 98
Altair, US 169
Aludra, AF 96, 97
AM 20, 131
AM-10 156
AM-18 157
AM-36 159
AM-372 161
AMA 155
Amarillo Victory, US 170

233

Index

Amazon River, Brazil 66
AMC 217
AMCU 157, 172
AMCU-46 156
Amehia see *Chief*
American, US 170
American Attorney, US 170
American Bureau of Shipping 95
American Civil War 26
American Eagle, US 170
American President Lines 184
American Press, US 3, 170
American Pride see *Rock Springs Victory*
American Veteran, US 170
American Victory, US 170
Amerocean, US 171
Amersea, US 171
Amethyst, HMS 211
Amgak, Korea 212
Ammunition 2, 10, 17, 33, 94, 98–101, 132, 142, 143, 166, 188, 215, 220, 224
Ampac Idaho, US 171
Ampac Nevada, US 171
Ampac Oregon, US 171
Ampere, ADG 202
Amphibious Armored Personnel Carrier 70
Amphibious Command (control) Ship 57, 58, 59, 150
Amphibious Craft 88, 150
Amphibious Group I 7, 17
Amphibious Feints 25, 92, 128, 145, 147
Amphibious Force 29, 88, 136, 222
Amphibious Landings 17, 18, 20, 25, 29, 58, 63, 70, 78, 89, 93, 139, 143, 145, 148
Amphibious Transports 147–149, 216
Amphibious Truck 70, 72
Amos G. Thoop, US 171
AMS 2, 17, 20, 23, 153, 155, 157, 158, 165
AMS-31 158
AMS-342 158
AN-5 see *Catalpa*
AN-9 see *Butternut*
AN-20, US 128; see also *Elder*
AN-27 see *Mulberry*
Anacostia, TAO 104
Andromeda, AKA 140
Angel of the Orient 61
Angus Glenn, Canadian 171
Angus McDonald, US 171
Ania 195; see also *Stathes Yamaglias*
Anittepe, Turkey 42
Ann McKim see *African Glade*
Anne Butler, US 171
Annie C., US 172
Annioc, US 172
Anniston Victory, US 172
Anti-Aircraft Weapons 13
Anti-Submarine 26, 41, 44, 45, 47, 48, 50, 52, 63, 66, 67, 152, 166, 213
Antonio Delfino, British see *Empire Halladale*
"Any Purpose Designated" 145

Anzac, HMAS 208
AO 103, 111
AO-50 see *Tallulah*
AO-139 110
AOE 103
AP 144
AP-188 114
APA 22, 28, 60, 139, 144, 148
APA-18 148
APA-37 145
Apache IV, US 134
APD 19, 145, 149, 150, 201, 204
APD-27 149
APL-23 129
Apnok, PF 219
Apollo, US 172
Apollo's Warriors: United States Air Forces Special Operations During the Korean War 202
Apra Harbor 157
Aquila, Chile 125; see also *Aventinus*
AR-9, US 125
ARC, Columbia 32
Arcadian Victory, US 172
Archer see *African Pilgrim*
Archer T. Gammon, TAP 114
Arcturus, class 142
Arequipa, AF 97
Argentina 90
Argentine Navy 65, 136
Argonaut see *African Patriot*
Argovan, Canadian 172
Ariadni see *Tombigbee*
Arikara, ATF 134
Arizpa, US 172
Arleigh Burke, DDG
Armada da la Republica de, Colombia 209
Armament 39
Armistice 12, 26, 212, 218
Army Air Corps 199
Army Ships 95
Army Transport Service 100, 119–121, 182, 183, 192, 197–199
ARS 44–49, 129, 133, 130
Arthur Middleton, class 146
Arunta, HMAS 208
Arv Carite, Venezuela 69
Asbury Victory, US 172
Asheboro, PC/PF 58
Asherville, class 34
Ashland, US 88, 90
Ashtabula, AO 104–107, 110–112, 124
Asian Pacific Theatre 86–87
Askari, ARL 129
AT 134, 135, 136
ATA 136
ATA-30 149
ATA-121 137
ATA-198 136
ATE 127
ATF 134–137
ATF-83 135
ATF-110 135
Atlantic Water, US 172
Atlanticus, US 172
Atlas II, ARL 129
Atmospheric Nuclear Weapons Test 82

Atomic see Nuclear
ATR 125, 126
Attack Transports 33, 139, 142, 144
Attleboro Victory see *American Attorney*
Aucilla, AO 104
Auckland, New Zealand 217
Audrey II, US 172
Augustine Daly, US 172
Auk, class 155–164
Australia 18, 208, 209
Australian Navy 7, 21, 214, 215
Auxiliary 34
Auxiliary Ships 93, 98, 136
Auxiliary Submarine 64, 67
Auxiliary Sweepers 152, 158
AV 131
AV-8 138
Aventinus, ARVE 125
AVP 131
AVP-28 131
Awards 58, 65–67, 69, 77, 84, 92, 105, 107, 114, 146, 154, 168, 169, 170, 175, 177, 179, 182, 183, 187, 188, 189, 190, 191, 220
Axis ships 151

B-36 6
Badger Mariner, US 172
Badoeng Strait, USS 155
Balao, class 64–69
Bangpakong, HMTS 218
Banner II, TASKL 100
Banning, PC/PCEC 58
Bannock, class 136
Barbados, government of 83
Barbara Fritchie, US 172
Barbara Lykes, US 172
Barbers Point 11
Barenfels, Foreign 172
Barges 9, 199, 200, 214
Barnard Victory, US 172
Barnegat, class 131, 132, 137, 138
Barney Krishbaum, US 172
Barracks Ships 33
Barrett, TAP 114
Bartlesville Victory, US 172, 201
Barton, US 23
Bashaw, SSK 63
Bass, US 9
Bass, Horace Ancel 150
Baton Rouge Victory, US 172
Battle coaster 168
Battle Creek, US 169
Battle Stars 12, 42–53, 55–58, 61, 64, 65, 68, 73–77, 79–93, 97, 99, 100, 101–107, 110, 112–126, 128–131, 133, 134–138, 140–146, 148–156, 158–164, 202, 206
Battleship 8, 24, 25, 33, 103, 105, 133
Bay, class 209, 211, 212
Bayfield, APA 145–147
Baylor Victory, US 173
Bayonne, PR 50
Bay Raktar, Turkey 87
Beach Master 57
Beach Red (Inchon) 81, 83, 85
Beatrice Victory, US 173

Beatty, US 54
Beauregard, US 173
Beaver Victory, US 173
Bedford Victory, US 173
Begor, APD 149
Belfast, HMS 18, 215
Belgium 214
Belgium Victory, US 173
Bellatrix, AKA 140
Belocean, Norway 173
Beloit, US 173
Benevolence, AH 60, 61
Benjamin Hawkins, US 173
Benson, Adm. W.S. 116, 119, 121
Berea Victory, US 173
Bering Strait, WAVP 131
Bert McDowell see *Hooper Island*
Bet Jeanne, Norway 173
Bessemer Victory, US 173
Besugo, SS 64
Beutny see *Prasaw* HMTS
Bexar, APA 145
Big Black River, LSM 91
Bikini Island 60, 93, 103, 111–112, 129
Binghampton Victory, US 173
Birchol, RFA 214
Bisbee, PE 51
Black Eagle, US 173, 186
Black Swan, HMS 8, 18, 211–213
Black Warrior River, LSMR 91
Blackfin, SS 63
Blackstone River, LSM 91
Blair House 17
Blanquillo, SS 65
Blenny, SS 64
Blockade 8, 20
Bloomington Victory, US 173
Blue Beach (Inchon) 19, 92
Blue Cross State, US 173
Blue Ensign, US 213
Blue Island Victory, US 173
Blue Star, US 174
Blueback, SS 63
Bluefield Victory, US 173
Bluegill, SS 64
Bob Hope, US 33
Bocaccio, SS 65
Bochum, Germany 86
Bolster, ARS 130
Bombardment 24, 26, 149, 163, 212, 213
Booker T. Washington, US 174
Borneo operations 143
"Bottom Dwellers" 152
Bougainville campaign 134, 143
Boulder Victory, US 101, 102, 114, 124, 148
Bowditch see *South Bend Victory*
Bowdoin Victory, US 174
Boxed Aircraft Transport 172, 178, 193, 195, 197
Boy, US 174
Bradley, Gen. Omar 70
Brainerd Victory, US 174
Brazil 66, 85
Brazil Victory, US 174
Bremerton, US 26, 29
Bridges 201

Brigham Victory, US 174
Bright Star, US 174
Brisbee, US 210
Bristol, class 43, 155
Bristol Gun Boat 43
Britain Victory, US 174
British Commando 89
British Commonwealth see Great Britain
British Navy 21, 50
British Royal Marines 25
Broadkill River, LSMR 92
Bronze Star 66, 145
Brown Ranger, RFA 214
"Brown Water Navy" 52
Brush, US 20, 139, 153
Brute II, TAKL 100
Bryce Canyon, US 127
B.T. Irvine, US 172
Buckeye Victory US 174
Buckle, class 54
Buckley, class 42, 45, 48, 49, 150
Bucknell Victory, US 174
Buckner Bay 26
Bucyrus Victory, US 174
Buenaventure, 108
Bugara, SS 64
Buoy Tender 206
Burak Reis, Turkey 68
Burbank Victory, US 174
Burco Trader, US 174
Bureau of Ships 77
Burke, Arleigh A. 6, 216
Burlington, PE 51, 210
Burnet see *Bangpakong*, HMTS
Bushnell, David 151
Butternut, AN 206

C1-M-AV1, class 141
Cabezon, SS 64
Cabildo, LSD 89
Cable Ships 199
Cacapon, AO 104
Cache, TAO 104
Cada Grande, class 89–90
Cagle, Malcolm W. 5, 24, 43, 58, 61, 62, 69, 99, 100, 154, 170, 177, 187, 202, 220, 221
Cahaba, TAO 104
Caiman, SS 65
Calaveras County, LST 516 78
Caliber 39
Caliente, AO 105
California see *Drew Victory*
California Bear see *Paducah Victory*
Californian, US 175
Callaghan, Adm. William M. 95, 96
Calvert II, US 145
Cam Ranh, Vietnam 85
Camano, class 100, 101, 102
Cambodia 191
Campaigns: CCP Intervention 12, 44, 45, 46, 49, 51, 53–59, 61, 73–77, 77, 80, 81, 83–86, 88–91, 97, 98, 101–104, 106, 107, 110, 114–118, 120, 124, 126, 129, 130, 131, 135, 136, 137, 139, 140, 141, 143–145, 147–150, 154, 155–158, 161; CCF Spring Offensive 12, 42, 43, 46,
47, 48, 49, 51, 55, 56, 57, 58, 61, 73–77, 81–83, 85–93, 98, 99, 104, 105, 107, 109, 110, 115, 117, 119, 120, 124, 125, 130, 131, 140–143, 146–148, 156, 157, 158, 160, 202; First UN Counteroffensive 12, 44, 45, 46, 49, 51, 53–58, 61, 73–77, 80, 81, 82, 84, 85, 86, 87, 88, 89, 90, 91, 92, 93, 97, 98, 99, 109, 110, 111, 115–120, 124, 128–131, 135, 136, 138, 141, 142, 143, 144, 145, 146, 147, 148, 149, 150, 154–158, 161; Korean Summer-Fall (52) 12, 43, 44, 45, 46, 47, 49, 51, 54, 57, 58, 59, 61, 73–77, 78, 80, 82–90, 92, 96, 97, 98, 99, 100, 101, 102, 104–107, 109–111, 115, 116, 119, 120, 124, 125, 126, 128–131, 135–138, 140, 143, 144, 145, 148–150, 155–157, 160, 161, 162, 163; Korean Summer-Fall (53) 12, 42, 43, 44, 46, 47, 49, 51, 54, 55, 56, 57, 58, 59, 61, 74, 75, 76, 77, 79, 80, 82, 83, 85, 87, 88, 90, 92, 96, 98, 99, 100, 101, 104–107, 109, 110, 111, 115, 116, 119, 120, 124, 125, 126, 128, 130, 131, 137, 138, 141, 143, 144, 146, 149, 150, 155, 156, 157, 159, 160, 162, 163, 164, 206; North Korean Aggression (US Defensive) 12, 44, 45, 47, 51, 53–59, 61, 73–77, 79, 80, 81, 83, 84, 85, 87–100, 103, 104, 106, 107, 110, 114–120, 124, 125, 126, 128–135, 137–146, 146, 148, 149, 150, 155, 157, 158, 159, 161, 162; Second Korean Winter 12, 42–48, 51, 54–56, 59, 61, 73, 74, 75–81, 85, 88, 89, 91, 93, 96, 97–102, 104–107, 109, 110, 111, 118, 119, 120, 124, 125, 128, 130, 131, 133–138, 140, 142, 143, 144, 147, 148, 149, 150, 154, 155, 157–160, 162, 163, 164, 202; Third Korean Winter 12, 43, 46, 47, 49, 51, 54, 58, 59, 61, 73–80, 81–90, 92, 96–102, 104, 105, 106, 107, 109, 110, 111, 115, 116, 119, 120, 124, 131, 135–138, 140, 143, 144, 145, 148, 149, 150, 155, 156, 157, 160, 161, 162, 163; UN Offensive 12, 47, 50, 54, 55, 56, 57, 58, 59, 61, 73, 74, 75, 76, 77, 79–81, 83, 85, 88, 90, 91, 97, 99, 110, 114, 117, 118, 119, 120, 124, 130, 134, 135, 136, 137, 140, 142, 143, 144, 145, 147, 148, 149, 150, 155, 158, 162, 218; UN Summer-fall offensive 2, 42, 43, 44, 46, 47, 48, 49, 51, 54, 55, 57, 61, 73–81, 83–93, 97, 98, 101–107, 109–111, 124, 125, 130, 131, 135, 136, 140, 141, 143, 155–160, 202
Canada 128, 209, 214, 215
Canadian Mail, US 175
Canadian Merchant Marines 209
Canadian Navy 21, 50
Candido de Lasla (Argentina) 90
Caney, TAO 104, 105
Canney 163

Cannon, class 42, 217
Canton, US 112, 114
Canton Victory, TAP 114, 175
Cap Norte see *Empire Trooper*
Cape Comfort, US 175
Cape Elizabeth, US 175
Cape Saunders, US 175
Caper see *Kelso Victory*
Capital Division, ROK 21
Captain Lyras see *Mother M.L.*
Capt. N.B. Palmer, US 175
Captain Tono, Columbian 51
Captain's Gig 203
Cardigan Bay, HMS 212
Cardinal O'Connell TAK 17, 100, 166
Cargo ships 100, 139, 166
Caribbean 98
Caribou see *Nathaniel B. Parker*
Carl Vinson, US 33
Carleton Victory, US 175
Carmick, DMS 21
Carmick, David 154, 156
Carolinas 58, 100
Carp, SS 65
Carpenter, DE 42
Carrier, Aircraft 2, 5, 8, 10, 18–20, 27, 33, 92, 99, 103, 105, 211, 213
Carrier Task Force see Task Force
Carrier Task Group see Task Group
Carroll Victory, US 175
Carter Braxton, US 175
Casablanca 44
Casco, class 132
Cassia County, LST 527 79
Castilla, US 136, 139
Castor, AKS 102, 103
Casualties 45, 47, 51–53, 55, 59, 60, 61, 59, 60, 61, 66, 79, 83, 92, 94, 137, 157–162, 164, 212, 213, 218, 221
Catalpa II, AN 206
Catamount, LSD 89
Catawba Victory, US 175
Catazpaii, AN 206
Catfish, SS 63, 65
Catherine Goulandris, US 175
Cavalier, US 145
Cayuga County, LST 529 79
C.C.N.Y. Victory, US 174
CCRAK (Combined Command for Reconnaissance Activities Korea 201
Cease Fire Agreement 28, 62
Cecil N. Bean, US 175
Cedar Creek, ATO 105
Centaur see *Harpoon*
Center for the Study of the Korean War 2, 16
Central Falls Victory, US 168
Central Intelligence Agency 3, 5, 9, 142, 200, 224
Central Victory, US 175
Chaho Island 162
Chain Trader, US 175
Challenge see *Castor*
Chang, Thailand 84
Chang Sa Dong 155
Changjon 153

Chanticleer III, ASR 133
Chara, AKA 140
Charles A. McCue see *Joseph Feuer*
Charles H. Marshall see *Transamerican*
Charles Lykes, US 175
Charles M. Conrad, US 175
Charles McNary, US 175
Charles S. Sperry, US 133
Charles Winson, ROK 175
Charr, SS 65
Chatterer, AMA 20
Chautauqua, WPG 52
Check Knot see *Sgt. Joseph E. Muller*
Check Sweeps 23
Cheju Do, Korea 85, 86, 87, 129
Chemung II, AO 105
Chepacket, TAO 105
Cherokee, US 134, 135, 136
Chevalier II, DDR 53
Chickasaw III, US 135
Chicks 23, 154
Chief, AM 159
Chikaskia, TAO 105
Chilean 124
Chin Cho 159
China, Communist 3, 4, 12, 21, 23, 26, 27, 99, 167, 211, 222, 223
China Victory, US 175
Chinau 138
Chindo 221
Chinese People's Army 28
Chinnampo 20, 23, 44, 55, 61, 70, 89, 91, 92, 128, 138, 140, 145, 149, 153, 155, 156, 158, 159, 211, 212, 220, 221
Chipola, TAO 105
Chiri San, PC 219
Chisholm, Donald 70
Chittenden County, LST 561 79
Cho do 29, 134, 135, 136, 212
Choctaw Victory, US 176
Choju Do 141
Chongjin 23, 51, 145, 149, 155, 160, 162, 164
Chongju 21, 85, 86, 87
Chonjin 162
Chosin Refineries 18
Chosin Reservoir 21
Choson Dynasty 3
Choto Island 162
Chowanoc, ATF 134, 135
Choysang, RFA 214
Christain, US 176
Christine, US 176
Christmas Eve 22
Christmas Islands 112
Christos M. US 176
Chu Yung see *Waxwing*
Ch'uksan, Korea 157
Chulpo 9, 221
Chumunjin, Korea 24
Chung Cheng 90
Chung Fu, ROC 82
Chung Nam Province, Korea 55
Chung Tung see *Sea Coronet*
Churchill, Winston 77

CIA, Central Intelligence Agency "cigarette" route 221
Cimarron II, AO 105, 110
CINCFE (Commander in Chief Far East) 17, 224
Cinhae 138
Cisne see *Piscataqua*
Citrus Packer, US 176
City of Alma, US 176
Civil Service Commission 95
Civil War, American 33, 52, 151
Clandestine (Covert) Activities 25, 144, 149, 201, 202, 203, 204
Clarion River, LSM 92
Clark, Adm. J.J. 223
Clark, Lieutenant 220
Clarksburg Victory, US 176
Clarksville Victory, US 176
Class 511 (LST) 78–86, 88
Class 542 (LST) 78–86, 88
Class 1081 (LST) 87
Classification Modifiers 34–37
Classification of Ships 34–37
Clearwater County, LST 602 79
Clearwater Victory, US 176
Clendenin, US 61
Clifford E. Ashby see *Trojan Trader*
Clove Hitch, US 176
Clovis Victory, US 176
Coast Guard, US (USCG) 8, 9, 10–13, 33, 34, 41, 43–47, 51, 52, 59, 95, 130–232, 141, 142, 145, 199, 204, 224
Coastal Sentry, US 176
Cocopa, ATF 135
Codington, US 176
Coe Victory, US 176
Coeur d'Alene Victory, US 176
Coffeyville Victory see *Mormacelm* 176
Cohocton, TAO 106
Cold War 225
Colgate Victory, US 176
Colina see *Kankankee*
Collett, USS 17
The Colonel and I 67
Colonial, LSD 89
Colqitt AK see *Kukui*
Columbia 50, 51, 119, 128, 209
Columbia River 88
Columbia Trader, US 176
Columbia Wolf see *Bluefield Victory*
Combat Stores Ships 96
COMINRON 3 81
Command Ship 57
Commandoes 25
Commissioned (ships) 31, 37
Commissioning Pennant 31
Commodore Perry 28
Commonwealth see Great Britain
Communism, Communist 1, 4, 9, 25, 26, 106, 150, 154, 210, 211, 221, 223
ComNavFE 7, 17
Compass, US 176
Competent, AM 160
COMSERVRON 103
Comstock, LSD 89
Condamine, HMAS 209

Condor, AMS 156
Condor Missile Tests 48
Conestoga see *Millicoma*
Coney, PPE 42
Congress 33, 77
Consever, ARS 85, 130
Consolation, AH 60
Consolidated Vultree 6
Constant Warwick, HMS 50
USS Constitution 154
Constitution see *Skagway Victory*
Constitution State, US 176
Conway III, DE 42
Cooper Union Victory, US 176
Copenhagen 210
Coral Sea, US 176
Cornell Victory, US 176
Cornhusker Mariner, US 177
Cornish Gig 203
Corsicana II see *Pecos II*
Corson, AVP 131
Corte Real, Portugal 45
Cortez see *Plymouth Victory*
Cossatot, TAO 106
Cotabato Del Sur, Philippines 79
Cotton Mariner, US 177
Cotton State, US 177
Coucal, ARS 131
Council Bluffs Victory, US 177
Cowanesque, TAO 106
Cowell II, DE 42
Crane, HMS 212
Crane ships 199
Crash Boat 202
Crash Boat-63 201, 202
Crash Boat-85 201, 202
Crash Boat Rescue Squadron 22 201
Cree, AT 136
Creighton Victory, US 177
Crescent City, class 145
Crook County, LST 611 79
Crosley, class 149, 150
Cruisers 7, 8, 18, 22, 24, 25, 26, 33, 103, 211
Cuba Victory, US 177
Cuban Missile Crisis 45, 54, 66, 146, 148
Curlew IV, AMS 156
Current, ARS 130, 177
Currier, DE 42
Currituck, class 132
Cutters 10, 12, 33, 41
Cyclone, US 58

D-Day 78, 79, 154, 155
Daengyong Do 162
Dale, class 214
Dalton Victory, TAK 100
DANFS 12, 34, 45, 55, 56, 58, 64, 66, 69, 85, 100, 135, 146
Dang jin-Gun, ROKN 55
Dartmouth Victory, US 177; see also *Choctaw Victory*; *President Arthur*
David B. Johnson, US 177
David Dudley Field, US 177
Daviess County, LST 692 79
DD see DDE
DD-495 155

DDE (Destroyer Escort) 34
Deadweight 31
Deal, AKL 100
Deal Island see *Kermit Roosevelt*
Dealey, class" 42
Dean, Maj. Gen. William F. 18
Decommissioning (as subject) 37
Defected 184
Defense, AM 160
DEG (Guided Missile Escorts) 34
Degaussing ships 163, 199, 202
DeHaven, US 17
DeKalb County, LST 715 80
Del Alba, US 177
Del Aires, US 177
Deliver, US 130
Delta II, AK 125
Democratic People's Republic of Korea see North Korea
Democratic People's Republic of Korea Railroad 66
Denebola see *Hibbing Victory*
Denfeld, Louis E. 6
Denise, US 177
Denmark 210
Department of Agriculture 8
Department of Defense 6, 45
Department of the Army 204
Department of the Navy 6
Department of Transportation 167
De Pauw Victory, US 177
Depth Charges 13, 21
Desert Storm, Operation 7
Designations, ship 34
Des Plaines River, LSMR 92
Destroyer Escorts 41, 89
Destroyer Minesweepers 152, 154
Destroyers 2, 4, 8, 10, 11, 12, 18, 22, 24, 26, 33, 41, 103, 133, 137, 154, 166, 201, 211, 213, 217
Deuel, US 146
Deuel, Harry P. 146
Devastator, AM 160
Devonshire (British troops) 215
Devonshire, HMT 215
Dextrous, AM 160
Diachenko, APO 149
Diachenko, Alex Maxwell 149
Diamond Mariner, US 177
Dictionary of American Naval Vessels 154
Digby County, US 177
Dimboola see *Empire Longford*
Diodon, SS 65
Diphda, TAKA 140
Disappeared 110, 190
Displacement 30, 31
Distillery Ship (AW) 202
Ditto, US 177
Diver, class 130
Dixie II, US 127, 128
DMS 154
DMS-33 154
DMS-35 155
DMS-38 155
DMZ 22
Dock Landing Ships 166
Docking Service 88, 89
Doctor Lykes see *Hamul*

Doolittle Raid 106
Dolly Turman, US 177
Donald E. Holland see *Sea Cliff*; *Sea Daring*
Donald McKay see *Polaris*
Doncella, SS 65
Dondor, AMS 156
Dorothy see *Flora C.*
Dorothy Stevenson, US 177
Douglas A. Munro, DE 42
Dowanesque, TAO 106
Doyle, DMS 154
Doyle, Adm. James H. 9, 17, 21, 58, 71
Drayton, Captain 151
Drew Victory, US 177
Drury Victory, US 178
Dubois, HNLMS 217
Dudley H. Thomas, US 178
Duke Victory, US 178
Dukes County, LST 735 80
DUKW 70, 72
Dumlupinar, TCG 65
Duncan III, DDR 54
Dunkirk 77
Dunn County, LST 742 80
Durango Victory, US 178
Durant, WDE 43
Durant, Pharmacist's Mate 43
Dutch 31, 119
Dutiful see *Laetres*
Dutton see *Tuskegee Victory*
Duval County, LST 758 80
Dyer, Adm. George C. 201

E-5 201
E-6 201
Earlham Victory, US 178
East Coast Blockading and Escort Force 51
Eastern Carolinas 101, 102
East Korean Support Group 8
East Point Victory, US 178
Eberie, US 149
EC2 (Emergency Construction) 168
Echodale, RFA 214
Economic Cooperation Administration 18
Ecuador 88, 206
Edison Mariner, US 178
Edmonds, DE 43
Edsall, class 42–47, 63
Edward L. Grant see *Lipari*, and *Lucille Bloomfield*
Edward L. Logan see *American Eagle*
Edward P. Ripley see *Flora C.*
Edwin Markham, US 178
Eileen, US 178
Eisenhower, Pres. Dwight 55
EK-12 52
EK-16 50
EK-23 50
EK-42 51
Elby, US 178
Elder, AN 128
Elderfields see *Helen Stevenson*
Eldorado, AGC 57

Electroencephalograph brain-wave machine 61
Electron, AKS 102
El Gato Blanco, Panama 83, 178
Elkhorn, AOG 112
Elko Victory, US 178
Elliott, Chuck 66
Ellkay see *Monongahela II*
Elly, US 178
Elmira Viceroy, US 178
Embarkation-Control Liaison 57
Emerson, Ralph Waldo 139
Empire Dunbar see *Wave Laird*
Empire Edgehill see *Wave Chief*
Empire Flodden see *Wave Baron*
Empire Fowey, HMT 215
Empire Halladale, HMT 215
Empire Herald see *Wave Prince*
Empire Jewel see *Empire Fowey*
Empire Law see *Wave Conqueror*
Empire Longford, HMT 215
Empire Marshall, British 178
Empire Metal Service see *Eaglesdale* RFA
Empire Naseby see *Wave Knight*
Empire Pride, HMT 215
Empire State Mariner, US 178
Empire State V see *Barrett*
Empire Trooper, US 215
Empire Viceroy, US 178
Empire Wallace, British 178
Empire Windrush, HMT 215, 216
Empire Witham see *Choysang* RFA
Endicott, DMS 155, 159
Endurance, RS 82
The Enemy Below 49
England *see* Great Britain
Enid Victory, US 178
Eninetok, Atomic Testing 58, 81, 132, 158, 163
Ensign Whitehead see *Pak Tu San*
Epperson, DDE 43
Epping Forest, LSD 90
Ernest G. Small, DDR 54
Escanaba, WPG 52, 104, 107, 111, 112
Escanaba Victory, AF 97, 178
Escort Carriers 20
Escort Division 43
Escort Squadron II 46
Esso Annapolis see *Chemung II*
Esso Fleet Oiler 107, 108, 109
Esso Raleigh see *Guadalupe*
Estero, AKL 100
Estes, AGO 58
Eta Jima see Firecrest
Ethiopia 119
Ethiopia Victory, US 179
Etlah, AN 129
Eugenie, US 179
Europe (n) area 8, 26, 52, 56, 79, 93, 117
Evacuations 17, 18, 22, 59, 90, 91, 97, 103, 140, 147, 184, 204, 212
Evelyn see *Plymouth Victory*
Everett, PF 51
Evergreen Star, US 179
Eversten, HRMS 217
Executive Order 10179 11

Exmouth Victory, US 179
Explosions 108
Express Buffalo see Rock *Springs Victory*
Ezra Meech see *Liberty Flag*

F (army naval ship) 32, 199
FA (army cargo ship) 199
Fabius, ARVA 125
Fairhope, US 179
Fairisle see *Yugoslavia Victory*
Falgout, WDE 13, 43
Falkland War 65
Fante, Italian 48
Far East Air Force 201
Far East Command, Naval Forces 7, 11
Far East Command, US 7, 17, 98, 104–107, 109, 111, 119, 125–127, 134, 136, 147, 152–157, 158, 159, 161
Faribault, AKA 141
Farragut, Admiral 151
Farrar-Hockley, Sir Anthony 208
Federal Voyager, US 179
Felix Risenberg see *Transatlantic*
Fentriss Maru, SCAJAP 216
Ferdinand Westfall, US 179
FFG (Guided missile frigates) 34
Field, James vii, 3, 62
Fifty-five gallon drum 103
Firecrest, AMS 156
Firedrake, AE 99
Fireflies 21
Fiske II, DDR 54
Fitch, WDE 43
Fleet Destroy Escorts 34
Fleet Marine Force 70
Fleet Striking Force 55
Fletcher, DDE 42, 43, 44, 46, 47, 48, 49
Flora C., US 179
Florida 80, 82
Florikan, ASA 133
Floyd County, LST 772 80
Floyds Bay, AVP 137
Flying Fish Channel 19
Ford County, LST 762 80
Formosa 97, 103–105, 159, 161, 223
Forrestal, James V. 6, 95
Fort Charlotte, RFA 215
Fort Duquense see *Cowanesque*
Fort Langley, REA 215
Fort Marion, LSD 90
Fort Necessity see *Cossatot*
Fort Rosalie, REA 215
Fort Sandusky, REA 215
Foss, DE 44
Foster, WDE 44
40th Parallel 24
FP (army passenger ship) 32, 199
France 42, 79, 134, 210
Francis A. Retka see *Liberty Bell*
Frank E. Spenser see *Anne Butler*
Frank Knox, DDR 54
Frank R. Stockton see *Amersea*
Frank Walsh see *Blue Star*
Fred C. Ainsworth, TAP 114
Frede Joyce see *George F. Duval*

Frederic C. Collins, US 179
Frederick Brouchard, US 179
Frederick Clover, RASC 216
Frederick E. Williamson, US 179
Frederick Funston, TAP 115
Free State Mariner, US 179
Freighters 144
French Morocco 43
Fribourg Trader, US 179
Frigate 7, 8, 24, 25, 34, 41, 50, 208, 209, 211, 217, 218, 219
Frontenac Victory, US 179
Frontier, US 128
Frostburg Victory, US 179
Frybarger, DE 58
FS (French) 32
FS (US Army Supply) 32, 199
FS-263 see *Deal*, AKL
FS-291 199, 200
FS-345 see *Banner II*
FS-379 see *Brute II*
FS-385 see *Sharps*
FS-395 see *Whidbey*
FS-525 199, 200
Fulton, class 133
Fun San (ROK) see *Sharps*
Funston, class 114
Furman see *Furman Victory*
Furman Victory, US 179

Gainesville Victory, US 179
Galen L. Stone see *Ocean Star*
Gallup, PF see *Prasae II*
Garcia D'Avilla, Brazil 85
Gardiners Bay, AVP 131, 138
Gasoline Tanker 103, 112
Gato, class 63, 64
Gauntlet see *African Grove*
Gearing, class 42–46, 53, 54, 55
Geer County, LST 799 81
Gemini Recovery 45, 55, 106
General A.E. Anderson, TAP 115
General A.W. Brewster, TAP 115
General A.W. Greeley, TAP 115
General B.M. Blatchford, TAP 116
General C.C. Ballou, TAP 116
General C.G. Morton, TAP 116
General C.H. Muir, TAP 116
General Daniel L. Sultan, TAP 116
General D.E. Aultman, TAP 115
General Edwin D. Patrick, TAP 116
General E.T. Collins, TAP 116
General George M. Randall, TAP 117
General George Patton, US 179
General H.B. Freeman, TAP 117
General H.W. Butner, TAP 118
General Hugh J. Gaffey, TAP 117
General J.C. Breckinridge, TAP 118
General J.H. McRae, TAP 118
General John Pope, TAP 115, 117, 118, 119, 121
General Leroy Elting, TAP 119
General M.B. Steward, TAP 119
General M.C. Meigs, TAP 119
General M.L. Hersey, TAP 119
General M.M. Patrick, TAP 119
General Motors 72
General Nelson M. Walker, TAP 119

Index

General R.L. Howze, TAP 119
General S.D. Sturgis, TAP 120
General Simon B. Buckner, TAP 120
General Squire, class 115, 118, 119, 120, 121
General Stores Ship 102
General Stuart Heintzelman, TAP 120
General W.A. Mann, TAP 120
General W.C. Langfitt, TAP 120
General W.F. Hase, TAP 121
General W.H. Gordon, TAP 121
General W.M. Black, TAP 121
General W.O. Darby, TAP 121
General William Mitchell, TAP 121
General William Weigel, TAP 121
Generating ships 199
George A. Lawson, US 179
George A. Marr see *Stathes Yamaglias*
George Clymer, APA 146
George Eastman, US 179
George E. Merrick see *Saxon*
George F. Duval, US 180
George K. Fitch see *North Sky*
George M. Cohen see *General George Patton*
George M. Culucundis, US 180
George W. Kendall see *Dorothy Stevenson*
Georgia 80, 82
German U-Boats 41
Germantown, US 31
Germany 85, 87, 212
"Ghost of the Korean Coast" 144
Ghu Hwa, ROC, Sgt. G.D. Keathley 124
Gigs 199, 203
Gilbert Islands, 42, 136, 142
Ginrich, Adm. John E. 128
Gladiator, AM 160, 161
Gladiator II, AM 160
Gleaves, class 154, 155
Glendale, USS 51, 218; see also *Tachin*, HMTS
Glory, HMS see *Wave Premier*
Gloucester II, PF 215
Gold "E" Efficiency Award 127
Golden City, US 180
Golden Mariner, US 180
Golden Noon see *Paducah Victory*
Golden Rocket see *Zelima*
Golfe de Juan 163
Governor Graves see *Sea Herald*
Grace (Typhoon) 18
Graffias, AF 97
Grainger, AK 106
Great Britain (British) 5, 8, 18, 30, 31, 65, 70, 71, 77, 78, 131, 151, 210, 213, 215
Great Falls Victory, US 180
Great Republic see *Pictor*
Greater Underwater Propulsive Power (Guppy) 62, 65–69
Greece 86, 112, 114, 119
Greece Victory, US 180
Greeley Victory, US 180
Green Bay Victory, US 180
Green County, LST 799 81

Green Harbor see *Cooper Union Victory*
Green Island see *Muncie Victory*
Green Ranger, RFA 214
Green Springs see *Marine Carp*
Green Star, US 180
Green Valley, US 180
Greenfish, SS 65
Greenharbor, US 180
Greenhouse 48
Greenlet, ASR 27, 133
Gresham, WAVP 132
Gretna Victory, US 180
Grinnell Victory, US 180
Groton, USS 210
Groton Trails, US 180
Guadalcanal 43, 93, 140
Guadalupe, AO 106
Guall 21
Guam 11, 42, 65, 106, 114, 134, 158, 162, 163
Guerrilla groups 9, 145, 201, 219, 220
Guinea Pig Squadron 191
Gulf Water, US 180
Gull II, AMS 156
Gunboat 52
Gunboat Diplomacy 52
Gunston, Hall, LSD 90

Haakon VII see *Gardiners Bay*
Haeju 159, 212
Hagaru-ri 21
Halalua Victory, US 180
Halcyon Panther see *Sapulpa Victory*
Halcyon Tiger see *New Zealand Victory*
Hall J. Kelley see Ditto
Hallion, Richard 15
Hamal see *Hamul*
Hamhung, Korea 20
Hamilton County see LST 802 81
Hamilton Victory, US 180
Hampden County, LST 803 81
Hampshire Country, LST 819 81
Hamul, AD 128
Han La San, PC 219
Han Yang, Taiwan 55
Hanchon 212, 213
Hanna, DE 44
Hannibal Victory, US 180
Hanson, DDR 54
Harbor craft 33, 128
Harlem Heights see *Suamico*
Harold D. Whitehead, US 181
Harold L. Winslow, US 181
Harold T. Andrews, US 181
Harpoon, US 181
Harris County, LST 822 81
Harry Kirby see *Christine*
Harry Tucker, US 55
Hart, HMS 8, 18, 212
Hartman, Adm. C.C. 207
Harvard Victory, US 181
Haskell, class 145, 146–149
Hass, Mike 202
Hastings Victory see *Sgt. Truman Kimbo*
Hattiesburg Victory, US 181

Havan, AH 60, 61
Hawaii 64, 134
Hawaii Bear, US 181; see also *Kelso Victory*
Hawaiian, US 181
Hawaiian Packer see *Delta II*
Hawaiian Traveler, US 169
Hawangpo 52
Hawea, HMNZA 217
Hawkeye Mariner, US 181
Hawkins, DDR 54
HDMS (Denmark) 32
Hecla, class 213
Hector III, AR 125
Hedgehogs 48
Helen Lykes, US 181
Helen Stevenson, US 181
Helicopters 23, 59, 61, 159, 210, 215
Hellenic Navy 67
Hendry D. Lindsley, US 181
Hennepin, TAK 101
Henrico, APA 146
Henry Adams see *Catherine Goulandris*
Henry M. Stephen see *Sea Faith*
Henry Tucker, DDR 55
Henry Villard see *Ampac Oregon*
Herbert J. Thomas, DDR 55
Hermitage, US 89
Heron II, AMS 157
Hewell, AKL 101
Heywood Broun, US 181
Hibbing Victory, US 181
Hickman County, LST 825 82
Higbee, DDR 55
Higgins Industries 93
High Point Victory, US 181
Hijacked 191
HIJMD (Japanese, Imperial) 32
Hillsborough County, LST 827 82
History of the United States Naval Operations in Korea 62
Hitchiti, AFT 135
HMAS (Australia) 32
HMCA (Canada) 32
HMNZS (New Zealand) 32
HMS (Great Britain) 32
HMT (Great Britain) 32
HNLMS (Netherlands) 32, 217
HNOMS (Norway) 32
Ho Do 26, 212
Hobart Victory, US 181
Hokkaido, Japan 65, 69
Holland 31
Holland, John 33
Hollandia 58, 135
Holmes County, LST 836 82
Holy Star, US 181
Honda Knot, US 181
Hong Kong 150, 213, 214, 215
Hong Kong see *Empire Longford*
Hong Kong Transport see *Colgate Victory*
Hood River Port Museum 59
Hooper Island, ARG 125
Hoosier Marnier, US 181
Hoosier State, US 181; see also *Carter Braxton*

Index

Hope, US 61
Hope Victory, US 182
Hopkins, Adm. J.M. 17
Hoquiam, PF 52
Horace A. Bass, APD 24, 144, 145, 150, 210
Horatio Allen see *Sea Gate*
Hospital 131
Hospital ships 10, 11, 33, 59, 60, 84, 212, 215
Houston, US 33
Howard T. Richetts see *Ampac Idaho*
HrMs/Zr.Ms. *see* Netherands
HTMS, Thailand 32
Hualcopo, Ecuador 88
Hubbard, Ron 140
Hull number (as a subject) 37
Hungnam (Redeployment) 20–25, 45, 46, 51, 52, 54, 57, 61, 72, 84, 91, 97, 106, 114, 115, 116, 117, 118, 126, 136, 140, 146, 154, 156, 158, 161–164, 167, 170, 172, 175–192, 194, 195, 196, 197, 216, 217
Hunter-killer submarines 33, 69
Hunter Victory, US 182
Huntsville see *Knox Victory*
Huron, US 53
Hurricane, US 182
Hwangto-do 26
Hyades, class 97
Hyman Rickover, USS 33

Ice Station Zebra 64, 67
Ike, US 182 see *Sea Cliff*
Illinois 80
Imchin, PC 219
Impeccable, AM 161, 162
In Harm's Way 148
Inchon 1, 3, 8, 9, 17, 18, 19, 21, 22, 25, 44, 51, 55, 57, 58, 60, 61, 70, 78, 79, 81, 84, 85, 87, 88, 89, 91, 96, 101, 103, 107, 114, 135, 136, 138, 139, 141, 142, 143, 145, 146, 148, 149, 153, 155, 158, 159, 167, 170, 173, 175, 177, 185, 187, 190, 191, 192, 195, 197, 200, 204, 209, 210, 212, 216, 218, 220, 221
Inchon-Kimpo-Seoul airfield 17
Incredible, AM 159, 161
India 8
Indian, class 52
Indiana 80
Indochina 210
Indonesia 84, 129
Intelligence 19, 23, 25
Interdiction 23
Interpreter see *Dudley H. Thomas*
Intrepid, US 59
Inverkeithing 214
Iowa 80
Iran Victory, US 182
Iraq 7
Irene Star, US 182
Iron County, LST 840 82
Ironwood, WAGL 206
Iroquois, WPG 53
Isaac Peral, Spanish Navy 67
Isaac Van Zandt, US 182

Israel Air Force 194
Israel Putnam, US 182
Italy (Italian) 42, 48, 67, 69, 136, 137, 163, 212
Iwakuni 138
Iwo Jima 57, 77, 80, 143, 145, 148, 157, 160
Iwon 19, 20, 25

James A. Lane see *Ocean Navigator*
James B. Weaver, US 182
James Baines see *Algol*
James E. Robinson, class 102
James Fennimore Cooper see *Mohawk*
James H. Cooper, US 182
James H. Price, US 182
James McHenry, US 182
James, O'Hara, US 121
James W. Cannon see *Transoceanic*
Janes' Fighting Ships 154
Japanese (Japan) 3, 4, 7, 8, 9, 21, 45, 50, 52, 55, 62, 64, 66, 66, 68, 81, 86, 91, 96, 100–102, 104, 111, 114, 127–129, 131, 134, 135, 141, 145, 148, 156, 158, 159, 161, 166, 191, 200, 201, 210, 213, 216, 219, 224
Japanese Coast Guard 8
Japanese Maritime Safety Agency 216
Japanese Minecraft (JML) 17
Japanese National Railroads 8
Japanese Red Cross 8
Jarvis, Jim 201
Jasper F. Cropsey see *Oceanic*
Java Sea 64
J.C.W. Beckham see *Sea Ranger*
Jefferson City Victory, US 182
Jefferson County, LST 845 82
Jelandside, US 182
Jenkins II, DDE 44
Jennings County 82; *see also* LST 846
Jeong Ju, ROK 55
Jeremiah M. Daily see *Atlanticus*
Jericho Victory, US 182
Jesus Gonzalas Otraga see *Chief*
Jimmy Carter, USS 33
Jishima see *Condor*
JMS 219
JMS 306 23
JMSDF (Japanese) 32
Joann see *Yugoslavia Victory*
Johan Maurits van Nassau, HNLMS 217
John Adams, Frigate 10
John B. Whidden, US 182
John Ball, US 182
John C., US 182
John C. Butler, class 42–49
John H. Marion, US 182
John H.B. Latrobe, US 182
John Hanson, US 182
John Howland, US 183
John Kulkundis, US 183
John L. Sullivan, YAG 98
John Lyras, British 183
John T. McMillan US 183

John W. Brown see *Twin Falls Victory*
John W. McKay, US 183
John W. Powell, US 183
Johnson, Louis 1, 166
Joint Advisory Commission, Korea (JACK) 200
Joint Chiefs of Staff 5, 17
Joliet Victory, US 183
Jonah E. Kelley, class 129
Jones, John Paul, US 62, 183
Joplin Victory, US 183
Jose, Marti, US 183
Joseph, US 169
Joseph Feuer, US 183
Joseph Lee, US 183
Joseph Priestley, US 183
Joseph Wantuck, APO 150
Joshua Slocum, US 183
Joy, Adm. C. Turner 9, 21, 63, 71, 151, 222, 223
Jumper Hitch, US 183
Juneau, USS 17
Junks 23, 92, 155, 199, 203
Jupiter, US 138
Jutlandia, (Denmark) 210

Kaesong, ROK 210
Kallak see *Mattaponi*
Kalma Gak Point, Korea 156, 157
Kang Hwa Man, ROK 220
Kangnung 17, 52
Kaniere, HMNZA 218
Kankakee, TAO 106
Kansas 80
Kansas City, Kansas 72
Kansong 52
Karin, AF 97
Kaskaskia, AO 106
Katharine B. Sherwood, US 183
Kathlena see *Bartlesville Victory*
Katsonis, Hellenic 67
Kearsarge, USS 33
Keel 32
Keel-laying ceremony 31
Keelung, Taiwan 103, 163
Kelso see *Hawaii Bear*
Kelso Victory, US 183
Kemp P. Battle see Sea Herald
Kemper County, LST 854 83
Kennebee, class 106
Kenneth Stevenson, US 183
Kenneth Whiting, AV 132
Kent County, LST 855 83
Kentucky 80, 82
Kenyon Victory, US 183
Keosanqua, ATA 136
Keppler, DDE 44
Kermit Roosevelt, ARG 125
Kern, US 184
Kern Hills, US 184
Keystone Mariner, US 184
Kezia (storm) 85
Khruschev, Nikita 132
Kiel 215
Kiland, Adm. Ingolf N. 58
Kilauer, AE see *Mount Baker*
Killer Submarine 64
Kilometers 31

Kim Il Sung 15
Kim Po see *Kite II*
Kimball R. Smith, SS 168, 184
King (nuclear test) 82
King, Adm. E.J. 166
King County, LST 857 83
Kink's Mountain see *Millicoma*
Kirin Do 92
Kishwaukee, AOG 112
Kite, ZMS 20, 157
Klamath, WPG 53
Klepper canoes 199, 203
Klondike, class 127
Knot, as subject 31
Knox Victory, US 184
Kobe, Japan 212
Kochang see *Mockingbird II*
Kodiak see LSM 161
Kodiak, Alaska 101, 143
Koiner, WDE 13, 44
Koje-do 85, 86, 87, 143, 148
Koje Deception 145, 147, 161
Kojo 23, 55, 90, 82, 140–142, 158, 159
Kokura, Japan 95
Korea, Occupation 55
Korean Service Medal 11, 12, 47, 66, 67, 131, 132, 140, 146, 150, 168, 210
Korean Strait 18
Korthi see *Westchester*
Kosong 52
Kosovo 7
Kukui, WAK 141
Kum Hwa see *Curlew IV*
Kum Kang San, PC 220
Kumchon 18
Kunsan Harbor Station 201
Kwajalein 105
Kyoshin Tan 159
Kyoto Wan 155
Kyushu 137

Ladybird, HMS 211, 212
Laertes, AR 125
Lafayette County, LST 859 83
Lafayette Victory, US 184
Lafitte, US 184
La Grandiere, FMS 210
Lahaina Victory, US 184
Lake Minnewanka, US 184
Lake Pennask, US 184
Lakeland Victory, US 184
Lakeside, Foreign Ship 184
Lakewood Victory, US 184
Lamoure County, LST 883 83
Landing Craft 129, 144, 147
Landing Craft Assault, LCA 70, 71
Landing Craft Infantryman, LCI 70, 71, 72, 76
Landing Craft Mechanized, LCM 70, 71
Landing Craft Repair Ship 129
Landing Craft Tank, LCT 71
Landing Craft Utilities, LCU 72
Landing Craft Vehicle Personnel 70, 201
Landing Ship Dock, LSD 71
Landing Ship Infantry, Light LSIT 93

Landing Ship Infantry LSI 72
Landing Ship Man see Landing Ship Medium
Landing Ship Medium LSM 71, 76
Landing Ship Medium Rocket, LSMR 1
Landing Ship Tank, LST 71, 77
Landing Ships 216
Landing Vehicle Tracked 70
Lane Victory, US 184
Lanta, Thailand 88
Laokawapan see *Cahaba*
La Perouse Strait 27, 65
Lardeo Victory, US 184
Lassenn, class 126
Latitude 11, 12
Launches 34, 199
Lavrakas, Commander 145
Lawrence Brengle see *Michael J. Goulandris*
Lawrence County, LST 887 84
Lawrence J. Gallagher see *Nigel*
Lawrence Victory, US 184
LCC-11 57, 146
LCM 88, 89
LCPI 146
LCPR 204
LCU 89
LCU 520 73
LCU 531 73
LCU 539 73
LCU 562 73
LCU 608 73
LCU 629 73
LCU 634 73
LCU 637 73
LCU 638 73
LCU 674 73
LCU 675 73
LCU 677 73
LCU 684 73
LCU 686 73
LCU 742 73
LCU 783 73
LCU 788 73
LCU 810 73
LCU 859 74
LCU 869 74
LCU 870 74
LCU 877 74
LCU 893 74
LCU 960 74
LCU 974 74
LCU 979 74
LCU 980 74
LCU 1009 74
LCU 1056 74
LCU 1080 74
LCU 1082 74
LCU 1085 74
LCU 1086 74
LCU 1103 74
LCU 1124 74
LCU 1125 74
LCU 1136 74
LCU 1156 74
LCU 1160 75
LCU 1162 75
LCU 1195 75

LCU 1236 75
LCU 1255 75
LCU 1273 75
LCU 1286 75
LCU 1287 75
LCU 1317 75
LCU 1374 75
LCU 1387 75
LCU 1396 75
LCU 1402 75
LCU 1421 75
LCU 1446 75
LCU 1451 76
LCUP 150
LCVPs 19, 23, 89, 93, 146
League Island, AKS 102
"Leaping Lenah" 55
Lee Sung Ho 19
Lenawee, APA 146
Leo, TAKA 141
Leon, APA 146
Leonardo L. Romero see *Chain Trader*
Letitia Lykes, US 184
Lewis, DE 45
Lewis H. Emery, Jr, US 184
Lexington, USS 33
Leyte 45, 51, 57, 79, 83, 99, 111, 134, 135, 142, 206
Leyte Gulf, USS 21
Liberty see *Simmons Victory*
Liberty Bell, US 184
Liberty Flag, US 184
Liberty Ship 98, 100, 125, 167, 168, 170–183, 186–198
Libra, class 142
Lighters 59, 199, 200, 203
Lighthouse Tenders WAGL 204
Lilica, US 185
Lincoln County, LST 898 84
Linfield Victory, US 185
Lingayen Gulf 80, 111, 143
Lipan, AT 134, 136
Lipari, US 185
List see naval register
Litchfield County, LST 901 84
Little America 141
LKA 142, 143, 144
LKA-93 see *Yancy*
LKA-94 see *Winston*
LKA-97 142
LML 219
Loch, class 211, 217
Loch Achanalt see *Pukaki* HMNZA
Loch Achily, HMS 213
Loch Achray see *Kaniere*, HMNZA
Loch Eric see *Hawea*, HMNZA
Loch Heilen, HMS 212
Loch Katrine see *Rotoiti* HMNZA
Loch Kilbirnie, HMS 212
Loch Laxford, HMS 212
Loch Lubnaig, HMS 213
Loch Scamadale, (British) 211
Loch Shin see *Tauto*
Lodestone, ADG 202
Logan, ZPA 146
Logistics Support 20, 95, 100, 133, 167, 208

242 Index

Loma Victory, US 185
Lone Star Mariner, US 185
Longboats 199, 203
Logistics 95, 208
Longitude 11
Longview Victory, US 185
Loran Station 206
Lott, Arnold S. 152
Louis Marshall see *George M. Culucundis*
Louisburg see *Schuylkill*
Lowe, WDE 45
Loyola Victory, US 185
LPA 139
LPA-194 148
LPA-210 149
LPA-212 147
LPA-220 148
LPR 150
LSD 10, 18, 22, 88
LSD 4 90
LSD 5 90
LSD 8 90
LSD 16 89
LSD 17 89
LSD 18 89
LSD 19 89
LSD 22 90
LSD 26 90
LSD 27 90
LSIL 1091 93
LSM 58 76
LSM 110 76
LSM 125 76
LSM 161 76
LSM 175 76
LSM 226 76
LSM 236 76
LSM 316 76
LSM 335 76
LSM 355 76
LSM 362 76
LSM 397 77
LSM 399 77
LSM 401, class 91, 92
LSM 419 77
LSM 422 77
LSM 429 77
LSM 463 77
LSM 448 77
LSM 501, class 92
LSM 546 77
LSM 547 77
LSMR 26, 90
LSMR 401 see *Bigh Black River*
LSMR 403 91
LSMR 404 see *Black Warrior*
LSMR 405 see *Broadkill River*
LSMR 409 see *Clarion River*
LSMR 412 see *Des Plaines River*
LSMR 525 see *St. Francis River*
LSMR 527 see *St. Joseph River*
LSMR 536 see *White River*
LSSL 77 see *Yung Huang Man*
LSSL 91 see *Kang Hwa Man*
LSSL 107 see *Yung Huang Man*
LST 9, 10, 22, 23, 28, 59, 60, 96, 207, 126, 129, 216, 220
LST 14 19

LST 120 see *Munsan*
LST 231 125, 129
LST 511, class 78
LST 516 78
LST 527 79
LST 529 79
LST 561 79
LST 602 79, 84
LST 611 79
LST 692 79
LST 715 80
LST 735 80
LST 742 80
LST 758 80
LST 762 80
LST 772 80
LST 799 81
LST 802 81
LST 803 81
LST 819 81
LST 822 81
LST 825 82
LST 827 82
LST 836 82
LST 840 82
LST 845 82
LST 846 83
LST 852 129
LST 854 83
LST 855 83
LST 857 19, 83
LST 859 19, 83
LST 883 83
LST 887 84
LST 898 84
LST 901 84
LST 902 84
LST 914 84
LST 918 84
LST 973 19, 88
LST 975 85; see also *Marion County*
LST 1048 85; see also *Morgan County*
LST 1068 85; see also *Orange County*
LST 1073 85; see also *Outagamie County*
LST 1077 85; see also *Park County*
LST 1080 86; see also *Pender County*
LST 1082 86; see also *Pitkin County*
LST 1083 86; see also *Plumas County*
LST 1084 86; see also *Polk County*
LST 1089 86; see also *Rick County*
LST 1090 86, 87; see also *Russell County*
LST 1096 87
LST 1097 see *League Island*
LST 1101 87; see also *Saline County*
LST 1122 87; see also *San Joaquin County*
LST 1123 87
LST 1131 125, 129
LST 1134 87; see also *Stark County*
LST 1138 88
LST 1141 88; see also *Stone County*

LST 1146 88; see also *Summit County*
LST 1148 88; see also *Sumner County*
LST 1479, class 102
LSU 19, 88
Lt. George W.G. Boyce, TAK 101
Lt. Raymond G. Beaudoin, TAP 122
Lucille Bloomfield, USL 185
Lucky George 146
Luosey, Michael J. 9, 219
Lumber Carrier, US 185
Lumberman, (Foreign) 185
Luxembourg Victory, US 185
Luzerne County, LST 902 84
Luzon 104, 134, 142, 143
Luzon, class 125
Luzon II, US 125
LVT 88, 93
Lynn Victory, US 185

Macalester Victory, US 185
MacArthur, Douglas A. 1, 7, 17, 18, 19, 20, 21, 47
Mack Bruton Bryan see *Transunion*
MacQuarie see HMAS *Culgoa*
Madaket, US 185
Magoffin, APA 146
Magpie II, AMA 153, 157
Mahoning County, LST 914 84, 85
Maine, HMS 212
Mainstay, AM 161
Makin Island 66
Malay Maru #2, SCAPAP 216
Malaysia 87
Malden Victory, US 185; see also *Sgt. Jack J. Pendleton*
Manatee II, TAO 106
Manchester, USS 155
Manchuria 23
Mandarin see *African Pilot*
Manderson Victory, US 185
Manila 49, 103
Mankato Victory, US 185
Mansfield, US 17, 139, 153
Manson, Frank A. vii, 5
Manuel Doblado see *Defense*
Manzanillo, Mexico 79
MARAD see Maritime Administration
Mare Island Navy Yard 142
Marianas 45, 100, 101, 104, 106, 132, 143, 157, 159, 166
Marias, TAO 107
Marine Adder, TAP 122, 123
Marine Beaver, US 61
Marine Carp, TAP 122
Marine Hawk, US 61
Marine Lion, US 60
Marine Lynx, TAP 122
Marine Phoenix, TAP 123
Marine Progress see *Ampac Oregon*
Marine Serpent, US 123
Marine Snapper, US 185
Marine Walrus, US 60
Mariner, US 185
Mariner class freighter 144
Marines 6, 19, 20, 21, 22, 72, 81,

90, 93, 99, 139, 144, 145, 146, 147, 150, 199
Marinship Corporation of California 107, 108
Marion County, LST 85
Maritime Administration (MARAD) 7, 79, 80, 98, 99, 101, 104, 113, 114, 132, 138, 148, 166, 167, 169, 170
Maritime Commission 96, 97, 98, 99, 101, 102, 104–119, 121, 122, 124, 126, 140, 141, 143, 144, 146, 147, 148, 149, 167, 168, 172, 174, 176, 180, 182, 184, 186, 188, 190, 198, 220
Maritime Self Defense Force 158
Mark II (Magnetic) 207
Marquette Victory, US 185
Marsh, DE 45
Marshall, George C. 5, 6
Marshall Islands 45, 100, 101, 102, 134, 142, 164
Marshall Plan 170
Marshall Victory see *Lt. Raymond O. Beaudoin*
Marshfield Victory, US 186
Martin Behrmen, US 186
Marven, US 186
Mary Adams, US 186
Mary Lunkenback, US 60
Maryland 64
Mathews, AKA 141
Masan, US 94
Mascoma, TAO 107
Massillon Victory, US 186
Mataco, ATF 135
Matchless see *Aludra*
Mattaponi, AO 107, 109
Mayfield Victory, US 186
"Mayor of Wonsan" 26
McCaffery, DE 45
McCandlish, Earl 202
McCann Rescue Chamber 135
McCoy Reynolds, DE 45
McGinty, DE 45, 46
McKean II, DE 55, 153
McKinley, US 22, 57, 58
M.E.Comerford, US 185
Mechanized Artillery Transport 90
Medal of Honor 33
Medical service 59, 84
Mediterranean 26, 54, 98, 107, 146, 161
Melody see *Blue Star*
Menard, APA 147
Menhaden, SS 66
Menifee, APA 147
Merapi, AF 97
Merchant 220
Merchant Auxiliary 215
Merchant Marine 27, 93, 95, 166, 167, 168, 187, 223, 224
Merchant Marine Association 107, 169, 170, 191
Merchant Marines and Lower Case Letters 167
Merchant Ship Sales Act 7
Meredith Victory, US 186
Merganser II, AMS 153

Meridian Victory, US 186
Merrick, AKA 141
Mesquite, class 206
Meteorological service 11
Mexico 79, 85, 134, 135, 160, 161
Michael J. Goulandris, US 186
Michael Moran, US 186
Michigan 82
Middlesex Regiment, First Battalion 213
Midland Victory, US 170, 186; see also *Back Eagle*
Midway 101, 112, 114, 123, 137
MiG-15 90, 212, 213
Mike (nuclear test) 82
Military Intelligence 224
Military Sea Life Command 96
Military Sea Transportation Service (MSTS) 8, 57, 80, 84, 85, 86, 94, 95, 96, 100–106, 107, 109, 110, 111, 113, 114–124, 140, 141, 143, 148, 149, 166, 167, 188, 199, 224
Millicoma, TAO 107
Milne Bay 125
Milton Foreman see *Shinecock Bay*
MinDiv 31 158, 162
MinDiv 32 159, 161, 162
Mindoro Landing 79
Mine Squadron 90
Mine Squadron Three 18, 20, 154, 161
Mine Squadron Five 163
Minefields 153, 154, 155, 158
Mines 20, 22, 25, 63, 137, 151–153, 158, 159, 216, 217, 219
Minesweepers 2, 4, 9, 24, 25, 33, 43, 81, 89, 90, 131, 151, 153–156, 160, 162–164, 199, 200, 216, 217, 219, 221
Ministry of Transport (British) 215, 216
Minnetonka, WPG 53
Minot Victory, US 186
Miscellaneous Auxiliary 98
Miscellaneous Section 145
Mispillion, AO 107
Mission, class 107, 108, 109
Mission Buenaventura, TAO 107
Mission Capistrano, TAO 107
Mission Carmel, TAO 108
Mission De Pala, TAO 108
Mission Dolores, TAO 108
Mission Loreto, TAO 108
Mission Los Angeles, TAO 108
Mission Purisima, TAO 108
Mission San Antonio, TAO 108
Mission San Carlos, TAO 108
Mission San Diego, TAO 108
Mission San Ferenando, TAO 108
Mission San Francisco, TAO 108; see also *Tamalpais*
Mission San Gabriel, TAO 108
Mission San Jose, TAO 108
Mission San Juan, TAO 108
Mission San Luis Obispo, TAO 109
Mission San Miguel, TAO 109
Mission San Raphel, TAO 109
Mission Santa Ana, TAO 109; see also *Soubarissen*

Mission Santa Barbara, TAO 109
Mission Santa Cruz, TAO 109
Mission Soledad, TAO 109
Mississippi 82
Mississippi River 72
Missouri 82
Missouri, USS 10, 21, 34, 37, 155
Mister Roberts see *Virgo*
Mobile Surgical Team 84
Mocking Bird, AMS 20, 158
Moctobi, AT 135
Modeste, HMS 212
Mohawk, US 186
Mohican, US 186
Mokpo 17, 153
Molala, ATF 137
Monarch of Bermuda 209; see also *New Australia*
Monongahela II, TAO 109
Monroe Victory, US 186
Monsoon, US 57
Montague, AKA 141
Monticello, US 89
Montrose, AFT 147
Moon see *African Moon*
Morecambe Bay, HMS 212
Morgan County, LST 1048 85, 89
Morgantown Victory, US 186
Mormacdale, US 186
Mormacelm, US 186
Mormacelm see *Coffeyville Victory*
Mormacmar, US 186
Mormacmoon, US 187
Mormacpine, US 187
Mormacport, US 187
Mormacrio, US 187
Mormacson, US 187
Mormacspruce see *Muncie Victory*
Mormactide, US 187
Mormacwave, US 187
Morning Light, US 187
Morning Star, AGC 50
Most Dangerous Sea 152
Mothball Fleet 37, 145, 161, 171
Mother M.L. US 187
Mother Ship 78, 133
Mount Baker, AE 99
Mount Hood, class 99
Mount Katmai, AE 10, 99
Mount McKinley, AGC 58, 60
Mount Rose see *Empire Windrush*
Mountain Mariner, US 187
Mountrail, US 147
Mounts Bay, HMS 212
Mousetrap depth charges 131
Move Over Darling 64
M.P. Crocker 12
MSCO 156–159
MSCO-54 165
MSF 154, 161, 163
MSF-122 163
MSF-131 164
MSF-318 160
MSF-341 160
MSF-372 161
MSF-376 162
MSF-382 163
MSF-387 164

MSTS see Military Sea Transport Services
Muhlenberg Victory, US 187
Muir Woods, TAO 109
Mulberries 134
Mulberry, AN 206
Muncie Victory, US 187
Munda 42
Munsan, LST 220
Munsee, AFT 137
Murchison, HMAS 209
Murphy's War 69
Murrelet, AM 161
Museum ship 184, 191
Mutiny 218
MVC-566 147
Myo Hyang San, PC 220

NA Reserve Fleet 132
Nae Tong, ROKN 52
Naifeh, DE 45, 46
Naktong 94
Nam Cho Yong 17
Nan Do 29
NASA program 46, 106
Nashua Victory, US 187
Nat Brown, Foreign 187
Natchang, AOG 112
Nathaniel B. Palmer, US 187
Nathaniel Crosley, US 187
National Defense Reserve Fleet 7, 96, 117, 119, 166
National Policy 9
National Security Act 5, 6
National Security Council 5
Nationalist China see Republic of China
NATO 5, 32
Nautilus, USS 63
Navajo 135
Navajo Victory, US 136, 137, 187
Naval Historical Center 220
Naval Intelligence 224
Naval Operations 6
Naval Register (List) 7, 8, 34, 37, 43, 44, 45, 47, 48, 49, 50, 51, 52, 55, 56, 64, 66, 67, 68, 79, 80, 81, 83, 84, 83, 94, 95, 96, 97, 98, 99, 101, 103, 104, 107, 109–114, 124, 125, 127, 128, 129, 130, 131, 133, 135, 140–144, 147, 148, 150, 156–65
Naval Regulations, US 8
Naval Service Organization 38
Naval Transportation Service 95, 106, 107, 108, 114, 115, 117–121, 140–143
Naval Unit Commendation 104
Navasota, US 110
Naver, HMNZA see *Pukaki* HMNZA
NavFE (Naval Forces Far East) 17, 68, 71, 216, 222
Navigator see *Warwick Victory*
Navy Cross 150
Navy Unit Commendation (Citation) 81, 88, 150, 154, 155, 156, 164
Nbiedermair, John 77

Negotiations 28
Neptune see *Apollo*
Net Tender, AN 128, 206
Netherlands Navy 105, 214, 217
Netherlands Victory see *Pelican State*
Nevadan, US 187
New Australia, HMAS 209
New Guinea 51
New Hampshire 82
New Hebrides 112, 136, 164
New Orleans 72
New Rochelle Victory, US 187
New World Victory, US 187
New York Ambrose lighthouse 11
New Zealand 18, 128, 214, 216, 217, 218
New Zealand Expeditionary Force 218
New Zealand Victory, US 188
Newaden, US 188
Newell, WDE 46
Newcastle Victory, US 188
Newport News 7
Newton see *Saugatuck*
Niagara Victory, US 188; see also Ocean *Victory*
Niantic Victory, US 188
Nicholas C.H. US 188
Nicholas Longworth see *Helen Stevenson*
Nicholas II, DDE 46
Nigel, US 188
Nikoklis see *Capt. N.B. Palmer*
Nimitz, Adm. Chester W. 66
Noble II, APA 147
Non-Commissioned, ship 37
Noon Day, US 188
Norcuba, US 188
Normandy invasion 44, 77
Norris, DDE 46
North Africa 77, 105, 163
North Carolina see Union
North Dakota 80, 145
North Heaven, US 188
North Korea 1, 2, 3, 4, 7, 9, 15, 16, 17, 19, 21–26, 28, 52, 63, 85, 86, 87, 98, 123, 128, 145, 159, 152, 153, 154, 164, 168, 184, 199, 201, 202, 203, 212, 213, 219, 220, 222, 223, 225
North Light, US 188
North Pilot see *Westchester*
North Pilot, US 188
North Platte Victory, US 188
North River see *Jericho Victory*
North Sky, US 188
Northpoint, Barbados 83
Northport, US 188
Northwalk Victory US 188
Norway 131, 135, 151
Norwich Victory, US 188
Nuclear (atomic) 6, 7, 10, 60, 61, 82, 103, 107, 111, 112, 128, 129, 130, 131, 135, 145, 163
Nutmeg Mariner, US 188

Oakol, RFA 214
O'Bannon II 46

Oberon, AKA 142
Ocala Victory, US 188
Occidental Victory, US 189
Ocean Betty, US 189
Ocean Chief see *Alstede*; *Mother M.L.*
Ocean Leader see *Joseph Feuer*
Ocean Lotte, US 189
Ocean Navigator, US 189
Ocean Rose see *Ocean Betty*
Ocean Seaman, US 189
Ocean Skipper, US 189
Ocean Star, US 189
Ocean Station 132
Ocean Victory 189; see also *Niagara Victory*
Ocean Villa, US 189
Oceanic, US 189
Oceanic Ondine see *Frontenac Victory*
Oceanside, LSM 175 76
Ocklawaha, US 189
Oerlikon 20mm cannon 71
Ogishima see *Pelican II*
Oglethorpe, AKA 100 18, 142
Oglethorpe, Bruce 57
Ohio 82
Oilers 94, 166, 213, 214, 215
Okanogan, APA 147
Okeechobee, US 53
Okinawa 6, 42, 45, 57, 58, 69, 77, 80, 81, 83, 86, 87, 93, 97, 100, 125, 131, 136, 144, 145, 146, 148, 155, 159–164, 180
Oklahoma 80
Okubo, Adm. Takeo 216
OL, class 214
Old Colony Mariner, US 189
Old Dominion Mariner, US 189
Old Dominion State, US 189
Olympic Pioneer, US 189
Omega, US 189
On the Beach 69
O'Neill, USS see *Dubois* HNLMS
Onslow, AVP 132
Ontonagon, US 189
Op-23 6
"Open and closed jigs" 162
Operating Rooms 60, 210
Operation Big Switch 86, 141, 145, 146
Operation Charger Log 112
Operation Chromite 91
Operation Crossroads 60, 104, 111, 112, 128–131, 134, 135, 145, 146, 162, 163
Operation Decoy 25
Operation Fishnet 150
Operation Greenhouse 10
Operation Highjump 141
Operation Ivy 82
Operation Lee 220
Operation Little Switch 86
Operation Magic Carpet 146
Operation Petticoat 67
Operation Torch 77
Operation Totem Pole 87
Operation Sandstone 106
Operation Sea Dragon 203

Index

Opossum see *Sea Coral*
Orange County, LST 1068 85
Ore Trader, US 189
Oregon 79
Oregon Victory, US 176
Oregonian, US 189
Oriental Destiny see *Kelso Victory*
Orion, Ecuador 206
Oshkosh Victory, US 189
Ospre III, AMS 20
Otsego, US 52
Ouachita Victory see *Green Valley*
Outagamie County, LST 1073 85
Overlin Victory, US 188

P&O Leader see *China Victory*
P&T Explorer, US 189
P&T Navigator, US 190
P&T Pathfinder, US 190
Pacific Carrier see *Liberty Flag*
Pacific Fleet, US 7, 98, 109, 141
Pacific Fleet Reserves 3, 44, 45, 49, 61, 68, 79, 82, 84, 85, 86, 90, 99, 100, 101, 126, 146, 161, 163, 164, 206, 213
Pacific Theatre 47, 49, 56, 58, 68, 72, 81, 87, 98, 105, 107, 109–111, 114, 117, 125, 126, 127, 131, 133, 135, 136, 137, 140–147, 149, 152, 156, 158, 160, 161, 162, 166
Pacific Victory, US 190
Pacrobin see *Pelican State*
Paducah Victory, US 190
Paenguyong Do 92
Pak Tu San 220
Pakistan 126
Palaus 137
Palermo 125
Palmere, Michael A. 10
Palmyr 114
Palon see *New Zealand Victory*
Pan American Victory, US 190
Panama, government of 83
Panay, US 212
Pangan (Thailand) 87
Panmunjom 24
Paravane 153
Paricutin, AE 99
Parish, class 78
Park Benjamin, US 190
Park County, LST 1077 85
Partisan 9
Partridge, AMS 20, 23, 153, 158, 161, 224
Pasig II, AW 202
"Passage to Freedom" 149
Passumpsic, AO 110
Patapsco, AOG 112, 119
Patrol and Reconnaissance Group 20
Patrol Gunboat 41, 52
PC-61 220
PC-62 220
PC-65 see *Nae Tong*
PC-66 see *Imchin*
PC-600 see *Myo Hyang San*
PC-701 9, 220
PC-702, ROK 83, 220
PC-703, ROK 19, 153, 220

PC-704 23
PC-705 see *Han La San*
PC-706 see *Myo Hyang San*
PC-799 see *Kum Kang San*
PC-810 see *Chiri San*, also *Kum Kang San*, also *Pak Tu San*
PCE-67 164
PCEC 58
PCEC 896 59
PCEF 898 59
PCS-1416 see *Swallow III*
PE (Frigate) 34
Pearl Harbor 27, 65, 66, 67, 68, 102, 104, 110, 112, 133, 134, 146, 166, 206
Pecos II, TAO 110
Pegor, US 190
Pelegia see *Sea World*
Peleliu 45, 58, 107, 156
Pelican Mariner, US 190
Pelican II, AMS 21, 157
Penconic Bay see *Trojan Trader*
Pender County, LST 1080 86
Pennants 31
Pennsylvania 84
People to People Health Foundation 61
Perch, SS 9, 17, 66, 203, 204
Perkins, DDR 55
Person, Warren R. JG 157
Pescapdures 131
Petaluma, TAOG 112, 190
Peter Del II, US 191
PF-61 220
PF-62 219, 110
PG-46 51
PG-146 51
Philadelphia Naval Shipyard 7
Philip II, DE 46
Philippine Sea, USS 21
Philippines 11, 51, 58, 77, 79, 80, 82, 104, 107, 112, 130, 135, 141, 161, 163, 206
Pickard, Steve 101
Pickaway, APA 148
Pickerel II, SS 63, 65, 66, 67
Picket Boats 2
Picket Radar Destroyers 41
Pictor, AF 97
Piedmont, AD 128
Pierre Victory, US 191
Pine Island, US 132
Pine Tree Mariner, US 191
Pinnaces 199
Pioneer Dale, US 191
Pioneer Valley, AO 110
Pirate, AMS 20, 159, 160, 224
Piscataqua IV, TAOG 113
Pitkin County, LST 1082 86
Piyale Pasas, Republic of Turkey 54
Planetree, WAGOL 206
Platte, US 110
Pledge, AM 20, 161, 162, 224
Plumas County, LST 1083 86
Plymouth Rock, US 89
Plymouth Victory, US 191
Poet Heim, HRMS 216
Pohang 18, 55, 58, 70, 99, 114, 142, 143, 145, 153, 158, 162

Pohang-dong 18, 25, 86, 219, 220
Point Defiance, US 88
Polaris, AF 98
Polk County, LST 1084 86
Pollux III, AKS 98, 101
Pomodon, SS 66
Pongam Do 85, 86, 87
Pontchartrain, WGP 53
Porter, US 26
Portland Tender, US 191
Portugal 45, 212
PR-3 201
Prairie Mariner, US 191
"Prairie Ships" 82
Prairie II, AD 128
Prasae II, HMTS 218
Pratt Victory, US 191
"Pregnant Perch" 66
Preminger, Otto 148
President Arthur see *Dartmouth Victory*
President Buchanan see *Skagway Victory*
President Garfield see *Thomas Jefferson*
President Harrison, US 191
President Jackson, TAPA 148, 149
President Jackson II see *Barrett*
Presidential Unit Citation (ROK) see Republic of Korea
Presidential Unit Citation (USA) 51, 67, 154, 159, 162
Primo Longobordo, Italy 69
Princeton, USS 21
Princeton Victory, US 191
Prisoner of War 28, 82, 85–87, 90, 103, 123, 140–143, 163, 164
Private Joe P. Martinez, TAP 124
Private Sadao S. Munemori, TAO 24, 82, 85, 119
Provo Victory, US 191
PS (Paddle driven steamer) 32
Psychological Warfare 201
PT-809 204
PT-810 204
PT-811 204
PT-812 204
Ptarmigan, AM 162
Public Health Service 95
Pudiano, SS 68
Puget Sound Naval Shipyard 7
Pukaki, HMNZA 218
Punts 199
Purdue Victory, US 191
Purple Star, US 191
Puru 163
Purvis Bay 42
Pusan 9, 17–19, 27, 28, 45, 51, 52, 61, 72, 79, 90, 94, 96, 97, 99–103, 114–117, 126, 134, 136, 139, 142, 145, 146, 159, 162, 166, 177, 179, 200, 210, 213, 215, 216
Pvt. Francis X. McGraw see *Wabash Victory*
Pyongyang 3, 18, 20, 25, 202

Quapaw, US 135
Queen Mary, class 72
Queenfish I, SS 67

Queens Victory 191
Quemoy 43
Quinn, Commander R.D. 66
Quonset Huts 78, 201

R-1 201
R-1-667 201
R-2 201
Raccoon see *Sea Ranger*
Radar 53, 55
Radar Picket Destroyer 53, 54
Radar Picket Submarines 63
Radcliffe Victory see *Sgt. Andrew Miller*
Radford II, DDE 47
Ragnor Naess see *sea Pender*
Raider Co, First 204
Rainier, AE 99
Rajah Jaro (Malaysia) 87
Ramora, USS 26
Ramsden, WDE 47
Rang Won, ROKN 56
Raven see *Bellatrix*
Reclaimer, ARS 130
Red Beach (Inchon) 19, 88
Red Cross 8, 210
Red Oak Victory, US 191
Red Rover, US 59
Redhead, AMS 20, 162
Redstart, AM 162
Reef Knot, US 191
Reefer 10, 94, 166, 181
Refrigerator Stores 96, 97, 100
Refugees 149
Regimental Combat Team, 9th 116
Regulus, AF 97; see also *Escanaba Victory*
Remora, SS 63, 67
Renshaw III, DE 47
Renville, APA 148
Repair Ships 127, 166
Replenishment Ships 94, 96, 97, 99, 103, 142, 224
Repose, AH 61
Republic of China (Nationalist) 2, 3, 9, 21, 23, 26, 27, 28, 63, 66, 82, 83, 90, 97, 124, 126, 162, 163, 164, 223
Republic of Korea (South) 1, 3, 6, 11, 15–17, 22, 23, 25, 28, 50, 52, 56, 59, 85–87, 103, 113, 146, 154, 162, 163, 168, 203, 204, 210, 219, 220, 222, 225; 3rd Division 18, 21; 6th Division 21; Capitol Division 21; First Army Corps 20, 21, 146; Presidential Unit Citation 49, 81, 97, 137, 150, 217
Republic of Korea Navy (ROKN) 9, 11, 19, 52, 55, 58, 186, 92, 99, 102, 115, 116,
118, 119, 120, 123, 125, 128, 130, 153, 156, 157, 158, 200, 219, 220, 221
Republic of Turkey 42, 44, 54
Rescue Ships 113, 130
Reserve Fleets 37, 43, 51, 58, 87, 91, 92, 97, 102, 105, 112, 114, 130, 142, 150, 159, 160, 164, 181, 184, 190, 191, 192

Retto 163
"Revolt of the Admirals" 6
RFA (Great Britain) 32
RFA Ranger, class 213
Rheinholt, US 191
Ribble, HMS see *Johan Maurits van Nassau*
Rice County, LST 1089 86
Rice Victory, US 191
Richard H. Davis, US 191
Richard J. Hopkins see *Atlantic Water*
Richey, WDE 47
Richmond see *Kaskaskia*
Rider Victory, US 192
Ridgefield Victory see *Colgate Victory*
Ridgway, Gen. Matthew 210
Rincon, AGO 113
Rincon (Hills), US 192
Rio Grande, AGO 113
Rio Panuco US 85
Rizal see *Murrelet*
Robert B. Forbes, US 192
Robert G. Ingersoll, US 192
Robin Goodfellow, US 192
Robin Gray, US 192
Robin Hood, US 192
Robin Kirk, US 192
Robin Mowbray, US 192
Robin Trent, US 192
Rochester, USS 21
Rock Springs Victory, US 192
Rockford, USS see *Apnok*
Roger P. Taney, WAG 53
Rogers, DDR 55
Ronald Reagan, USS 33
Ronquil, SS 67
Roosevelt, Franklin Delano 168
Roosevelt, Theodore 32, 199
Rose Knot, US 192
Rotoiti, HMNZA 218
Royal Air Force Flying Boat 214
Royal Army Service Corps 216
Royal Canadian Air Force 209
Royal Marines 66, 150, 156, 203, 211, 214
Royal Navy 41, 210, 211, 216
Royal Prasae see *Prasae*
Royal Thai Army Regiment, 21st 18
Rubber boats 145, 199, 201, 204
Ruddy, AM 162
Rushmore, US 89
Russell County, LST 1090 86, 87
Russia see Soviet Union
Rutgers Victory, US 192
Ryder, AKL 101
Ryukyu-Formosa Area 63

S (submarine) 33, 203, 212
Sabalo II, SS 67
Safeguard, ARS 131
Sailor's Splice, US 192
St. Augustine Victory, US 192
St. Brides Bay, HMS 213
St. Clair County, LST 1096 87
St. Francis River, LSMR 92
St. Joan, US 169
St. Joseph River, LSMR 92

St. Paul, USS 21, 29
Saipan 42, 80, 81, 101, 102, 106, 134, 220
Sakhalin, USSR 65
Saline County, LST 1101 87
Salisbury Sound, US 132
Salmon, US 68
Salvage operations 134
Salvage ship 85, 127
Sam Kak San 220
Samchok 17, 217
Sampan 23, 199, 204, 220
Sancaktar, Turkey 86
The Sand Pebbles 52
Sandoval, APA 148
San Joaquin County, LST 1122 87
San Mateo Victory, US 192
Santa Catalina see *Jupiter*
Santa Clara Victory, US 192
Santa Fe, Argentine Navy 65
Santa Rosa see *Lipari*
Santa Venetia, US 192
Santos Delgollado see *Gladiator*
Sappa Creek, TAO 110
Sapulpa Victory, US 192
Sargo, SS 68
Sariwon 18
Sarsi, AT 23, 137, 164, 224
Sasebo, Japan 17, 20, 99, 101, 126, 128, 129, 134, 136, 149, 159, 163, 206, 214
Satyr, AN 129
Saugatuck, TAO 110
Saxon, US 192
Scabbardfish, SS 67
SCAJAP 71, 81, 216, 219
Schuyler, US 193
Schuyler Otis Bland, US 193
Schuylkill, TAO 111
Scotland 151
Scott-Moncrieff, Admiral 212
Scrap 45, 48, 49, 53, 61, 65, 66, 69, 79, 81, 84, 86, 87, 88, 96, 107–110, 114, 139, 141, 145, 149, 150, 154, 156, 159, 163, 164, 168, 169, 179, 171, 172, 173, 174, 176–198, 211–215
Sea Bon, US 193
Sea Champion, US 193
Sea Cliff, US 193
Sea Comet II, US 193
Sea Coral, US 193
Sea Coronet, US 193
Sea Daring, US 193
Sea Darter see *Henrico*
Sea Devil I, SS 67
Sea Dolphin see *Leon*
Sea Faith, US 193
Sea Fort, US 193
Sea Fox, SS 68
Sea Furie, US 21
Sea Garden, US 193
Sea Gate, US 193
Sea Glamor, US 193
Sea Glider, US 193
Sea Globe, US 193
Sea Herald, US 193
Sea Leader, US 193
Sea Legend, US 193

Sea Life, US 193
Sea Manor, US 193
Sea Merchant, US 194
Sea Merit, US 194
Sea Monitor, US 194
Sea Mystery, US 194
Sea of Okhotsk 63
Sea Panther see *Hamul*
Sea Pender, US 194
Sea Ranger, US 194
Sea Splendor, US 194
Sea Star, US 194
Sea Victory, US 194
The Sea War in Korea vii, 5, 62
Sea Wind, US 194
Sea Wizard see *George M. Culucundis*
Sea World, US 194
Seaborne, US 194; see also *Selma Victory*
Seaplane Tender 127, 131, 132
Seaton see *Sea Merchant*
Second Echelson Movement Group 187
Sebastian Lerdo de Tejada see *Devastator*
Sebec, TAO 111
Secretary, Department of the Navy 6, 33
Secretary of Defense 1, 95, 166
Secretary of State 3
Sedgwick County, LST 1123 87
Seebees 79
Segundo, SS 68
Seige 106
Selma Victory, US 194; see also *Seaborne*
Seminole, AKA 142
Seneca see *Rock Springs Victory*
Senzan Maru, SCAJAP 216
Seoul 3, 19, 27, 103
Sgt. Andrew Miller, TAK 101
Sgt. David C. Shanks, TAP 124
Sergeant George D. Keathley USAT 17, 124, 166
Sgt. Howard E. Woodford, TAP 125
Sgt. Jack J. Pendleton, TAK 101
Sgt. Joseph E. Muller, TAP 124
Sgt. Sylvester Antolak, TAP 124
Sgt. Truman Kimbro, TAK 102
Service Force Pacific 136, 159
Service Squadron 112, 166
Seton Hall Victory, US 194
Seventh Fleet, US 7, 17, 18, 27, 34, 45, 55, 58, 63–65, 68, 97, 100, 104, 105, 110, 111, 112, 222, 223
Severn, TAO 111
Seymour D. Owens, US 54
Shadwell, US 97
Shamchok 219
Shark, US 33
Sharon Victory, US 194
Sharps, AKL 102
Shawnee Trail, TAO 111
Shenandoah, class 127, 128
Shinano Maru, SCAJAP 216
Shinecock Bay, US 194
Ship Gender 30
Ship Numbering Systems 37

Shipping Control Administration of Japan (SCAJAP) 8, 9
Ships Data Book 7
Ship's Identity 32
Ship's Overall Length 31
Shoalhaven, HMAS 8, 209
Shon, Admiral 219
Shouldice, D'Arcy V. Lt. Commander 20
Shoveler, AM 163
Si Hung, ROK 92
Sichang, HMTs 218
Sicily 72, 145
Sicily, USS 145
Siege of Wonsan 25, 26
Sierra Nevada see *Empire Halladlae*
Silver Robin see *Pelican State*
Silverstein, DE 47, 68
Simmons Victory, US 194
Simon Benson see *Sea Merit*
Sin-do 26
Sinanju 18
Sind see *Prasae*, HMTS
Singapore 214
Singapore Navy 82
Sioux Falls Victory, US 194
Sixth Fleet 26
Skagit, AKA 142
Skagway Victory, US 194; see also *Constitution State*
Sloop 33, 211, 212
"Slot" 42
Small, US 23
Small Seaplane Tender 131
Smith, Adm. Allan E. "Hoke" 20, 25
Smith, Gen. O.P. 58
Smith, Gen. Walter Bedell 200
Smith Caper see *Kelso Victory*
Smith Leader see *China Victory*
Snelling, US 89
Snorkel 63–69
So Yang see *Rincon*
Sok Cho Ri 146
Sok To 29, 92, 212
Sokcho 136, 161
Solomons 49, 113, 136, 206
Somerset see *Coastal Sentry*
Sonar 159
Songi 111
Songjin, NK 23, 44, 47, 51, 52, 55, 70, 91, 137, 140, 155, 158, 159, 160, 161, 163, 210, 221
Sonsan 150
Soubarissen, TOE 111
South Bend Victory, US 195
South China Sea 64, 65, 66
South Dakota 146
Southerland, DDR 56
Southwestern Victory, US 195
Southwind, US 195
Soviet Mine Fields 63
Soviet Minelayer 23
Soviet Submarines 63
Soviet Union 1, 3–5, 10, 11, 12, 15, 19, 20, 23, 26, 27, 50, 51, 52, 63, 66, 68, 69, 81, 105, 109–111, 152, 217, 219, 220, 222, 223
Soya Strait 67

Spain 139, 147
Spanish American War 10
Spanish Navy 67, 177
Sparrow, HMS 213
Spartanburg Victory, US 195; see also *Cotton State*
Special Boat Squadron, UK 203
Special Operations 9
Sperry, AS 133
Sphinx, ARL 123
Spiegel Grove, US 89
Spook Missions 201
Sproston, DDE 48
Stark County, LST 1134 87
StarKist Foods, Inc 97
State Department 26
Stathes Yamaglias, US 195
Station Nan 13
Station Ship 112
Station Sugar 43, 53
Station Tanker 104, 110, 112
Station Victor 45, 53
Station Victory 43, 45
"Steaming Demon" 140
Sterlet, SS 68
Stern, US see *Van Zijll* HNLMS
Stetson Victory see *Sgt. Sylvester Antolake*
Steuben County, LST 1138 88
Stickleback, SS 68
Stillwater see *Cache*
Stock Star, US 195
Stone County, LST 1141 88
Straits of Formosa 63
Stricken, ship 37, 41–52, 56, 65, 68, 79, 80, 81, 83–92, 97–100, 102–107, 109, 111–114, 116, 121, 123–131, 133–137, 141–147, 149, 150, 159, 161, 163, 164, 165, 202, 206
Struble, Adm. A.D. 2, 8, 17, 20
Sturgeons Bay Ship Building and Dry Docking Company 101
Suamico, TAO 104–107, 110, 111
Subic Bay 65, 135
Submarine 2, 7, 9, 10, 24, 26, 27, 33, 61, 62, 63, 65, 68, 133, 151, 213, 219, 222
Submarine Chaser 58, 219
Submarine Combat Patrol Pin 67 or 68
Submarine Command 68
Submarine Rescue 127, 133
Submarine Tender 127
SubSinkEx Project Thurber 64
Sue Lykes see *Stock Star*
Suez Affair 212
Suisun, US 132
Suisun Bay 7
Sullivan, John L. 6
Summit County, LST 1146 88
Sumner County, LST 1148 88
Sunapee, US 53
Sunion, US 195
Superiority at Sea 223
Supreme Commander, Allies, Japan 19
Surfbird, AM 163
Susquehanna, US 195
Sussex II, AK 142

Suwon 154
Suyong 142, 186
Swallow, AMS 21, 159
Swathmore Victory, US 195
Sweepers 23, 89
Swift, AM 163
Sword Knot, US 195
Sydney, HMAS 208
Symbol, AM 163
Syngman Rhee 15

Tabitha Brown, US 196
Tachin, HMTS 218
Tachin, Thailand 51
Tacoma, class 50, 51, 52, 219
Tacoma III, PF 52, 220
Taddei, US 196
Tae Chong do 135
Tae-do 26
Taenchon-do 92
Taedong, ROKN 52, 220
Taedong River 3
Taejon 18
Taeju 91
TAGM II see *Twin Falls Victory*
Taineron, US 196
Taiwan, Republic of 4, 55, 66, 84, 98, 106, 128, 185, 223
Taiwan Strait 132
Takelma, ATF 135
Talladega, APA 148
Tallulah, US 196
Taluga, TAO 111
Tamalpais, TAO 112
Tampa, Fl 171
Tanchon, Korea 145, 153
Tandjung Nusanive, Indonesia 84
Taney, WAG 53
Tang, SS 68
Tangun 3
Tanker 10, 27
Tanks 78
TAO 103
TAOG-4 114
TAP 22
TAP-188 114
Tar Heel Mariner, US 196
Tarakan Island Campaigns 80
Tarawa 93
Task Force 52 155
Task Force 58 105
Task Force 70.9 68
Task Force 77 8, 20, 22, 29, 44, 47, 48, 55, 97, 100, 103, 222
Task Force 79 20
Task Force 90 21, 22, 28, 71, 91, 92, 136, 222
Task Force 92 20, 42, 51
Task Force 95 21, 26, 42, 48, 112, 145, 154, 222
Task Force 96 18, 67, 222
Task Force 96.5 8
Task Force 96.8 8, 211, 212
Task Force Organization 38
Task Group 57.3 132
Task Group 96.8 20
Task Group Organization 38
Task Group York 65
Taupo, HMNZA 218

Tavispan see *Petaluma*
Tawakoni, ATF 136
Tawasa, ATF 136
Taylor, DDE 48
Telemachus, HMS 213
Telfair, APA 148, 149
Tenders 127, 128
Tennessee 82
Terrebonne Parish class 78
Texas 80, 82
Texas, US 196
Thackrey, Adm. Lyman A. 21, 57
Thailand, Navy 50, 51, 87, 88, 218
Thi Nai, ROKN 79
Third Fleet 158
Thirty-Eighth Parallel 3, 15, 16, 17, 18, 19, 27, 158
Thomas Jefferson, APA 149
Thomas M. Cooley see *Ocean Betty*
Thompson, AKA 21, 23, 89
Thompson, DMS 155
Thronson, Francis 167
Thuban, AKA 142, 143
Thunderbird see *Jericho Victory*
Tiger, SS 49
Tilefish, SS 68, 69
Timber Hitch, US 196
Time Charter Ships 22, 166
Tinaztepe, Republic of Turkey 44
Tirpitz (German) 216
Tiru, SS 69
Titania, AKA 13 18, 143
To Jang Po 159
Tobato Maru, SCAJAP 216
Tobruk, HMAS 208
Tochi PF-16 50
Tokchok Island 220
Tokyo Bay 28, 105
Tolland, class 142, 143
Tolovana, TAP 112
Tomahawk, US 112
Tombigbee, US 114
Tonnae 200
Tontij, class 113
Tora! Tora! Tora! 46
Tornado see *Stock Star*
Torpedo boats PT 33, 203
Torpedoes 33
Tortuga, LSD 90
Toucan, AM 164
Towanda Victory, US 196
Train 2
Tran Quang Kahi (Vietnam) see *Bering Strait*
Transamerican, US 196
Transatlantic, US 196
Transcolumbia see *Marine Lynx*
Transnorthern see *China Victory*
Transoceanic, US 196
Transoceanic Period 9
Transpacific, US 196
Transunion, US 196
Trapp, LST 88
Trench, class 67, 69
Triaina, Hellenic Navy 67
Trigger, SS 144
Trinity Victory, US 196
Tripoli 10
Triumph, HMS 18

Trojan Trader, US 196
Tromp, Admiral 31
Troop ships 215, 218
Troop transport 114, 124, 143, 149
Truce talks 28
Truman, President 6, 7, 11, 17, 19, 24, 47, 55, 63, 167, 168
Tsingtao 102
Tsushima Straits 27, 138
Tucson Victory, US 196
Tugs 2, 10, 127, 134, 135, 137, 166
Tulane Victory, US 196
Tunnels 201
Turban 143
Turkey (Turkish) 65, 68, 69, 86, 105, 119, 128, 131, 134
Tuskegee Victory, US 196
Twin Falls Victory, US 197
Tyne IV, HMS 213
Typhoon 18
Typhus 137

U-505 128
"Ugly Duckling" 168
Ulithi 111, 114, 135, 156, 163
Ullong do 137
Ulvert M. Moore, DE 48
Unadilla III, ATA 137
Underwater Demolition Team 145, 149, 150, 153
Ung-do 26
Unicorn, HMS 213
"Unification debates" 6
Union, AKA 143
Union Victory, US 196
United Fruit Company 98, 188
United Kingdom 212
United Nations 2, 3, 8, 9, 15, 18–20, 22, 24, 25, 27–29, 45, 52, 63, 64, 67, 69, 70, 98, 113, 128, 134, 136, 138, 149, 167, 199, 202, 203, 204, 210, 217, 218, 222
United Nations Escort and Blockade Force 46, 48, 51
United Nations Medal 66
United Nations Security Council 17, 24
United States 3, 5, 6, 7, 8, 10–12, 14, 15, 17, 25, 27, 28, 33, 41, 42, 50, 52, 62, 93, 95, 103, 110, 128, 139, 151, 153, 159, 166, 208, 217
United States, SS 168
United States, USS 6
United States Air Force 2, 6, 8, 18, 28, 201
United States Army 6, 80, 84, 85, 102, 111, 114, 118, 120 121, 122; 1st Cavalry Division 96, 142, 146, 148, 153; 2nd Infantry Division 115, 116, 117, 139; 3rd Infantry Division 22, 146; 7th Infantry Division 19, 20, 21, 22, 170; 8th Army 19, 20, 21, 145, 224; 8th Cavalry Regimental Combat Team 25; 10th Corps 19, 20, 21, 58; 21st Infantry Division 146; 24th Infantry Division 18, 96; 25th Infantry Division 96; 45th Infantry Division 145, 146;

8227th Army Unit 204; Army Port Command 18
United States Army Transport 102
United States Concrete Pipe Corporation 101
United States Lighthouse Service 204
United States Marine Corps 173
United States Naval Submarine Force Information Book 69
United States Navy 2, 5, 6, 8, 9, 12, 13, 28, 31, 37, 41, 85, 96, 99–110, 112, 114, 115, 118–121, 123, 127, 129–138, 140–147, 151, 154, 159, 166, 173, 174, 179–184, 86, 188, 194, 197, 203, 214, 216, 218, 219, 224
United States Navy and Marine Corps Award Manual see Awards
United States Navy Ships: Sunk or Damaged During the Korean Conflict vii
United States Trust Territories 98, 100
Ural-Altaic language 3
USO, US 197
USAT 32; *see also* United States Army Transport
USCGC 32; *see also* United States Coast Guard
USN Monitors 128
USNS 32; *see also* United States Naval ShipF
Utah state 82
Utah Beach 43
Ute, AS 137
Uvalde, AKA 154

Valdosta Victory, US 197
Valley Forge, USS 21, 196; see also *Tallulah*
Vammen, DE 48
Van Fleet, General 224
Van Galen, HRMS 217
Van Zijll, HNLMS 217
Vanderbilt Victory, US 197
Vasco da Gama (Portugal) 212
Venezuela Navy 69
Vercharmain, Foreign 197
Vesuvius IV, AE 100
Vicksburg, USA 26
Victoria see *Alamo Victory*; *Ethiopia Victory*
Victory Ship (as subject) 147, 174, 166, 168
Vietnam 7, 44–49, 52–55, 61, 66, 68, 69, 72, 79–88, 92, 97, 98, 99, 100, 104, 106, 107, 110, 112–114, 117, 118, 128–132, 134–137, 141–146, 148, 149, 170, 177, 184
Vinh Long see *Satyr*
Virginia 80
Virginia City, US 197
Virgo, USAKA 143
Vladivostok, Russia 23, 26, 63
Volador II, SS 69
Volunteer Mariner, US 197
VP-47 26
Vulcan, class 125

W (Coast Guard) 34
Wabash III, AGO 114
Wabash Victory, US 197
Wachusett, WPG 53
Wacosta, US 197
WAGL 204
WAGL-297 see *Ironwood*
WAGL-307 see *Planetree*
Wahine, HMS 218
Wahoo II, SS 69
Wake Forest Victory, US 197
Wake Island 11, 47, 55
Walke, US 153
Walker, DE 48
Walker, Gen. Walton 21
Wallace M. Tyler see *Sea Star*
Waller, DE 49
Walsa-ri 92, 163
Walter B. Cobb, APO 150
Walter F. Perry, US 197
Walter M. Christiansen 193; see also *Sea Comet*
Waltham Victory, US 197
Walton, DE 49, 197
Wantuck, US 201
Wantuck, John 150
War Patrol 63, 64, 65, 67, 68, 69
War Patrol Combat Insignia 66
War Shipping Administration 101, 102, 106, 119, 120, 163, 169–192, 194–197
Warramunge, HMAS 208
Warrior, US 197
Warwick Victory, US 197
WAS see War Shipping Administration
Washburn, AKA 144
Washington, George 30
Wasp, USS 33
Water boats 199
Watertown see *Niantic Victory*
Watson, Lavinia Fanning 31'
WAVD 131
Wave, class 214
Wave Baron, RFA 214
Wave Chief, REA 214
Wave Commander, REA 214
Wave Conqueror, REA 214
Wave Duke, REA 214
Wave Knight, REA 214
Wave Laird, REA 214
Wave Liberators, class 214
Wave Monarch, REA 214
Wave Premier, REA 215
Wave Prince, REA 215
Wave Regent, REA 215
Wave Sovereign, REA 215
Waxbill, AMA 159
Waxwing, AM 164
Weather Balloons 13
Weather Station 13, 43, 45, 58
Weathersby, Katharine 223
Weiss, APD 150
Wellesley Victory, US 197
Wesleyan Victory, US 197
West Coast Support Group 12
West Germany 87
West Korean Support Group 8
West LynnVictory, US 198

West Pac 67, 69
Westchester, US 198
Western Island Attack Group 136
Western Ocean, US 198
Western Rancher, US 198
Western Trader, US 198
Westport Victory, US 198
Whale boats 199, 206, 207
WHEC 131
Wheeling see *Seton Hall Victory*
Whetstone, LSD 90
Whidbey, AG 98, 141
Whidbey Island, class 90, 98
Whiggle boats 199, 207
White Marsh, US 90
White River, LSMR 92
White Sands Bay, HMS 204, 213
Whiteburst, DE 49
Whiteside, AKA 144
Whiting, class 131
Whittier, Alaska 143
Wild Pigeon see *Uvalde*
William Clagett, US 198
William Coddington, US 198
William Eaton, US 198
William Frederic Kraft see *Evergreen Star*
William H. Carruth, US 198
William H. Wilmer, US 198
William Hodson see *Sea Coronet*
William L. McLean, US 198
William Lester, Foreign 198
William R. Rush, DDR 56
William Seiverling, DE 49
William Sproule see *Christian*
William Thorton see *Western Trader*
Willoughby see *Gresham*
Wilson Victory, US 26; see also *Private Sadao S. Munemori*
Wiltsie, US 144
Winchester see *North Pilot*
Windsor Victory see *Macalester Victory*
Winged Races see *Firedrake*
Wingless Victory see *Bartlesville Victory*
Winnebago, WPG 53
Winona, WPG 53
Winston, AKA 144
Wisconsin 80, 82
Wiseman, DE 49
W.L. Mccormick see *Yankee Pioneer*
WLB 204
WLR 204
Wolfgeher, Paul Collection 16
Wolmi-do 19, 90, 91, 212, 218
Wolverine Mariner, US 198
Wonsan 3, 8, 18–20, .22, 23, 25, 26, 29, 42, 48, 49, 51, 52, 55, 58, 70, 78, 84, 89–92, 97, 106, 107, 111, 118, 121, 126, 136, 137, 139, 134, 135, 140, 145, 146, 148–167, 184, 199, 212, 216, 219
Wooden Sweepers 152, 153
Woodstock Victory, US 198
World War I 131, 133, 151
World War II 5, 6, 7, 10, 12, 34, 41, 42–56, 58, 60–62, 64–68, 70, 72, 77–93, 96–100, 103–107,

109–114, 116, 118, 126, 128–144, 146, 147, 148, 151, 153, 156–162, 164, 166, 168, 180, 191, 199, 202, 203, 206, 207, 210, 212, 215–218, 223
World War III 63
Worth, Cedric R. 6
Wrangell, class 100
Wusueh, HMS 212
Wyoming 79

Xantus, class 126
Xavier Victory, US 198

YAG-37 see *John L. Sullivan*
YAGR-14 see *Dudley H. Thomas*
Yakushima see *Osprey III*
Yale Victory see *Archer T. Gammon*
Yalu River 21, 23
Yancy, AKA 144
Yang Do Island 154
Yangtze River 211
Yangyang 52
Yankee Pioneer, US 198
Yankee Station 99
Yard Class Minesweepers (YMS) 17, 219
Yellow Sea 19, 103, 138, 155
YMS 17, 151, 163, 217

YMS-1, class 157
YMS 1 to 479 165
YMS-100 ROK 157
YMS-148 see YMS-516
YMS-186 ROK 158
YMS-192 ROK 156
YMS-218 ROK 156
YMS-231 ROK 156
YMS-301 ROK 220
YMS-302 ROK 220
YMS-303 ROK 221
YMS-305 ROK 217
YMS-306 ROK 217, 221
YMS-307 ROK 221
YMS-359 ROK 165
YMS-369 ROK 157
YMS-374 ROK 157
YMS-400 ROK 157
YMS-410 class 158
YMS-415 ROK 155
YMS-417 ROK 157
YMS-419 ROK 158
YMS-420 ROK 158
YMS-441, class 158
YMS-461 ROK 159
YMS-501 ROK 221
YMS-502 ROK 221
YMS-503 ROK 221
YMS-504 ROK 153, 221

YMS-505 ROK 153
YMS-509 ROK 221
YMS-510 ROK 221
YMS-511 ROK 221
YMS-512 ROK 221
YMS-513 ROK 9, 221
YMS-514 ROK 221
YMS-515 ROK 221
YMS-516 ROK 221
YMS-518 ROK 221
Yo do 23, 79, 163, 210
Yokohama, Japan 146
Yokosuka, Japan 50, 61, 64, 66, 134, 139, 142, 143, 154, 206
Yon Yama Maru, SCAJAP 217
Yong Do 145
Yong yong 136
Yongcho Do, Korea 85, 86, 87, 220
Yonghong Island 220
Young, Richard O. 0
Yugoslavia Victory, US 198
Yuma, class 130
Yuma II, ATF 136
Yung Huang Man, ROK 221
Yurishima 156; see also *Chatter*

Zeal, AM 164
Zelima, AF 98

www.ingramcontent.com/pod-product-compliance
Lightning Source LLC
Chambersburg PA
CBHW081548300426
44116CB00015B/2805